MARY LOU McDONALD

A Republican Riddle

SHANE ROSS

Atlantic Books
London

Published in hardback in Great Britain in 2022 by Atlantic Books,
an imprint of Atlantic Books Ltd.

10 9 8 7 6 5 4 3 2

A CIP catalogue record for this book is available from the British Library.

Trade paperback ISBN: 978 1 83895 589 2
E-book ISBN: 978 1 83895 590 8

Printed and bound by CPI Group (UK) Ltd, Croydon CR0 4YY

Atlantic Books
An imprint of Atlantic Books Ltd
Ormond House
26–27 Boswell Street
London WC1N 3JZ

Contents

INTRODUCTION:
The Riddle of Mary Lou   1

CHAPTER 1:
The Skeleton in the Cupboard   19

CHAPTER 2:
From the Cradle to the Altar: A Politics-Free Zone   48

CHAPTER 3:
Into the Arms of Gerry Adams   80

CHAPTER 4:
The Anointing of Mary Lou: The Fast Track to Europe   110

CHAPTER 5:
Desperately Seeking a Dáil Seat   143

CHAPTER 6:
The Mansion in Cabra   179

CHAPTER 7:
A Star Takes the Dáil by Storm   224

CHAPTER 8:
Adams Calls the Shots   256

CHAPTER 9:
Playing the Cemetery Game   287

CHAPTER 10:
To Hell and Back   322

CHAPTER 11:
A United Ireland or Bust   355

ACKNOWLEDGEMENTS   397
INDEX   404

THE RIDDLE OF MARY LOU

Mary Lou McDonald never wore a balaclava. She never pulled a trigger. She never planted a bomb. She has never even been in prison. Indeed, it is unlikely that she has ever incurred as much as a speeding fine.

Today she leads a party full of hardened IRA veterans. Some are still puzzled by her selection as leader of Sinn Féin. Others are pleased that she is in control. She will never qualify for membership of the Felons Club, the exclusive hostelry in the heart of west Belfast frequented by IRA ex-prisoners. No doubt she would be warmly greeted as a guest, but she sports none of the wounds of war required for automatic admission.

The Felons Club is a semi-private hostelry at 537 Falls Road. According to its bye-laws, it was established 'to foster and maintain among Irish Republicans friendships formed during imprisonment or internment as a result of their service to the Irish Republican cause'. It is a meeting place for many Irish Republicans, particularly IRA members who served time in prison. Full membership is restricted 'to those who have been imprisoned or interned for their Irish Republican beliefs'.

Outsiders are allowed in, but 'shall not be supplied with intoxicating liquor in the club premises unless upon the invitation and in the company of a member'. The rule would seem to more comfortably belong in posh, gentlemen-only, exclusive London clubs than in a bolthole for former IRA paramilitaries.

Mary Lou McDonald's failure to have been part of the IRA campaign is her greatest liability, and her greatest asset. She will never be the full 'Shinner'. She will never command the same awe or respect as Gerry Adams or Martin McGuinness with republicans north of the border. Former occupants of the Maze prison are acutely aware that she never had blood on her blouse, not having suffered the indignities, physical brutality and pain of the long campaign. Adams and McGuinness were both war heroes who would qualify for the Felons Club. Yet these two former IRA leaders, from Belfast and Derry respectively, are the men who thrust greatness upon the well-spoken young woman from Rathgar in middle-class Dublin, handing her a mandate to lead both the IRA veterans and Sinn Féin newbies to the next stage in the party's pursuit of power, north and south.

In the Republic, Mary Lou's detachment from the grisly IRA war of terror is an imperative if she is to win the Taoiseach's office. In the refined, hedge-clipped avenues of suburban Dublin there is little tolerance for the physical violence championed by her mentors, Adams and McGuinness, in the North over three decades. The gross injustices of Bloody Sunday and other British Army atrocities are deplored, but there is still no appetite for ambiguity or double-think on a policy that risks returning Ireland to former days. Mary Lou's task is to convince Ireland's citizens that she is a peacemaker, while reassuring militant Northern nationalists that their fight was not in vain; that the promised land of a united Ireland is coming and that it could not have been done without their sacrifices. Today she stands on the verge of being the first ever female Taoiseach, the first Sinn Féin cabinet minister in the Republic, but, more importantly, the president of a party that is in power simultaneously both north and south of the Irish border. History beckons.

Yet precious little is known about Mary Lou the person. The contradictions in her life – so far – prompt countless challenging questions. She is dogged by unsolved riddles.

As the author of this book, I must make a confession – not of a vested interest, but of a prejudice, a weakness, perhaps. I have known and liked Mary Lou McDonald for many years. I worked with her while we were both in opposition on the Dáil's Public Accounts Committee (PAC) from 2011 to 2016. She was excellent company, lively and amusing. As a performer in the sittings of the committee, she was second to none. She would go straight for the jugular. Witnesses feared her sharp tongue and her speedy ripostes. She was well briefed by the highly competent Sinn Féin back office, which was grooming her for greatness. I confess to a similar love of the limelight, but she was a media darling with a talent for the sound bite that left me and others in the halfpenny place. We competed for the cameras, but it was a pointless contest. Mary Lou McDonald was a combatant without parallel for media coverage. Along with the PAC chair, John McGuinness, and others, we were given a dressing-down by the chief justice, Frank Clarke, for our aggressive questioning of Rehab boss Angela Kerins. The judicial rebuke didn't take a feather out of Mary Lou. She was refreshing, irreverent and fearless.

When I became a minister in 2016, my relations with Mary Lou and Sinn Féin remained good. Despite sitting on the opposition benches, the party supported my push for reform of the blatant political patronage in judicial appointments and of drink-driving laws. In turn, I willingly received Sinn Féin delegations, much to the horror of some of my Fine Gael cabinet colleagues. When Mary Lou asked me if, as minister for sport, I would visit a boxing club in her Dublin Central constituency, I willingly did so.

Consequently, in 2021, when I decided to write this biography,

I had anticipated her co-operation, albeit limited. I understood that Sinn Féin is an ultra-secretive organisation that likes to control its own message. In June 2020, I rang Mary Lou, asking her to meet me for half an hour without divulging why. I wanted to tell her what I was about face to face. She graciously agreed, although at the time she was particularly busy in crisis talks in Northern Ireland, negotiating the proposed Irish Language Act.

The Dublin Bay South by-election was in full swing at the time. Mary Lou was campaigning intensely on the ground, so wanted to meet somewhere close by in the embattled constituency. She opted for a private house meeting, rather than a public café, providing her with a short break from pounding the pavements. We met, alone, in a 'safe' house belonging to my son, Hugh, in Ranelagh, Dublin 6.

When she arrived, I told her of my intention and the reasons for writing this book, primarily because she was likely to be Ireland's next Taoiseach. She looked doubtful. She was bemused but non-committal about her attitude to the project. She was modest, suggesting that she might even be too boring for a biography. I said that I would appreciate it if she would open a few doors, in particular to her family, because stories of her upbringing, her publicly un-known siblings, her mother, her father and her husband would be compelling. I had met her charming and highly intelligent younger sister, Joanne, a couple of times, her mother, Joan, and younger brother, Patrick, briefly, but knew nothing about the rest of her immediate family, let alone her reclusive, heretofore almost invisible, husband, Martin Lanigan. All six people merited a little exposure if we were to paint a fuller picture of the people who helped to shape the mysterious Mary Lou.

They have turned out to be a fascinating family, with talents and shortcomings that make her formative years assume a new importance.

Mary Lou asked me not to go into the details of her parents' separation. I assured her that, though details about her background were essential to the narrative, I had no curiosity about any animosity between her mother and father; the book was intended to be neither a polemic nor a hagiography. And it was not designed to advance or to torpedo her ambitions to be Taoiseach. If there were important stories, good or bad, they would be published. I would speak to her critics, as well as her family and supporters. I specifically mentioned the case of Máiría Cahill, the woman raped by an IRA man when she was only sixteen years of age. Otherwise, if Mary Lou was discovered to have 'guns in the cupboard', of course, that would have to emerge, but I was not looking for them. She responded that there were none.

Overall, Mary Lou seemed a bit taken aback. She would need to 'consult' with a few (unnamed) people and would get back to me within a few days with a response about whether she could open any doors. She glanced at my son's garden and mentioned that her husband, Martin, was a good gardener. It was the first time I had ever heard her mention him. We parted as friends. Following the publication of this book, I hope we can remain so.

The omens are not good.

Mary Lou phoned me a week later with the result of her consultations. She did not identify the people to whom she had spoken. She was not willing to assist me with the book. She felt it was 'premature'. She would not be asking anyone to speak to me, nor would she be telling anyone to refuse. I told her that I would almost certainly have questions to put to her when I had finished my research. She said there was no guarantee that she would agree to answer them.

I interpreted Mary Lou's response as an attempt to dissuade me from putting pen to paper. I knew there would be a negative reaction from Sinn Féin, a party that likes to hold a rigid control over its members, regardless of rank. It would be a harder task if she were to put a muzzle on anyone, but she had now 'consulted' with certain people and had reached a conclusion. I could guess

the names of some of those to whom she had spoken about the proposed biography. I expressed disappointment and we wished each
other well.

Mary Lou's career so far poses many puzzles. The most
frequently asked question is how a middle-class, privately schooled
woman has emerged as the leader of a united Ireland movement
that has traditionally been driven by Northern working-class males,
many of them unapologetic advocates of IRA violence?

Another question has attracted even more immediate attention.
Do the IRA veterans, the volunteers, the backbone of Sinn Féin in
Northern Ireland, approve of her? Is their acceptance of her leadership conditional? Or, worse still, do the Northern hard men control
her? What is the new leader of Sinn Féin's true relationship with
them? Is she mistress or servant?

We seldom catch a clear glimpse of the powerful Sinn Féin old
guard, former members of the supposedly disbanded IRA Army
Council. One such rare occasion occurred, ominously, as recently
as 30 June 2020, at the funeral of former IRA intelligence chief
Bobby Storey.

Storey was an icon of republican folklore, even in his lifetime.
He was indisputably in the IRA 'army'. He was a legend because he
had masterminded some spectacular dramas, including the mass
escape of thirty-eight IRA prisoners from Long Kesh prison in
September 1983. He had continued to plan meticulous illegal
operations, such as the £26 million Northern Bank robbery, carried
out in 2004, long after the 1998 ceasefire, which Storey supported.
The IRA tried to spin him as some sort of Robin Hood character
because of his 'success' in the bank heist, but opponents insist that
he was a thoroughly nasty piece of work, known darkly as an IRA
'enforcer' for good reason.

Mary Lou showed up at Storey's funeral in Belfast. As leader
of Sinn Féin, it would have been hard for her to plead a prior
engagement, yet it was a paramilitary parade with trappings to

match. No volley of shots was fired over the coffin, but the identical black trousers, white shirts, black ties and Easter lilies worn by the citizens of west Belfast lining the streets bore the hallmarks of an army of disciplined followers, rather than of an angry rabble or a gathering of family friends in mourning.

An almighty row broke out about the lack of social distancing at Storey's funeral at a time when Covid restrictions were in force. Many expected that prosecutions would follow, with the names of Mary Lou and Northern Ireland's deputy first minister, Michelle O'Neill, in the frame. The prosecutions never happened. Yet Mary Lou looked distinctly uncomfortable in the photographs taken of herself closely bunched with former IRA chiefs outside the Storey family home, marching behind the funeral cortège.

Her discomfort was understandable. It was probably caused by the company she was keeping rather than by any fear of catching Covid for a second time.

The coffin carriers at the funeral were the key. Their identity was a message from the hard men. The people carrying Storey to his last resting place were not his family and not Mary Lou or Michelle O'Neill, the democratically elected leaders of Sinn Féin north and south. They were republican veterans. No non-combatants needed to apply as the final coffin carriers. Their exclusively military status was a gesture of defiance, evidence that the IRA Army Council perhaps still existed. The coffin carriers were the elite of the de-commissioned army. Gerry Adams was joined by Storey's fellow Maze escaper, Gerry Kelly, to carry Storey on his final journey. Seán 'Spike' Murray, who was convicted of explosives offences, Martin Ferris, who served ten years for smuggling arms in 1984, Seán 'The Surgeon' Hughes, the unelected republican leader from south Armagh, and Martin 'Duckster' Lynch, who served ten years for possession of a rocket launcher, also shouldered the burden.

Mary Lou looked on. So did 'non-army' Sinn Féin TDs from the Republic, Pearse Doherty, Rose Conway-Walsh and Matt Carthy.

Was this a signal to Mary Lou that, while she was welcome at their solemn gig, the 'army' still ran its own show? The funeral was on its terms. When in Belfast, do what the Belfast boys do. It provoked the question: had they fully accepted the leadership of the middle-class woman from south Dublin? Or were they still operating in a parallel paramilitary universe?

Mary Lou parried later hostile media questions about her attendance at the funeral of an IRA leader with the reply that Bobby Storey was 'a champion of the peace process'. Which was rather stretching it. He was a lot more than that.

A few days after Mary Lou had told me that she would not stand in my way of talking to anyone, I decided to hit the phones in pursuit of the coffin carriers from the North. I rang MLA (Member of the Legislative Assembly) Gerry Kelly's constituency office in north Belfast. He was not there, but I left a message with a request for him to ring me.

Gerry Kelly is a man with a serious IRA record. He was sixty-nine in April 2022, part of an ageing group of former IRA activists whose influence is a topic of hot debate. He was convicted of the 1973 Old Bailey bombings along with the even-better-known Price sisters, Marian and Dolours. Kelly was sentenced to two life sentences plus twenty years. According to the Sinn Féin account, he went on hunger strike for 206 days in Britain and was force-fed 167 times. He was transferred to the Maze prison outside Belfast. While escaping with thirty-seven others in 1983, armed with a smuggled handgun, he shot a prison officer, who survived despite serious head wounds. Kelly went on the run for three years, but was re-arrested in the Netherlands in 1986. After his release in 1989, he joined the Sinn Féin negotiating team and has been a key republican figure ever since. I hardly expected an early response from a busy MLA, but within half an hour my mobile rang. It was Gerry Kelly.

I explained to him that I was writing a book about Mary Lou

McDonald. I would be in Belfast in the coming days and would appreciate a meeting with him and his Sinn Féin colleague, Seán 'Spike' Murray. I was chancing my arm.

Kelly was charming: 'there should be no problem'. He even promised that he'd talk to Seán Murray about meeting me.

I had hit the jackpot on day one. The Army Council was coming out to play.

A few days later, when I rang back to fix the time and place of the appointment, Gerry had vanished. In response to a second call, he was in Kerry on holiday. I was asked to ring him on his return. Several more calls encountered the same brick wall. There was little point in me, a journalist, setting out in hot pursuit of a man who had given the European forces of law and order the slip for years when he was on the run.

In the following days and weeks, a pattern emerged. The replies to my calls to IRA diehards from Belfast and Derry were unambiguous and unanimously negative. Even Gerry Adams showed hints of humour. Since we follow each other on Twitter, I sent Adams a direct mail:

Hi Gerry
I do hope that your wife Colette is better now [she had contracted Covid] and all well with you. I know that you were reluctant to speak with me about my book on Mary Lou. I can assure you that it is neither polemic nor eulogy. In any case is there any chance we could meet for a cup of coffee in Belfast? I shall be up the week after next and the week after that. If necessary, the words 'Mary Lou' need not be uttered. Best wishes, Shane

By chance, I knew from that day's *Sunday Independent* that it was Adams's seventy-third birthday the following Wednesday. So I added: 'How about Wednesday? I could bring you a birthday present?!! Congrats, Shane.'

Gerry Adams is known for many things. Humour is not one of them.

I received the following reply: 'Nope Shane. Grma xo ga.' I was puzzled. What in the name of God was 'Grma xo ga'? Was it a coded message or had the great man's finger slipped on his mobile phone's digits?

When I received the message, I was lunching with my family. I put the question to them collectively.

My daughter, Rebecca, interpreted the puzzle: '"Grma" is go raibh maith agat – thank you. "xo" is a kiss and a hug and "ga" is Gerry Adams,' she said.

'Brilliant. Give me a response in Irish?' I asked her.

My wife, Ruth, whose Irish is good, provided it. 'You should reply "Tfr xoxo sr", meaning "Tá failte romhat xoxo sr". Translated into English, it's "You are welcome, hugs and kisses, Shane Ross".'

I sent the message. 'Hugs and kisses' was probably a bit over the top.

Other early responses from Northern Ireland replicated the Gerry Adams/Gerry Kelly line. Conor Murphy, minister for finance in the Northern Ireland Executive, convicted of being in possession of explosives and sentenced to five years' jail in 1982, said no. Former Sinn Féin policy officer Danny Morrison, whose sentence in 1990 for kidnapping an IRA informer was later quashed, also said no. Martina Anderson, the Derry MLA convicted of conspiring to cause explosions, said no. Arthur Morgan, a former IRA prisoner who served seven and a half years in Long Kesh, replied after four calls. Arthur, a former TD with whom I had enjoyed many cups of coffee in the Leinster House members' bar, said that 'Mary Lou was in Brussels when I was in the Dáil. I was working flat out at the time to hold the seat.' Arthur said no; he couldn't help me.

Those who qualified for the Felons Club had got the message. They were all singing from the same hymn sheet. Those who were once 'army' were behaving like, well, an army.

I contacted others, this time in the Republic, all non-combatants, people who, like Mary Lou, had never worn a balaclava. Initially, no one said no. It was looking good.

Sinn Féin TDs David Cullinane and Aengus Ó Snodaigh initially said yes. In both cases we arranged to meet, but both men pulled out. Cullinane soon left a message saying he had 'mentioned it to the Press Office. She [Mary Lou] had no problem with Shane but . . . I might give it a miss. Best of luck with the book, regardless.'

Aengus Ó Snodaigh TD was due to meet me in the TriBeCa restaurant in Ranelagh. He sent a text that morning: 'Have to cancel today. Will ring later to apologise in person.' He never did.

I spoke to other Dáil deputies, including Rose Conway-Walsh, Donnchadh Ó Laoghaire, Seán Crowe and Réada Cronin. None said no. All four promised to return with a reply. None did.

Elisha McCallion, the deposed senator from Derry, forced to resign by Mary Lou in October 2020 over a funds scandal, initially said yes, but changed her mind within a few days, claiming that 'the party is not linked into this project'. Elisha is former bomber Martina Anderson's niece.

When I rang Deputy Pearse Doherty, he was in a hot snot over a piece I had written in the *Sunday Independent* about the Sinn Féin civil war raging in Derry. He said he wasn't interested in the book.

The exercise was revealing. The non-combatants in the South were doing somersaults to fall into line with the ex-prisoners in the North.

Happily, as time passed, some initial naysayers quietly changed their minds and opened up. I spoke to former Sinn Féin ministers, MLAs and TDs. Others gave off-the-record briefings, while many who had left Sinn Féin in recent years came forward. I spent two hours at a secret venue talking to a former active member of the IRA's Army Council, a household name.

My series of calls suggested that when there is a different agenda between North and South Sinn Féin, the demands of the

Northern faction often prevail. Today's Southern leaders, like Mary Lou McDonald, Pearse Doherty, Eoin Ó Broin, David Cullinane and Rose Conway-Walsh, have never seen action, while influential leaders in Northern Ireland are identified with the military wing. Some of the ex-army Sinn Féin leaders, such as Conor Murphy and Gerry Kelly, are now democratically elected MLAs but remain loyal to their past and to their actions. Gerry Adams had uniquely managed to straddle the military and political wings in order to speak for both the Northern and Southern Sinn Féin parties. Adams, a Northerner, led Sinn Féin in the Dáil while retaining supreme influence over the military wing in the North and South. Despite his protests that he was never in the IRA, nobody (except apparently Mary Lou) believes him.

When Mary Lou insists that the IRA has disbanded, it reassures her supporters in the Republic, but her influence over some elements north of the border is undoubtedly diminished as a result. While writing this book, I spent a great deal of time in Derry and Belfast discovering what politicians and people think of Mary Lou McDonald. Is she acceptable to Sinn Féin members as their leader, or is she a late arrival, a carpetbagger riding in on horseback for the endgame, hoping to clean up on the back of their struggle? Are the hard men of the North exploiting her? Is she merely a vehicle of convenience in the battle which they, not she, have fought for a united Ireland? Is her popularity and acceptability in the Republic their ticket to power when the two parts of Ireland come together?

It is equally important to discover how Ulster Unionists see her. Is she perceived as even more threatening to the union than Adams because she is poised to capture the office of Taoiseach in the Dáil while simultaneously holding the leadership of the largest political party in the Northern Ireland Assembly? Would they prefer Adams, the IRA devil they know from Belfast, or the less familiar woman from Dublin? Or does her distance from the Troubles make her more palatable to them?

Above all, there remains a more fundamental question about Mary Lou McDonald. Is she a true believer, a real republican or an adventurer, an opportunist, like many other politicians? Did she spot an opening for a young middle-class Southern woman in Sinn Féin over twenty years ago and go for the gap with gusto? Did she tailor her convictions accordingly? At first glance, her commitment to the republican cause seems shallow, even suspect. When Mary Lou is asked about her republican pedigree and convictions, she appears to be on tricky terrain. She invariably instances the hunger strikes in 1981 as her 'road to Damascus moment'. Yet at the time of the IRA prison protests she was only twelve, a schoolgirl in Notre Dame des Missions school in suburban Dublin. Her insistence that the news of the prisoners' deaths on the television screen were seminal events in her childhood is well known. Moreover, in an interview with Freya McClements of *The Irish Times* in April 2021, she boldly beefed up the imagery, painting a powerful picture of the effect on her family. 'I remember,' she said, 'the day that Bobby Sands died. I can still see my brother running out to tell me, shouting the news . . . I was still a child and didn't fully understand the politics of what was happening, but felt viscerally the fact that something was extraordinarily wrong in our country.'

It was undoubtedly a memorable moment in the life of the young Mary Lou, but strangely, 'visceral' or not, the memory seems to have lain festering, casually shelved for at least fifteen years. There is no recorded instance of her nursing or suppressing any dormant republican fervour or any remotely connected sense of injustice during her teenage years or as a university student. Her political passion was not woken from its slumbers until late into her twenties, after her marriage to Martin Lanigan in 1996, when she joined Fianna Fáil, the Irish National Congress and, finally, Sinn Féin in quick succession. During those missing years, the Troubles in Northern Ireland were raging, wrongs were being perpetrated on both sides, and the minority in the North was pleading for more support from sympathetic Irish men and women in the Republic. There were openings galore for nationalists, young and old, to promote the cause of a united Ireland. Mary Lou McDonald was at worst unconcerned, at best a 'sneaking regarder' of Irish unity, more energised at the time by urgent matters like her studies, her courtship with Martin and her social life. She was a normal student, determined to enjoy the experience, particularly in Notre Dame des Missions and in Trinity College Dublin, where she received a privileged education, undisturbed by high-minded ideological vocations like republicanism or social equality.

She backs up her 'road to Damascus moment' narrative with tales of her republican family background, citing both her mother's and her father's Fianna Fáil roots. This might explain her first political decision to join Fianna Fáil, but not the haste with which she left the party and switched to Sinn Féin. Her passage to the top of Sinn Féin at breakneck speed was highly unusual in a party building up from the grass roots in the early years of this century. She had bags of talent, but so did many other newcomers to the party at the time. They were forced to take the dreary county- or city-council route. Mary Lou was not.

If she was initially a political mongrel who transformed herself into a republican thoroughbred, her family life is a key component to understanding her political versatility. Critical commentators frequently dub her an 'enigma' because they have never been able to fathom how a charming girl from upmarket Rathgar made the jump over to what many of them consider the dark side. Some are horrified that such a thing could happen, but maybe they should start looking for answers in the obvious places. None of them have probed the impact on her of the two principal men in her home life: her father, Paddy McDonald, and her husband, Martin Lanigan. Nor have they sought to determine the influence of her mother, Joan, or her strong-minded sister, Joanne, or her other siblings. All we know is what Mary Lou has told us. Her own account of her early life is determined by a very powerful airbrush. It is supported by an even more powerful broad brush.

Mary Lou had an exceptionally supportive extended family network. She would come to need it. She had four aunts (sisters of her father), most living near her Rathgar home, who played a noble part in providing security and back-up during her childhood. On her mother's side, she had two married uncles with children, a farming family living in deepest Tipperary, where she spent most summer holidays. It is simplistic to put her later puzzling choice of political allegiance solely down to the charisma of Gerry Adams and Martin McGuinness, or to a young idealistic woman's failed experiment with Fianna Fáil causing her to flee into the arms of Sinn Féin.

Yet she did join and leave Fianna Fáil, the political party of both her parents, within little more than a year. Again, two different explanations of her short-term loyalty to Fianna Fáil have emerged. Most party members have maintained, until now, that she left Fianna Fáil because she was in a hurry, frustrated because her progress was being blocked by the late Brian Lenihan Junior. They insist that she felt Lenihan saw her as a threat rather than an asset in his Dublin West constituency. Others believe her own version: that Fianna Fáil was weak on the national question, that its members were not true republicans. So she switched horses.

Surprisingly, Mary Lou is not a fluent Irish speaker, a skill that might have been expected to be a priority for a nationalist with high aspirations. Nor is there any evidence that her sympathy for Northern nationalists was accompanied by, or based on, frequent visits to Northern Ireland in her youth.

She has always protected the men in her life from public scrutiny. Her carefully hidden father is an unpredictable character who might merit a biography in his own right. He fully earned the half-chapter he has been afforded in this book. Mary Lou has given him the full airbrush treatment.

Her husband, Martin Lanigan, the father of the couple's two children, Iseult and Gerard, has been even less visible than Mary Lou's father. He appears almost nowhere in public with her, which has prompted inevitable curiosity.

Her mother, Joan, is regularly wheeled out by Mary Lou with gratitude for being a stable force when her father was absent. Despite the disruption caused by her parents' separation when Mary Lou was ten, she always doggedly insists that she had a happy childhood and that hers was a very close family. Presumably she excludes her severed father from the happy family unit but, when pressed, says that she loves him. His compulsive recklessness before and after his separation from Joan cannot have aided the cause of a happy upbringing for their four children. According to Mary Lou, her mother was not an active republican but supported 'Amnesty International and was very involved in the Burma Action Group'. She worked as a teacher and in a medical centre after the children were reared.

Her younger sister Joanne's mysterious membership of a far more militant republican socialist group than Sinn Féin has never before been properly explored. Mary Lou has openly declared her closeness to Joanne and her children. She never discusses her sister's unconventional republican activities. They too receive the overworked airbrush.

Mary Lou McDonald's skilfully spun narrative of her early years is the story of a highly conventional education and childhood. She rattles off the CV of a girl from Rathgar who attended a private convent, followed by obtaining a degree from Trinity College, spending a postgraduate year in Limerick and working a few short-term, humdrum jobs. A pretty ordinary middle-class biography. Hence the surprise that she opted for Sinn Féin, the party currently associated with rebels and underdogs.

Mary Lou's early life and activities do not sit comfortably with her political destination. The unvarnished truth is far from this almost universally accepted, but unchallenged, version of her life before politics, which is hopelessly incomplete, with many aspects of her background and political activities hitherto unexplored and unexplained.

The road that may lead her to the Taoiseach's office is littered with riddles. The IRA riddle and her real relationships with the military wing of Sinn Féin is only one conundrum in the story of this complex woman's rise to the top.

CHAPTER 1

THE SKELETON IN
THE CUPBOARD

Mary Lou McDonald's father, Patrick 'Paddy' McDonald, was no angel. He married Joan Hayes on 3 April 1967. The wedding took place in the Roman Catholic church in Monkstown, County Dublin, five days before Joan's twenty-first birthday. Paddy was only twenty-three. Their first child, Beatrice (Bea), was born on 31 August 1967. She was designated male at birth and confirmed her transition in 2021. Her sister Mary Lou was born on May Day 1969 in the National Maternity Hospital in Dublin's Holles Street.

Mary Lou has always portrayed her mother as an unsung saint. The two pivotal figures in her early life could not have lived more different lifestyles. Paddy was wild, Joan a rock of common sense. Both are still alive.

Researching this book, I have met gardaí who arrested Paddy, lawyers who defended him and publicans who loved him. Mary Lou's father is what is often euphemistically called a 'character'. He has left a trail of trouble wherever he trod. Some of those he has met along the way describe him as a daredevil, others as a lovable rogue; a number mutter unprintable expletives under their breath. Mary Lou prefers not to talk about him.

Paddy was reared in middle-class Rathmines by his parents, Bernard and Annie. He had four older sisters, Maeve, Nora, Joan and Phyllis. Maeve, the oldest, died in February 2022, while Phyllis, the youngest, predeceased her in December 2019. The surviving aunts of Mary Lou speak of their niece with great fondness. They are, understandably, more reticent, but equally affectionate, when their wayward brother's name is mentioned.

Paddy started his working life as a small building contractor, following in his father's footsteps. He entered the workforce in his teens and had already built his first house when he was twenty-one. Business was buzzing in the early years of his marriage. He saved money and made a profit of £5000 in the first six months of 1970. He, Joan and their two children lived in comfortable rented accommodation in Eaton Brae, Rathgar, a slightly higher rung up the south Dublin social climbers' ladder than his former Rathmines homestead. The McDonalds were upwardly mobile. Paddy's progress was not hindered by his Fianna Fáil contacts or, more pointedly, by his membership of the party of builders and strokers. He played rugby for Palmerston. Kevin Fitzpatrick, former president of the club, remembers him as a 'rough diamond. He was a prop forward, a square-jawed man; he could be very funny. He was in and out of the first team.'

Mary Lou was barely a year old when, on a summer night in 1970, Paddy's world collapsed. Her father was a passenger in the back of a Volkswagen that was involved in a head-on crash. The accident nearly killed him. It was around midnight when he saw the approaching headlights, as the Volkswagen tried to overtake another car. His next memory is nearly twenty-four hours later. He regained consciousness in the Meath Hospital, hearing the voices of his wife and his sister Phyllis by his bedside. He learned that he had been hurled through the windscreen. A priest had given him the last rites. Mary Lou was nearly fatherless at the age of one. Her mother, Joan, escaped widowhood by a whisker.

In November 1985 Paddy told *Magill* magazine that he had suffered multiple life-changing injuries in the crash. His back and neck were badly damaged. But, like many self-employed people, he needed to return to work rapidly. He had a wife and two children to support and a valuable countrywide contract with Telefusion (Ireland) to fulfil. Ten days after the crash he was back on the job.

Life for Paddy would never be the same again. The injuries he had suffered caused him to feel dizzy at work. He could no longer climb up poles or crawl along roofs because of the vertigo he would suffer. He was unable to monitor the activities of his workforce. He under-priced jobs, something he had never done before his mishap, and lost all confidence in his ability to function effectively. Despite medical treatment and physiotherapy, after two months he began to realise that his health was not improving, and so his livelihood was threatened. He decided to go down the compensation route.

An employee of Paddy's steered him into the arms of a lawyer called Brendan O'Maoileoin of Michael B. O'Maoileoin Solicitors, an introduction Paddy would rue in the years to come.

Brendan O'Maoileoin was even more 'colourful' than Paddy. He was a former member of the Fianna Fáil national executive and a two-time candidate for the Seanad. He lost his seat on the national executive in 1970 and was easily defeated in his Seanad bids on both occasions. He lived in a grand-sounding house in Dundrum named Altamont Hall and sent his sons to Stonyhurst, the upmarket English Roman Catholic public school. He was later to become embroiled in a row at Dublin's United Arts Club when he was expelled for 'behaviour unbecoming of a member'. He sniffed snuff and drank plenty.

Paddy told *Magill* that, owing to his injuries, he had decided to stop working on site. O'Maoileoin was confident of a satisfactory outcome to the compensation claim, but advised waiting until both drivers in the accident had faced pending prosecutions. It seemed a wise course to take, although it meant that Joan, Bea and Mary Lou were now surviving on Paddy's savings. In 1971, all criminal actions surrounding the crash were completed, so Paddy's compensation case was poised to commence. According to Paddy, he restarted his business, although he himself was physically incapable of participating actively in it.

It was a bad decision. The business staggered from month to month. Paddy, wary of ladders, was unable to supervise most of the work. Jobs went wrong with regularity. Paddy felt that his workers were exploiting his inability to climb on to the roofs to monitor their activities. At the same time, the preferred solution – a chunky compensation award – seemed, strangely, to have stalled. O'Maoileoin was suspiciously busy when Paddy McDonald came calling. The optimistic Fianna Fáil lawyer seemed to be ducking and diving.

Legal proceedings were moving tortuously slowly. They dragged on into 1973, with no explanation for the delay. Three years after the accident, Paddy had not been awarded a red cent. It was the year that he and Joan were blessed with twins, Joanne and Patrick, born on Hallowe'en day. Suddenly Paddy had six mouths to feed. He was finding it difficult to support his wife and children.

Around this time brushes with the law began happening to Paddy with alarming frequency. Drink was an ever-growing menace. His troubles were coming in big battalions. Never a man to abstain from alcohol, he landed himself in embarrassing scrapes.

While researching Mary Lou's family history, I met a garda who had arrested a sozzled Paddy over fifty years ago for the relatively minor offence of refusing to get off a bus in Rathmines. It was Christmas Eve and Paddy was blotto. The garda put him in a cell and left him to cool off while he resumed his patrol. When he returned at around 2.30 in the morning, Paddy was out of the cell haranguing the puzzled duty sergeant. The garda who had arrested Paddy told me a bit about him, his Fianna Fáil connections and that he 'drove an old van and was in the building business'. Because it was Christmas Eve, the guards let him go.

On 28 February 1973, the day of the general election, Paddy landed in a spectacular scrape. He was a loyal and loud Fianna Fáil supporter, specifically working for candidates Philip Brady, Ben Briscoe and Gerard Buchanan in the constituency of Dublin South-Central. Paddy drove a truck carrying the Fianna Fáil posters around the constituency. After parking it illegally near the Harold's Cross dog track on election night, he defiantly got back into the truck when a tow-away vehicle arrived to take it to the compound. A row broke out. Paddy refused to remove himself to allow the truck to be taken away. The truck, the posters and Paddy all ended up locked in the corporation compound.

The following day – 1 March 1973 – the *Irish Independent*, tongue-in-cheek, told the story, together with a large picture of the truck, the offending posters and the bold Paddy, embedded in the driving seat. Headed 'The Van behind the Wire', the story read:

Fianna Fáil's drive to get its supporters out to vote in the Dublin South-Central Constituency was blunted last night . . . by a vigilant traffic warden.

He spotted a large van festooned with posters of the three candidates, Ben Briscoe, Phil Brady and Gerard Buchanan parked in a rush-hour clearway and promptly called in the tow-away vehicle.

It did not go down very well with the party's supporters who saw their well-oiled election operation being disrupted at a vital time.

As the tow vehicle edged its way towards the van at Harold's Cross Road about forty people protested.

But the law had its way, and off the van was taken to the Corporation compound at Christ Church Place where it became briefly the 'van behind the wire'.

However, within minutes of its capture Fianna Fáil workers were bailing it out and it was soon making its way once again around the constituency.

Forty years later, Mary Lou McDonald aped her father's election-eve drama when, not only did she refuse to leave the Dáil when suspended, she also implanted herself in the chamber itself for several hours, challenging the ushers to remove her physically. She brought Dáil proceedings to a close. Both acts of defiance escaped unpunished.

Paddy and his candidates had the last laugh. Both Brady and Briscoe were elected. Gerry Buchanan was beaten but was appointed a judge a few years later.

During 1973, things went from bad to worse for Paddy McDonald. He was still receiving physiotherapy and medical treatment for the accident. His business was in free fall. In 1974 his money ran out. Further inexplicable delays in the legal case were causing him huge stress. So were the Montessori school fees for Bea and Mary Lou. Paddy, full of bravado, regaled his pals in the pub with cock-and-bull stories of how he had tossed a coin with the school principal for the kids' nursery school fees. His savings spent, Paddy borrowed from the bank.

The business was limping from one disaster to another. He still had a few hard-won Eastern Health Board contracts and a job at the Dundrum mental hospital, but even they went wrong as his physical health failed to improve, despite medication.

O'Maoileoin became even more elusive. He made excuses for delaying appointments; he was never available. Paradoxically, according to Paddy, the two men remained on good terms, exchanging stories about Fianna Fáil friends on the rare occasions when they actually managed to meet. In one instance, O'Maoileoin had given McDonald a solicitor's undertaking as comfort for a bank loan. He used the money borrowed on the back of this promise to tackle a job in Arklow. It was never finished. He wasn't paid.

While Paddy McDonald was sinking, Brendan O'Maoileoin was flying: he had moved to a newly renovated office in Dublin's Lower Fitzwilliam Street. Paddy's visits to him became less friendly, but more frequent and frenetic. Paddy was calling every day; the temperature was rising. On one occasion, he became involved in an altercation with the receptionist when he tried to leave the office with his file. The endless delays continued, defying explanation.

As Paddy tells it, he was beginning to flounder in 1975. He could not sleep and he was taking Mogadon in increasing quantities. He was receiving treatment from a top psychiatrist. His marriage was in danger and he was drinking like a fish.

Just as Paddy thought he might crack up, a meeting was arranged with O'Maoileoin and his barristers in the Four Courts. Paddy recalls a mention from the lawyers of an offer of a £3000 settlement, but he told them of the scale of his personal incapacity, that he needed more than £30,000, considering his permanent state of ill health, his four children and the loss of his normal working-life expectancy. His senior counsel reassured him that he would get him 'a fair settlement', but warned him that the taxman would take a big slice of any notional £30,000 award.

Paddy McDonald didn't give a hoot about the taxman. He would deal with him in due course. He was now desperate for money; he didn't even have the cash for his bus fares. He couldn't pay the rent on the family apartment for Joan, Mary Lou and her siblings. He hassled and harried O'Maoileoin to no avail, until his faith in his solicitor was finally shattered. He even considered, in his own words, 'doing away with O'Maoileoin'.

Drink was landing him in more trouble. In early 1976, he was back in court, this time for all the wrong reasons. On 17 February, the *Evening Echo*, a Cork newspaper, and the *Irish Independent* both carried a story about an excitable neighbour of the Russian Embassy, on Dublin's Orwell Road, storming into the high-security citadel in the early hours of the morning. This time, Paddy McDonald was in hot water.

Headed 'Russia Embassy parties keep children awake', the *Evening Echo*'s narrative ran as follows:

Late night parties in the Russian Embassy in Dublin keep young children in the neighbourhood awake until the early hours, an accused man claimed at a Dublin court yesterday.

He went to the Embassy to lodge a complaint but was surrounded by 'six KGB men' after he had thrown a length of rubber at an official inside the grounds, he told Justice T.P. O'Reilly at Rathfarnham Court.

Before the Justice was Patrick McDonald, a building contractor of Ard na Gréine, Eaton Brae, Orwell Road, Rathgar. He was charged that between 1 and 2 a.m. on August 28 last at Orwell Road – a public place – he was guilty of disorderly behaviour while drunk.

He was also charged that on the same occasion he used insulting words or behaviour with intent to provoke a breach of the peace or whereby a breach of the peace might be caused. McDonald, who defended himself, disputed the first charge by pointing out that the offence of being drunk was not committed in a public place but within the grounds of the Russian Embassy, a place where the general public have no access. This charge was dismissed.

Dealing with the second charge, Justice O'Reilly asked McDonald could he show cause as to why he should not bind him to keep the peace.

The defendant said his house was only a very short distance from the Embassy on Orwell Road. His four young children, he said, could not sleep because of the 'constant parties being held in the Embassy'.

The disturbances were so bad on this particular night that he decided he would have to do something to rectify the matter. He approached the Embassy lodge and knocked on the door but got no reply. Then he walked up the driveway to the Embassy itself. He tried to explain the point to an official – 'but this man only laughed at me.'

McDonald added; 'I took up a piece of rubber and threw it at him and almost immediately was surrounded by six KGB men.'

He was very glad when the Gardaí arrived.

Inspector Thomas Noone, prosecuting, said the Gardaí had never received any complaints from residents about disturbances at the Embassy – even though there were a number of families with young children in the neighbourhood. If the defendant wanted to complain, he could have phoned the Gardaí, who would have handled the matter for him.

Justice O'Reilly also dismissed the charge and made no order binding to the peace after McDonald gave an undertaking that there would be no repetition of his conduct in the Embassy grounds.

The *Irish Independent*'s account was even more colourful. At the top of page 3, it entitled its piece 'Saw Red at the Russian Embassy'. It told of how McDonald 'blew his top' about 'Russian high-jinks' and how Garda Aubrey Steedman added that Paddy had been 'shouting about the KGB and seemed to want to be arrested'. He also appeared to have had 'drink taken'.

Garda Steedman wouldn't have needed to consult the Special Branch to come to that conclusion.

Paddy McDonald gave an assurance to the court that he would not repeat his behaviour and he walked away an innocent man.

The episode illustrated that while Paddy McDonald was often a drunken buffoon, he was nobody's fool; he had spotted that his offence was not committed in a 'public place', as written on the charge sheet. The Russian Embassy was the opposite: it was a private fortress which he had penetrated. He secured his own acquittal without the need for expensive lawyers. No doubt he entertained punters in the pub for months afterwards with tales of how he had outwitted the KGB and the gardaí. He had no fear of the courts. McDonald was to spend much of the next decade fighting his corner in front of the beaks.

The court merry-go-round began in earnest in 1977, seven

years after the car crash. Mary Lou was by then an eight-year-old and, although she has spoken little of her home life during this period, it must have seemed far from stable, even through the eyes of such a young child. According to Paddy, his marriage was now in deep trouble, but he had talked to Joan about buying a small shop with the compensation money which, he claimed, would enable him to support his family again. But his personal crisis deepened and he began to behave increasingly recklessly. Paddy says he was told that the court had awarded him 'hardship' money until the compensation case was settled, so, even though he no longer trusted the word of his own lawyers, desperate, he accepted a cheque from O'Maoileoin for £1,100. He went straight to a Rathmines bank to cash it, only to find that it was crossed and would have to go through an account, impossible before closing time on a bank holiday weekend. He stormed back to O'Maoileoin's office in a rage. His solicitor capitulated and arranged for it to be cashed before the bank's doors closed that day.

The court case was held the next week. Marcus Webb, an eminent psychiatrist who specialised in alcohol dependence, was there. So was Derek Robinson, a Meath surgeon, presumably to give evidence about the car accident. There was an accountant, Donal Ward, Paddy McDonald's GP Dr Berber, two senior counsel, one junior counsel and O'Maoileoin.

Paddy McDonald was puzzled. The senior counsel were not the ones he had expected. He had demanded a hearing before judge and jury, but had been willing to settle the case if a realistic sum was offered, at least enough to set him up in a business to support his family.

Soon after his senior counsel opened the case, it was adjourned. When it resumed, none of the counsel or other potential professional witnesses were present. Just McDonald, O'Maoileoin and the junior barrister.

Then the bombshell dropped. O'Maoileoin took the stand and

revealed that the compensation case had been settled in 1975, two years earlier. Paddy McDonald had been kept in the dark; he promptly told the court that the lawyers had settled the case without his authority. He remembered only the £1,100 cheque, which he had understood was 'hardship' money to tide him over until a settlement was reached. He was shattered, emerging from the court dazed, his hopes of a rescue package dashed.

The court had told him that it was open to him to pursue O'Maoileoin for negligence, not misconduct.

O'Maoileoin vanished into thin air. Paddy went home that night devastated. According to his own account, his wife Joan asked what hope there was now for her, Bea, Mary Lou, Patrick and Joanne. The settlement money was a pipe dream. The family had no future. Seemingly, O'Maoileoin had ruined them.

Paddy McDonald may have been an incorrigible and battered rogue, but he refused to give up. Although it was almost impossible in those days to find a solicitor willing to sue a fellow lawyer, he resolved to try. For once he was lucky. Through his Fianna Fáil connections, he knew John Fitzpatrick, a highly respected solicitor with Vincent & Beatty, a reputable firm. John Fitzpatrick took on the case, a decision that probably did not endear him to his peers, but it was a courageous call by a man of integrity. Fitzpatrick was later to be Dublin City sheriff and returning officer for Dublin City constituencies.

The pursuit of O'Maoileoin began. Paddy McDonald headed back to the High Court. This time he had a team of heavy-weight lawyers in good standing with their peers. Nicholas Kearns, a senior counsel with a high reputation, advised the team assembled by John Fitzpatrick. (Kearns was later to become a supporter of the Progressive Democrats and president of the High Court.) Nevertheless, there were further delays; it took months to access Paddy's file, eventually achieved with the help of an unnamed Fianna Fáil politician.

Paddy McDonald's marriage to Joan had finally cracked under the strain. In 1979 they separated when he moved out of the family home, leaving Joan to bring up Mary Lou, aged ten, and her three siblings on her own.

Undeterred, Paddy soldiered on. He was finally back in court in 1980, running an action to establish negligence against O'Maoileoin and another for damages. The High Court found in his favour, adjudging O'Maoileoin to have been negligent. O'Maoileoin appealed the decision to the Supreme Court. On 11 March 1982 *The Irish Times* carried the result of the appeal:

> Court rejects appeal by Dublin solicitor
>
> The Supreme Court yesterday dismissed with costs an appeal by a Dublin solicitor against a finding by a jury in the High Court that he had settled a personal injuries action without the authority of his client.
>
> The appellant was Michael B. O'Maoileoin, who carries on practice as a solicitor at Lower Fitzwilliam Street, Dublin and against whom an action was brought by Patrick McDonald, a building contractor, Eaton Brae, Orwell Road, Dublin.
>
> Mr. McDonald claimed that he retained Mr. O'Maoileoin to act for him in an action for damages for personal injuries and that Mr. O'Maoileoin, without his authority, settled the action for £4,250 and costs in 1976.
>
> The court was told that Mr. McDonald refused to accept the settlement and had insisted that his action should proceed. When the action came up for trial, the defendants claimed that it had been settled. An issue was directed as to whether, or not, the action had been settled and the President of the High Court (Mr. Justice Finlay) held that it had.
>
> Mr. McDonald then brought proceedings against Mr. O'Maoileoin, and another issue was directed as to whether Mr. O'Maoileoin had settled the case without authority. This

was tried before Mr. Justice D'Arcy and the jury found in Mr. McDonald's favour.

The Chief Justice (Mr. Justice O'Higgins) said that the basis of the appeal was that on the evidence given before the jury only one answer could be given to the question as to whether Mr. O'Maoileoin had settled without authority, express or implied. It had been submitted on Mr. O'Maoileoin's behalf that an affirmative answer by the jury was perverse.

The judgement was plain sailing in Paddy McDonald's favour, but there was a sting in the tail. The chief justice had some harsh words to say about his evidence. The article went on:

The Chief Justice asserted that the evidence of Mr. McDonald left much to be desired; it appeared at times to be unreliable. It appeared at times to be impossible to accept in certain particulars, but consistently throughout his evidence was the assertion that he had given no authority for the acceptance of the sum.

He would dismiss the appeal. Mr. Justice Henchy, who agreed with the Chief Justice, said the accident had happened in 1970 and it was now 1982. A great part of Mr. McDonald's life would have been spent in one form of litigation or another. All this seemed to be inconsistent with the due administration of justice. If damages were to be determined – as they would – on what basis could they be determined? Since 1970 inflation had driven all concepts of money topsy-turvy and he could not see how any jury in 1982 or 1983, as it might be, could assess damages now when the real time for assessing damages should have been in 1975 or 1976.

It was within the competence of the jury, he said, to decide that the limit of Mr. O'Maoileoin's instructions was to proceed with the negotiations, but not to settle without the imprimatur of the client. That was what they had found.

Mr. Justice Griffin, who also said he would dismiss the [i.e.

O'Maoileoin's] appeal, said the court was not entitled to interfere
with this finding. It seemed to him that Mr. McDonald would be
entitled to such damages as he would have recovered in 1976, not
in 1983.

The exact compensation remained unsettled until 1985 when
the amounts were finally decided by the High Court. Paddy
McDonald was awarded £15,000 damages and £12,000 special
damages to include loss of earnings. On top of that he was awarded
£22,780 for interest and costs.

It was a pyrrhic victory. It may have been groundbreaking in
successfully calling a solicitor to account, but it left Paddy and his
separated family still buried in deep financial trouble. He complained that the sum awarded for his loss of earnings was paltry,
considering that back in 1970 he had made £5000 profit in the first
six months alone. His life was in bits. His family was split asunder,
partially at least due to the pressure caused by the stress of his
accident and by unscrupulous lawyers. He spoke of his eighteen-
year-old child Bea, who had just started third-level education, of his
twelve-year-old twins and of his elder daughter, Mary Lou, aged
sixteen, who had just finished her Inter Cert; according to him,
at that time she wanted to do law in university. He confessed to
being 'very bitter' and having obligations to his wife, Joan, but he
couldn't 'fulfil them'.

One of the reasons he could not fulfil the obligations was that
O'Maoileoin didn't pay up. In 1987 Paddy petitioned the High
Court to bankrupt O'Maoileoin and he won his case. In 1988 the
issue was further complicated when it emerged in court that Paddy
McDonald had accepted unspecified sums from O'Maoileoin in
discharge of his claims. It is not known what agreement he had
finally reached with his former solicitor. However, O'Maoileoin's
bankruptcy still stood undischarged. There were other creditors in
the queue.

O'Maoileoin resurfaced to practise as a barrister in the United Kingdom for many years and even became a member of the underwriters Lloyd's of London. Lloyd's coughed up to pay for many other claims against O'Maoileoin when the official assignee in bankruptcy caught up with him.

Thirteen years after he had been declared a bankrupt – in 1999 – with extraordinary audacity, O'Maoileoin applied to Ireland's courts for the annulment of his bankruptcy. In March 2006 his application was finally refused by Supreme Court Justices Niall Fennelly, Fidelma Macken and none other than McDonald's one-time senior counsel Nicholas Kearns, by then a judge of the highest court in the land.

If Paddy McDonald, for all his faults, had not begun to put a halt to O'Maoileoin's gallop in the late 1970s, there might have been many more victims of his unscrupulous practices. Paddy may have been a rascal, a drunk, an adventurer, but alongside the abundance of booze there was a streak of human decency in his blood.

Paddy's story since his separation from Joan in 1979 is one of finding work wherever he could, at home and abroad. He has done construction work in Ohio, has worked in restaurants and pubs in Galway and the United Kingdom, has operated in the Middle East, most notably in Saudi Arabia and in Hong Kong. Not surprisingly, when he landed in alcohol-free Saudi, he was not long discovering the joys of 'Sid', short for 'Siddiqi', the Saudi answer to Ireland's illegal drink, poteen.

With typical panache and misplaced initiative, Paddy is even believed to have started a weekend 'speakeasy' – an illegal drinking club – in a London café.

After his separation, his businesses continued to spring up in different guises and at various addresses. He had registered his original building company, Patrick B. McDonald & Co., in his parents' home in Spire View Avenue, Rathmines, when he was first married and living in Rathgar, but, following his separation and change of abode, he started another outfit called Ultimate Security, registered at his sister Nora's address in Wainsfort Avenue, Terenure. It was while wearing his security hat that he managed to land a gig as caretaker for the grandson of a former British Conservative prime minister, Andrew Bonar Law (in office 1922/23). His grandson, also Andrew Bonar Law, lived with his wife, Joanna, in Shankill Castle, County Dublin. The Bonar Laws liked Paddy and his new English partner, Shirley. The couple stayed for about eighteen months, caretaking in Andrew and Joanna's cottage, often babysitting the Bonar Laws' grandchildren. He had been installed in the Bonar Laws' cottage rent-free because Andrew was aware of the need to protect himself from the perils – in those days – of inadvertently giving rights for life to paying tenants. Inspired thinking. The father of the future leader of Sinn Féin and the deeply committed unionist Tory prime minister's grandson struck up an excellent relationship because both men were good chess players.

With such a mixed cocktail of unorthodox enterprises on her father's CV, Mary Lou McDonald has always been understandably reluctant to talk about him. It is difficult to know what effect his antics had on her childhood, but they were hardly positive. It is inconceivable that she was unaware not only of his drunken escapades, but also of the specific episodes of his erratic behaviour which were being reported in the press with alarming regularity. The media coverage of his exploits must have caused anguish not only in the McDonald household but also among his older sisters living in ultra-respectable Churchtown and Terenure. Mary Lou was young enough to have been shielded from the Russian Embassy high jinks when she was only seven, but friends, relations and Rathgar neighbours would not have taken kindly to such unwelcome publicity later brought upon them by a fellow resident.

One of Mary Lou's relations tells a colourful tale of Paddy's late-night arrival at home with the well-known Mr Pussy, Dublin's

1970s sensational drag queen, after a performance in the legendary Baggot Inn.

Mr Pussy (aka actor Alan Amsby) recalls the night: 'I remember causing quite a stir,' he confesses. 'I suppose it would be like bringing Boy George or Lady Gaga into your home in this day and age.'

Mary Lou was too young to remember Mr Pussy's nocturnal visit, but she was a street-savvy teenager when Chief Justice Tom O'Higgins publicly dubbed her father's sworn evidence as being at times 'unreliable'. He was half-hero and half-villain, but his behaviour must have caused plenty of angst to Mary Lou's mother and her children. Her husband constantly sailed far too close to the wind for comfort. They must have lived in dread of where he would pop up next.

Since Mary Lou's arrival in public life, her difficulties about addressing her father's role surface every time she is asked the inevitable questions put to pivotal public figures about their parents and their own formative years. She is awkward and unusually defensive on the subject.

On Mary Lou's first appearance on Ireland's popular *Late Late* television show in 2014, her father was airbrushed out of her narrative. Asked to talk about her family, she said she had 'two fantastic brothers, a lovely sister and a wonderful mother'. Then she pointed out to the programme's host, Ryan Tubridy, that her mother was in the audience. The cameras duly obliged by zooming in on a proud, smiling Joan. Paddy didn't get a mention. He was a non-person. The Mary Lou airbrush was working overtime.

In 2018, a tame interviewer from the official Sinn Féin magazine, *An Phoblacht*, suggested that she 'tell us about your childhood'. Her reply was by now a successfully tried-and-tested formula: 'My mother Joan is fantastic. She is a very steadying influence for me and our family. Our extended family are close. I have two brothers and a sister with whom I had good craic growing up. We had a very regular, happy childhood. I loved my school and we had great friends. I did all of the things kids should do and should not do as I was growing up.' The broad brush had joined the airbrush. She was determinedly painting a picture of normality on the home front, while avoiding any detail. In the process Paddy McDonald had been vaporised. That was the official version, as printed by the party's propaganda organ. Paddy was surplus to republican requirements.

Mary Lou has often deftly deflected questions about her father from less gentle interviewers than *An Phoblacht* with sad tales of her parents' separation in 1979 and how such divisions in the family were a stigma at the time. She is not averse to playing the victim. Sometimes she has a nice line in ironic diversion about how Pope John Paul II was visiting Ireland preaching old-fashioned Catholic values at the time of her parents' marital break-up. When pressed, she volunteers vaguely that her father was either 'mainly in the building trade' or even – as she told Kathy Sheridan of *The Irish Times* in 2021 – that 'he did very well and very badly, depending on the times', implying that he was subject to the prevailing economic winds. In puff pieces about Mary Lou, her father has sometimes even been elevated to the status of 'a successful surveyor', which is stretching his skill set.

When she was asked about her father's occupation by former Fine Gael MEP Mary Banotti in her book *There's Something about Mary*, she closed up like a clam, offering the following: 'Various things. He mainly worked in construction. Now he lives in County Galway.' Full stop. She didn't even reveal that he was running a bed and breakfast there.

Banotti must have felt the vibes. She steered the thirteen-page interview elsewhere. Mention of Paddy was a conversation stopper.

In Deaglán de Bréadún's well-researched book *Power Play: The Rise of Modern Sinn Féin*, a second author was unable to prise any significant information about her father from Mary Lou. She corrected the description of him as a 'surveyor', pointing out that 'building contractor' was more accurate. And that was all anyone was going to elicit from Mary Lou about her father. The family renegade was relegated to a mere footnote. Up until now, the skeleton has been kept tightly locked in the cupboard.

In marked contrast, Mary Lou's mother, Joan, and her side of the family have been regularly mentioned in political dispatches.

Joan Hayes was reared on a farm in the Glen of Aherlow, County Tipperary. She was educated by the Dominican nuns before becoming a secretary, working for Aer Lingus in Dublin. She was wooed, swept off her feet and married to a dashing Paddy McDonald at the age of just twenty.

Like Paddy, Joan was from Fianna Fáil stock. Different Fianna Fáil stock. For Paddy, Fianna Fáil was not only in his blood but it also offered a network where contracts could be secured with connections. Joan's attachment to the party was an old-fashioned tribal loyalty. Where Paddy mixed with men on the make in Dublin, Joan was solid, Tipperary and traditional. Her folk, the Hayes family from west Tipperary, had an interesting history dating back to the civil war. They were on the republican side and had the wounds to prove it.

The Glen of Aherlow is a missing piece in the riddle of Mary Lou. It is relatively unexplored as an influence on her thinking. Her mother was the link that provided Mary Lou and her siblings with access to this historic and enchanting part of Ireland. It is a place of breathtaking beauty and tranquillity. It is hard to think of a bigger contrast in atmosphere between the unpredictable happenings in Ard na Gréine, her home in Rathgar, and the dignified quiet of the place in Tipperary that Mary Lou often identifies as her 'second home'.

The Glen of Aherlow is republican hero Dan Breen country. It is famous for its ambushes in the War of Independence and the civil war. In the sanitised *An Phoblacht* interview, Mary Lou volunteered, 'My mother is from Tipperary so we would spend all our summers in the Glen of Aherlow'. And then, she introduced a woman who may have affected her more than any other, adding, 'with my grandmother Molly, who was a huge influence in my life.'

Much of the rest of the *An Phoblacht* interview was the usual cringe-making apple pie that might be expected from Sinn Féin's in-house journal. Yet Mary Lou returned to Molly for a second time. Asked 'What were the political influences on your life growing up?' she again inserted Molly into the script, replying, 'My grandmother Molly, who lived in the Glen of Aherlow. She was hugely important in terms of how I understand life and politics. I learned a lot from that deep republican sentiment that Molly had. My mother is also very political, not just in terms of national politics, but international. Growing up we would sit at our kitchen table and debate things that were happening across the world.'

It is quite possible that Mary Lou was indulging herself in the luxury of a little retrofitted republicanism in the pages of *An Phoblacht*, a media outlet that required her to demonstrate her nationalist credentials to the party faithful. Yet the story of Granny Molly is potentially a far more convincing explanation for her supposedly strong republican views than the flimsy yarn she often spins about her 'road to Damascus moment'. She still insists that the plight of the IRA hunger strikers in 1981 (when she was only twelve) was the motivator for her joining Sinn Féin in 1999 when she was thirty.

As a sceptic of the Mary Lou version of her background, I decided to head for rural Tipperary, to the Glen of Aherlow and the village of Lisvernane (where her mother had been reared), to find out whether Mary Lou's claim to these strong republican roots was a porky, a romantic fantasy, a flag of political convenience or a genuinely influential part of her make-up. Was the leader of Sinn Féin spinning a line to the faithful? Did anyone in the village of Lisvernane even remember Mary Lou?

Before making the journey to the Glen of Aherlow, I read an interview which Mary Lou gave to Martin Quinn of the Tipperary

Live radio station on 25 October 2020. Recalling her time spent in the Glen of Aherlow, she said that, while she is a very proud Dub, she also considers Tipperary to be 'home'. She might not repeat the following words quite so loudly in her constituency of Dublin Central as she did to Martin Quinn in Tipperary:

> Every summer we would travel by train or car to Tipperary to the home of my grandmother, Molly Hayes. Molly (*née* Black) was married to John Hayes and they farmed in Gortavoher.
>
> Coming to a farm in the Glen of Aherlow was pure magic, and enriching and exploring the Glen and roaming the fields and the mountains was something out of a story book.
>
> In travelling down to Tipperary, once we caught sight of the magnificent and iconic Christ the King statue, we always felt that we were home and, on arrival, Molly would be standing outside to welcome and greet us. It was the start of our summer adventure and the memories are long-lasting and wonderful.

Mary Lou explained that Molly's house is still regarded as home to them, because her mother was born there and her cousin still lives there.

She told Martin Quinn that her summers in the Glen gave her a great feeling and understanding of rural life which she has carried with her in her political career. And then she laid on the romantic sentimentality, as only Mary Lou can do:

> While we roamed the hills and fields around the Glen of Aherlow, we also herded the cows with my Uncle Liam and watched the milking progress, from milking by hand to automation, and the lorry arriving to collect for the creamery. It wasn't all about life on the farm, it was also about going to Mass in Lisvernane dressed in our Sunday best, going into Moroney's shop in the village and also going into Tipperary town. The trips to Tipp were a major highlight

for us as it meant a visit to Kiely's and to the bakery there. My great-grandmother was Hannah Kiely so we always got special treatment when we were there and Larry Kiely would come out in his white coat to welcome us and to give us some pocket money, which we very gratefully received! I remember that my first time seeing a person of colour was when I was in the Glen. I was fixated by this incredibly beautiful-looking woman, dressed very colourfully and she had a beautiful smile. My grandmother explained that she had married a local man and was living in the area. These are all very precious memories that I treasure from my time on holidays there.

Mary Lou insisted that she had a deep affection for the Glen. She had been dropping local names by the bucketful. A bit of poetic licence for local radio would be understandable, but she was reminding them that her mother's family were, indeed, long-established residents of Dan Breen country.

Her claims that she had republican leanings as a result of her time in Tipp were about to be tested. Martin Quinn asked the leading question. Did she learn about the history of republicanism in the Glen of Aherlow and of people like Dinny Lacey, who was killed in an action against Free State troops at Ballydavid, Bansha, and the O'Dwyer brothers from the same area who were murdered by crown forces on 18 October 1920, and was she aware of this history during her childhood in the Glen?

She never blinked: 'Yes, I would have been aware of the names and of the stories of Dinny Lacey and the O'Dwyers and others such as Dan Breen. My grandmother was a strong republican, but she didn't speak much about the war because she had her own trauma during that period.'

This was far from a soft interview with *An Phoblacht*. This one was being given two years later to an independent radio station where she was open to challenge.

And Mary Lou was not shy about discussing it. Referring to her grandmother, Molly, she opened up a completely new front: 'Her half-brother James O'Connor was executed by the Free State side during the civil war and this had a lasting effect on her. He worked on the railway and was engaged to a local girl, Esther Quirke. It was a devastating loss and one that Molly carried with her all her life. Our family still talk about James and about the trauma visited on the family at that time.'

Mary Lou warmed to the theme: 'In order to understand history and to appreciate and know what was involved in the struggle for Irish independence it is therefore important to remember and commemorate this week Seán Treacy and the O'Dwyer brothers, and all those who gave so much for the cause of independence a hundred years ago. We owe them so much and we must never forget their role in the struggle.' It was a tour de force.

To my shame, I had never heard of James O'Connor. If what Mary Lou was saying was true, she herself could claim solid republican ancestry and street cred. Her urban middle-class image was only part of the picture. James O'Connor might not, after all, be yet another case reminiscent of familiar, but exaggerated, claims by Irish nationalists that their grandparents – or even their grand-uncles – were in the GPO in 1916; her family's close emotional connection with O'Connor could be an authentic story. It was time to either confirm it or blow it out of the water.

I phoned Tipperary county councillor Joe Hannigan, an old friend and a walking encyclopaedia of Tipperary, about my making a fact-finding visit to the area. He immediately sent me a fascinating book called *The Troubles in the Glen*, one of the most beautifully illustrated pieces of local history that has ever passed through my hands. It tells the story of the Lisnagaul ambush, of the death of Dinny Lacey, and it tells tales of the Black and Tans' terror and even the activities of Cumann na mBan in the area. The book is a magnificent labour of love. Stories are written without bitterness, but with pride, about the actions of local people in the fight for Irish independence. Nearly all the forty-five chapters are written by residents of the Glen. It was completed in November 2020 to commemorate the hundredth anniversary of the Lisnagaul ambush. Mary Lou had no hand, act or part in the book. The lion's share of the work was done by a local editorial committee. The name of the chair of the committee jumped out at me. It was none other than James Hayes, Joan Hayes's brother and Mary Lou's uncle.

Mary Lou's uncle James 'Jimmy' Hayes is aged seventy-nine. He has lived his entire life in the Glen of Aherlow after leaving school at fourteen to help on the family farm. One of the pieces he wrote in the book includes how heated discussions on the War of Independence were a constant feature in the Hayes household. It is evident from the book that the Hayes family is deep into republican history.

As I turned the pages, I came across a surprising chapter, this time about a hero of the civil war, not the War of Independence. Jimmy had obviously exercised his editorial prerogative to include the story of none other than James O'Connor, his own uncle and the grand-uncle whom neither he nor Mary Lou ever knew. The author of the piece was Jimmy's wife, Breda Hayes. It gives a tragic, but eloquent, account of James O'Connor's short life.

James O'Connor was the son of Patrick and Bridget O'Connor (*née* Keogh). His father, Patrick, died in 1911 at the age of thirty-nine. His mother, Bridget, a thirty-four-year-old widow, remarried a forty-four-year-old bachelor, William Black, within six months. They had four children, including Mary Lou's grandmother Mary (Molly), who married John Hayes in 1942. Molly and John had three offspring, Jimmy (Mary Lou's uncle) in 1943, Joan (Mary Lou's mother) in 1946 and Liam (another uncle) in 1948.

James O'Connor worked on the railway and joined the IRA. He fought against the Black and Tans in the War of Independence and the Free State forces in the civil war. He was a member of the

IRA's Rathbride column, composed mostly of former railway workers. They were based in a dugout belonging to a family of small farmers – the Moores – on the Curragh, County Kildare.

On 13 December 1922, a detachment of troops from the Curragh were searching the Moores' house for arms and discovered the dugout. Eight men, including James O'Connor, surrendered. The Rathbride IRA column was armed to the teeth with rifles, cables and ammunition, bought from a Free State soldier serving in Naas barracks. The eight prisoners were taken to the waiting truck but an arm of one of the men, Thomas Behan, was broken by a blow from a rifle butt on the way. When he could not climb into the truck, he was struck again and, according to official reports, he died on the spot. The more likely cause of his death was that he was shot by Free State forces in cold blood later that day. The other seven were taken to the Curragh and charged in front of a military tribunal with illegal possession of ten rifles, two hundred rounds of ammunition, four bomb detonators and one explorer, a semi-automatic rifle. All seven, including twenty-four-year-old James, were sentenced to death. They were executed, one by one, on 19 December. They were buried in the Curragh military camp, but exhumed and reburied in 1924 in the Grey Abbey cemetery in County Kildare to be, for ever after, known as the 'Grey Abbey Martyrs'. It was the biggest group execution of the entire civil war.

According to Breda Hayes's account in *The Troubles in the Glen*: 'News of the execution of James O'Connor by the Free State came to his mother, Mrs. Black, and family the following day. The entire family were totally devastated. James had been engaged to a local girl, Esther Quirke, and she was deeply traumatized. He used to visit home whenever he could and his younger brothers and sisters looked forward to his visits and what he might bring to them. The late Father Jimmy Brett, a neighbour, recalled being in the house that day and there was a terrible grief in the household. He was a very popular young man.'

James had written a final letter to his mother the day before his execution.

Curragh Camp,
18 December 1922

Dear old Mother,

A few short lines, dear Mother, bidding you a last farewell. I am going to Eternal glory in the morning with six other true-hearted Irishmen. Don't fret, Mother, I am quite happy being at Confession today and Holy Communion in the morning, after which I will go to our Eternal Father in Heaven. I would love to see your face, Mother, and all my little brothers and sisters, not forgetting poor old William. But God's Holy Will be done. Keep the holy Faith and put all your trust in the Blessed Mother. She will guide and protect you as she did poor Jim. Somebody might call to you some day that saw the last of me and my six companions who are coming with me. But God send the day soon that I will see your face and all the little children's faces in the Heaven above where we shall know no parting. Remember me to all kind friends around you and ask them to pray for the eternal repose of our souls, and to keep to the holy Faith. Also remember me to poor Esther, Ned and Joe. Mother, I never felt in better form – just the same as though we were all going home for Xmas. But thank God and His Blessed Mother we are going to the happy home. My trunk and clothes are all here. I hope you get them all. I will also send you my Rosary Beads with a little medal attached for Esther Quirke. So now, dear Mother, I must say Goodbye for the last time in this life to you and all my little brothers and sisters, kind friends and relations. But don't fret, Mother, I could not be happier.

Don't forget, Mother, to go to Confession and Holy
Communion as often as possible and show your love for the
Almighty God and send all children and everybody around
you. Tell them from me to love, honour and serve God here
on earth to be rewarded with everlasting glory in Heaven.
Tell Father Maloney I was asking for him and to pray for
the souls of the following men who will be executed on
19 December in the Curragh Camp: Brian Moore, Patrick
Mangan, Patrick Bagnall, Patrick Nolan, Jackie Johnston,
James O'Connor and Stephen White and most of all poor
Thomas Behan who was shot without seeing a priest on
Tuesday 15 December 1922, the night we were all arrested.
I will leave the rest to the officer in charge of the Prison,
trusting that he will see that you get all my belongings.
A last farewell now, Mother, to all at home.

    With love from
    Your soldier son, James O'Connor

P.S. Don't forget to write to Father Donnelly, Chaplain,
Curragh Camp. I told him all and he will see you some day,
Mother. I am writing this about one hour before execution.
Farewell, Mother and all. Your fond son, Jim.

This was the trauma that Mary Lou's grandmother, Molly
Hayes, carried in her heart.

On the same page as the story of James O'Connor in *The
Troubles in the Glen* is a colour picture of nine people gathered
around a gravestone erected in his memory in the Kilmoyler
churchyard in the Glen of Aherlow. It is a mixture of councillors,
locals and relations of James O'Connor. In the centre is a younger
Mary Lou McDonald.

I asked Joe Hannigan the best way to learn more about the
area and its history and how to verify Mary Lou's links with the

heritage and politics of the people there. He arranged that Pat Moroney, a former teacher and current pillar of the local community, should give us a whistle-stop tour.

Armed with *The Troubles in the Glen* and other research into Mary Lou's contacts and relations, we met Pat at the statue of Christ the King with its magnificent view of the Galtee Mountains. He gave us a tour of the entire area, including the Lisnagaul ambush memorial, the old RIC barracks, the cross marking the spot where Dinny Lacey was shot, the James O'Connor memorial stone, the stable where the O'Dwyer brothers lived and died, the church where Mary Lou was taken to Mass as a child and Moroney's bar and shop where she bought sweets after the Masses.

The Lisvernane area is a treasure trove of reminders of the War of Independence. Around every corner lies the site of an ambush or a story of bravery or martyrdom. Not only was Pat aware of Mary Lou's connection with the area, he could also tell us that she had returned since childhood holidays on several occasions. We learned that on one visit she had judged a *Strictly Come Dancing* event in aid of the local GAA club and had exchanged repartee with the participants and supporters afterwards. They had loved it. In 2008 she had given the oration at a republican shrine, the annual commemoration of the Lisnagaul ambush.

And then Pat took us to her Uncle Jimmy's house to meet the brains behind the book and his wife, Breda, the woman who wrote the chapter about James O'Connor. Jimmy and Breda signed my copy of their book.

Jimmy regretted the civil war, judging it a pointless loss of life, when nobody gained anything.

On a later visit to Lisvernane, I met Mary Lou's other uncle, Liam Hayes, and his wife, Marian, who live down the road in the family home where Mary Lou spent her summer holidays as a child. Over tea and biscuits, Marian showed me the yard where Mary Lou had played with her young cousins. Apparently, Mary Lou was always the teacher when they played school.

We had a polite chat about local history and republican folklore. As patrons of the book, Liam and Marian signed my copy willingly, giving us an opening to talk about republicanism and Mary Lou. Liam fondly recalled the telegram from Dublin that he and Marian had received the day Mary Lou was born. Like his brother, Jimmy, he felt that the civil war had achieved little or nothing. He spoke passionately, but calmly, about a united Ireland and admired Mary Lou because she was on the side of the underdog.

Knowing the grief that Liam's mother, Molly, had suffered at the execution of James O'Connor, I took the bull by the horns and asked Liam about James, the uncle he never knew because he was executed at the age of twenty-four. He openly volunteered that James's death still upsets him. I asked him if Mary Lou was really close to his mother, Molly, the republican, as she had so often claimed. Liam confirmed the closeness, adding that Mary Lou was as close to Molly as he, her son, ever was.

My jaw dropped.

Mary Lou's well-crafted account of the sources of her republican convictions has some of the hallmarks of desperation and some of the characteristics of authenticity. The deep and lasting effect of the hunger strikers on her childhood is something we must take at face value while recognising that its credibility rests on her word alone. The evidence to support her insistence that she was exposed to strong republican influences on both sides of her family is more convincing.

Her family history alone might explain her first toe dipped into the warm, welcoming waters of Fianna Fáil. It hardly provides the sole motivation for her final destination – Sinn Féin.

CHAPTER 2

FROM THE CRADLE TO THE ALTAR: A POLITICS-FREE ZONE

Mary Lou's reluctance to reveal more than the bare minimum about her family and her upbringing has opened a vacuum that has enabled many misleading yarns about her to gain traction. Her childhood and education, both enjoyed in the constituency where I was a Dáil deputy, were a frequent talking point among the chattering locals. Her family home and her school, Notre Dame des Missions, both lay within the same prosperous Rathgar–Churchtown neighbourhood. She was the local girl who had made it to the top of the political tree. The locals liked Mary Lou, but they didn't like her party.

The slightly bitchy, but accepted, local narrative was different from the Sinn Féin-approved official political version. It normally went as follows:

Mary Lou, leader of Sinn Féin, grew up in a large house in Rathgar, one of the most affluent suburbs of south Dublin. Her parents were separated. Her father was a successful builder (in some versions upgraded to a chartered surveyor) who could easily afford to pay for the private convent education that the supposedly republican socialist TD had enjoyed. Her mother was sufficiently well off not to need a full-time job outside the home. Mary Lou sailed through life, from big house to privileged private school to Trinity College Dublin, the most long-standing and well-known university in Ireland. Her mother was still living in the big house, although all four of her children had left the nest and were enjoying different, but highly successful, lives. Mary Lou had glided from Fianna Fáil into the least likely of all political homes – Sinn Féin.

Sinn Féin has never yet won a Dáil seat in Mary Lou's childhood home patch. Most of her neighbours there probably voted Fine Gael. Their main concerns were about the iniquities of property and income taxes. Social consciences did not cause them loss of sleep. They were stunned by her rise in politics, puzzled that a respectable community like theirs could produce such a pleasant, well-spoken girl who ended up as an apologist for the despised IRA. She was the girl who got away.

Of course, the prevailing chronicle of her background was only partly true. Her father was far from a well-heeled builder, effortlessly paying all the household bills and school fees. More often than not, he was an unemployed building contractor. He was gone, but not forgotten. His finances were dire, his income erratic, giving rise to serious insecurity in the McDonald home.

The house, Ard na Gréine, where Paddy parted ways from Joan, Bea, Mary Lou, Joanne and Patrick in 1979, was indeed one of the finest in Rathgar. It features in *On the Banks of the Dodder: Rathgar and Churchtown*, the excellent book by local historian Ged Walsh. It stood on its own grounds on Orwell Road, next door to the Russian Embassy, the centre of many current tales of espionage and protests over the invasion of Ukraine. From 1884 to 1900 it was a school, run by a Miss Barton, eventually ending up in the hands of the celebrated hotelier and property developer P.V. Doyle. He built houses on the grounds, resulting in today's Eaton Brae estate.

When Ard na Gréine was offered for sale in September 2015,

it carried a price tag of €2,250,000. The house was described in the
sales brochure by the estate agents Sherry FitzGerald in Terenure as
a 'two-storey over garden level, late Victorian detached property
standing on a site of approximately 0.15 hectares located off the
exclusive Orwell Road'. The brochure went on to list all the magnificent nearby amenities and private schools, including Notre
Dame des Missions, Mary Lou's parents' school of choice. Despite
its assertion that Ard na Gréine was 'rich with history', the sales
pitch somehow overlooked that it was the childhood home of no
less topical a figure than the then vice-president and now current
leader of Sinn Féin. Perhaps the estate agents feared that such a
historical nugget might bring down the price.

The fable of the McDonalds living in 'a mansion in Rathgar'
was debunked when the truth came tumbling out. Ard na Gréine
has been divided into apartments for many decades, long before the
McDonalds began to live there in the early 1970s. Mary Lou's
parents were tenants in a house that had been converted into flats.
They never owned a house of their own, let alone, as folklore has it,
a palace in the leafy suburbs.

Today, Mary Lou's mother lives in the same dwelling. Joan is
a life tenant in one of the apartments. Mary Lou and her siblings
were not to the manor born. They were ordinary flat-dwellers with
a good address. And their out-of-work, out-of-sight father often
struggled to pay the rent.

No doubt Joan shielded her children from the unpredictable
activities of their father. Mary Lou consistently credits her mother
– not her father – with the determination that all four of them
would receive a first-class education. The result of Joan's endeavours
was remarkable. Inside the apartment was a dedicated place for
each child to do their homework.

The family work ethic was strong and it paid off. One of
Paddy McDonald's proudest boasts, even today, is that all four
of his children received degrees from Trinity College Dublin, an

opportunity that neither he nor Joan had ever been lucky enough to be offered. Bea blazed a trail for the rest of the family into third level. After she had been sent to St Mary's College, Rathmines, run by the Congregation of the Holy Spirit, where she played rugby and was in the choir, she went to Trinity. St Mary's annual fees today stand at €5,450. Somewhere, despite their financial difficulties in the 1970s and 1980s, the McDonald clan found money for Bea's and Mary Lou's expensive educations. It is difficult to fathom how they could afford it.

Bea entered Trinity in 1985 and emerged with a second-class honours (first division) degree in microbiology in 1989. She went on to add qualifications galore to her name, including a PhD in pharmacology from University College London, a graduate diploma in law and a post-doctoral fellowship from the Johns Hopkins University School of Medicine in Baltimore, Maryland. She has held various private practice positions in the US and the UK. According to her own website, she is a consultant with 'considerable experience in contentious proceedings', which appears to be a family talent. As a European patent attorney and qualified US patent agent, Bea McDonald is now based in Wokingham, Berkshire, running her own intellectual property company. She doesn't sound as good a person to meet for a pint as her father, but she almost certainly has greater earning potential. Her nationality was recorded as 'British' in her original application to be registered as a director of the company in July 2016. Within three weeks, it was hurriedly amended to 'Irish', as befits a sibling of the leader of Sinn Féin.

Mary Lou's two younger siblings, twins Patrick and Joanne, took very different paths in life. Before his time in Trinity College, Patrick was at Templeogue College, another local school, run by the Holy Ghost Fathers. Patrick's degree from Trinity was in biblical and theological studies/classical civilisation in 1998.

He began his working life with the Irish Film Board in 2000 and worked on the financing and production of over sixty projects there, including *Bloody Sunday, The Count of Monte Cristo* and Disney's *King Arthur*. After that, he branched out on his own, becoming an independent film producer in Ireland, setting up his own company, Rubicon Films, and making *The Mighty Celt* for BBC Films. Like Bea, he emigrated, but Patrick's destination was Australia, where he launched Wolfhound Pictures in 2011. In 2013 he produced the award-winning science-fiction film *Predestination*, starring Ethan Hawke. He has lived in Australia ever since, writing screenplays and producing numerous films for screen and television. In 2013, Mary Lou lamented his departure for Australia. Talking to *Hashtag 2013*, the Dublin Business School magazine, she commented that 'He had to emigrate due to the economic downturn. He had a business that was doing well and when the crash happened it suffered and he was forced to leave, like many people in Ireland.'

A few years ago I met Patrick with his mother in Churchtown's Howards Way restaurant when he was back home for a break. We had a brief conversation. The next day in Leinster House, I couldn't resist pointedly remarking to the proudly left-wing Mary Lou how good it was to see so many of her family enjoying the fruits of private enterprise. She graciously laughed.

Patrick's twin, Joanne, was different from her three siblings. She is a fascinating mixture of worthy ideals and high achievement. Mary Lou is always at pains to single out her younger sister for declarations of special affection. She told author Deaglán de Bréadún, 'I love my sister and we're on great terms. She's got two lovely children. I've got two children. We're very close; we're a very, very close family.' Mary Lou always manages to heap praise on Joanne without giving any actual details of her virtues. Strangely, she never mentions her sister's little-known, but very radical, politics.

Joanne's career has none of the predictable normality of her twin brother. She has managed to combine a high-powered business agenda while pursuing left-wing causes.

Joanne was a pupil at St Louis school in Rathmines, run by the St Louis Order of Nuns. All four children were destined for schools with a strong Roman Catholic ethos, a preference shared by Paddy and Joan, both of whom retained a remarkably strong attachment to their faith.

The children's education combined traditional Catholicism with a high standard of teaching, offering all four of them the opportunity to score enough Leaving Certificate points to lift them into third level. While the elder two enjoyed the benefits of private education, Joanne and Patrick went to non-fee-paying schools, possibly reflecting the rapidly deteriorating financial fortunes of the McDonald family in the 1980s.

Joanne is remembered by one fellow pupil at St Louis as 'exceptionally bright, and an active participant in the venture scouts', a branch of scouting that concentrates on challenging events such as hiking, rock climbing, camping and pioneering.

Joanne flew through Trinity College without a hiccup. She took a second-class honours (second class) degree in microbiology in 1995 and headed for Dublin City University, where she gained a master's degree in molecular biology in 1996. Not satisfied with this, she ticked another academic box from the University of Liverpool, with a PhD in cell biology and anatomy.

Joanne looked likely to be an academic, but, instead, she initially specialised in executive recruitment in academia itself, soon expanding her experience into the not-for-profit and pharmaceutical industries across the public and private sectors. Her varied CV claims 'significant experience in executive recruitment nationally and internationally within the Life Sciences, Engineering, Education and the public sector'.

Joanne was, superficially, a fairly typical but highly motivated woman with a mission to be a hotshot in the executive search market. But there is far more to her than that.

Joanne McDonald has been climbing rapidly up Ireland's

corporate ladder. However, her LinkedIn CV lacks precise dates between her doctorate and her time as a director of Science Recruitment IRELAND (SRI). SRI is a global agency with its headquarters in Dublin. It specifically emphasises, among its priorities, the need for diversity, sustainability, inclusivity and global health. It has a particular interest in non-governmental organisations in Africa and developing nations. It was at SRI that Joanne earned a good reputation as a civic-minded, ethical expert in such nuanced sectors.

She stayed with SRI for six years, from 2007 to 2013. During that period – in December 2010 – she and her partner, Gary Ronaghan, had their first child, Pádraig Ben, and in July 2012, their second, Ella Mary. Her impressive CV reveals a gap, not telling us what she did in the four-year space between leaving SRI in 2013 and moving to another executive search agency, Ardlinn, in 2017, as head of research sciences and the public sector. She and Gary had a third child, Rossa Tomás, in 2016, giving them three children under the age of six. The children are being educated at a gaelscoil in County Dublin.

Joanne was highly regarded in Ardlinn. Founder and director Áine Brolly was obviously sorry to lose her in 2020. She told me: 'Joanne was exceptionally bright. She came to Ardlinn with a PhD in an area of biochemistry. Her focus was on the senior levels of the pharmaceutical sector. She also led our public sector recruitment practice.'

Ardlinn is a branch of Ireland's biggest recruitment company, the publicly quoted CPL Resources (now sold to Japanese group Outsourcing Inc.). It operates at the highest level of Irish business, especially serving the needs of multinational companies, with offices throughout Europe, selecting candidates for executive jobs with annual salaries as high as €250,000. Joanne was moving into the corporate big time.

In 2020 Mary Lou's sister landed the jackpot. Novartis, one of the largest pharmaceutical companies in the world, came calling. The US–Swiss global giant offered her the position of 'senior talent acquisition business partner' in Ireland. She grabbed it with open arms.

Novartis may have been an enormous business change for Joanne. She began to work for a company with a different ethos; it is market-led; its shares are quoted publicly; it gives share options and performance bonuses to selected employees. Novartis has inevitably been involved in activities of a controversial nature which former employees of the more politically correct SRI might find hard to stomach. These include lobbying links with the Trump administration, when Novartis paid $1.2 million to Trump lawyer Michael Cohen, often described as the former president's 'fixer'. Cohen was supposed to deliver healthcare consultancy services, which he was unable to do. In 2018, he was sentenced to three years in prison for tax evasion.

Joanne's acceptance of a position with Novartis is not a cause for criticism. There is no earthly reason for the younger sister of the leader of Sinn Féin to fret over Mary Lou's views of multinationals or even over Novartis's activities in the United States. Few multinationals are scandal free. She appears to be a highly competent, scrupulously honest executive. Far more interesting is how Joanne McDonald has managed to reconcile her career in the multinational world with her own lesser-known left-wing ideology, political allegiances and activities.

Joanne McDonald was, unknown to many, an active member of Sinn Féin at the same time as Mary Lou, but little publicity has been given to the younger sister's membership of the party. Indeed, it came to public attention in a limited way only when she left Sinn Féin in dramatic circumstances in June 2006. There are surprisingly few instances of her popping up, even as a low-profile Sinn Féin member, around the time that Mary Lou joined, probably because Joanne has never been an attention-seeker or a grandstander. Yet she appears to be a true believer.

Although references to Joanne's time in Sinn Féin are sparse, they leave no room for doubt. On 2 June 2005, *An Phoblacht* carried an account of the annual conference of the Institute for British–Irish Studies in UCD. It reported proudly about how the high-powered Sinn Féin delegation, led by West Tyrone MLA Barry McElduff, had included 'Laois Councillor Brian Stanley, Monaghan Councillor Matt Carthy, Rathmines activist Joanne McDonald and Derry activist Joe Doherty'. Joanne was in exalted company. Both Stanley and Carthy were later to become TDs, while Joe Doherty was already an IRA hero. Barry McElduff, an MLA at the time, was destined to be removed from his Westminster seat in 2018 after posting a thoroughly distasteful video of himself balancing a Kingsmill loaf on his head on the anniversary of the IRA massacre of ten Protestant workmen in Kingsmill, County Armagh.

Like her elder sister, Joanne was held in high esteem in Sinn Féin, yet, ironically, her commitment to the ideals of Sinn Féin, but not to the party itself, proved stronger than Mary Lou's. Just one year later, in June 2006, while Sinn Féin MEP and party chairperson Mary Lou was determinedly climbing up the greasy poll, Joanne bolted.

When she bade farewell to Sinn Féin, Joanne had not yet started to ascend the ranks of high-powered companies, let alone multinationals. If she was nursing such ambitions, they might have tempted her towards the political centre.

Far from it. She went the other way. Joanne's chosen exit from Sinn Féin led her to Éirígí, a breakaway group. While Sinn Féin is the Irish for 'ourselves', Éirígí is the Irish for 'rise up', a more militant, more activist slogan. Éirígí was led by high-profile, ultra-left-wing dissidents whose politics were ideological, not pragmatic, and geared towards more protests, frequently directed against corporate outfits, often multinationals. Many members of Éirígí were unhappy with the Good Friday Agreement, seeing it as reinforcing partition. Éirígí placed less emphasis than Sinn Féin on the border with Northern Ireland and more on social justice. Its protests were more aggressive than the average run-of-the-mill demonstrations. They included the occupation of banking premises, like Anglo-Irish Bank's headquarters, and confrontation with multinational Royal Dutch Shell's activities in bringing gas ashore in the West of Ireland, a campaign that attracted widespread publicity.

Éirígí was a self-proclaimed 'socialist republican' group. On 21 June 2006, *Magill* magazine revealed that Éirígí, promoting a 'Reclaim the Republic' campaign, 'included Joanne McDonald, the sister of Mary Lou McDonald, the party's MEP'.

Magill went on to speculate that Éirígí 'is believed to have been provoked by tensions within Sinn Féin concerning a move to the right in policy and the insistence of the party leadership that the option of entering a coalition government with Fianna Fáil be maintained'.

A clear dividing line between the two McDonald sisters had opened up. Mary Lou, the hard-headed careerist politician with a seat in the European Parliament, stayed put. Joanne, the idealist, took the republican socialist exit to activism and militant resistance.

Éirígí got off to a terrible start. While its leader, Brian Leeson, insisted that Éirígí was not, as many mistakenly assumed, in favour of violence, it found great difficulty in shaking off the accusation. Two former members of Éirígí were charged with the killing of two British soldiers at Massereene Barracks in Antrim in 2009. Both had left Éirígí before the shooting, but the mud stuck. Éirígí may even have initially attracted a few unsavoury dissidents who were anticipating a paramilitary wing, but any such intentions were not tolerated by its leadership.

As a member of Éirígí, Joanne McDonald sank much of her radical energies into the Shell to Sea campaign, the movement that emerged in Mayo after the discovery of the Corrib gas field. It cleverly targeted Shell, exploiting the globally unpopular multinational's plans to build a natural-gas pipeline in the West of

Ireland. Shell to Sea followers, many of them members of Éirígí, took strong action to prevent Shell, Statoil and Marathon from building a refinery at Bellanaboy in County Mayo.

Initially, in May 2005, Mary Lou and fellow Sinn Féin MEP Bairbre de Brún had brought the activities of Shell and Statoil (a Norwegian company) in Mayo to public attention in a letter to the Norwegian government. They used the arrest and imprisonment of five Mayo farmers (soon to be known nationwide as 'The Rossport Five') as a hook to highlight the issue. At this time, Joanne was still in Sinn Féin. For a brief period, the sisters were in unison about Royal Dutch Shell. Mary Lou's and Bairbre de Brún's pleas fell on deaf ears. Shell, Statoil and Marathon continued to operate despite the protests in Mayo.

In May 2006, Mary Lou issued a stronger, more forthright statement full of unusually left-wing rhetoric about Shell and multinationals in general. Observers have since suggested that there was a sense of alarm in her wording. Was she trying to prevent a split? Was she trying to pre-empt the foundation of Éirígí just one month later?

'The people of Rossport,' she thundered, addressing an issue hundreds of kilometres away from her Dublin constituency, 'are rightly concerned by this whole process, which saw five members of their community jailed last year for refusing to allow a dangerous pipeline to be run through their community and their refusal to bend the knee to multinational companies to exploit Irish national resources.' She vowed 'to bring the Rossport case back to the European Parliament, if necessary'. And then, undoubtedly address-ing unhappy Sinn Féin insiders, she pinned her colours to the masts of the protest marchers: 'It is essential that the momentum is now built upon to ensure that there is a widespread campaign of opposition to the imposition of a dangerous pipeline . . . Sinn Féin stands beside the community of Rossport.'

But it was too late. One person who did not have faith in

Mary Lou's ability to thwart Shell, Statoil and Marathon was her own sister. Six weeks after Mary Lou's rousing words of support, Joanne and other disillusioned Sinn Féin rebels left the party and formed Éirígí. Its earliest initiative was to lead loud, confrontational campaigns against multinationals like Shell. Éirígí seized (some would say infiltrated) the leadership of the Shell to Sea campaign.

While Mary Lou now took a back seat on the Corrib gas issue, Joanne moved into top gear. She had a close family link to the campaign. Her partner, Gary Ronaghan, an engineer with another multinational, Ericsson, was an equally hardened opponent of Shell. He too was an Éirígí activist.

In 2007, Gary was struck by a lorry in an anti-Shell sit-down protest. He complained to the garda ombudsman about an incident which, according to Éirígí, 'saw Ronaghan's life placed in extreme danger'. The claim of life-threatening injury was, maybe, a little fanciful. Gary was taken to Mayo general hospital after his foot was trapped under the rear wheel of a lorry. It was bruised and swollen and suffered tissue damage. Gary lived.

Four years later, in August 2011, Gary Ronaghan was again reported as wounded in action when he was on another Shell to Sea mission. According to an account – written by Éirígí – 'Gary Ronaghan, an Éirígí activist, was attacked on top of the fence and subsequently received five stitches to a cut on his upper lip and suffered damage to his teeth.'

Joanne was never as physically involved in protests as her partner, but she was no less committed. She was elected treasurer of Éirígí in 2009. She chaired public meetings on the Shell pipeline and acted as a guest speaker on several panels. Her presentations, some of which are available on YouTube, were thoughtful and calm. At one meeting in Dublin's Liberty Hall, former Green Party MEP Patricia McKenna remembers telling her after she had spoken that she 'recognised her voice'. Joanne responded that she did not think that they had met. Patricia told her that she 'sounded very like Mary Lou McDonald'. To which Joanne replied proudly, 'I am her sister.'

At another meeting, Joanne shared a platform with Maura Harrington, the well-known protester and hunger striker who received several jail sentences for her actions in opposing Shell. Joanne wrote letters, signed petitions and lodged objections, constantly keeping the Éirígí flame burning.

Mary Lou did little more than pay lip service to the Shell to Sea campaign. When it bubbled over again in 2011, she surfaced for a harmless Dáil motion, a routine attack on energy minister Pat Rabbitte for what she regarded as the Labour Party's sell-out. But Mary Lou and Sinn Féin members were already slowly moving down the road to becoming an establishment party; they were rarely, if ever, seen on the road to Rossport. They left the heavy lifting to Joanne and others in Éirígí.

Eventually, the Shell to Sea movement lost out to the multinational. The Shell stake was sold to a Canadian pension fund. Gas is flowing and the protest campaign has withered. Éirígí is now holding similar protests on other issues, such as housing. It is a political party but has hardly landed a glove on Sinn Féin support. Joanne and Gary have found other outlets for their revolutionary fervour, including membership of the Gernika Group, which brings Irish and Basque activists together in a united front against the possible re-emergence of fascism. Basque separatist movements have always enjoyed co-operation with Sinn Féin.

The political parting of the ways when the sisters were in their thirties did not disrupt their deep friendship. It has survived intact. They may no longer share an identical political philosophy, but their policy differences will not break the bond between them.

Until now, Mary Lou has allowed us only a sanitised peep at her own upbringing. And she has mostly shared with us those politically convenient bits, like her idyllic family holidays in republican Tipperary. She repeats the same story of her parents' separation ad nauseam.

While Mary Lou's father is often erased from the story, his parents and sisters are normally excluded from her narrative about her upbringing. Paddy McDonald's four elder sisters are an important, but often unrecognised, part of Mary Lou's earlier years. They doted on Paddy, the baby of the family, the tearaway afterthought, whom they fondly nicknamed 'Buddy'. They extended their affections to his offspring.

Luckily for Joan McDonald, all four of Paddy's sisters lived within a stone's throw of Ard na Gréine. Only one of the sisters, Joan Butler, was married with children. Joan Butler is deeply religious. A lifelong member of the Legion of Mary, she has been in the choir at the local Church of the Good Shepherd in Churchtown for forty years. She is proud of Mary Lou and, when I spoke to her in her own home, she referred frequently to the beautiful young girl who was staunch and honest. 'She was a very happy child and we called her "the giggler". All I can see is her laughing. They'd come up here, mum and kids. She'd play tennis on the road out there. She could certainly talk.'

Sunday Independent journalist Barry Egan has similar memories to Joan Butler's of Mary Lou's happy disposition. Writing in August 2019, he recalls his childhood as one of Joan's neighbours:

A memory I have of Henley Park is playing, chasing and the like as a six-year-old with Mary Lou, her big brother Bernard, my little sister Marina and Mary Lou's first cousins Shirley and Tracey Butler. The latter two went to Notre Dame around the corner with the smiley child who would go on to be the leader of Sinn Féin one day. My memory of Mary Lou is that she was a real giggler. She never stopped giggling. A happier child you could never hope to meet. She would find everything funny and would be in a constant and joyous state of laughter. Which is, looking back, a pretty good state to be in. You'd only have to look at her and she'd burst into a fit of giggles. When I switch on the telly now I sometimes miss the old Mary Lou.

Joan Butler recalls holidays with Mary Lou, her siblings and Joan's eight children in Rossnowlagh, County Donegal. 'She'd play tennis on the beach,' she told me. And then she added, 'I pray for her every night to St Michael the Archangel. I had the abbot of Mount Melleray say Mass for her recovery from Covid.' In the spring of 2020, St Michael and the abbot answered Joan Butler's prayers. Mary Lou made a full recovery.

Joan Butler is a gem. In the summer of 2021 I was fortunate to spend an evening talking to her about her family. Despite Joan's sisterly loyalty to her uncontrollable brother, despite the separation, she spoke admiringly of his former wife, insisting that she is a 'brilliant, strong woman'.

About an hour into our conversation, she was beginning to wax lyrical about Mary Lou when her mobile phone rang. She took the call, but, mistakenly, left on the speaker.

The female voice on the phone opened up: 'I'm just checking on you. Are you alone?'

'I'm fine,' replied Joan, 'he's [referring to her husband, Pierce, who died a few months later] upstairs.'

Voice: 'I'm ringing you about that fella who's coming to your house tonight' – obviously regarding 'that fella' as an enemy of the people. I shifted on my armchair.

Joan: 'That fella is a very nice guy. He's sitting here with me now.'

There was a pause. I swear I heard a gulp.

Voice: 'Mary Lou isn't going to be saying that.'

The conversation ended fairly abruptly. Joan is a formidable adversary, no pushover, who makes up her own mind. I warmed to her.

Unfazed by the short interruption, Joan then launched into a eulogy about Mary Lou's husband, Martin Lanigan. 'He is a wonderful man; she could not manage without him. He takes over the children at home.'

I began to wonder why Mary Lou had kept this family treasure in the background for so long. Her aunt Joan, a practising Christian, speaks ill of no one.

Aunt Joan and her family provided a home from home and eight easily accessible cousins for Mary Lou to visit as a child. Her decidedly middle-class house in Churchtown's Henley Park was midway on Mary Lou's route home to Orwell Road from Notre Dame des Missions. As a schoolgirl, she was regularly to be seen playing in the cul-de-sac which provided a perfect location for the cousins to hang out together in safety.

Joan Butler was not the only aunt to give Mary Lou additional love and security. Paddy's other sisters were equally hospitable. A ready-made network of the McDonald sisterhood always rose to the occasion. Her late aunt Maeve, aunt Nora and her late aunt Phyllis also adored their brother's children as if they were their own. A second house, inhabited by Nora and Phyllis, in nearby Wainsfort Road, Terenure, provided the location for many happy childhood memories, particularly at the weekends.

Maeve McDonald, who died on 14 February 2022, spoke to me three months before she died. She had nothing but good to say about her brother Paddy's separated wife: 'She is a lovely lady. She was teaching English to French students.' Maeve remembered Mary Lou and Joanne 'making shops down the garden in Wainsfort Road with cardboard boxes. They both had lovely voices too.'

Maeve recalled taking the two eldest children to Dublin Zoo. She also recollected Bea and Mary Lou having a sale of work when Mary Lou remarked, 'Our mum and dad have to sleep in the same bed and we want to buy a bed for our poor mum.'

Maeve worked for the *Irish Independent* and *Evening Herald* newspapers as a copy-taker, a highly skilled, high-speed job taking down articles over the telephone.

In the mid-eighties Maeve McDonald asked Liam Collins, a reporter in the *Evening Herald*, if he would look after her schoolgirl niece, who was coming into the *Independent* offices in Middle Abbey Street, Dublin, for work experience. Maeve was a glamorous figure in the big noisy newsroom, shared by reporters from the *Evening Herald* and the *Irish Independent*, making phone calls, bashing out reports and bickering with one another.

The copy-taker's job was to take news and sports stories dictated over the phone from reporters at 'markings' outside the office, from court reporters and from correspondents covering news and sports stories at home and abroad. Quite often they were using public phones, so it was important to keep on the right side of Maeve McDonald and other copy-takers to ensure that a story was typed quickly and efficiently to meet newspaper deadlines, because if they didn't like you, they could leave you hanging on the line while they took other copy. Liam Collins said:

> I remember Maeve asking me would I look after her niece for a day and being struck by her unusual name, Mary Lou. I had grown up, so to speak, in the Midlands and had only ever heard the name from showband singers belting out the Gene Pitney standard 'Hello Mary Lou, goodbye heart', which is one of the reasons the name stuck in my mind.
>
> It was a long time ago, but I remember her as an attractive teenager and her aunt Maeve was very protective of her. A newspaper office back then was a rough and ready place, and, as far as I recall, she would have been one of the first transition year students I encountered. What I remember is that she was quite intense and focused. I showed her around and explained the process and we may even have gone out on some innocuous job together. But it wasn't what I would call a memorable encounter. Some

transition year students are fired up with ideals and want to get into journalism to change the world and you remember that intensity.

Mary Lou certainly didn't have that at the time. She seemed like a nice middle-class kid trying to figure out what she would do in life, and because her auntie worked in the *Independent*, it was a convenient place for her to give journalism a try. I don't think she was terribly impressed by the controlled chaos that surrounded her and I'm not sure if she even finished the week.

Looking back, I think if she was ever interested in journalism, she was quick enough to figure out that there were easier ways to make a living.

I don't pay close attention to up-and-coming politicians or Sinn Féin, but when Mary Lou McDonald was elected to the Dáil in 2011, I knew exactly who she was and remember being quite shocked that she was a Sinn Féin TD. By then I was working in the *Sunday Independent* and I rang Maeve, because I decided to write a piece about her [Mary Lou] for the paper.

I wanted to focus on what I regarded as the first few 'normal' Sinn Féin TDs among the fourteen elected to the Dáil on that occasion, because until then most of their TDs were connected to the IRA or the hunger strikes. I remember that even then her family background seemed to be mysterious; there were no details of her mother and father, she seemed to have arrived on the political scene fully formed.

I asked Maeve if she could fill in any of the missing details about Mary Lou – I wasn't looking for dirt, just the normal stuff that reporters like to know about the people they are profiling, who their mother and father were and that sort of thing. Maeve wasn't forthcoming. I can't recall the details, but she told me that she didn't want to get involved and we left it at that.

Later, in 2013, during the Central Remedial Clinic controversy, I was working as the opinion editor of the *Irish Independent* and remember watching Mary Lou's performance at the committee

investigating salaries paid to senior executives at the charity. I
thought she was impressive. I rang the Sinn Féin press office to ask
if she would do what we call a 'comment piece' for the *Irish
Independent* for the following day. They seemed quite shocked to
get a call from the 'Indo' and I was quite surprised myself when
they came back and said 'yes' and I received an op ed which was
delivered on deadline and to exactly the specified word count. At
the time I remember thinking maybe she really was paying attention
all those years before during our brief encounter when she was
doing work experience in the newspaper.

Paddy's other sisters, Phyllis and Nora, were rocks of reassur-
ance for Joan and her children when they were very young. Both
were in good jobs. Phyllis, who died in 2019, had been a highly
successful chiropodist and had run a shoe shop in nearby
Rathfarnham. Nora, still living in Terenure, was an accountant and
a sportswoman. According to one family member, Nora is still the
go-to person on Paddy's side of the family. At one time she worked
on the books at the controversial charity Rehab.

Mary Lou may have lost the permanent presence of her father
at the age of ten in 1979, but the benefits of having an extended
family of four attentive aunts living within walking distance of her
home should not be underestimated. And, furthermore, her two
solid, comfortably-off uncles and their wives offered welcoming
summer holidays in County Tipperary every year. If anything was
lacking, emotionally or materially, she had an abundance of willing
back-up.

One member of the McDonald clan told me that Paddy's and
Joan's branches of the family became gradually more distant from
each other after he left the family home. There was no rift, but the
family member felt that Joan wanted to be as independent as
possible.

Following Paddy and Joan McDonald's decision to send Bea

to St Mary's, another fee-paying school within a stone's throw of Ard na Gréine, Notre Dame des Missions, was a practical choice for Mary Lou. The schools had a similar history. Notre Dame stood aloof from the popular free secondary school scheme announced by education minister Donogh O'Malley in 1967, because the scheme was not initially approved of by the Church. Notre Dame was a small school with modest classroom numbers. Consequently, it provided individual attention, gaining a reputation for high academic standards combined with a strong religious ethos. It had a good reputation in debating, sport and choral singing. Most of its pupils were the daughters of middle-class local residents. Leadership of Sinn Féin was not an ambition for which the school would have prepared its pupils. According to one of the teachers, the Notre Dame pupils came from families who were mostly 'scrimpers and savers'. The parents made sacrifices to pay the school fees. Its former pupils numbered many high achievers in Irish life, including celebrity singers the Vard Sisters, best-selling novelist Cathy Kelly, economist and journalist Maev-Ann Wren and author Mary Morrissy. Fiona Dawson, daughter of Irish and Lions rugby star Ronnie Dawson and the global president of Mars Food, attended Notre Dame. Not surprisingly, all four daughters of former Fianna Fáil minister for transport Seamus Brennan were pupils (they lived next door to the school).

Mary Lou fitted comfortably into the Notre Dame ethos. Her teachers, without exception, liked her. A more peculiar, but almost unanimous, view among the staff – with one exception – was that there was no detectable sign at the time that she would turn out to be a public figure. She displayed not a hint of republicanism or social radicalism during her years at the school.

Sister Carmel Looby, who was principal during Mary Lou's time, is complimentary: 'She was a good child. You remember the less co-operative! She loved English and was keen on debating. She was mature for her age and was confident enough to say what she felt. She was a very good debater. On one occasion she knocked on my office door, saying she wanted to make a complaint. The teachers had not put her on the debating team. I admired her for that and suggested that she go back and talk to the teacher involved. She was interested in history and loved her English. She was a good worker.'

One of those teachers who remembered Mary Lou well was the late Máire Cranny, who taught her speech and drama. Máire's daughter, the well-known broadcaster and former senator Marie-Louise O'Donnell, invited me into Máire's nursing home, run by the Little Sisters of the Poor in Roebuck Road, Dublin, in July 2021, to talk to her mother about Mary Lou. Sadly, Máire died on 2 March 2022.

The very mention of Mary Lou's name lit up the face of the ninety-eight-year-old former speech and drama legend. She indicated that Mary Lou was very intelligent and did a lot of debating. Or, as she bluntly put it, 'she was an excellent arguer'. That was hardly a surprise! Mary Lou had taken part in musical dramas, public speaking and choral verse choirs which Máire had produced at the school. On one occasion, Mary Lou had a part singing in the musical *Oklahoma* in a joint production with St Mary's College. By a happy coincidence her sister Bea was in the St Mary's choir. One surprise from Máire was that Mary Lou 'never looked for attention'.

According to Mary Lou herself – in a much later interview when she was an MEP – her favourite teacher was Sister Una Rutledge. Mary Lou said that Sister Una was 'patient, encouraged all of us and treated us as equals'. When I spoke to Sister Una, she returned the compliment. She described Mary Lou as 'our best debater' and, alone of all her teachers, 'wasn't surprised she went into politics'. Sister Una taught English to Mary Lou, her favourite subject.

Former school principal Brian Cox remembers her primarily as a 'debater and someone who was always interested in the world around her, but she didn't strike me as a future politician. Some, like Mary Lou, begin quietly, nurturing their ambition until they are ready to emerge.'

Other teachers, who did not want to be named, describe Mary Lou as understated, another 'as quiet as a mouse', one even saying that she was conscientious, always did her homework but in staff meetings was often dubbed as 'bland'. Others said that she 'coasted through'. She certainly never set the world on fire academically, according to several of her teachers; one mentioned that 'she flattered only to deceive'.

The teachers were aware of her difficulties at home, especially the parental separation and the financial problems that had arisen from her father's escapades. They spoke highly of her mother. Sister Looby remembers Joan as 'a very supportive parent, very involved in the school', adding that she never had to send for her.

Mary Lou speaks with painful vagueness about her years at Notre Dame, possibly because she finds its private, fee-paying status politically awkward. On one occasion, she relented slightly. In an interview twenty years later she volunteered that English was her favourite subject, named John Lennon as her childhood idol and played it safe by picking 'Free Nelson Mandela' as her favourite schooldays song. Asked if she would send her children to the same school, she dodged the question by saying that she planned 'to send my children to a local school on the northside of Dublin', a promise she later fulfilled. In the same interview, she said that the best things about her school were her 'friends, debating and long summer holidays'. And then, with a gentle dig at her alma mater, she let it slip that the worst thing about her education was 'a limited mix of people from different social and ethnic backgrounds'. Slightly ungrateful and below the belt, maybe, but Mary Lou McDonald MEP was by the time of the interview a grown-up left-wing politician, no longer a member of the south Dublin bourgeoisie.

When Notre Dame school closed in 2019, after it fought a

losing battle for survival, no one on the committee opposing the school's closure ever asked Mary Lou McDonald TD, vice-president of Sinn Féin, to rush to the barricades. At the time, neither she nor the school seemed comfortable with the relationship. She has always appeared uneasy with her privileged education and might not have wanted to defend a private school, while some of the parents against closure told me that they were reluctant to enlist a Shinner to their ranks.

Despite her strong debating skills, Mary Lou had sailed through Notre Dame without a whiff of republicanism in her formative teenage years. Nor had she displayed any aptitude or enthusiasm for the Irish language. Her very public long-delayed discovery that the death of hunger striker Bobby Sands, when she was at Notre Dame aged twelve, was an apparent 'road to Damascus moment' had never surfaced in the schoolroom.

At the end of her time at Notre Dame, Mary Lou failed to gain the Leaving Certificate points she needed to take the subject she wanted to study at the university of her choice. She was forced to repeat the exam a year later at Rathmines Senior College. At the end of the course at Rathmines, she gained enough points to win admission to the Department of English at Trinity College Dublin.

While Mary Lou's academic record at TCD was hardly stellar, her political interest was a non-starter. She played little part in college life and appears to have disdained all the available opportunities offered by political clubs and societies to pursue those principles in which a young idealistic woman might have believed. She is typically cloudy about her time in TCD, telling Mary Banotti in her book *There's Something about Mary*: 'When I was in college I had no interest whatsoever in political parties. My view then was that individual issues were what mattered and that you had a better chance of seeing a result by working on an issue. And, to be honest, I was doing other things which I found far more engaging and interesting.' When asked what these things were, Mary Lou replied,

'Being with my friends, going out. I was involved in some of the societies in college, but I never threw myself in hook, line and sinker. I enjoyed my books, I enjoyed my friends and I enjoyed my freedom of being at university.'

Mary Banotti failed to ask her what societies she had joined or what 'individual issues' mattered or what issues she had 'worked on'.

On the surface, Mary Lou was spoofing.

When she was asked a similar question by journalist Olaf Tyaransen in an interview with *Hot Press* magazine in June 2004, she responded:

> I would have been involved in different campaigns, say, when I was at university – and afterwards.
>
> Olaf Tyaransen: What kinds of campaigns?
>
> Mary Lou: Well, for instance in my university days the big things were – and still are – issues around student accommodation, issues around grant levels, all of those sorts of issues. And then . . .

Mary Lou was struggling.

She travelled through TCD unnoticed and unambitious. She caused no waves, not even a ripple, either within or outside her lectures.

Ivana Bacik, president of TCD's Student Representative Council 1989/90, when Mary Lou was there, is now leader of the Labour Party. She says, 'I don't remember Mary Lou from my time in Trinity . . . she may have been involved in campaigns but not very centrally, at least during my time as I remember.' Bacik was deeply embroiled in issues that might have appealed to a progressive young female student, in particular the pro-choice views that Mary Lou was to promote later in life. Somehow, in TCD all those opportunities passed her by.

Journalist and broadcaster Sarah Carey was another contemporary in Trinity. She never once crossed paths with Mary Lou McDonald. When I asked her about any possible encounters, she was surprised to learn that Mary Lou had even been to TCD:

> I attended Trinity College between 1988 and 1992 reading History. The department is in the (not very large) Arts Block close to the English Department where Mary Lou was studying. During that time, I was active in the college's main debating societies, the Phil and the Hist. I was a class rep and active in the Students' Union, including sitting on the electoral commission which ran all union elections across the college. I was involved in Players, the main drama society. I lived in rooms in Front Square in 1991/92. I contributed to the college's publications like *Trinity Times* and *Piranha*.

Sarah added:

> I was a regular in the Junior Common Room, where the lefties hung out with their Nicaraguan flags on the wall. I drank in the Buttery with the engineers and in the Stag's Head with the debaters. In summer term, we'd head to the Pav [Pavilion] and sit out in the sun and watch the cricket.
>
> At no time was I aware of Mary Lou McDonald's presence in Trinity. I had a great time in college, though I left with a stomach ulcer and a 2.2 degree. Maybe she spent her time more soberly and wisely, but it was a relatively small place at the time, so I was genuinely shocked to learn we were contemporaries. That's no reflection on her obviously.

Perhaps Mary Lou's 'Damascus moment' had been hibernating for ten years, but her strongest suit, her passion for debating, which developed so well at Notre Dame, had positively ebbed. Certainly, the republican flame that the IRA hunger strikers of 1981 were supposed to have ignited was extinguished.

Even her lecturers were not overtly impressed by her diligence or her abilities. She told de Bréadún that one of her English literature teachers, current Independent senator David Norris, was 'Brilliant – it wasn't so much that he taught, he performed!' When I asked David Norris to make a comment on Mary Lou, his admiring pupil, he replied: 'In relation to Mary Lou, I did not teach her, so cannot accede to your request.' Mary Lou must have been sitting silently at the back of a crowded class.

Other lecturers are understandably reluctant to speak good or ill of any specific student. One key academic in the English department was lukewarm. His report on Mary Lou's progress in her final year was far from a ringing endorsement of her performance, commenting:

> Not much from her in class, attendance uneven. Worked hard at her essays, though the results were uneven; capable of original argument, but sometimes out of focus and misconceived.

On her study of a specific poet, he commented that she 'had read a lot of criticism, including some fairly out-of-the-way critics and couldn't really handle it. As a result, she lost focus on the poets themselves. Still, marks for effort. 59.'

Mary Lou took a gap year out after her third year in Trinity and taught in Spain. She was in no hurry to hit the big bad world, despite already losing twelve months repeating the Leaving Certificate exam. Eventually, in 1993, she sat her finals, achieving a moderately good degree, a 2.1 in English literature, but at the unusually mature age of twenty-four.

Among those scoring identical grades to Mary Lou's tally in her final Trinity exams was none other than an ex-IRA bomber, Shane Paul O'Doherty. O'Doherty, a mature student, had served fifteen years for IRA bombings but had repented and made peace with many of his victims. He insists that he never encountered

Mary Lou during his four years in TCD. She certainly never mentions him.

Other students of her year find it hard to remember her. One with a patrician background showed a rare distaste: 'She wore an Aran jersey, she could be very sweet, a saccharine sweetness which I didn't trust. She could be slightly sulky, sarky. I detected a hidden sectarian bustle.'

Mary Lou did not take advantage of the amazing openings offered at TCD, but she did encounter a significant obstacle, which maybe provides a partial explanation. In 1990, during her second year at Trinity, in Peter's Pub in Dublin's Johnson Place – off South William Street – she met her future husband, Martin Lanigan. The World Cup – Italia '90 – was on the screen in the pub. They were introduced by a Basque friend of Mary Lou's, who was dating a good pal of her future husband's. According to her, Martin was 'in high dudgeon', roaring and shouting at the referee. She thought he was going to have a stroke. They soon became an item. The romance lasted throughout her remaining years in Trinity, survived her year away in Spain and afterwards at the University of Limerick, until their marriage in 1996.

Neither Martin, nor most of his friends, were students at Trinity. Much of the couple's courtship was carried on outside the Trinity milieu. She told Rodney Edwards of the *Impartial Reporter* that Martin 'was different, from the northside and seven years older'. What Trinity lost, Martin gained.

After she graduated, Mary Lou still had little appetite for the rat race. Her year in Rathmines Senior College and her gap year in Spain had already provided a two-year buffer from the perils of the outside world. After Trinity, she opted for a further extension of her education, a master's degree in European integration studies at the University of Limerick. Her choice of subject was a country mile away from her Trinity studies. When de Bréadún expressed surprise at the switch from English literature to European studies, she replied: 'I go on instinct on lots of things. I didn't have a masterplan, where I have carefully plotted out every step of a career path.' She was realistic and humble enough to admit, 'That's self-evident.' She appeared to be floundering.

What was 'self-evident' was that Mary Lou had *no* plan, let alone a 'masterplan'. Like so many others with primary degrees, she hadn't a clue what to do next, a typical graduate who had given little thought to her role in life while she savoured the student experience. What is also beyond doubt was her continued detachment from politics of any sort. Her thesis in Limerick addressed the status of trade unions in a deregulated market, with reference to Aer Lingus. Written in 1995, it is still available for inspection in the University of Limerick, and was read by a researcher for this book. It was remarkably consistent with a speech she made in the Dáil on 28 May 2015. It showed a real interest in the fate of workers, as opposed to trade unions, 'which,' she wrote, 'should not act as apologists for capital dominance even when this policy is insisted by government.'

Twenty years later, she told TDs during the debate on the sale of Aer Lingus shares that 'fears of compulsory redundancies, fears of outsourcing, fears of a real, effective running down of workers' terms and conditions are justifiable, because if IAG [the global company that took over Aer Lingus] and the government have their way it will, necessarily and by definition, trigger a process of consolidation.'

Her supervisor, Professor Eoin Devereux, co-director of the Centre for the Study of Popular Music and Popular Culture, a young academic at the time, says: 'I was asked to supervise Mary Lou's thesis . . . I remember Mary Lou as being a highly committed and able postgraduate student. I met her again a few years ago on one of the water charges protests in Dublin and we both had a laugh at the fact that I still remember the title of her thesis all those years later.' It was a mildly controversial subject, but not one to reignite the emotions of a closet republican with an eye on Fianna Fáil or Sinn Féin. Nevertheless, she threw in her lot with the University of Limerick and European integration. It imposed a certain geographical distance between Martin and her, but she returned to Dublin to see him every weekend.

The University of Limerick awarded her a 2.1 degree. According to herself, she enjoyed her year there. Her favourite memory was 'the city and the people'. She was the only Dub in her class and she settled into university accommodation, sharing a house with women from Germany, China, Monaghan and Ennis. There were large numbers of Erasmus students from abroad. This time her fees were paid by a bursary. The course included a full week's field trip to Brussels to witness the European Parliament and Commission at work.

Mary Lou's good friend in the University of Limerick, fellow student of European integration and current Raidió na Gaeltachta presenter, Máirín Ní Ghadhra, clearly remembers 1994 as not only the year she hung out with Mary Lou, but also as the year that Limerick won the Fitzgibbon Cup – the higher education hurling championship – for the second time. Máirín recalls Mary Lou's mastery of the English language as 'amazing. I always associate great language with people who speak it properly and I always associate it with Mary Lou.' Like Mary Lou's aunts, Máirín has a lasting memory of her friend's long curly hair.

The two students used to play a lot of Abba's hits and 'walked in the rain' to pass the time. On Europe, Máirín observed that Mary Lou was more of a sceptic than she was herself. She had an interest in social affairs, but didn't appear to have any obvious angle. She definitely had 'no love for any political party'.

The two friends laughed a lot. More significantly, in line with her time at TCD, Mary Lou seemed more interested in Martin Lanigan than in politics. Máirín remarks that Martin was a really 'lovely guy', but nevertheless she and other friends were surprised when Mary Lou returned to Limerick after the Easter break with a 'huge diamond ring on her finger'. She observes that 'the rest of us weren't ready for the engagement'.

Máirín Ní Ghadhra, a native Irish speaker, strongly defends Mary Lou from those detractors who point the finger at her weakness in the Irish language. She insists that 'she has come on in leaps and bounds and definitely understands conversations in Irish', although Máirín has never yet interviewed her for Raidió na Gaeltachta.

The two women do not meet so often now, since both are busy in the political/media circus. She says that she used to meet Mary Lou for lunch but no longer does, although they slip into an easy friendship over a cup of coffee when they do get together.

Mary Lou's relaxed attitude to earning a living remained, even when she left the University of Limerick. Once again, she did not seem to be hell-bent on an immediate permanent and pensionable job. She appeared to have modest ambitions. In 1995, armed with her master's in European integration, she applied for a part-time post in the Institute of International and European Affairs (IIEA).

The IIEA had been set up as a think tank in 1990 by former Labour Party chairman and TD Brendan Halligan. Patrick Keatinge, the director of research in the mid-1990s at the then Institute of European Affairs, recalls interviewing and offering a job as a researcher to Mary Lou: 'I was very impressed at the initial interview stage. Mary Lou had the most relevant graduate studies, she was self-possessed and she had a general vitality. From watching her work at the Institute, I was not surprised at her elevation to the European Parliament at a relatively early age.'

There is no indication that Mary Lou had her eyes on a seat in Europe at the time, but undoubtedly her (albeit limited) experience in the IIEA gave her an edge when running for the European Parliament nine years later.

She was never going to bust a gut at the IIEA. The job was part of a community employment programme, for only nineteen and a half hours a week. It was not well paid, but provided enviable knowledge to anyone pondering the career opportunities offered by the rapid expansion of Europe into all facets of Irish life. Perhaps Mary Lou had spotted this.

Odran Reid, first administrator of the IIEA, worked alongside Mary Lou at the time. He says she was a 'lovely person with untapped ability'. Her work was 'good, but not spectacular. She had basic drafting skills.'

Former foreign policy editor of *The Irish Times* and a board member of the Institute for British–Irish Studies in UCD, Paul Gillespie was an active member of the IIEA in the 1990s and editor of *Britain's European Question: The Issues for Ireland*, published in 1996. Mary Lou was hired to do research for the book. She happily worked with British embassy officials on the publication (five years later, as a republican activist, she was handing them in letters of protest) and even, on one occasion, accompanied Paul, former Taoiseach Garret FitzGerald, historian Ronan Fanning and other co-authors on a trip to major offices in Whitehall and Westminster. Paul Gillespie says that Mary Lou was a 'proficient researcher and that her eyes would have been opened by working on this. I got on well with her.' He says she was a member and convenor of meetings of the social policy committee, where she took the minutes. She was emphatically non-political in a party sense, and there were no indications of her later Fianna Fáil or Sinn Féin convictions.

Odran Reid endorses Gillespie's view. However, he says that she was interested in politics, but he felt that her sympathies might have lain with Labour. He was 'surprised that she later joined Fianna Fáil, a party towards which she seemed antagonistic. She appeared to me to be left of centre, but not very. There was certainly no sign of her later passion for a united Ireland. She would have been regarded as pro-Europe.'

In early 1995 Mary Lou McDonald's time at the IIEA ended.

She was nearly twenty-six years old and had, somehow, still managed to avoid the drudgery of a full-time job. She had effectively no life experience, was destined to be married within a year, but appeared as uncertain as ever about the career path, if any, she favoured. Her academic record at Trinity and at the University of Limerick was good-to-average, but not enough to contemplate a future as a lecturer or a professor.

Then she made a surprise decision. In 1995, a year before she married Martin Lanigan, she resolved to return to the warm womb of academia. This time, she headed for Dublin City University (DCU), having decided that the next staging post was for her to become *Doctor* Mary Lou McDonald. DCU accepted her as a PhD student under Professor Kathy Monks, Dean of the DCU Business School. The average doctorate can take between four and eight years. Mary Lou committed to embark on the excruciatingly dull topic of 'Industrial Relations and Human Resource Management'.

By the time this third academic journey of her life was due to be completed, she was expected to be married and over thirty-four years of age. At long last she had settled on a plan; her future looked tediously secure: a conventional life beckoned as a happily married middle-class suburban housewife living in a semi-detached house on the northside of Dublin. She would tackle the doctorate over the long term. Her future verged on the humdrum. There was not the slightest hint of the extraordinary change of direction looming just around the corner. But, first and foremost, she was going to marry the man she loved.

CHAPTER 3

INTO THE ARMS OF GERRY ADAMS

Mary Lou McDonald and Martin Lanigan were married in the University Church, St Stephen's Green, Dublin, on 29 May 1996. The service was attended mainly by family and close friends. A reception was held afterwards in the historic Tailors' Hall on the edge of Dublin's Liberties. On their marriage certificate, Martin, thirty-four, describes himself as being on the 'Clerical Staff, Bord Gáis Éireann'. Mary Lou, twenty-seven, is recorded as a 'Graduate Student' in Dublin City University. They hardly sounded like a power couple.

Mary Lou certainly didn't marry Martin for his money or his politics. He had neither. They started their married life by purchasing a small dwelling at 34 Halliday Square in Dublin's Stoneybatter district.

Martin Lanigan came from a family of market gardeners living in the beautiful Strawberry Beds in west Dublin on the banks of the Liffey. Martin's father, Gerard, and his paternal grandfather, William, had both earned modest livings from tiny pockets of land providing flowers – mostly tulips – for Dublin's Smithfield market.

The Strawberry Beds is a close-knit community. It has been

captured in a local history book, *The Strawberry Beds*, written by long-time resident Patrick Troy. He identifies the Lanigans as among the older-established inhabitants of the community.

For twenty-five years in the 1970s, 1980s and 1990s, the local community held an annual Strawberry Fair, a summer fête to bring the community together, to parade its wares and attract visitors. Activities in which Martin Lanigan's family participated included the tug-of-war, local bands, golf, sheaf of wheat contests and pony riding. Unfortunately, the fair had to end in 1995 because of an accident, followed by a steep insurance claim.

At the heart of the community lie three pubs – The Wren's Nest, Anglers Rest and Strawberry Hall – the local school and, more recently, a community centre. In a 1968 photograph of the schoolchildren in the Lower Road school, no fewer than six members of the Troy family and three of the Lanigans, including Martin, feature. Falling numbers meant that in 1971 the school was merged with St Bridget's National School in Castleknock.

Among the pupils who knew Martin Lanigan at St Bridget's was Conor Lenihan, former Minister of State under both Bertie Ahern and Brian Cowen from 2004 to 2011. Lenihan remembers Lanigan as 'a good character, a decent guy; we were in the same class. The Lanigan family were really country people in a burgeoning urban community. We were both in the Gaelic football team. We went to the same parties.'

Martin Lanigan was never destined to follow his father and grandfather into a career in market gardening because the pickings from the family business were shrinking by the year. One neighbour insisted that 'Martin never picked a strawberry', although Mary Lou regularly credits him with good gardening skills. His father's landholding was not expected to provide a living for the next generation. After finishing his schooling, Martin headed straight for a steady job as a clerk in the state-owned Bord Gáis Éireann.

Martin had four sisters, Bernadette, Geraldine, Ann and

Carmel. Ann, to whom he was very close, died young. His elder sister Bernadette, who lived in the family home in the Strawberry Beds until recently, worked in the Royal Victoria Eye and Ear Hospital on Dublin's Adelaide Road, winning the Nurse of the Year title. Geraldine is less visible, as is Carmel, who emigrated to Australia.

Unlike Mary Lou, Martin did not have a university degree, but he had other talents. Music had always flourished in the Strawberry Beds, where bands sprouted up among the youth living there. Martin formed the last band from the Lower Road with some of his neighbours: John Mooney, a brother of fellow resident and later Fianna Fáil TD Mary Mooney, Maurice Troy, brother of Patrick, the author of *The Strawberry Beds*, and Michael Byrne. They called themselves the New Hollande Band after the original name of The Wren's Nest pub where they drank. Martin had a good voice and could be heard practising with the band in the community hall every Friday. In 1982 the band, which produced its own music, gave a long-remembered concert on the banks of the Liffey near The Wren's Nest weir. Patrick Troy notes with surprise that 'although there was no official policing for the event, there was no trouble at all'.

The Wren's Nest was one of the centres of social life in the Strawberry Beds. A friend of Mary Lou's remembers Martin as 'a bloody good singer; he was influenced by The Pretenders and The Police. He was a talented songwriter too. Like the rest of the band, he had no political opinions on anything. Mary Lou', she says, 'would come out to his gigs with her friends from TCD. She was great craic, very amiable.' She adds that Martin was no sportsman. He was generally 'laid-back, happy in the background'.

Mary Lou has never lived in the Strawberry Beds, but her five-year courtship with Martin and their later marriage meant that lots of local residents had met her. Many liked her; one or two resented her intrusions. She is clearly remembered on a tug-of-war team at the Strawberry Fair and for mucking in at local events. When I visited the owners of The Wren's Nest, Stella and Una O'Rourke, one Sunday morning, they described Mary Lou as 'delightful company' and recalled going to the greyhound races with her and Martin. Along with many of the pub's customers, they had taken a minibus to Martin and Mary Lou's wedding.

A resident from one of the other families told me that 'Mary Lou came on to the scene as Martin's girlfriend. The endorsement of the Lanigans gave her an entrée.' Nevertheless, this person felt that maybe Martin was 'punching above his weight', although she added, by the way, that he was 'very good-looking'. Nevertheless, Mary Lou 'blended well with the people here. She seemed more Fianna Fáil than Sinn Féin, confidently middle class.'

Occasionally the unity of the residents of the Strawberry Beds community splintered. In the 1990s there was a burning issue. Much of the Liffey Valley is protected by a Special Amenity Area Order, approved by none other than Fianna Fáil minister Padraig Flynn in 1990, restricting building in the area to preserve its unique appeal. The order became the subject of a major row after it was signed. In his book, Patrick Troy says that 'This Order would eventually ensure the end of families that lived for generations on the Lower Road.' It meant that

sons or daughters of farmers, market gardeners, publicans and long-time residents could no longer build locally and were forced to purchase outside the Strawberry Beds. Local people were unable to compete with the stronger purchasing power of outside wealth. There are now only seven families on the road that can claim to have an unbroken line to their ancestors of sixty years ago. It is now believed that even the wren or the robin would have difficulty getting planning permission to build its nest in springtime. By conferring on it the Special Amenity Area status with its stringent legislation, the keepers and carers of the valley have been selectively

excluded from their role as guardians. There was never any need
for such legislation as strict adherence to normal planning legislation
would have been adequate. The vision of the legislators has not
been realised, as there are now fewer visitors to the area than in the
sixties or seventies. There are fewer amenities and services available
now for travellers to the Strawberry Beds.

Martin and Mary Lou were potential victims of this development to which Patrick Troy refers. The couple soon moved out of
Stoneybatter but not to the Strawberry Beds. Instead, they settled
for a semi-detached house in a nearby estate, Riverwood in
Carpenterstown, Castleknock. Their new residence had none of the
charm of the Strawberry Beds, but was situated in a cul-de-sac
in the depths of a local suburban concrete jungle, just three kilometres away.

A number of impassioned residents' meetings were held on the
planning hot potato. It split the Strawberry Beds community. Some
demanded that the Special Amenity Area Order could be breached
if long-established locals wished to build a single dwelling, while
others were adamant that their area should remain untouchable.
One of those who wanted looser restrictions for locals was none
other than the new arrival, Mary Lou McDonald. She is remembered
by many in the Strawberry Beds as a self-appointed spokesperson
for the unhappy long-time-resident families who saw their sons and
daughters departing for less desirable locations. Those families
wishing to build one-off houses welcomed her articulate interventions
at local spats. Others resented a non-resident paddling her own
canoe in the sacred Strawberry Beds.

At the meetings Mary Lou, the extrovert outsider, was vocal
on the subject, while Martin, the introvert resident, was practically
silent. She did the talking for them both.

The meetings ended inconclusively, but with an agreement
between the warring factions that no one would actually object if

long-standing residents applied for individual, one-off permissions for family members.

It was probably Mary Lou's first high-profile entry into local politics, in a constituency – Dublin West – where she would later unsuccessfully contest a Dáil seat.

The parochial politics of planning in the Strawberry Beds and Dublin West was a battle primarily fought by councillors, although the sitting TDs often felt obliged to become involved in council matters. Dublin West was no exception. It was overendowed with household names, political giants on the national stage. Fianna Fáil's Brian Lenihan Junior had inherited his Dáil seat from his father, Brian. Other powerhouses in the constituency included Independent TD Joe Higgins, the late Fianna Fáil deputy Liam Lawlor, the late Fine Gael TD Austin Currie and Labour TD, later Tánaiste, Joan Burton.

The Strawberry Beds was Lenihan country. Brian Junior lived on the banks of the Liffey. He drank in The Wren's Nest, where a picture of the much-loved young minister still hangs on a wall of the pub. There was probably no room for another talented Fianna Fáil TD, like Mary Lou, in the Castleknock/Strawberry Beds area.

Even after her marriage, there was no sign that Mary Lou had her eye on Fianna Fáil, on a Dáil seat or even on membership of the local council. She made no urgent moves towards a political – or indeed any other – career while she and Martin settled down, seemingly content with the life of newly-weds in search of a house of their own. A couple of kids down the line and maybe a second income were probably on the agenda. At this time, Mary Lou was continuing her doctorate in DCU, a long-term project. She had no permanent source of income, no outlet for her obvious talents, which, arguably, lay more in public service, in debate, in interaction with people, than in academia. She had never held a full-time job. Martin was busy, working for the gas company for much of the day.

Staff at DCU say that they hardly ever saw Mary Lou because pursuit of a doctorate is a fairly solitary activity. Doctoral students normally have a supervisor, as Mary Lou did, but do not attend lectures. They meet almost no one and are rarely on campus. As an experience, for Mary Lou it must have been a stark contrast to the more recent joys of being a carefree, unattached, gregarious undergraduate.

Eighteen months after Mary Lou's marriage to Martin, in November 1997, a major event occurred in her life. Her beloved grandmother Molly Hayes died. Molly was the militant Tipperary nationalist who had exerted a major influence over her in her formative years.

Mary Lou was deeply upset by her grandmother's death. In an interview with journalist Rodney Evans of Fermanagh's *Impartial Reporter* in 2020, she opened up about her grief. Two decades later it was still hurting:

> My grandmother died the year after I got married. Molly was her name. She and I were very close; she was a big influence on my life. That was a huge loss, and I remember actually on the day that she died, I had heard that she was struggling, and I made my way down to Tipp, and I just missed her by probably about 40 minutes or so. I was devastated like, not that it would have made any difference, I mean she was going, she was dying, but I felt for a long time that I should have got there quicker . . . I was distraught. She was the typical type of matriarchal figure, great crack, huge influence on me and my ideas without me even realising. She's the type of woman where – you know they barred smoking on trains – but she'd get the train up from Limerick Junction to Dublin, I'd go and collect her and she'd tell me 'I smoked my fag and I left the packet there, just to let them know.' So, I'd say 'well okay', she was at a stage I wasn't going to argue with her, but she thought it was a pure effrontery of some buck to tell her she couldn't smoke her cigarettes.

But, anyway, she was a great woman. So yeah, I was upset, I mean it didn't scar me indefinitely, but it was just one of those moments. Loss is hard you know, but again I've been very, very lucky.

There is no reason to doubt her expressions of grief. Her story is almost identical to the one she gave to *An Phoblacht*. There is one difference: talking to the *Impartial Reporter*, traditionally a strong unionist paper, she omits to mention that Molly was a militant republican. When speaking to *An Phoblacht*, she lays on the republican sentimentality with a trowel. Granny Molly, selectively told, has to be spun with care.

Exit one matriarch, enter another – this time from the Strawberry Beds – who was about to profoundly alter Mary Lou's life.

Martin Lanigan had a good friend called Joe Comiskey. They had been at the Lower Road school together. Joe owned a small construction company registered at Woodlands, the Lower Road, Strawberry Beds. His mother, Nora, who lives at that address, was secretary of the company. Joe and Martin remain pals, both children of established families in the community. Naturally enough, when Martin and Mary Lou became an item, socialised in the Strawberry Beds and got married, Nora Comiskey began to know Mary Lou well. Nora Comiskey recalls that she first met Mary Lou when she and Martin were watching a football match in the Strawberry Hall pub in the early 1990s. They did not want to be interrupted, but they were! She remembers her first impression was that Mary Lou was 'good-looking' and that he was 'reaching high'. Nora was a guest at their wedding. All four were regular customers at The Wren's Nest, where Fianna Fáil held many of its meetings.

Nora, now in her late eighties, a matriarch of Fianna Fáil, is also a matriarch of the Strawberry Beds, a lifelong pillar of the community; she was brought up there. Her family had a proud tradition of providing domestic service for the large estates in the area. Her father, James White, worked for the nearby Plunkett estate. She herself had been a worker at Rowntrees' sweet factory, cycling to work every day. A member of Fianna Fáil for over fifty years, Nora Comiskey is way out on its republican wing. As a person, she is immensely engaging, great company, a trifle outrageous and utterly fearless about expressing her strong convictions. She has conquered cancer three times.

Nora Comiskey and Mary Lou got on like a house on fire. They still do. They often talked politics. In 1997 Nora was in her mid-sixties, Mary Lou in her late twenties. At the time, Nora was a younger matriarch, but already a hardy warrior. She had fought many republican battles in a party fast moving away from its nationalist roots. She tells a colourful story of fleeing from the RUC in high heels after a republican demonstration. Nora regarded herself as one of the custodians of the republican soul of Fianna Fáil. She may have been a thorn in the side of Brian Lenihan Junior during his supremacy in the constituency, but Nora had historical, not local, wars to wage. Her brand of hard-line republicanism was in retreat. Extradition of IRA terrorists to Northern Ireland was increasing, a battle that Fianna Fáil had effectively conceded. Nora Comiskey had been fighting a rearguard action on that front, with most of her allies coming from outside the party, many of them from Sinn Féin. She did not hide her admiration for Gerry Adams and Martin McGuinness. Adams attended her husband Ollie's funeral. As a result, so did the Garda Special Branch, which keeps subversives under surveillance.

Disaffected republicans within Fianna Fáil in the 1980s had plenty of differences with the government of the day, whether it was led by Fianna Fáil or Fine Gael. Nora Comiskey's ultra-republican activities seemed to be indulged by Fianna Fáil as a tolerable noise in the background, despite her close association with many known subversives. In August 1988 she had sat on an anti-extradition platform in Monaghan town alongside Joe Cahill. No republican was more militant than Cahill. A former chief of staff of the IRA, he had been sentenced to death for killing a police officer in 1942. Alongside Cahill and Comiskey on that day sat former Westminster MP and one of the founders of the Irish Republican Socialist Party Bernadette McAliskey, a leader of the Irish Women Workers' Union Pádraigín Uí Mhurchadha, and journalist Tom Carron, a brother of Sinn Féin's Owen Carron, the MP elected to take Bobby Sands's Westminster seat after the hunger striker died.

At that time, Charles Haughey was Taoiseach and leader of Fianna Fáil, and during the meeting Nora Comiskey fired a warning shot across his bows. According to the *Irish Independent*, she threatened Haughey with a political uprising if he proceeded to implement extradition from the Republic to the North, insisting that 'it would be the death knell of the party'. The newspaper described her as 'a surprise speaker' at the rally. They didn't know her very well. Nora Comiskey had the brass neck to turn up anywhere. She was carrying the torch of former ministers Neil Blaney and Kevin Boland, who had left Fianna Fáil in disgust after the 1970 Arms Trial.

A year later, in 1989, Nora had surfaced in a much more formal setting. This time, according to the *Irish Press* newspaper, it was with Gerry Adams himself, the president of Sinn Féin, generally seen as a permanent member of the IRA Army Council. With others, they attended the launch of a new umbrella group called Comhdháil Náisiúnta na hÉireann, the Irish National Congress, to fight not only extradition, but partition itself. Among their number were Frank McManus, a former Unity MP, west Belfast priest Father Des Wilson and Father Patrick Ryan, the republican priest fighting extradition to Britain. According to the *Irish Press*, 'one of the meeting's organisers, Ms. Nora Comiskey, a member of both the national and Fianna Fáil anti-extradition committees, said that the Comhdháil was not intended as a political party but would operate along the lines of the African National Congress (ANC)'. She knew full well that wrapping the Nelson

Mandela garment around her shoulders would protect her flank from accusations of subversion. This enabled her to keep within the acceptable levels of rebellion, while skilfully remaining inside the Fianna Fáil tent. 'Each group and individual involved,' she said, 'will retain their own policies, but we would hope in certain elections to maximise support for the strongest candidate. We believe that all our ills stem from partition – violence, unemployment, emigration and the waste of hundreds of millions of pounds maintaining the border, as well as the massive loss of revenue to the country as a result of violence.'

In early 1990, the Irish National Congress held its first conference. More than 400 people turned up to hear speakers urge Britain to withdraw from Ireland, to call for the release of the Birmingham Six, for a ban on the use of plastic bullets and for the Irish government to take a case against Britain to the European Court of Human Rights. The conference was attended by delegates from Sinn Féin, People's Democracy and former members of Fianna Fáil. A fifteen-person executive was elected, which included Nora Comiskey, the well-known artist Robert Ballagh, trade unionist Matt Merrigan, firebrand Bernadette McAliskey and Patricia McKenna, later to become a Green Party MEP. There was a significant Sinn Féin contingent on the INC executive, including a highly sulphurous Rita O'Hare, wanted in Northern Ireland for the attempted murder of a British soldier in 1972, and future Sinn Féin Stormont minister for education Caitriona Ruane. In the centre of all the activity was Nora Comiskey, flirting with republican fellow travellers and playing footsie with the IRA itself.

Nora Comiskey was relentless in pursuit of the united Ireland agenda. She joined former government minister Kevin Boland on an expedition to fill in border roads cratered by the British Army. She wrote letters from the INC to Taoiseach Charles Haughey urging him, as president of the EU in 1990, to demand British withdrawal from Ireland. She continued to take the fight to the floor of the

Fianna Fáil ard fheis in 1993 when she denounced the party, asserting that people who had died for Ireland 'would turn in their graves' if they knew of current government attitudes to Northern Ireland.

When Nora Comiskey met Mary Lou McDonald, she was an untouchable maverick within Fianna Fáil. It was she who brought Mary Lou into the party. They were a perfect match. The republican conscience of Fianna Fáil instantly clicked with the younger woman – with credible nationalist pedigree – in search of a mission. Nora saw her potential, her credentials and her ability. She also saw her as an articulate young ally in her efforts to drag the party back to its republican roots.

Mary Lou didn't need much persuading. In 1998 she threw herself into the political fray. In the same year, she abandoned her doctorate. She must have felt comfortable with Nora Comiskey's strong associations with the leaders of the military wing of Sinn Féin, such as Joe Cahill, Martin McGuinness and Gerry Adams. Her start–stop life's journey had taken yet another twist. The career that had never paused anywhere for long was heading towards bare-knuckle politics.

Backed by Nora Comiskey's patronage, Mary Lou made an immediate impression – sometimes positive, at other times negative – on grass-roots members of the party. One former Fianna Fáil TD from the area who watched her in action summed up her appearance in the local party: 'She was introduced into the party by Nora Comiskey, who was her mentor and her minder. Nora saw her potential. She was very articulate, but her brand of republicanism was too militant for us. She tabled lots of motions. She was very outspoken. I remember motions coming up at Comhairle Dáil Ceantair [constituency executive] meetings. I remember people telling Mary Lou to 'stay quiet' when she had caused mayhem at the monthly meetings, but she and Nora stood their ground. I think she may even have been sanctioned.'

Former local councillor and Dáil candidate Deirdre Doherty

Ryan, a running mate for Brian Lenihan in the 2002 general election, backs up this view:

> Mary Lou was brilliant. I was chair of the Women's Group and she was the great white hope for women. All the Fianna Fáil women were willing to put their shoulder to the wheel for her, if she wanted to go forward for election. We were all stunned when she left. She was very active locally for a while. One week she was at a Fianna Fáil Comhairle Dáil Ceantair meeting, then the next week she was a candidate for Sinn Féin. I often wonder if Mary Lou was put in to learn the ropes. I met her recently and she gave me a big hug. Mary Lou was introduced to the party by Nora Comiskey, who had very strong republican views and equally strong republican contacts. I am a republican too, but was a strong supporter of Brian Lenihan.

As I tracked the Mary Lou path into Fianna Fáil, all roads led to Nora Comiskey. It was time for me to visit the local matriarch in her charming cottage in the Strawberry Beds.

Before my visit, I had spoken to Nora Comiskey on the telephone. She was friendly, but understandably wary. When I arrived, unannounced, at eleven o'clock on a fine August morning, Nora was preparing for a local health staffer to visit. She was unfazed by her rather unexpected guest, asked me into her house and immediately suggested a glass of whiskey. I warmed to her. It was the first time in forty years that anyone had offered me alcohol so early in the day, but it may have been a big hint that she had little respect for the stricter drink-driving laws that I had introduced as minister for transport. I gave her a copy of my last book, *In Bed with the Blueshirts*, to smooth my passage. She instantly reminded me of my embarrassing past, that I had been a Blueshirt myself twenty-five years earlier. Immediately I was on the back foot. Her banter was good-natured. She was a refreshing cross between an old warhorse and a benign battleaxe.

Nora Comiskey has nothing to hide. She was born a republican and will die as one. Her sitting room is full of the mementoes of martyrdom. The Proclamation of the Provisional Government of the Irish Republic hangs on one of the walls; on another is a framed copy of an Easter 1916 *Evening Herald* with the headline 'TWO MORE EXECUTED'. She is a political matriarch to her fingertips. Nora is mightily proud that Mary Lou joined Fianna Fáil as her protégée. She told me that they had talked a lot about politics beforehand and were on the same political wavelength. Both were against extradition and wanted to support Irish prisoners in British jails. Nora believed that extradition should be avoided by making wanted IRA offenders stand trial 'here in their own country', although she remarked with a sigh that 'they would probably get a tougher trial here under the Criminal Law Jurisdiction Act than in Northern Ireland or in Britain'. She was the prime mover in the unsuccessful campaign to save wanted IRA man (later a TD) Dessie Ellis from extradition to the United Kingdom, where he was subsequently acquitted of terrorist charges.

Contrary to Fianna Fáil's normally hostile spin that Mary Lou had taken off from Fianna Fáil in a huff because Brian Lenihan was standing in the way of her ambitions, Nora told me that he had wanted to promote her to the council because he too saw her potential. He didn't want her to go to Sinn Féin. He would even have been happy to invite Mary Lou on to the general election ticket as his running mate.

Nora's version of events is backed up by long-time Fianna Fáil member, supporter and friend of Brian Lenihan, Mary D'Arcy. She remembers Mary Lou as 'great fun and very pleasant'. Mary D'Arcy was secretary of the Kevin Barry Porterstown cumann which Mary Lou joined.

Mary D'Arcy recalls a conversation between Lenihan, Mary Lou and herself in The Wren's Nest around the time that Mary Lou was on the verge of jumping ship. Lenihan had just discovered that

Mary Lou was about to bolt. Typically direct, he took the bull by the horns: 'Mary Louise, for God's sake don't leave us and join that crowd of hoodlums in Sinn Féin.'

Mary Lou replied bluntly: 'Brian, Fianna Fáil are not republican enough for me.'

The man, whose family members had seen themselves as republicans since the foundation of the state, was taken aback. 'I am,' he said, 'a Wolfe Tone Republican. I am a constitutional republican, uniting Protestant, Catholic and Dissenter.'

She wasn't prepared to wait. Within weeks, she was in Sinn Féin.

Even Nora Comiskey, her patron, didn't stop her, but it is doubtful whether she really tried. She readily admits that when Mary Lou was showing signs of impatience about Fianna Fáil's commitment to a united Ireland, she had 'told her that she was in the wrong party'. Perhaps Nora was too, but she stayed put, although she says that Mary Lou suggested that she should join her in Sinn Féin.

Nora had not only led Mary Lou into Fianna Fáil, she had, naturally enough, steered her towards the Irish National Congress, her alternative sphere of republican influence – a second front. Although the INC was officially non-party political, it is often portrayed as a halfway house between Fianna Fáil and Sinn Féin. In reality, it probably had far more members sympathetic to Sinn Féin than to Fianna Fáil.

When Mary Lou arrived, members of the INC executive could not believe their luck. Here was a young woman with words at will, with republican principles, beating down their door. They instantly put her on their male-heavy, middle-aged executive. She was exactly what they needed. Nora was guiding her protégée deeper into republican territory. In turn, Mary Lou was moving fast towards her final destination.

Her rapid progression from Fianna Fáil to Sinn Féin via the Irish National Congress raised eyebrows in both parties. Some

Fianna Fáil members felt that she was simply experimenting, trying it out; others felt that she had no intention of staying in the party for long. Conspiracy theorists felt that a hidden hand had planted her in Fianna Fáil to cause as much disruption as possible and embarrass them on their vulnerable republican flank.

There are certainly tough unanswered questions about Mary Lou's original and final intentions within the wider republican political network. There remain to this day unexplained anomalies overhanging her membership of Fianna Fáil.

Her opaque transition from Fianna Fáil to Sinn Féin is another of several events about which she is reluctant to enlighten the sceptical. She plays down her Fianna Fáil membership as though it had never existed. She has been rewriting history, her story presented differently depending on her audience.

In December 2008, Mary Lou gave an interview to *An Phoblacht*, the official voice of Sinn Féin. The newspaper outlined the authorised Sinn Féin/McDonald biography. In the interview she rattles off her 'happy childhood' in Rathgar, her holidays in Tipperary, her 'education' (no mention of Notre Dame, the private school), her 'university studies' (no mention of Trinity, the bastion of privilege), her utterly obscure 'work for the trade union movement', her 'haunting imagery' of the hunger strikers, her 'republican-minded' family. And she adds how her poor mother was 'fit to be tied over the hunger strikes'.

And then the amnesia. She addressed the faithful, the Sinn Féin readers, on the thorny issue of her past membership of Fianna Fáil with the following final, definitive words: 'I never joined the Fianna Fáil party . . .' She spelled it out loud and clear to the republican readership.

She must have been hoping that readers of *An Phoblacht* don't read books, at least not books written by Fine Gael stalwarts. A few months earlier she had answered a question from Fine Gael's Mary Banotti for her book *There's Something about Mary*.

Banotti asked her straight out: 'Did you join Fianna Fáil?'

Mary Lou replied, 'I did.'

Her two statements are flat contradictions, impossible to reconcile.

In the *An Phoblacht* interview, she added with characteristic lack of detail: 'When I was in my twenties a friend of mine invited me to a Fianna Fáil meeting and I went to a couple more meetings, but it was very clear I was in the wrong place.' Her yarn was cunningly vague, classic broad-brush. The 'friend' is not identified and no precise dates are given. Just a casual 'couple' of meetings. She makes it sound as if she sat quietly on a sofa at a few informal party get-togethers, listened carefully and took a measured decision that Fianna Fáil were pseudo-republicans. She may have had a point about that, but a more relevant question was whether she herself was a real believer, or was she merely an opportunist in a hurry, taking Fianna Fáil for a ride?

She went on rapidly, with her well-practised mastery of diversion, to mention that she had 'got involved in the Irish National Congress' where she said she had 'met people from Sinn Féin'. Nameless people again, of course. She presented the INC as her heaven-sent corridor to the republican utopia.

Her denial of her membership of Fianna Fáil is staggering in its brazenness. It omits to mention the nature or the occasion of the casually phrased 'couple' of meetings she attended. The truth is that she was an active member of Fianna Fáil for at least eighteen months – 1998 to early 2000.

Although she insisted that she was never a member of Fianna Fáil, basic research shows that she was a member of the Kevin Barry cumann of Fianna Fáil in Porterstown, Castleknock; that she attended cumann meetings from 1998 to 2000; that she spoke eloquently at the Comhairle Dáil Ceantair at the time.

Apart from all the cumann meetings, the women's groups, the Comhairle Dáil Ceantair gatherings and others, she, somehow, clean forgot to tell *An Phoblacht* that she had been honoured by her Fianna Fáil colleagues with the gift of a precious speaking slot at the Fianna Fáil ard fheis in November 1998. She had seized the opportunity to criticise the RUC. Quite a memory lapse.

A man with a clearer memory, Gerry McGeough, the well-known pro-life advocate and lifetime republican, adds fuel to the debate about the timing of Mary Lou's transition from Fianna Fáil to Sinn Féin. He remembers Mary Lou back around November 1998, the month she spoke at the Fianna Fáil ard fheis. Gerry was president of the Trinity College Dublin Sinn Féin cumann. Mary Lou arrived at a Trinity debate hotfoot from visiting Sinn Féin headquarters in Parnell Square. He says that 'She had obviously been sent down to get to know a few people. She hadn't a clue who I was. I mentioned my book *Defenders* and she asked about it in a tentative way. She thought I was a loyalist! Caoimhghín O Caoláin, Sinn Féin's only TD at the time, and unionist MP William Thompson were there. She was one of those people who talk to you and are always looking over your shoulder to see who is there. She made a beeline for Caoimhghín.' He adds, 'Mary Lou popped up again when she invited me to speak at the annual Seán Russell Commemoration in 2001. She was definitely a Sinn Féin party member by that stage.'

Mary Lou's hope must have been that none of *An Phoblacht*'s readership in December 2008 had read the *Irish Times* report of her speech to the Fianna Fáil ard fheis ten years earlier:

A Ms. Mary Lou McDonald, Dublin West, speaking on reform of the RUC, said the RUC was composed exclusively of people from one tradition and they were utterly incapable of carrying out fair policing. There had been victims who had died at the hands of the RUC. There needed to be a root and branch change to the policing system.

Quite a coup for someone who had never joined the party. The denial doesn't wash. Mary Lou McDonald was a full participant in Fianna Fáil, not a disinterested observer at a 'couple' of meetings.

Mary Lou's outright denial of her membership of Fianna Fáil could be explained as a pragmatic political reinvention. In December 2008, when she gave the *An Phoblacht* interview, Fianna Fáil was rapidly becoming toxic. Her past association with the party, which had been popular in 1998, could have been fatal. It was the year of the bank guarantee, of individual financial scandals, the year of the property meltdown. It was the year when austerity was looming, when unemployment started to rocket and when the recession began. It was the year when Bertie Ahern was forced to resign. The Fianna Fáil heroes of 1998 had become the villains of the intervening decade. The tribunals had exposed certain Fianna Fáil members as corrupt to the core. Mary Lou's 'interview' with the house-trained scribes from Sinn Féin's *An Phoblacht* was part of her campaign to be re-elected to the European Parliament in 2009. Any association with Fianna Fáil was political death, its brand contaminated.

The truth is that she had been up to her neck in Fianna Fáil. Even more interesting were other sensitive meetings she attended at the same period, at least one arranged by Fianna Fáil national executive member Mary White. Both women, committed republicans, wanted to support the minority nationalist population of Portadown, who were trapped in one of the most infamous black spots of sectarianism, the Garvaghy Road. Mary Lou McDonald and Mary White shared strong feelings about the Orange marchers passing through nationalist areas after the Sunday church service at Drumcree. Understandably, they saw the marchers as triumphalist and provocative. They joined forces to show solidarity with the nationalist people. Mary Lou was reported by the *Sunday Independent* to have made contact with Brendan McCionnath, a Sinn Féin member who was leading the resistance to the Orange marchers. She maintains that the lack of interest from other

Fianna Fáil members in the plight of the residents of the Garvaghy Road helped to convince her that the party was not serious about Irish unity.

It was no coincidence that Mary Lou linked herself to Mary White, a well-known cheerleader for the Adams agenda on Northern Ireland. Sometimes Mary White even openly praised Adams, the leader of a despised rival party, in public fora. Her rebelliousness paid off. Her election to the next Seanad was achieved when a large block of Sinn Féin votes transferred to her in typical disciplined fashion. A few years later, in 2003, she gained even greater notoriety when she headed out to Colombia to show support for the so-called 'Colombia Three'. By then Senator White, she demanded that the Fianna Fáil government should seek the release of Niall Connolly, Jim Monaghan and Martin McCauley after they had been charged in Colombia with training left-wing FARC terrorists in the art of bomb-making. Both Monaghan and McCauley had already been convicted of terrorist offences. No wonder the Sinn Féin councillors voted for Mary White en masse.

Mary Lou was hanging out with Fianna Fáil activists like Nora Comiskey and Mary White, of whom Gerry Adams and Martin McGuinness would approve. She was choosing to throw herself into one of the uglier hotbeds of sectarian conflict in Northern Ireland. She was jumping in at the deep republican end of the Fianna Fáil pool, despite having no *locus standi*. Not even a county councillor, she puzzled many of the less outspoken Fianna Fáil foot soldiers, who were fighting more parochial battles about medical cards, housing and water rates. While they were knocking on doors or attending Castleknock residents' meetings, the articulate newcomer was swanning about on a solo run, uniting Ireland.

Some of them would have preferred that Mary Lou should fight for a council seat under the Fianna Fáil banner, but she did not see herself as a humble councillor. Nor were her activities looking like those of someone seeking approval from the Fianna Fáil leadership, nor anticipating a long career in that party. She was rocking the boat.

Her behaviour provoked some discontented murmurings in the ranks of the Soldiers of Destiny. Several Fianna Fáil members, while silently suspicious of her presence, were resentful of her abilities. Others challenged her. Angela Rowley, a lifelong party member, persistently asked which Fianna Fáil cumann Mary Lou had joined that entitled her to speak at meetings. According to one party member, Angela Rowley was regularly politely told to button her lip: Mary Lou was a talented young woman whom they should encourage. If Nora Comiskey was ever asked for confirmation of her protégée's party membership, she would scoff at the question, asserting that membership always took a bit of time. The matriarch was fiercely protective of her republican apprentice.

It was obvious that, whatever else she did, Mary Lou was not going to hang around Castleknock securing medical cards for constituents. She wanted a united Ireland and was making waves on several fronts. The minutes of the Irish National Congress show that she joined its executive in July 1998. She was parachuted in, again courtesy of Nora Comiskey. She joined other republican luminaries, like future INC chairperson Cathal McCarthy, artist Bobby Ballagh and her own constant minder and mentor, Nora, at the top table.

Minutes of the July 1998 executive meeting when Mary Lou landed reveal that retiring chairperson Bobby Ballagh had recently been at an informal meeting with a leading member of Sinn Féin. According to the minutes, Ballagh reported that 'Sinn Féin were anxious to rebuild links with non-party republicans and groups such as the INC, in the aftermath of the confusion and dissension surrounding the referendum on Articles Two and Three of the constitution [which claimed the territory of Northern Ireland]. Sinn Féin are willing to meet us and are interested in maintaining constructive links.'

The arrival of Mary Lou on to the executive on the same day that Sinn Féin was love-bombing the INC may not have been a coincidence. The same minutes record that she would join a three-person sub-committee to prepare the INC document for the Patten Commission on the future of the Royal Ulster Constabulary. The minutes also record that the INC would hold a public meeting in Dublin's Mansion House in August to highlight the issue of sectarian violence. Possibly of more significance, it was also noted that 'Sinn Féin have given a commitment on postering' for the meeting. Sinn Féin were fast movers. They were on a charm offensive, wooing the INC and its executive.

Increasingly, the INC was looking like a vehicle being eyed by Sinn Féin for its own ends. The presence on its executive of Rita O'Hare, a senior Sinn Féin official with convictions for IRA activities, gave it a darker flavour. Some members feared that O'Hare was there to observe and report back to Sinn Féin's military wing. O'Hare is reported by reliable sources to have been impressed by Mary Lou.

One man who was determined that the INC would not become a Sinn Féin front was executive member and latterly INC chair Cathal McCarthy. A fierce opponent of sectarianism and a committed republican, McCarthy wanted to ensure that the INC was not captured by any one political party. Writing in 2016 on a blog, 'The Pensive Quill', edited by former blanketman and Long Kesh prisoner Anthony McIntyre, McCarthy had some choice words to write about Sinn Féin and Mary Lou. He was yet another member of the INC in Sinn Féin's sights at the time.

> From 1993 to 2010 I was a member of the National Executive of the Irish National Congress and during that time I had a lot of direct dealings with Sinn Féin.
>
>   The INC was a lobby group that promoted constitutional republicanism through the ideals of 'freedom, unity and peace'.

Phoenix Magazine once described the INC as an organisation for 'middle class republicans that baulked at the idea of joining Sinn Féin', but nothing could be further from the truth. The INC was a liberating space where republicans from all parties came together to discuss our differences and agree a strategy to end political violence and partition.

In the late nineteen nineties the wife [Cindy] and I used to go on holidays every August to west Belfast for the week-long festivities of Féile an Phobail. The festival always ended with the annual anti-internment commemoration rally and in 1999 our participation in this event made the front page of the Sinn Féin newspaper, *An Phoblacht/Republican News*.

I didn't realise it at the time, but this was to be the beginning of a love-bombing campaign to get me to join Sinn Féin.

It was suggested to me on numerous occasions by a variety of their members that I should consider joining the party, that I would be a great asset. The ego massaging switched to outright bribery in 2000 when I 'won' a weekend away to Glasgow to see Celtic play.

I had witnessed the draw being rigged and I was taken aback when I was the 'winner'. For fun, I refused to accept the prize unless it was changed to a trip for two so that I could take my wife. That would be no problem I was told, all I had to do in order to collect my greatly increased prize was to join Sinn Féin!

I politely refused.

In a second piece, Cathal McCarthy outlined the strange behaviour of Mary Lou McDonald after a controversial decision by Dublin City Council to unveil a plaque to commemorate the foundation of the Orange Order in Dublin's Dawson Street:

In 2000 I was Vice-Chair and PRO of the INC. Mary Lou McDonald (then a member of Fianna Fáil) was the INC's chairperson. Mary Lou and I were invited to attend a meeting with Sinn Féin party officials to try to dissuade the INC from holding a protest against the civic endorsement of Orange Order sectarianism by Dublin City Council.

Sinn Féin was of the opinion that the Celtic Supporters' Club intended to disrupt proceedings and that the ensuing violence would reflect badly on organisations that were there to engage in peaceful protest. The INC was of the opinion that this was mere speculation and that any violence, if it occurred, would be publicly condemned by us. We informed Sinn Féin that we would be going ahead with the protest.

It was after this meeting that I was contacted separately and invited to join Sinn Féin. I was offered £35,000 (we still had the punt) per annum to become a Sinn Féin activist and organiser in Limerick City.

I refused the offer. I had come to the conclusion the previous year that Sinn Féin's Ard Chomhairle (their ruling body) was not so much Republican and Nationalist as it was Marxist and Communist. More importantly, I am pro-life and Sinn Féin are pro-abortion-on-demand, so even if they doubled their money on offer, I was never going to join.

I rang Mary Lou to tell her about this development and she informed me that the same offer had been made to her and that she had accepted it; she asked me not to tell the other members of the INC Executive, as her membership would not become official for another 3 months and that she would announce it then (normally there is a 6 month 'vetting' period, but Mary Lou's membership was being fast-tracked).

It seems that Mary Lou was not being transparent. Was she, at a minimum, hopelessly conflicted as an undeclared applicant for membership of Sinn Féin?

Cathal McCarthy continued:

Less than a week before the protest I got a panicked phone call
from the INC's Secretary Sile Carson, informing me that a majority
of the INC's National Executive were now opposed to holding the
protest, that Mary Lou had been ringing around and convincing
people that it was a bad idea.

I assured Sile that the protest would go ahead as had been
unanimously agreed at our last meeting, even if it was just the two
of us; members were free not to participate, but any decision to call
off the protest would require another meeting and another vote.

I did my own ring-around and convinced everyone to take
part. Of course, I felt I had no option but to reveal Mary Lou's
membership of Sinn Féin to the other members.

I presented Mary Lou with two options, either resign as
chairperson or lead us in protest – she chose the latter and in
Dawson Street, Dublin on 28 May 2000 Mary Lou made her
international and national television debut.

Mary Lou resigned from the INC shortly after that, but she
kept in contact: she had been parachuted into the Joe McDonnell
cumann [named after the fifth hunger striker to die] by the Ard
Chomhairle as their candidate in the 2002 general election and she
was terrified. The cumann had already selected their candidate and
they were not exactly happy about having their decision over-ruled.

As a means of breaking the ice, Cindy [Cathal's wife] and I
agreed to make a banner for the cumann for Mary Lou to present
to them as a gift and Sinn Féin compensated the selected candidate
[for being removed and replaced] with an all-expenses-paid, two-
week holiday in Spain.

When I refused to help her cumann with an anti-bin charge
campaign they were mounting, because I wasn't a member and
it felt like I was being dragged in and because I had other things
to be doing, I explained my reasons and I never heard from Mary
Lou again.

Cathal was not the only republican to be blanked by Mary Lou when he no longer served any useful purpose for her or Sinn Féin.

Former Independent Alliance minister Finian McGrath, vice-chairperson of the INC in 1999/2000, had a similar experience. Finian had stood shoulder to shoulder with Mary Lou and Cathal, on 28 May 2000, in the protest against Orange sectarianism at the unveiling of the plaque to commemorate the founding of the Orange Order. Finian was on the INC executive with both Mary Lou and Cathal at the time. He was on the soft left, the socialist wing, that believed in the James Connolly vision of a united Ireland. A primary school teacher, Finian would book the room for their meetings in the Teachers' Club in Dublin's Parnell Square. He describes Mary Lou in those days as 'very young and articulate. She was warm and sociable. She loved the craic with the lads. She would join us for a "smoke" all the time. She was very, very republican, but socially left of centre. We used to say that Mary Lou was "SNQ" (Sound on the National Question)! I would slag her and Nora Comiskey about Fianna Fáil not being serious about a united Ireland. She took it well. She was very popular in the INC.' Finian's words about Mary Lou being 'very, very republican' ring true. Contemporaries at DCU at the time recall her harbouring doubts about some of the provisions of the Good Friday Agreement, including the abolition of Articles 2 and 3.

Cathal McCarthy relays a story of Finian McGrath's later unhappiness with Sinn Féin's changed attitude to him, a fellow republican, in the build-up to the 2002 general election. In line with their policy of cherry-picking the brightest and the best from the INC, Sinn Féin had invited Finian himself to run for the party, but he had declined. They then threatened to run their own candidate and destroy his chances. Finian wrote to Cathal before the election, asking him to try to persuade Sinn Féin, as comrades in the INC, not to run a candidate against him. Finian believed the republican vote might be split. 'A two-nationist Labour' candidate might even

win. Cathal suggested that Finian should contact his old pal Mary
Lou.

Mary Lou, by then out of the INC, failed to return Finian's
calls. Sinn Féin went ahead and ran a candidate against him, a
fellow republican. The Sinn Féin candidate tanked while Finian
took the final seat. By 2002 the INC was no longer a lobby group
that Sinn Féin wanted to infiltrate. Its exploitation as a fertile
recruiting ground for the party had been prevented by Cathal
McCarthy and others. The more worthy experiment of creating an
umbrella group, where republicans of all hues and parties could co-
operate, had faltered.

Mary Lou's term as chair of the INC followed a now familiar
career pattern: her tenure in all her adventures was short but
eventful, often surrounded by controversy. In Fianna Fáil she was a
dissident almost before she joined; she had found an outlet for her
radical instincts in fellow dissident Mary White on the Garvaghy
Road. In the INC she was made secretary in 1999 before taking the
chair in 2000. Her short period there was marked by internal
dissension in which she was directly involved. Elsewhere, she never
lasted long in the same posting. Outside politics, she gave up her
doctorate at DCU in 1998 in midstream. She had lasted only a year
as a researcher in the Institute of European Affairs. From 1998 to
2000, she had spent a short, but uneventful, spell, again as a
researcher, at the Irish Productivity Centre (IPC), one of those
doomed IBEC/ICTU[1] ventures that was eventually liquidated.

One executive at the IPC says that at the time she was in the
middle of 'transitioning from Fianna Fáil to Sinn Féin'. He was
tight-lipped about how the relationship ended, commenting that it
was 'unexpected', but 'by mutual agreement'. She celebrated her
thirtieth birthday in 1999 with a CV marked by a lack of staying
power that would have sent flashing amber lights in the direction

---

1   Irish Business and Employers Confederation and the Irish Congress of Trade
    Unions.

of any prospective employer. She was still every inch the restless republican.

Alternatively, was she so confident of her ultimate destination that the erratic ups and downs of the journey were of no consequence to her? Her chopping and changing certainly never worried Sinn Féin.

Mary Lou's route to her final political home is clouded in mystery. Most of it is of her own making. Her willingness to rewrite history is an obstacle to any biographer putting clarity ahead of contradiction.

Nora Comiskey, the woman who guided her through her republican baptism, may have eased her passage to Sinn Féin. She recalls telling Mary Lou that she was in the wrong party if she wanted a united Ireland. It is difficult to imagine that Nora did not have a quiet word with Gerry Adams after Mary Lou showed increasing signs of impatience with Fianna Fáil.

Mary Lou, as always, has been woolly on the subject. She explained her change of political party to Deaglán de Bréadún: 'I suppose, first of all, I knew some of the lads through the Irish National Congress, although that wasn't the crucial thing.' She felt Sinn Féin actually had their act together. And they knew what they were doing.

Some members of her family still say that her republican sister, Joanne, was the decisive influence in Mary Lou switching parties.

It is particularly hard to accept her professed route from Fianna Fáil to Sinn Féin because of her own account of the transition. In her interview with *Hot Press* journalist Olaf Tyaransen in June 2004, he asked her about her sudden shift. She explained that 'Having discovered I was in the wrong party, I then went to Sinn Féin in 1999.'

Her suggestion that 1999 was her year of entry into Sinn Féin presents further problems of credibility. In 2000 Mary Lou was still a member of Fianna Fáil, the party she has denied ever joining. The minutes of Fianna Fáil's Kevin Barry cumann, Porterstown, Castleknock, as late as 26 January 2000, show that party member Mary Lou McDonald proposed another member, Edward McManus, as a constituency delegate to the Fianna Fáil national executive.

It is not illegal to be a member of two political parties at the same time, but it is highly irregular. Perhaps Mary Lou herself was confused. If Cathal McCarthy's story is accurate and she asked him to keep her application to join Sinn Féin a secret in 2000, maybe she was technically not a Sinn Féiner at that moment; but that does not explain how she could be an active member of Fianna Fáil in 2000 (according to the minutes of a local cumann meeting) if she 'went to' Sinn Féin in 1999 (according to herself).

Her request for Cathal's silence on her pending membership of Sinn Féin might have been more acceptable if she had immediately stood down from the INC pending a decision on her application. Yet it is highly likely that she was, as he says, already being secretly 'fast-tracked' into Sinn Féin.

Not long afterwards, she announced that she was resigning from the INC chair. She felt the chair was inappropriate because she had decided to seek selection as a public representative for Sinn Féin. With super-efficient speed, she was then nominated by the Joe McDonnell Sinn Féin cumann as its candidate for Dáil Éireann for the constituency of Dublin West. Not for the first time, nor for the last, the parachute was produced to hasten Mary Lou's promotion. There were rumours of resentment from Sinn Féin troops on the ground, but no rebellion.

A lot of behind-the-scenes preparation is needed for such Machiavellian manoeuvrings within political parties. Talks with unnamed figures within Sinn Féin must have been going on for several months before Mary Lou landed at yet another republican citadel.

At the time, she was extraordinarily fortunate. She had

witnessed from the inside exactly how Fianna Fáil operated locally, its hopes, plans and strategy in the Dublin West constituency, where she herself was soon to be a rival candidate. Not a bad start for a defector to Sinn Féin to have been deeply embedded behind enemy lines for a couple of years before the battle began.

Whatever the truth of Mary Lou McDonald's extraordinary somersaults around the republican merry-go-round, she had now landed. She may have left behind some Fianna Fáil members who felt betrayed, a shell-shocked INC, an abandoned PhD supervisor and brief tenures in several research and teaching bodies, but she was being embraced by Sinn Féin. The days of short-term performances in long-term assignments were over. Mary Lou knew it. She was embarking on a long-term project that was pointing her towards the Taoiseach's office.

CHAPTER 4

THE ANOINTING OF MARY LOU: THE FAST TRACK TO EUROPE

Mary Lou was right about Fianna Fáil. The so-called republican party's journey towards a united Ireland resembled a tortoise travelling on tranquillisers. She could huff and puff about the Royal Ulster Constabulary at the Fianna Fáil ard fheis, she could stir it up about the Garvaghy Road and Drumcree at Fianna Fáil cumainn, she could take aim at the Orange marchers, but Fianna Fáil had been partitionist in all but name. She truly wanted speedier action on Irish unity, but progress was tortuously slow. Fianna Fáil wanted a united Ireland, but not just yet . . .

Nevertheless, her decision to join Sinn Féin in 1999/2000 made little political sense. Fianna Fáil was on a roll. It had won the 1997 general election and was, albeit unknown to her or to anybody else, set for over a decade in power. Bertie Ahern had been a prime mover in negotiating the Good Friday Agreement in 1998. Fundamental change in Northern Ireland was at last in prospect, with a new Assembly and cross-border bodies agreed by unionists. There was even a ceasefire that might last. And McDonald was a member of the party in the driving seat.

Yet, instead of celebrating the Good Friday breakthrough

and seeking further progress by the same route, she decided to defect to the enemy. It was a major change of gear. Sinn Féin was a small party with a dark past and a doubtful future. Its leaders believed in the ballot box when it suited them, but they also believed in the Armalite, which suited them more often. The IRA hadn't gone away.

Sinn Féin had been lurking below the radar in Ireland's political underworld for several decades. For most of the period known as the Troubles, it was led by Adams and McGuinness, IRA leaders and political pariahs of the time. As apologists for IRA atrocities, Sinn Féin's bosses were banned from the airwaves under section 31 of the Broadcasting Authority Act (1960). There had been a cross-party political consensus in the Dáil about not giving the terrorists 'oxygen' – until 1994 when Labour Minister for Arts, Culture and the Gaeltacht Michael D. Higgins decided not to renew the ban on Sinn Féin under the act. Ireland's future president considered it to be an infringement of free speech.

The effect of granting Sinn Féin access to the broadcasting media was not as alarming as some of us had forecast, but it brought the party in from the political deep freeze. Journalists who had claimed that they would expose Sinn Féin's arguments once they were allowed to challenge them in live interviews failed abysmally. Adams, McGuinness and others proved, for the most part, masters of the new media.

Despite their sudden access to all broadcasting outlets, there was no surge of support for Sinn Féin in the South. In the 1997 general election, the first since Sinn Féin had been allowed full media coverage, they won only one Dáil seat, that of Caoimhghín Ó Caoláin in Cavan–Monaghan. Fianna Fáil was returned to power.

Mary Lou knew that Sinn Féin had been political outlaws for over a decade. She knew the savagery of the party's history in pursuing a goal she shared, a united Ireland.

Sinn Féin had condoned violence and killings for decades. She was joining the party that carried a torch for the killers of twelve civilians murdered at a Poppy Day remembrance ceremony in Enniskillen in 1987; she was tolerating the party whose armed wing included the perpetrators of the Kingsmill massacre of ten Protestant workers; she was endorsing the party that approved the brutal murder on a Sligo holiday of Lord Mountbatten, Lady Brabourne, Mountbatten's eldest daughter's mother-in-law, and two teenage children – his grandson Nicholas Knatchbull and fifteen-year-old deckhand Paul Maxwell; and she forgave the party that sheltered the murderers of mother of ten Jean McConville, executed in 1972 as an informer and then 'disappeared' by the Provisional IRA. Did Mary Lou have any moral compass? Did she ask any of the hard questions of McGuinness and Adams before she signed up? Did she mention the IRA's Warrington bombers, who had murdered two children, twelve-year-old Tim Parry and Johnathan Ball, aged three? The history of the party she was joining was shamed by its tolerance of barbarity. She bit her tongue, held her nose, blocked her ears and joined the party with her eyes open.

Sinn Féin had not suddenly become a normal democratic party, even after the Good Friday Agreement. It still had an armed wing and arsenals galore at the time when Mary Lou swore allegiance to it. She would have been fully aware of that. Once you joined Sinn Féin, you gave support to the IRA; it was automatic. In 1986 Gerry Adams had specifically insisted: 'If you leave Sinn Féin, you leave the IRA.' Loyalty to one was not possible without loyalty to the other.

When Mary Lou switched to Sinn Féin, it did not mean she was obliged to become 'army' – an active member of the IRA – or take part in manoeuvres, but she would be compelled never to condemn even its most bloodthirsty activities. She didn't need to join the army, but she had to wear the boots.

And wearing the boots meant that she had to accept the culture, the past and the traditions of Sinn Féin and the IRA. One of the most insidious was the continued existence of an 'IRA Army Council'. Shrouded in necessary secrecy, the IRA Army Council authorised courts martial, executions, tarring and feathering and multiple bank robberies. Nobody doubted that Gerry Adams and Martin McGuinness, who welcomed Mary Lou into Sinn Féin, doubled up as key members of the seven-man Army Council. They ran the entire Provisional Sinn Féin movement, army and non-army. Gerry controlled the IRA, despite Mary Lou's incredible assertions that she believed him when he constantly denied his membership of the terrorist group. That loss of credibility was the price she paid for membership and for her rapid preferment.

Mary Lou kept her part of the bargain. For twenty years she never flinched when she was asked the hard questions. She backed the former terrorists' actions, however indefensible they were. What did Sinn Féin deliver in return?

They delivered in spades.

The existence of a private army and its weapons dumps was not the only difference between Sinn Féin and Fianna Fáil, the party Mary Lou left behind; nor was it the link with criminal activity, an association that damaged Sinn Féin's reputation but was widely believed to have bolstered its bank balances. It had a political structure that would have made the ultra-secretive old Workers' Party blush. In theory, it was quasi-democratic. In practice, power was centralised in the hands of very few people.

Theoretically, power within Sinn Féin is divested to its annual ard fheis, the policy-making body of members that meets once a year. The ard fheis elects the seven-person National Officer Board and twelve members of the Ard Chomhairle (national executive). Equally theoretically, the Ard Chomhairle runs the party. It is made up of the National Officer Board, the twelve members elected from the ard fheis, members from the four Cúigí (regional executives), the parliamentary groups north and south, the National Councillors' Forum and the National Youth Committee. Crucially, eight

members of the Ard Chomhairle may be co-opted by the leader.
Between the eight co-opted members, the National Officer Board
and the parliamentary group's nominees, little dissent is ever voiced
at Ard Chomhairle meetings.

In 2001, the year Mary Lou was brought on to the Ard
Chomhairle, it consisted of forty-one members. It was headed by
three of the military wing, party president Gerry Adams and vice-
presidents Martin McGuinness and Pat Doherty, backed up by
party chairman Mitchel McLaughlin, himself a non-combatant.
Other members of the military wing on the Ard Chomhairle included
Joe Cahill, Martin Ferris, Dessie Mackin, Alex Maskey, Gerry Kelly
and Rita O'Hare.

The Ard Chomhairle sits about ten times a year. The party's
day-to-day business was delegated to the Coiste Seasta (standing
committee) which meets every fortnight. It is smaller, with only
eight members, but includes the usual loyal suspects: the party
chair, the general secretary, the director of administration, the
directors of finance and human resources from both parts of Ireland,
and three members elected by the Ard Chomhairle itself.

One former Dáil deputy told me that the Ard Chomhairle was
carefully controlled by the National Officer Board, all seven of
whom sit on the Ard Chomhairle. Once a decision was made, everybody was obliged to fall into line. Dissent was almost unknown.
Leaks from Ard Chomhairle meetings never happen, a clear improvement on the traditional parties' permanent pandemic of leaks.

In practice, when Mary Lou joined up as a humble member of
the party, power was concentrated in the hands of Adams and
McGuinness. It was unheard of for the leadership to be defeated in
any Ard Chomhairle discussions. The power of the leader to co-opt
members to the Ard Chomhairle cemented his position, if that was
necessary. In Adams's case, his leadership had stood unchallenged
for thirty-four years. He would leave in his own time.

Several members of the Army Council sat on the Ard

Chomhairle. In theory, they made the military decisions while the Ard Chomhairle controlled all other matters. In practice, the Army Council dictated the pace on the non-military agenda. No one would expect the less vocal Ard Chomhairle members to challenge a united front of Adams, McGuinness, Martin Ferris, Gerry Kelly and others who had served decades in jail for the cause. Throughout the Provisional movement there was an aura of respect for those who had been engaged in the armed struggle.

Sometimes the 'army' Sinn Féin members mocked the non-combatants who had never pulled a trigger. Behind the scenes at party ard fheiseanna, less respectful IRA volunteers could be heard dubbing them as 'draft dodgers'. Party chairman Mitchel McLaughlin was often disrespectfully referred to as 'Dan Quayle', nicknamed after the former US vice-president, who is believed to have enlisted in the National Guard in order to duck action in the Vietnam War.

Longevity of service for those in power was accepted. For more than three decades, Adams straddled the military/political divide. He lasted even longer at the top of Sinn Féin than the notoriously ageing Chinese Communist Party leaders. As a TD for Louth and a member of the Army Council operating in Northern Ireland, he dominated both wings of Sinn Féin north and south. The cult of personality around him and the charisma of McGuinness guaranteed that the Ard Chomhairle was effectively a rubber stamp.

Mary Lou, the restless republican, was an unlikely fit with the straitjacketed Sinn Féin structure. Her arrival might have been expected to signal trouble. Her limited role in Fianna Fáil had been that of a free spirit, a budding dissident. She thrived on twisting their tails on the national question. Her speeches tended to be scathing of the party for being soft on the border. She had led a lobby group (the Irish National Congress) that was critical of the Fianna Fáil government's stance on the North. Fianna Fáil tolerated her carry-on because she was a small cog in a large wheel and, as a party, they allowed discussion and limited internal dissent. She was also a high-calibre contributor and a young woman with talent, the type the party did not want to lose. Mary Lou repaid their indulgence with impatience, but her choice of Sinn Féin as a place of refuge had the potential seeds of disaster in it. When she looked at the iron discipline of Sinn Féin, she should have shuddered.

Worse still, if she surveyed the Sinn Féin parliamentary party, she should have been equally reluctant to jump ship from Fianna Fáil. In 2001 Sinn Féin had one TD, Caoimhghín Ó Caoláin, the sole electoral success in the Republic. Ó Caoláin was a product of the much-trumpeted 'ballot paper in one hand and Armalite in the other' party policy. Sinn Féin had abandoned its boycott of Leinster House in 1986, but had succeeded in landing only a single TD in the four general elections since then. The policy was not working in the South, despite sensational successes in Northern Ireland in the 1997 Westminster elections.

Worse still, Ó Caoláin was a political nonentity. His chosen career outside politics, with the Bank of Ireland, provoked much mirth from observers, making predictable jokes every time his colleagues in the Sinn Féin 'army' section pulled off another bank heist. Ó Caoláin, a long-time county councillor, had reached the Dáil the hard way, having stood unsuccessfully in 1987, 1989 and 1992. He was a tireless worker. Brendan Smith, a long-time constituency rival and former Fianna Fáil cabinet minister, is full of surprising praise for him, recognising that 'at a local constituency level he is honourable and decent'.

No doubt he was, but that is all he was allowed to be. In the twenty-eighth Dáil, from 1997 to 2002, Ó Caoláin made little impression, merely parroting the party line. He was his master's voice to the last syllable. The real Sinn Féin action was offstage. Although Mary Lou had ambitions to reach the Dáil, it would be difficult to imagine that she fancied the role of being a mere mouthpiece for darker forces on the outside.

Sinn Féin never had much time for its Dáil deputies. To this day, they are treated as little more than lobby fodder. They read speeches written elsewhere and vote as instructed from on high. If they refuse to wear the boots, they get the boot. Ask Peadar Tóibín or Carol Nolan, both TDs who held sincere pro-life views. They upped sticks and left the party, disillusioned that Sinn Féin's diktat on the issue of the right to life should overrule their personal beliefs.

Dáil deputies and councillors who quit the party have told various media outlets about the centralisation of power in the hands of a few hard-nosed Sinn Féin leaders. One told me that the Ard Chomhairle was in reality either appointed by the leader or selected by 'rotten boroughs' or insiders who – in practice – bow to the will of the seven-member National Officer Board. The power is wielded from the top down and the system is 'akin to the democratic centralism' of the Workers' Party. It has a Stalinist ring to it, similar to the old Eastern European communist parties.

Sinn Féin parliamentary party meetings are not held in the same format as its rivals'. In the case of Fianna Fáil, Fine Gael and Labour, the deputies and senators hold private weekly meetings where politics and policies are debated and adopted. In Sinn Féin there was only one TD in 2000/01 – a man who was practically ignored; but even today, the parliamentary party of thirty-six TDs and four senators remains a toothless group compared to other layers of the movement. It meets, but with TDs' personal advisers present. These individuals are appointed by the party, not the TD. They report to the hierarchy. The TDs fall into line and accept their role as political eunuchs.

Sinn Féin chiefs are not ashamed of this model. In 2020 the party's long-time director of finance, Dessie Mackin, told *The Irish Times*'s Colm Keena that Sinn Féin does not want its TDs controlling the party. They want a party of 'activists'. Unfortunately, being a Sinn Féin 'activist' often means being a former member of the IRA.

In 2002 when Mary Lou first stood for Sinn Féin, she failed to win a seat in Dublin West, but her party returned five TDs to the Dáil in the general election. Those to join Ó Caoláin were Martin Ferris (Kerry North), Arthur Morgan (Louth), Seán Crowe (Dublin South-West) and Aengus Ó Snodaigh (Dublin South-Central). All of them had worked their passage into the Dáil the hard way. Each had been a county councillor and all had stood for the Dáil on previous occasions. Two, Martin Ferris and Arthur Morgan, had been members of the IRA Army Council.

Mary Lou didn't do county councils. Nor did she do army councils. She didn't do rigid party discipline. She didn't do any-thing Sinn Féin did, except campaign for a united Ireland. If she had been elected and joined the parliamentary party, she would have been a republican of a different stripe. A damsel in distress with the dinosaurs.

So why Sinn Féin?

Her explanations are rigidly consistent. Her maternal grand-mother, Molly, and the horror of the hunger strikers are the stock reasons she has given ad nauseam over the years. They have – once or twice – been buttressed by another, equally unconvincing, explanation. It was served up for the readers of *An Phoblacht* just after Mary Lou had been elected president of Sinn Féin in February 2018. After wheeling out Granny Molly for the umpteenth time, she fed the faithful with a new yarn. Asked by the Sinn Féin propaganda organ, 'Why did you decide to become active in Sinn Féin?', she responded: 'I remember the first time that I saw Gerry and Martin speak. It was in the Mansion House, and I went along with a friend of mine. The place was packed and I remember saying to my friend on the way out, "This is real; this isn't political rhetoric. This is history in the making". At that point I decided not only that I would be politically active, but that Sinn Féin would be my political home.'

No dates. No topic. No name of her 'friend'. Classic Mary Lou vagueness, the customary sweeping statement with no supporting evidence. The 'interviewer' from *An Phoblacht* helpfully asked no probing supplementaries.

The 'Gerry and Martin making history' line in sycophancy may please loyal members of the republican flock, but should be taken with a pinch of salt by ordinary decent sceptics.

The Fianna Fáil explanation that her departure from the party was due to frustration at the presence of Brian Lenihan has a ring of truth, but no more. Mary Lou certainly wanted to be a TD. She most definitely never wanted to be a county councillor. She saw no prospect of political advancement in Fianna Fáil in the Dublin West constituency. Fianna Fáil would have fixed her up with a council seat, even maybe a Seanad seat if she had started to behave herself. In the meantime, she might have been forced to wait decades for Lenihan to retire, for she was not to know that he would die tragically young in 2011. If she had stayed in Fianna Fáil, there was every prospect of years of party infighting, door-to-door drudgery and no guarantee of ultimate success.

Besides, she needed a job, even a career. Her constant flip-flopping and her inability to hold down any positions for more than two years were beginning to look like problems. She was married, over thirty years old, but still in search of a vocation or an opening that would suit her natural talents. She was a fine orator, good with people, but had no professional expertise, only a limited knowledge of European affairs, English literature and human resources, and had hardly risen above baby steps on the ladder of any of them.

Fianna Fáil was unlikely to offer her any permanent, paid position. She had been a pain in the neck, continually reminding fellow party members of their betrayal of the republican gospel. The local foot soldiers liked her personally, but the top brass in Upper Mount Street would never give her a leg up. She had probably antagonised them, if she had even appeared on their radar.

It is impossible to imagine today, but in the year 2000 the name of Mary Lou McDonald was as little known as the name of

Mrs Martin Lanigan. She had made minimal impact on the wider political world. Beyond the lively discussions at the Fianna Fáil meetings in The Wren's Nest, she was very small beer. The Soldiers of Destiny wanted to keep her on board, but they were never going to sacrifice Brian Lenihan for her.

Sinn Féin offered her two highly attractive prizes: a permanent job and a potential path to the top. Fianna Fáil would have retained her services as a volunteer, but she would have been forced to stay working for tedious, tottering ships that would sink in the night, like the Irish Productivity Centre or the ICTU training unit. Sinn Féin had bucketloads of money and was building up its permanent staff at a rapid rate.

Obviously, the improving financial health of Sinn Féin brought security of tenure in its wake, jobs in abundance and a far less complicated path to the summit. There were republican families, but no political dynasties were standing in her way in Sinn Féin south of the border. There was plenty of redundant military talent and bombing expertise hanging round, but that was being slowly discarded. The party's TDs-in-waiting were nearly all men. Sinn Féin was not to see a woman TD elected in the 1997, 2002 or 2007 general elections.

Above all, Mary Lou must have seen that she was facing a serious choice between being a minnow in Fianna Fáil or a big fish in Sinn Féin. Both Fianna Fáil and Fine Gael had long histories of suppressing new talent. Mary Lou was in a hurry. Time was not on her side. If she wanted to be a Fianna Fáil TD, she would have to battle vested interests, local warlords and even headquarters itself, particularly if she needed to move constituency. In Sinn Féin, she could probably take her pick of the pack.

Mary Lou McDonald opted to become a big fish in a small pond, but why did Sinn Féin really want her?

On the surface, she was not a good fit. Posh and privileged was hardly Sinn Féin. But such simple profiling does not take into account the strategic genius of Adams and McGuinness. It is often not fully grasped how committed both the giants of the republican movement were to peaceful change after the 1998 Good Friday Agreement. Perhaps they secretly felt that they had lost the war. No doubt they saw the advent of peace as their path to power in both Northern Ireland and the Republic; but that meant that the party would have to win more Dáil seats. Their strategy was patient and durable. Peace ensured that the second pillar of the 'Armalite and the ballot box' mantra was the only one left. They had struggled for three decades, fighting the terrorist war to a standstill. Now it was time to pursue the ballot box with the same long-term horizon.

To break through into government in the Republic required transforming Sinn Féin into a party that stopped supporting violence but championed the causes of the domestic underdog. It meant continuing to fight the sectarian war by peaceful means in Belfast and Derry, but by grasping day-to-day conventional issues in Dublin and Cork. It was a partitionist strategy, but absolutely necessary to challenge the established parties North and South. They would win seats in Northern Ireland not by appealing to unionist votes, but by stealing votes from the Social Democratic Labour Party (SDLP). They were unscrupulously content to compete for the affections of the Roman Catholic population. In the Republic, they needed educated, articulate candidates with no 'war' records, but with other competences. The party was on a big recruitment drive.

Mary Lou fitted into the southern strategy perfectly. She was manna from heaven. In turn, she was in a position to make reasonable demands on Sinn Féin before signing up.

The complex manoeuvrings that went on behind the scenes as Mary Lou transitioned into Sinn Féin will probably never be revealed, but we can see the results. We can also be certain that she would never have been given such favourable treatment by Sinn Féin unless Adams, McGuinness and others had hatched Project Mary Lou.

A parachute into the looming Dáil contest was not the only help from headquarters that Mary Lou received when she joined the party. Her public promotion began almost immediately. She was just a few months in Sinn Féin when her photograph appeared in *An Phoblacht*. It was not a picture of her working on the ground with the Sinn Féin troops of Dublin West where she was now the party's candidate. Instead, it was an image of her mixing with the mighty.

In November 2000 Sinn Féin launched its twenty-six-county budget submission for 2001. The photograph, dominating a full two-page spread in *An Phoblacht*, featured Sinn Féin president Gerry Adams, Caoimhghín Ó Caoláin and aspiring TD – their best chance for a Dublin seat – Aengus Ó Snodaigh. In the middle of the picture Adams – grinning from ear to ear – beamed down at a completely new face. She was young, female and well dressed. The caption simply described her as 'party representative Mary Lou McDonald'. Behind the four Sinn Féin members was a huge poster with the slogan 'Share the Wealth in Budget 2001'. Mary Lou was centre stage in an important photocall. It was the first of countless similar photographs to follow in the coming years. She was destined to be pictured with Adams at every possible dogfight, north or south of the border. She had no obvious qualification for presenting a budget submission, no known financial expertise, no democratic mandate. She looks slightly embarrassed by the intense attention, but that awkwardness quickly passed.

The occasion may have been billed as the launch of Sinn Féin's pre-budget submission, but in reality it was the launch of Project Mary Lou. It was Adams's clear message to the Sinn Féin troops that he and Martin McGuinness had landed an important new recruit and that she had their blessing.

It was the beginning of a long softening-up process. Mary Lou became a frequent feature, making discreet appearances in *An Phoblacht*. As Sinn Féin's 'Dublin West representative', she popped up with monotonous regularity in the pages of the Sinn Féin news-paper in several carefully chosen locations. These varied from letters to the editor about the Treaty of Nice to being pictured with Sinn Féin vice-president Pat Doherty at a conference. More significantly, in March 2001 she attended a commemoration for IRA Volunteer Tom Smith who, according to *An Phoblacht*, was 'gunned down by Free State soldiers on St Patrick's Day' 1975 while trying to escape from Portlaoise prison. Alongside her at the microphone stood Councillor Nicky Kehoe, formerly a convicted IRA member. Mary Lou was rubbing shoulders with the military wing.

Mary Lou McDonald was displaying, publicly and upfront, that she had bought into the IRA narrative, that she was on board for all the legacies of the Troubles. She was fulfilling her part of the bargain.

The 2002 Dublin West general election battle was a dry run for the new kid on the block. There was never a remote possibility that an almost unknown candidate like Mary Lou could take a seat for Sinn Féin at the time. She had recently moved house to settle in a middle-class Dublin West estate called Riverwood in Castleknock, but she was neither a household name nor a local councillor. Nor, before joining Sinn Féin, had she played a meaningful role in com-munity activities. Her husband had been brought up in the area, but her own links with it were tenuous. Whatever connections she had made were the result of marrying into the local Lanigan family. Unfortunately, Martin Lanigan was one of the least political creatures on God's earth. He later proved to be a fantastic father, but with little interest in his wife's profession.

Apart from her lack of roots in the constituency, Mary Lou carried the added embarrassment of her recent defection from a Fianna Fáil cumann in the same patch. One day she was in the Fianna Fáil camp in The Wren's Nest, the next she was supping with the Sinn Féin crowd in Mulhuddart village. She found that she was often explaining her political volte-face on the doorsteps.

The figures were hopelessly stacked against her. In the previous general election, in 1997, Sinn Féin candidate John McCann had won only 5 per cent of the vote. Nevertheless, win or lose, bar a political earthquake, her patrons at the top of the party planned to ram her through the ranks to become a national figure.

The 2002 Dublin West skirmish was a test for both parties to this unlikely alliance. Mary Lou was not yet ready for unveiling to the mass national media, but if she jumped the loyalty hurdle and performed reasonably in the election, she would be groomed for the top tables in Sinn Féin. And, of course, a full-time job was waiting for her in the party whenever she wanted it. It was a job with sky-high career prospects.

Even before the 2002 general election, Mary Lou had been quietly given a key position high in the Sinn Féin hierarchy. After just one year in the party, in 2001, she became a member of the Ard Chomhairle, another promotion that would not have happened without the specific approval of Adams and McGuinness. It was probably unprecedented for a complete lily-white, who did not sport the wounds of war or the scars of electoral battles, to be welcomed into the party's ruling body. Such rapid recognition may not have helped her in the oncoming battle in Dublin West, but it certainly indicated that other contenders for top positions in the party should keep one eye on the 'Situations Vacant' columns.

The newcomer's meteoric rise did not go unnoticed in the ranks. Dessie Ellis, a former IRA prisoner, a county councillor at the time and later a TD, told me: 'Mary Lou was obviously with Gerry; she was being groomed for the big picture.'

In return, Mary Lou was required to show blind loyalty to the leader and to party policy. No more would she enjoy the freedom of poking holes in her party's failure to live up to its ideals, as she had done in Fianna Fáil. Gerry Adams was not made in the benign Bertie Ahern or Brian Lenihan mould. If any member opted to challenge Adams, he or she was history. Nobody did. Mary Lou rigidly kept the faith for eighteen years. It paid off. She had done a political deal. She had taken the Shinners's shilling. Once she was bought, she stayed bought.

Both Mary Lou and Sinn Féin's all-powerful strategists were playing the long game. The Dublin West election was merely a preliminary sideshow where the young 'arriviste' would be blooded.

And blooded she was. There were some seriously heavy hitters in the field for the three-seater. Fianna Fáil's Brian Lenihan, the Socialist Party's Joe Higgins and Labour's Joan Burton were favourites to win. Sheila Terry of Fine Gael was given an outside chance; Tom Morrissey of the Progressive Democrats was a possible contender. In an article in *The Irish Times* ten months earlier, Mark Hennessy had dismissed Mary Lou's chances of winning a seat as next to zero, suggesting that Joe Higgins had already banked the anti-establishment vote.

And he had. The result was an anti-climax. Brian Lenihan topped the poll with a quota on the first count, even though he had taken a running mate, Fianna Fáil loyalist Deirdre Doherty Ryan. Joe Higgins was a comfortable second, with Joan Burton securing the third seat. Fine Gael's Sheila Terry failed to hold the Fine Gael vote at the 1997 level of 17 per cent and it dropped to 12 per cent on a bad day for the party.

Mary Lou's vote was not spectacular. She had made little impact outside her immediate community. She managed to improve the Sinn Féin share from 5 per cent in 1997 to 8 per cent, but it was nowhere near the number required to be in the hunt for a seat. Indeed, she was eliminated before either Morrissey or the second Fianna Fáil candidate, Deirdre Doherty Ryan, Brian Lenihan's loyal sweeper.

Doherty Ryan was pleased to edge ahead of her old Fianna Fáil colleague after her shock defection to Sinn Féin, but she says that she remained friends with Mary Lou. Indeed, she insists that in that head-to-head election 'Mary Lou asked people to give their second preferences to me, just for old time's sake. If I meet her today, she will still give me a hug.'

Mary Lou delivered. True to her word, when she was eliminated, a big whack of her second preferences transferred to Deirdre Doherty Ryan. If Mary Lou had stayed in Fianna Fáil, she might have been Lenihan's running mate instead of Deirdre. But Mary Lou was never going to be the political equivalent of a golfer's caddy.

Tom Morrissey says that Mary Lou polled exceptionally well in her own Riverwood patch: 'There was an 80 per cent turnout in her estate against 40 per cent in the constituency overall. It was fantastic for a first-time runner in a non-Sinn Féin area.'

The outcome was far from being a failed experiment for Sinn Féin or Mary Lou. She had flown the party flag, as required. She had increased the party's vote in a tough area; but she had no intention of hanging around and flogging a dead horse. She had taken a hit for the party. Now it was Sinn Féin's turn to give her the career break she felt she had earned.

They wasted no time. The marriage was consummated. Mary Lou's last job had been as a teacher in the Education and Training Services/ICTU training unit. It proved no more enduring than her previous roles. This time her career was for keeps.

The new government was formed on 6 June 2002. On 1 August, *An Phoblacht* introduced Sinn Féin's enlarged team in Leinster House. Sinn Féin had created a brand new job for Mary Lou as a 'political strategy co-ordinator'. Speaking to the Sinn Féin newspaper, she introduced herself as the party's rather grandiosely titled 'political oversight manager'. Project Mary Lou was moving up a gear. She explained the nature of her role: 'It's about operating 32-county politics. So obviously there's a need for the work and politics we're involved with in Stormont to integrate with the work and politics in Leinster House. But it also has implications in terms of each of our council groups.'

Nobody who read her explanation could be any the wiser about what she would be doing in the new Leinster House complex. Suffice it to say that neither Finian McGrath nor I (both Oireachtas members at the time) have any memory of ever seeing Mary Lou McDonald in Leinster House before her eventual arrival as a deputy in 2011.

The official blurb about her qualifications for the job embellished her academic prowess: 'She is currently working on a doctorate in Human Resources, which she says helps in terms of getting structures to operate properly and ensuring that work is done in a co-operative way, in a comradely way.' It was August 2002. According to all published curricula vitae of Mary Lou, she had actually given up her doctorate at DCU many years earlier. *An Phoblacht* sometimes takes the odd liberty in the interests of the party.

Whatever her real role, Mary Lou was already firmly established as the party's favourite daughter. She had been given a job with a wide brief because the party leadership wanted to slot her into a key position whenever one became available. While there would be no repeats of the Dublin West blooding, it was clear that Mary Lou was destined for a parliamentary high-profile role, not to be a policy wonk in a back office in Dublin's Kildare Street.

In the meantime, she needed to get to know the Sinn Féin troops North and South. There was a natural curiosity among them about this middle-class woman's speedy ascent. They knew that she was Adams's pet project, so their murmurs were muted, but in the Northern ex-army brigades there were a few rumblings of resistance. These would have to be nipped in the bud.

Mary Lou launched herself on a countrywide charm offensive. In October 2002 she arranged the 'Working Together for a New Ireland' conference in the Hillgrove Hotel in Monaghan town. Its aim was to bring together Sinn Féin representatives, North and South, to discuss the all-Ireland agenda. It was opened by Gerry

Adams, followed by Northern Ireland Assembly Group leader Conor Murphy and by Martin Ferris. The three IRA veterans were joined on the platform by the mandatory Caoimhghín Ó Caoláin. Seated in their midst, blending in with the 'old guard', was Mary Lou.

Part of the conference was devoted to the lack of women in parliament in both parts of Ireland. Gerry Adams pointedly interjected at one stage to insist that Sinn Féin 'need women elected. It means women being in winnable seats.' And, more ominously for some of those present, 'this means men moving to one side'. Mary Lou could have written his script.

It was no coincidence that the young woman chosen to chair the afternoon session was the party's fastest-rising star. *An Phoblacht* gave the conference – and its organiser – the full treatment. Afterwards, Mary Lou lost no time in networking with the curious delegates. According to all reports, the charm worked wonders.

Following the conference, a permanent Sinn Féin forum of TDs, MLAs and councillors, with a fifteen-member officer board, was ordered by the party's Ard Chomhairle. Mary Lou was appointed to set it up. It was in place in just over six months. She was now pivotal and embedded in the party's all-Ireland operations.

The grooming intensified. Mary Lou accompanied the top brass on their high-level outings. She began to appear in carefully stage-managed photographs, particularly where Adams was present. Along with the other bigwigs, she greeted the new leadership of the Irish Labour Party, led by Pat Rabbitte, at Sinn Féin headquarters on the Falls Road in January 2003. In February, she hit the big time when she was included in the Sinn Féin delegation to meet British Prime Minister Tony Blair and Taoiseach Bertie Ahern at Hillsborough. She was now part of the Sinn Féin peace team.

No one now doubted that Mary Lou was heading for the top. There was idle speculation in political circles that she might be destined for a council seat in Dublin in 2004 as a base for a safe

Dáil seat in 2007. It seemed a natural progression, giving her three years to work the local constituency, but it was not to be. Mary Lou didn't do councils.

On 11 March 2003 the die was cast. More than a year in advance, Sinn Féin nominated Mary Lou McDonald as its candidate for the European elections, due in June 2004.

The decision hardly caused a tremor in the political world. All the preparation, the wall-to-wall coverage from *An Phoblacht* and the Adams/McGuinness anointment, had put her in an unassailable position within the party, but it had not yet made her a familiar face to the public. That was all going to change.

Sinn Féin issued an utterly unremarkable press release with the news. They managed to make her career to date sound unexciting, even conventional. The press statement was cliché-ridden, but offered no hostages to fortune.

The next day's *Irish Independent* carried a twenty-six word filler: 'Sinn Féin yesterday selected a relative unknown to run as an MEP candidate for Dublin. Mary Lou McDonald (33) ran unsuccessfully in the last General Election.'

The tone was dismissive. The wider world hardly noticed the 'relative unknown' who was a failed Dáil candidate. Rival hopefuls for Europe, like Gay Mitchell of Fine Gael, Eoin Ryan of Fianna Fáil, Labour's Proinsias de Rossa and the Greens' Patricia McKenna were hardly quaking in their boots.

Meanwhile Sinn Féin had cleared the decks. Other ambitious party members with an eye on Europe could bury their hopes. Gerry Adams, the master strategist, had a long-term plan: the 'relative unknown' was going to be a name on everybody's lips within a year. Mary Lou was being installed as the new face of Sinn Féin. She would not simply be a candidate for Dublin. The exposure she would receive in the mainstream media as the party's candidate for Europe would become the alternative image of Sinn Féin nationwide. This was a bigger battle than a Dublin spat.

'Adams watchers' say the former Sinn Féin president always thought at least five years ahead. Project Mary Lou was a big part of his long-term master plan.

After the convention and nomination in March, it was back to the grindstone for Mary Lou. On 20 March 2003 she repeated her previous attendance at the annual commemoration of IRA Volunteer Tom Smith. This time she was not playing second fiddle to Councillor Nicky Kehoe. She chaired the proceedings in Glasnevin cemetery. The supporting colleague on the day was Aengus Ó Snodaigh, one of only two Sinn Féin TDs elected for Dublin in 2002, the other being Seán Crowe, himself a former candidate for the European Parliament. Ó Snodaigh, who was expected to deliver a significant Dublin vote to Mary Lou, would frequently be seen by her side in the battle for the votes of the capital's citizens in the coming year. Nothing was left to chance.

Whether the next event in Mary Lou's life was as carefully planned as her political preparations we shall never know; but it was an occasion of great joy. On 8 June 2003 she and Martin welcomed their first child into the world. Iseult Lanigan-McDonald was born. The name Iseult puzzled family and friends alike. It was an unusual, probably unforeseen, choice. There might have been an expectation in the Lanigan-McDonald clan that Mary Lou would wish to call a daughter after one of the strong women in her life, like her mother, Joan, or her grandmother Molly, the republican whom she claimed had such a huge influence over her thinking. Perhaps they should not have been so taken aback. In Celtic mythology, Iseult is a beautiful princess. Her mother is the Queen of Ireland.

Mary Lou's political plans took a pause, but no more, to allow for the disruption of a new arrival in the family. Back in 2003 she was entitled to fourteen weeks' maternity leave. Feminist or not, good mother that she was and still is, she was not going to be 'rested' for long. Just six weeks after the birth of Iseult, on 16 July, she was back on the trail with Aengus Ó Snodaigh, denouncing the country's 'deepening housing crisis', particularly in Dublin. Maternity leave or not, neither ordinary Dubliners' housing needs nor the European election campaign would defer to Princess Iseult.

Mary Lou looked tired in the photographs published of that press conference, but her campaigning did not stop there. On 16 August she undertook one of the most dangerous risks of her entire political life. It had the potential to blow the European election bid apart and to torpedo Project Mary Lou McDonald.

On 24 July a small advertisement appeared in *An Phoblacht* announcing yet another republican commemoration. It read: 'Annual Seán Russell commemoration. Assemble 3.30pm. Saturday 16 August. Five Lamps, North Strand, Dublin for march to monument in Fairview Park. Speakers: Dublin EU candidate Mary Lou McDonald and Brian Keenan.'

What madness was afoot?

The cocktail of Seán Russell and Brian Keenan was poisonous. Former IRA boss Seán Russell had been a Nazi collaborator. Brian Keenan was an ex-IRA chief of staff with blood on his hands. Mary Lou had a perfect excuse to duck away from this political minefield: she was on maternity leave. No one would challenge that.

Instead, she went ahead. It was widely believed in republican circles that she was being put to the ultimate loyalty test. Her party had just gifted her its nomination for a seat in the European Parliament, possibly one of the most coveted plums in Irish politics. It was payback time. She would have to show her own bona fides by standing shoulder to shoulder with two of the most unsavoury supporters of terrorism in the history of the republican movement.

Seán Russell had died on a German U-boat in 1940 on his return to Ireland. He had been in Germany encouraging the Nazis to invade Ireland as a bridge for taking over Britain. By the time he had arrived in Germany seeking help, Hitler's plans for the Holocaust were well in train. Russell was seeking an alliance, bragging about the IRA's more than 300 wartime bombings in the United Kingdom. The worst example of his handiwork was the slaughter of five people with a bomb planted in shops in Coventry. His memory was honoured annually at a ceremony beside his statue in Dublin's Fairview Park.

Brian Keenan was chosen as the lead celebrant of Russell's life for the 2003 ceremony. His IRA record was among the most savage of the entire Troubles. He organised guns from Libya. In the 1970s, imitating Russell's terror campaign of thirty-five years earlier, he had masterminded multiple bombings in Britain, which resulted in many deaths, both military and civilian. Pubs, hotels, railway stations and restaurants were legitimate targets for Keenan's London gang. In 1980 he was eventually captured and convicted of terrorist acts, including six killings. Keenan was sentenced to eighteen years' imprisonment, but served only twelve.

Apologists for Keenan insist that late in his terrorist career he became a committed convert to the peace process, but on the way he had bombed his passage to the table, leaving carnage in his wake. Tellingly, even as he was apparently emerging from his belief in terror tactics, he wrote from Leicester prison about how 'We must never forsake action, but the final war to win will be the savage war of peace'. It seemed that violence was a justifiable means to achieving political ends. For Keenan, peace was just another weapon in the armoury of war.

At that now infamous memorial in 2003, Keenan delivered a eulogy to Seán Russell. With Mary Lou standing beside him, he talked about the part Russell had played during the 1920s and '30s in the ideological disputes surrounding the Republican Congress, the formation of Saor Éire and his role as IRA chief of staff in the disastrous campaign in England during the Second World War. 'I don't know,' Keenan admitted, 'what was in the depth of Seán Russell's thinking down the years, but I am sure he was never far from Pearse's own position, who said "as a patriot, preferring death to slavery, I know no other way. There are things worse than bloodshed, and slavery is one of them. We are not and will not be slaves."'

Brian Keenan was still advocating violence. Mary Lou McDonald never as much as raised an eyebrow, following him with her own speech, which put more emphasis on the Sinn Féin party's electoral strategy in the next year than on Seán Russell.

It was possibly the lowest moment in her political career, before or since. She was trapped. If she had refused to attend the commemoration, she would have been suspect. It might have been game over. She had been asked to stand in silence as one of the most militant of all IRA leaders relived the blood sacrifice and invoked the name of Patrick Pearse in a paean of praise for a Nazi sympathiser. She had been humiliated, nailed to the cross by her doubting colleagues. Her acquiescence signalled submission. Alternatively, like Keenan, she was a true believer, but that seems less likely.

The Sinn Féin godfathers knew that there was now no going back for their protégée. She was compromised, a passive spectator, an apologist for IRA horrors. After that, she would have no problem explaining away Enniskillen, Jean McConville or any other IRA atrocities. They were deeply regrettable but . . . the grooming phase was over. It was full steam ahead for Europe. All obstacles to Project Mary Lou had been overcome.

The fallout from the Seán Russell memorial was more muted than might have been expected. Some journalists were deeply critical, including Jim Cusack in the *Sunday Independent* and Kevin Myers in *The Irish Times*, but the criticism scarcely got legs until late into the 2004 European Parliament election campaign.

In the meantime, Mary Lou continued to juggle Iseult with her work. Throughout her political career she has relied on her husband, Martin, and her mother, Joan, to share the childcare. In the 2003/04 period, Máiría Cahill remembers Mary Lou arriving upstairs in the

Felons Club in Belfast with her baby in tow. She thrust Iseult into Máiría's arms and proceeded to work the room of mostly senior male Sinn Féin members. She was a master at such interactions, never off duty.

Her attachment to Adams appeared to have become stronger. At the count for the Assembly elections in Northern Ireland in November 2003 she was constantly by his side, at a time when Sinn Féin overtook the SDLP in the popular vote for the first time. Sinn Féin increased its tally to 23.5 per cent, easily beating the SDLP, which lost nearly 5 per cent to 17 per cent. Adams himself topped the poll in West Belfast, where Sinn Féin provided the first four candidates past the post in a six-seater. Beaming out at the television cameras and press photographers as Adams soaked up the glory was Mary Lou. At the press conference Adams gave after his triumph, she brazenly 'doughnutted', looking elegant and attentive. She was surely hoping that some of the magic dust would pass on to her campaign in the South. According to the *Sunday Business Post*, 'Many Northerners, including perhaps the odd shinner, scratched their heads at her inclusion in the Assembly celebrations, but the party's strategy was clear: the campaign for the next election was already on.'

Her relentless appearances in the media at Northern events boosted Mary Lou's profile. Sinn Féin was on a roll in the North and she never missed an opportunity to milk it. Then in December, as political talks intensified, Mary Lou, candidate for the European Parliament, arrived in Downing Street. She was part of a five-person delegation of Gerry Adams, Martin McGuinness, Dodie McGuinness (McGuinness's sister-in-law and head of the Sinn Féin Bureau in England) and Caoimhghín Ó Caoláin. According to republican sources, she and Ó Caoláin 'reminded Tony Blair of his promise to co-operate with the Barron Inquiry into the Dublin–Monaghan bombings, on which he had not delivered'.

So Mary Lou, a mere Irish hopeful for Europe, was giving the

British prime minister a ticking off about his failure to keep his promises. Not a bad item for a candidate's CV.

As usual, the nation's cameras had spotted her. The following day *The Irish Times* published a letter from a sceptical reader:

THE OXYGEN OF PUBLICITY

Madam, On TV last night (December 17) I saw a young lady (unelected) accompany Mr. Adams to Downing Street. This was the same lady I saw beside him at his recent re-election in Belfast. Could this be Mary Lou McDonald, a candidate in next year's European elections?

What would the media say if Bertie Ahern, Enda Kenny or Pat Rabbitte went on with this kind of posturing? Outrage, I am sure, but of course Sinn Féin get away with it.

Yours etc. Brian McCaffrey

The letter was on the money. Even Bairbre de Brún, Sinn Féin's Northern Ireland candidate for Europe, was not in the Downing Street party. Sinn Féin was betting the bank on Mary Lou.

Funnily enough, Mary Lou had more credentials as a candidate for Europe than most first-time runners. She had a master's degree in European integration studies from the University of Limerick, she had been a researcher in the Institute of European Affairs for a short period and she was Sinn Féin's representative at the National Forum on Europe, but those were not the cards she was playing to the electorate. As the election approached, her campaign continued in precisely the same vein as before. It concentrated on high-profile media events, national issues and sound bites.

By their nature, European elections are media-driven. The populations are huge in comparison to Dáil constituencies. The candidates do little door-to-door canvassing unless the media are present to report to a wider audience on the reception the hopefuls receive. When that happens, the party handlers carefully select an estate where their candidate is likely to receive a warm welcome. Television debates are crucial.

The ground rules of the European contest in the four-seater Dublin constituency might have been created especially for Mary Lou McDonald. As a debater, she was light years ahead of rivals whose experience on county councils or in the Dáil did not seem to equip them for serious combat. She had been formidable at debating since her schooldays. Her convictions might be flexible, but her ability to present a case to a wide audience was mighty. She may have entered the European election battlefield with the disadvantage that many electors would never vote for Sinn Féin, but she had a clear edge in the field of serious media skills.

Mary Lou had other advantages. She was young and female. Aged thirty-five, she was still younger than most others in the field. Only one of the fancied contenders, Fianna Fáil's Royston Brady (thirty-two), was younger than her and only one of the other women runners, outgoing Green Party MEP Patricia McKenna (forty-seven), was judged to be in with a chance. Otherwise, Labour's Proinsias de Rossa (sixty-four) was defending his seat, Fine Gael's Gay Mitchell (fifty-two) was considered a certainty, while Eoghan Ryan (fifty-one) was in a battle with Brady for the Fianna Fáil pool of votes. The Socialist Party's Joe Higgins (fifty-five) was an outsider. Apart from Brady and McKenna, Mary Lou's opponents were sometimes seen as a group of ageing has-beens or Dáil deputies on their way out to grass. Sinn Féin or not, Mary Lou appeared fresh, articulate, even fluent by comparison.

Television exposes such basic, but unspoken, differences with a brutality that often cruelly translates into votes and seats. Silent visual messages can be powerful. Mary Lou was a big hit on the box. She excelled on RTÉ's flagship *Questions and Answers* television programme, where the familiar faces appeared tired, older and overwhelmingly male.

Nevertheless, Sinn Féin had a battle on its hands. In the 1997 European elections, their Dublin candidate, Seán Crowe, had garnered only 6.64 per cent of the first-preference votes. Mary Lou would need to double that number to secure a seat because Sinn Féin, notoriously, was never transfer-friendly.[2] To counter this, all the political openings in the party's gift were placed at Mary Lou's disposal. The other Sinn Féin candidates for Europe – Pearse Doherty, David Cullinane and John Dwyer: all good communicators – received far fewer media opportunities.

The ard fheis – in late February – was held in Dublin, Mary Lou's patch, and her opening speech was specifically timed to coincide with peak audience television. She seized the opportunity, raising the temperature in Dublin's RDS, the quintessentially middle-class venue in a prosperous suburban area, so carefully chosen. She let the main parties have it with both barrels.

Mary Lou was fired up. Earlier in the same week, Taoiseach Bertie Ahern had demanded that, six years after the Good Friday Agreement and seven years since the second ceasefire, the IRA should call a halt to its activities. He had warned Sinn Féin's chief negotiator, Martin McGuinness, that the recent IRA kidnapping of a dissident republican, Bobby Tohill, would undermine the political process.

Referring to Ahern's remarks, deliberately made a few days before the ard fheis, Mary Lou condemned the 'unfounded attacks on Sinn Féin that were dominating the headlines this week'. She retaliated by declaring that the party rejected the status quo and denounced the 'lazy, self-serving, self-promoting, egomaniac politics

---

2   Transfers occur under the electoral system of proportional representation in which a person's vote can be transferred to a second or further competing candidate (according to the voter's stated order of preference) if the candidate of first choice is eliminated during a succession of counts or has more votes than are needed for election. Sinn Féin has rarely been transfer-friendly because it tends not to be voters' choice as a second or even a high preference. It attracts first preferences from loyal supporters but tends not to be favoured for even a high preference by supporters of other parties, like it or hate it.

of Fianna Fáil and the PDs, Fine Gael and the Labour Party in the South and the DUP, UUP and the SDLP in the North, who think they have fooled the people of this island into believing there is no alternative.'

Good rabble-rousing oratory. Great television. No prisoners, but no content. She said nothing of substance, but the rhetoric was vigorous. Three and a half months out from election day, she was unflinchingly picking up the gauntlet.

Nevertheless, Ahern's intervention marked out uncomfortable territory for Sinn Féin. The continued activities of the IRA were certain to alienate the middle-ground voters whom Mary Lou was seeking to convince.

Six weeks later, on 20 April, Paul Murphy, Secretary of State for Northern Ireland, rose to his feet in the House of Commons. He had received the first report of the Independent Monitoring Commission (IMC) concerning paramilitary activity in Northern Ireland. For some reason it had been completed early, at the request of both governments. Its findings did not suit Sinn Féin. It revealed that paramilitary activity among both republican and loyalist groups was 'worryingly high: approaching one murder a month; some three victims a week both from shootings and assaults'. The report asserted that Sinn Féin and the Progressive Unionist Party had links with paramilitary groups. It tellingly stated that 'had the Assembly now been functioning, we would have recommended in respect of Sinn Féin and the Progressive Unionist Party measures up to and including exclusion from office'.

Hardly music to the ears of Sinn Féin candidates seeking inclusion in office in the Irish Republic.

Bertie Ahern immediately described the report as 'extremely disturbing' and 'worrying' and added that he accepted its findings – that leading members of Sinn Féin were also leading members of the Provisional IRA. In truth, just six weeks before an election, he was surely disguising his glee.

Sinn Féin's top brass were despondent. Gerry Adams was reported to be incandescent with rage. He even cut loose at RTÉ's chief news reporter, Charlie Bird, about an interview he had carried out with Bertie Ahern about the IMC report. The IMC's suggestion that sanctions should be taken against Sinn Féin were seen as below the belt in an election campaign. A party spokesman lost the head, dubbing the IMC a 'poodle of British intelligence'. It was a hollow claim about a four-person body consisting of Joe Brosnan, former secretary general of the Department of Justice, Dick Kerr, former secretary general of the Central Intelligence Agency, John Grieve, former deputy assistant commissioner of the Metropolitan Police, and Lord John Alderdice, former speaker of the Northern Ireland Assembly.

The report was a body blow to Sinn Féin.

Robbie Smyth, Sinn Féin's general secretary, conceded that its findings would have a 'negative impact' in the June election. But the official line was that they had the wind at their back; that it was a reversal, but that Mary Lou would still be elected. The party would simply redouble its efforts.

The IMC report gave ammunition to all Sinn Féin's opponents. Attacks from Bertie Ahern did damage. As an architect of the peace process, he carried weight when he subtly undermined those who were endangering the project. Other attacks, such as the more shrill utterings of Progressive Democrat minister Michael McDowell, served only to solidify Mary Lou's base and drive doubters into her camp.

Sinn Féin's standing in the polls wobbled. An *Irish Times*-MRBI poll, published on 22 May, showed Mary Lou trailing in fifth place on just 11 per cent, not enough to win a seat. She was behind Fine Gael's Gay Mitchell on 19 per cent, Fianna Fáil's Royston Brady on 18 per cent, Labour's Proinsias de Rossa on 14 per cent, with Fianna Fáil's second candidate Eoin Ryan on 13 per cent. Just behind her, ominously, lurked the Greens' Patricia

McKenna on 10 per cent. If those figures were repeated on polling day, Mary Lou was toast. Even if Fianna Fáil returned only one successful candidate, McKenna was certain to overtake Mary Lou on transfers. McDonald needed a far bigger first count lead over McKenna.

The confidence in the Sinn Féin camp had taken a knock. Expectations were dampened. Robbie Smyth, writing in the next edition of *An Phoblacht*, concentrated, instead, on the possible local council election gains on the same day. Reflecting on Mary Lou's prospects, he was circumspect, noting on 27 May that 'With the Sinn Féin vote still clearly growing in Dublin, an EU seat seems possible. The *Irish Times*-MRBI poll conducted last weekend put Mary Lou McDonald at an 11 per cent poll share.' He was preparing the troops for a cliffhanger rather than a coronation.

Some of Sinn Féin's opponents, scenting blood, felt it was time to move in for the kill. When Mary Lou handed in her nomination papers, Eoin Ryan objected to the description of her occupation on the ballot paper as a 'peace negotiator' and a 'full-time public representative'. It was getting personal. Ryan, lagging behind his Fianna Fáil running mate, Royston Brady, in the polls, had decided that an anti-Mary Lou stance would pay dividends. Targeting the voters in Fianna Fáil who despised Sinn Féin but were preferring his running mate to himself, he asked, 'What peace has Mary Lou negotiated and with whom?', adding 'The Sinn Féin candidate's claim to have been elected by the people to any office is utterly bogus.' John Fitzpatrick, the returning officer, was unmoved by Ryan's complaints. He responded that no formal rules were in place to decide what titles candidates could use. Fitzpatrick added that there had been no problem with Mary Lou's self-descriptions previously in Dublin West. Ryan was put back in his box.

Another opinion poll, this time from Lansdowne Market Research for RTÉ's *Prime Time* and the *Irish Examiner* newspaper a few days later, showed Ryan making no inroads into Royston

Brady's vote. He decided to double down. In the *Sunday Independent*, only five days before polling on 11 June, an increasingly desperate Ryan attempted to bury Mary Lou. He went for bust, resurrecting Seán Russell and Brian Keenan, ghosts whom Sinn Féin had tried to exorcise from the contest. It was a full-frontal assault, a tactic that other candidates had feared to adopt in case it would boomerang. Accusing Mary Lou of 'warped principles', Eoin Ryan demanded an explanation from her for why she had 'stood shoulder to shoulder with a brutal IRA bomber less than nine months ago to honour a friend of the Holocaust'. Referring to the 'horrors of Nazism', he accused Mary Lou of celebrating a 'Nazi collaborator'.

Ryan had done his damnedest. As before, it was Royston Brady, his running mate, who was the real target in his sights. If he made enough noise and drew sufficient attention to himself, the Fianna Fáil faithful might rally to his call and desert his colleague. After all, wasn't it he, not Brady, who was making the running for Fianna Fáil and challenging the devil herself? It might even benefit Mary Lou; but she was not the target, merely the vehicle for lifting Ryan above Brady.

Mary Lou showed no sign of panic at the poll that gave Patricia McKenna, her real rival for the final seat, a lead over her in crucial first preferences. If the results were repeated on election day, she would be back as Sinn Féin's political oversight manager, licking stamps in the back office. She continued her highly effective media appearances.

They worked. On polling day, Mary Lou scored the most spectacular victory of the election throughout the entire island. She comfortably took the fourth and final seat, outpolling the Greens' sitting MEP Patricia McKenna by nearly 20,000 votes. Where the polls had put them running neck and neck in first preferences, the final outcome gave Mary Lou 14.32 per cent, more than 4 per cent ahead of McKenna on 9.59 per cent. As predicted, McKenna received more transfers, but never came close to overtaking her.

Mitchell topped the poll for Fine Gael and de Rossa took the third seat for Labour. Ryan overtook Brady, beating him by a distance for the second seat. His strident attacks had landed, establishing him as the leading Fianna Fáil candidate. Equally, they seemed to have helped Mary Lou, uniting much of the anti-establishment vote behind her and allowing her to overshadow Patricia McKenna, Joe Higgins, Labour's second candidate Senator Ivana Bacik and other opponents of the government. Her media appearances had been crucial.

The European election was a historic breakthrough for Sinn Féin. They had won their first ever seat in the European Parliament. Almost forgotten was a second seat – in Northern Ireland – where Bairbre de Brún coasted home. They were now not only big winners on the island of Ireland, but a small force of two MEPs in Europe.

In the South, Sinn Féin finished with 11.1 per cent nationally, a healthy gain of nearly 5 per cent. Mary Lou's extraordinary performance had eclipsed the other three Sinn Féin candidates. None of them won a seat, but South candidate David Cullinane, on 6.7 per cent, East candidate John Dwyer, on 8.7 per cent, and North-West candidate Pearse Doherty, on 15.5 per cent, all signalled that Sinn Féin youth was on the march. The party's new wonder woman had lifted the vote throughout the country. Project Mary Lou McDonald had delivered beyond Gerry Adams's wildest dreams.

CHAPTER 5

DESPERATELY SEEKING A DÁIL SEAT

Sinn Féin didn't rest on its laurels for long, though the party was entitled to a moment of satisfaction. Project Mary Lou had lifted all boats. Not only did the party suddenly have two MEPs, it had also run three other candidates for Europe. While none took a seat, Donegal's Pearse Doherty, aged twenty-seven, and Waterford's David Cullinane, aged thirty, both household names today, came to national attention for the first time with strong electoral showings in 2004. A younger breed of Sinn Féin was emerging in the provinces.

More importantly, the local elections, held on the same day as the European elections, marked a big breakthrough for the party. Mary Lou was flavour of the month in cosmopolitan Dublin, but Project Mary Lou was bigger. It had spread far and wide. Sinn Féin had doubled its local authority numbers, mainly at the expense of Fianna Fáil. While Mary Lou had blazed a countrywide trail with her own compelling media appeal that the crusty older warriors of the IRA could never match, a new civilian army on the ground had also been mobilising in parallel for a decade. The war was over. The party had money to burn. The future was Sinn Féin.

As Mary Lou headed for Brussels in July 2004 with a spring in her step, she should have been looking forward to five years of hard slog on the coalface in Europe. She and Bairbre de Brún had opened a new front. They could work the corridors of the European Parliament, preaching the Sinn Féin gospel. It would be a tough sell. They would need allies, but Sinn Féin was now a recognised, though small, force in Europe. Nobody in the party was better equipped than Mary Lou McDonald to charm and cajole the commissioners, the MEPs and even the bureaucrats.

There was one catch. The first item on the Sinn Féin agenda was not how to make maximum use of Mary Lou's talents in Brussels. Perversely, it was how to bring her home with indecent haste. The real action remained in Belfast and Dublin.

Mary Lou's election was a public relations and psychological triumph for the party, but the contest itself had exposed the limited political value of seats in the European Parliament. The three Dublin MEPs elected alongside her, Gay Mitchell, Proinsias de Rossa and Eoin Ryan, were all ex-ministers. None was in the first flush of youth or any longer a significant figure within their own party. Europe offered different attractions to them. None would stand for the Dáil again. Happily out of the front line, they willingly hid their lights under bushels.

Mary Lou needed the limelight. Europe was a media backwater where worthy, but unseen, committee work demanded the bulk of MEPs' time. Some MEPs' nominations were rewards for recognition of a lifetime's work for their parties first and the nation second. Sometimes they were not overworked and escaped with far less intense scrutiny than they merited.

The European elections themselves attracted widespread, but only passing, media attention. They were often political beauty contests, offering a gladiatorial and entertaining blood sport. Yet when the battles were over, the MEPs' distance from the island of Ireland and the real political action back home often meant that they were left to their own devices, undisturbed. They had moved to the world of Eurobabble, of European directives, subsidiarity, directorates-general, qualified majorities and other indigestible jargon. Much of it was drudgery, no place for an aspiring TD, less still for any ambitious journalist seeking spicy stories. It suited many of the MEPs to be less accountable. The downside was that their work, if any, was not appreciated by a media in search of sensation over substance.

Mary Lou was well aware of the disadvantage of being 'stuck out in Brussels' for several days each week. She had been at the centre of Ireland's European election frenzy because the battle, as usual, had not been fought on European controversies but on national differences between warring personalities. And she was hot political property. No one was more capable of causing an almighty uproar from time to time in Brussels or Strasbourg, but in the European Parliament she was competing for media attention with more than 750 MEPs. Even Mary Lou's formidable communication skills would be stretched. Sinn Féin found itself with its greatest asset suddenly deported and stuck on the European mainland. Project Mary Lou needed redirection.

Obviously she could not just thank her voters, immediately resign, pack her bags and head for home, handing over to her little-known designated substitute, her political assistant, Killian Forde. She needed the authority and the platform of being an elected public representative. She had performed a superhuman task in winning a European seat, but Europe had served its purpose. Sinn Féin had won the election with its charismatic discovery, but now they wanted her back home to lead the fight for seats in the Dáil.

A plot was hatched. Mary Lou would do her European duties for an acceptable period to avoid any charges of deviously exploiting the great European project. She would travel, perform the minimum necessary chores in Brussels as an MEP, and give as much time as she could to Sinn Féin at home at the weekends, when she would also spend time with her daughter Iseult and her husband Martin. Corners would have to be cut.

They were, but first Mary Lou and her fellow Sinn Féin MEP, Bairbre de Brún, had to do a little European parliamentary house-keeping. One of their first, but most important, choices was to decide to which group they would hitch their wagon in the parliament. Formal membership of a group in the European Parliament was not compulsory, but it provided benefits, including voting leverage with its block numbers, committee positions and added resources.

The duo went in search of friends. The exercise was a reality check for them. They found that an association with Sinn Féin was far from being in universal demand.

Sinn Féin, perhaps surprisingly, was not a welcome bedfellow for the European Free Alliance/Green Group, which included the Scottish Nationalist Party and the Welsh Plaid Cymru. Mary Lou and Bairbre de Brún received a cold shoulder from them, despite their shared enthusiasm for independence from Westminster. The pair found themselves unwanted because any party linked with the IRA was untouchable in the United Kingdom, even among the nationalists there.

Elsewhere, the larger Christian Democrats (already allied with Fine Gael) and the Liberals were incompatible with Sinn Féin's outlook. Fianna Fáil had joined up with the smaller right-wing 'Europe for a Union of the Nations' Group, thereby blocking that option.

Sinn Féin was excluded from the large socialist group because it was not a member of the Party of European Socialists. The presence in this group of both Ireland's and Britain's Labour parties was significant. Neither country's Labour Party comrades would touch Sinn Féin with a bargepole. Everywhere McDonald and de Brún turned, doors were closed in their faces.

In the end it was Hobson's choice. Three months before the

election, Sinn Féin had prudently pre-empted the problem of being a political pariah if it ever came to forming European alliances. In March 2004 its senior party members had met with the European Parliament's United Left group in Dublin and Belfast. The group consisted of a mix of hard-left ex-communists and other unusual individuals, including the colourful, militant French Trotskyist Arlette Laguiller, sometimes known as 'Red Arlette' or even 'Arlette the Starlet'. She had stood five times for the French presidency. The meetings Sinn Féin hosted for the group in Ireland oiled the wheels for the party's eventual membership of the United Left–Nordic Green Left Group (GUE/NGL).

Other eccentric political entities embraced by the GUE/NGL included the Democratic Socialist Party, successor to the Marxist–Leninist SED party that had ruled East Germany with a rod of iron for forty years. Another relic of Marx and Lenin among Sinn Féin's chosen allies was the Communist Party of Bohemia and Moravia, which emerged from the Communist Party of Czechoslovakia and the Communist parties of France and Italy. This was the exotic crew with whom Mary Lou and Bairbre de Brún bedded down.

Even today, after the 2019 European elections, the GUE/NGL retains its unconventional make-up, although it changed its name in 2021 to the more mainstream-sounding 'The Left in the European Parliament – GUE/NGL'. Four Irish MEPs in the class of 2019 have joined this wide-ranging team. Sinn Féin remain attached in the shape of Chris MacManus from Sligo, while three former Independent TDs – Clare Daly, Luke 'Ming' Flanagan and Mick Wallace – are in the same gang.

Back in 2004, Sinn Féin did not feel the urge to broadcast widely about the unusual composition of its political allies in Europe. No doubt it would not have been music to the ears of their major benefactors, particularly their nationalist, pro-business patrons in the United States.

Indeed, they hid their associates in the undergrowth. When

Mary Lou was telling *An Phoblacht* about all the hard work she
and Bairbre de Brún had achieved on their first day in the parliament,
she reached for the Sinn Féin airbrush: 'Having found our bearings,
we met with other members of the European United Left/Nordic–
Green Left (GUE/NGL) group. They quickly made us feel very
welcome and were able to help with all of our queries and concerns.
Without such help, it could have been very easy to become lost in
the bureaucracy of the place.' She made them sound like cuddly
tour guides, not ideologues from a forgotten age.

Still, she didn't manage to conceal her new friends from the
folk back home. On 15 June 2004, less than a week after the
election, the *Evening Herald* went to town on the middle-class
Rathgar girl's European soulmates. With a huge headline, the
newspaper hardly minced its words: '**MARY LOU JOINS UP
WITH COMMUNISTS**' was splashed across the front page. The
subheading embellished the narrative: 'Sinn Féin aligns with hard
left, including Italian Stalinist party in Euro Parliament'. The
communist cat was out of the bag. The piece went on to explain
that 'Mary Lou will sit with a party in Brussels drawn from the
former communist one-party states across Europe.'

It was a 'gotcha' moment for the paper.

Mary Lou was never a communist. Several of her critics suggest
that even her personal commitment to Sinn Féin socialism is
lukewarm at best. When it comes to the contest within Sinn Féin
between socialism and nationalism, the nationalist argument nearly
always wins. Reunification comes first, socialism second, if
anywhere, in Mary Lou's priorities. She will ramble on until the
cows come home about the less controversial 'equality', but the
word socialism is rarely in her lexicon. Nevertheless, that would
never prevent her from coming to a pragmatic parliamentary
arrangement with diehard communists in Europe. Ever flexible in
her views, always one to seize a political opportunity, she saw the
practical advantage of joining the GUE/NGL. Such a liaison hardly

committed her to nationalisation, increased taxes on high earners or even wealth taxes. Indeed, today's Sinn Féin party, which opposes local property taxes, can hardly convincingly claim to be in favour of dramatic redistributions of wealth. Her May Day birthday is the closest she comes to socialism.

In the meantime, Mary Lou set out on the day job. On 21 July 2004, in Strasbourg, she opened her first speech to a plenary session of the European Parliament in Irish, followed by a short formal statement. In a two-minute offering, she plunged straight into the memory of Bobby Sands, crediting him with the politics of equality, justice and freedom. She had skilfully marked out her territory in a couple of paragraphs.

Her next speech, in November – four months later – addressed the activities of the European Ombudsman. No other plenary addresses are recorded in 2004. In January 2005 she spoke about the United Nations Framework on Climate Change, while, towards the end of the same month, she raised the issue of the murder of Belfast lawyer Pat Finucane. These were followed by short contributions on health and safety in the workplace and the rights of minorities. A one-minute speech praising the IRA followed in September. In that speech she did not pull her punches: 'Mr President,' she declared, 'the Irish Republican Army has taken another initiative to assist peace in Ireland. Today's courageous decision to verifiably and definitively dispose of its weaponry represents a major advance for the peace process in Ireland. The enormity of what the IRA has done should neither be underestimated nor undervalued. I should like to take this opportunity to praise the IRA for taking risks when others shirked their responsibilities.' She then attacked the Democratic Unionist Party (DUP). Par for the course. It was strong stuff, obviously targeted at any reluctant peacemakers still lurking in the darker, dissident corners of west Belfast and south Armagh.

She finished 2005 with another sixty-second intervention about

Irish Ferries and a slightly longer oration on equal opportunities. In all, she made only three short speeches at the plenary sessions held in 2004 and eight equally brief contributions in 2005.

After a short time, it was obvious to Sinn Féin strategists that their worst anxieties were being fulfilled. Brussels was a backwater. As they had feared, Mary Lou was spending too much time away from the cameras and distant from the important action in Dublin. Her activities in Europe were not maximising the media oxygen or the profile that Sinn Féin needed in Ireland.

She was making only a limited impact at home. In keeping with Sinn Féin's evolving policy, away from hostility, to 'critical engagement' with the European Union in 2005, Mary Lou led the campaign in Ireland against a new European constitution. She featured in Northern Ireland peace talks when she could fit in an appearance, but even during her early 2004/05 period she was often caught between too many commitments at home and abroad. It was becoming more and more obvious that it was time to bite the bullet. Europe was a sideshow.

As a first step, in the summer of 2005 Mary Lou received yet another leg up from her political patrons. Despite her duties in Europe, she was assigned a key post back home. She was appointed to succeed Mitchel McLaughlin as chair of the party. This was a clear signal to others that not only was she still the hierarchy's favourite daughter, but also that Project Mary Lou remained the number one priority for delivering the seats they needed in Leinster House.

But, first, she herself needed a Dáil seat. Yet, in which constituency?

It was 2005. A general election was not due until May 2007. As a Dubliner, Mary Lou would obviously be required to contest a seat in the capital. Several spots on Sinn Féin constituency tickets had already been earmarked by long-standing city and county councillors, who had been working flat out for years.

Highest hopes for a Sinn Féin gain centred on Councillor Nicky Kehoe, confidently expected to capture a seat in Dublin Central because he had failed by only a tantalising 79 votes in 2002. In Dublin South-Central, Aengus Ó Snodaigh was already *in situ* for Sinn Féin, as was Seán Crowe in Dublin South-West. Dublin South-East, Dublin South and Dun Laoghaire were seen as no-go areas, too prosperous for Sinn Féin, although Dublin South included Mary Lou's childhood home on Orwell Road. Dessie Ellis, a tireless worker, was considered a good bet to take a seat from Fianna Fáil in Dublin North-West. Since Mary Lou lived in Castleknock, Dublin West was home territory for her, but it had proved way beyond her reach in 2002. The other Dublin constituencies were probably no-hopers for Sinn Féin. The party had a problem.

Mary Lou had always floated above the local council merry-go-round. She could never compete on constituency work with any of the other Sinn Féin hopefuls. There was no point in the Ard Chomhairle (following instructions from on high) replacing a diligent party worker with Mary Lou, unless she was almost certain to win the targeted seat. There would be deep resentment locally; she might even meet resistance from anyone ordered to withdraw in her favour. She was box office on the big screen, a magnetic national performer, but, unlike others, had no local votes in the bank, no core base anywhere. Dáil battles did not replicate European election patterns. Mary Lou McDonald was a media creation who had done less than most to soil her hands down among the grass roots. Now the party was planning to parachute her from her lofty European perch into an unsuspecting, close-knit community in Dublin.

Fortune favoured Mary Lou. In November 2005 Sinn Féin strategists had a stroke of luck. Councillor and poll-topper Nicky Kehoe, the man who had come so close to success for Sinn Féin in the 2002 general election, apparently had been having second thoughts about becoming a Dáil deputy.

Kehoe had a chequered history. He had served jail terms in

Portlaoise prison for serious IRA offences, including the attempted kidnapping of billionaire Galen Weston in 1983 and the possession of explosives. He was released from prison in 1992 after twelve years. He was born and bred in Cabra, a poorer part of the Dublin Central constituency. After coming out of prison, he involved himself in community work, in particular St Finbarr's GAA club in Cabra. In 1999 Sinn Féin persuaded him to stand for the local council. He sailed in, making him the automatic Sinn Féin candidate for the 2002 general election. He contested Dublin Central, but was pipped for the final seat by Dermot Fitzpatrick of Fianna Fáil. Kehoe ran for re-election to Dublin City Council in 2004 and increased his first-preference vote mightily, from 2,380 to 3,609, nearly 20 per cent of all the votes cast and comfortably over the quota. His personal poll in the area had increased by many multiples of the tantalising seventy-nine-vote shortfall at the 2002 general election. He looked like a shoo-in for 2007.

Sinn Féin had always regarded Nicky Kehoe as a 'banker' for the 2007 general election rematch. But then something surprising happened. At some point in 2004, according to himself, he lost his hunger for a Dáil seat. He wanted to spend more time with his family. He told *An Phoblacht* that it was time for a 'younger' person to reap the benefit of all his hard work. Such selflessness is rare in politics.

On the date of Kehoe's shock decision not to go ahead with his Dáil bid, he was a geriatric of only forty-eight. By the time of the 2007 election itself, the 'younger' Mary Lou, the anointed one, was thirty-eight, well established and married with two young children.

Nicky Kehoe spun an unlikely tale to *An Phoblacht*: 'Realising that we'd need an alternative candidate, Christy Burke, myself and a few others sat down and looked at who would be the best candidate with the best chance of winning a seat here.' Nicky Kehoe's version hardly gels with fellow councillor Christy Burke's own account that it was Gerry Adams who asked Burke to show

Mary Lou the ropes. If Gerry asked a Sinn Féin soldier to jump, they inevitably asked him 'How high?'

Nicky Kehoe continued to *An Phoblacht*, the Sinn Féin font of truth: 'We decided we needed someone high profile who'd get us maybe that extra thousand votes or so. We asked Mary Lou McDonald to come into this constituency. It was put to the leadership and there were a few meetings to discuss it. We brought Mary Lou in. The papers have been trying to spin a notion that I was sidelined. No one sidelined me. Nobody could sideline me in this constituency because there would be no support for that sort of move. We nominated her and we gave her our full support.'

Nicky Kehoe was right. Shafting someone of his stature would have been tricky. Nevertheless, the leadership was determined that the make-up of Sinn Féin TDs should no longer be predominantly IRA veterans. Martin Ferris and Arthur Morgan were enough. Nicky Kehoe had been a prominent member of the IRA.

The story was spun that Kehoe wanted to head off to do a history degree in Trinity as a mature student. Whatever the truth of his explanation, he joined a lengthening list of casualties who had stood aside to make way for Mary Lou McDonald.

Once again, the decks had been cleared for her. The leadership moved quickly. On 19 November 2005 Sinn Féin made it known to the media that their member of the European Parliament Mary Lou McDonald would be seeking the party's nomination in Dublin Central for the next general election. The selection convention was fixed for twelve days later, 1 December, in Aughrim Street Parish Centre in Dublin's Stoneybatter. The announcement gave any other members of the party thinking of running less than a fortnight to make up their minds.

Mary Lou was selected as the candidate by a margin of two to one over token opposition from a trade union activist, Ray O'Reilly. She was nominated by two local councillors – none other than former candidates Nicky Kehoe and Christy Burke – both ex-IRA and both of whom would have been considered willing runners themselves. Job done. Mary Lou, in Brussels for less than eighteen months, was on her way back to Dublin.

A general election was not expected for another year and a half – the summer of 2007. Candidate selection elsewhere in Dublin Central suddenly began in earnest. Some parties' runners were already long established. New ones needed to be told to get cracking and hit the streets. There was great confidence in the Sinn Féin camp. After all, in theory, Mary Lou needed only seventy-nine votes over Nicky Kehoe's 2002 tally to steal the second Fianna Fáil seat.

But it was not as simple as that. Kehoe had always been one of the hardest grafters in Dublin City Council. He had worked for every vote. Perhaps Sinn Féin was a little intoxicated by Mary Lou's historic June 2004 European election victory. Maybe they felt that she was unbeatable; but winning in Europe was a different matter from winning locally.

More importantly, Dublin Central was no ordinary constituency. It was the kingdom of the magician himself, Bertie Ahern. Bertie was not only the master of the last-minute overnight leaflet drop, but he knew every corner of the constituency. He had been nursing it, street by street, for three decades. Indeed, so obsessed was he with the local scene, even when he was Taoiseach and president of the European Council, that one Saturday morning he is rumoured to have abruptly left a breakfast meeting with the Finnish prime minister at Helsinki airport, apologising that he had an important appointment in Dublin. He hopped on to the government jet that was waiting on the tarmac to keep a canvassing date with his local leafleting team at the corner of Griffith Avenue in northside Dublin. Unfortunately, the team had heard on the radio that Bertie was due for an important morning meeting in Helsinki. It was pouring with rain. They gave themselves a lie-in. Bertie's plane arrived at the airport at 10.30 a.m. to be met by his state car. He was dropped on the corner of Griffith Avenue at the appointed hour

Sunny spells and scattered showers. Cool, with frost in places tonight.
(See back page)

Irish Independent

Vol. 82. No. 52   THURSDAY, MARCH 1, 1973   PRICE 4p C

ELECTION SPECIAL 73

The van behind the wire!

NATION AWAITS VITAL RESULT

By CHRIS GLENNON
Our Political Correspondent

A NEAR RECORD poll was estimated early today as the polling booths closed throughout the country after 12 hours of voting. Indications through the 42 constituencies are that the average percentage vote was in the high seventies, possibly even higher than the 77 per cent. recorded in 1969.

Our top

election

service

IRELAND'S top political newsteam—which won wide acclaim

From many constituencies, there were reports of averages above 80 per cent., but overall, it seemed unlikely that the all-time record of 81.3 per cent. set in 1933 would be bettered.

For this election was conducted on a register more than a year old, a fact that led to protests in several areas since many people over 21 found that they were not entitled to vote.

Unless they had reached 21 before September, 1971, they were not included on the register that came into effect in April of last year. The new register, which will include the 18-year-olds, will not become effective until April 15 next.

In Dublin, where any swing would be most marked and have the greatest effect there were indications of an overall poll in the mid-70s.

Dublin South-East was one of the lowest at about 65 per

FIANNA Fáil's drive to get its supporters out to vote in the Dublin South Central constituency was blunted for a time last night . . . by a vigilant traffic warden.

He spotted a large van, festooned with posters of the three candidates, Ben Briscoe, Phil Brady and Gerald Buchanan, parked in a rush-hour clear way, and promptly called in the tow-away vehicle.

It did not go down very well with the Party's supporters who saw their well oiled Election operation being disrupted at a vital time.

As the tow vehicle

edged its way towards the van in Harold's Cross Road about 40 people protested.

But the law had its way, and off the van was taken to the Corporation compound at Christ Church Place, where it became briefly the "van behind the wire."

However, within minutes of its capture Fianna Fáil workers were bailing it out and it was soon making its way once again around the constituency.

Picture—by Matt Walsh—shows the Fianna Fáil canvassing van leaving the Dublin Corporation's vehicle compound at Christ Church place, last night.

Joan puts vote before

A 24-YEAR-OLD Cashel bride broke her journey to the Church for her wed-

Soldier shot on lollipop patrol

A BRITISH soldier shot dead while on patrol at the Cromlin Road near Ardoyne yesterday afternoon was named last night as Lance Corporal Alan Kenington (20), a bachelor, from Somerset.

He was a member of the 3rd Battalion of the Light Infantry and was on a "lollipop patrol" keeping Protestant and Catholic schoolchildren from clashing after school.

Lance Corporal Kenington had just come out of a shop in the area and was handing around bars of chocolate to his companions when four high-velocity shots were fired from Elmfield Street and Butler Street. He was standing with the patrol at the junction of Butler Street and the Cromlin Road.

An ambulance arrived on the scene, but the soldier was hit in the heart by one of the four shots and was dead on arrival in hospital.

An Army spokesman said last night that lollipop patrols ex-

of an Army mobile patrol war shot on the Springfield Road. The soldier was travelling in a vehicle which came under fire, but he was not seriously injured.

Following 3 hours of sporadic rioting in Ardoyne yesterday evening, fresh trouble broke out in the Protestant Belmont district on the east side of the city.

The rioting started after two armed and masked men planted a bomb in an off-licence in Beechfield Avenue, Belfast. They

gave a ten minute warning and the bomb exploded ten minutes after that. No one was injured.

Severe internal damage was caused but structural damage to the building was superficial. The security forces moved into the area and were attacked by a stone throwing crowd of about 50 youths. The Army replied by firing rubber bullets and the rioters dispersed.

MORE NORTH NEWS
ON PAGE TWO

Locked in the vehicle compound. Mary Lou's father, Paddy McDonald, in the driver's seat of the Fianna Fáil election truck detained in the pound after being towed away on election night 28 February 1973, as reported in the following day's *Irish Independent*.

Mary Lou, aged two, holding her Aunt Nora's hand. In the background – left to right – her aunt Joan Butler, her paternal grandmother Annie McDonald and her mother Joan.

Mary Lou's parents Paddy and Joan, as a young married couple.

Summer holidays in Tipperary with siblings and cousins.

Left to right
Top row: Mary Lou, Bea McDonald, John Hayes.
Second row: Eddie Hayes, Joan Hayes, Jerry Hayes.
Bottom row: Joanne McDonald, Caroline Hayes, Paddy McDonald.

Childhood home. Ard na Gréine in Rathgar, Dublin, where Mary Lou and her siblings were raised in an apartment.

Books in the air: Mary Lou, aged eighteen, throws her school books aloft to celebrate her Leaving Certificate results in August 1987.

Mary Lou (left), a student at the time, with members and friends of her future husband Martin's band, the New Hollande, from Dublin's Strawberry Beds. Pictured in Sheehan's pub in Chatham Street, Dublin.

Mentor, matriarch and shepherd. Nora Comiskey, the veteran Fianna Fáil republican, who guided Mary Lou on her journey from Fianna Fáil to the Irish National Congress to Sinn Féin.

Mary Lou with her reclusive husband Martin (and their son Gerard) voting in the European elections in 2009.

BEFORE: the small bungalow on Cabra Road bought by Mary Lou and Martin.

AFTER: the mansion following Mary Lou and Martin's refurbishments.

Cumann Na Meirleach Poblachtach Eireannach
Irish Republican Felons Club
Draft Of
Cuspóirí agus Rialacha
'Objects And Rules'

Cuspóirí / Objects

1. To foster and maintain among Irish Republicans friendships formed during imprisonment or internment as a result of their service to the Irish Republican cause.

2. To provide social and recreational facilities for those who have been imprisoned or interned for Irish Republican beliefs.

3. To provide for members such welfare facilities as the committee may consider necessary.

4. To support all lawful efforts directed towards the establishment and international recognition of an all Ireland Republic.

Ballraíocht / Membership

5(A). Full membership shall be restricted to those who have been imprisoned or interned for their Irish Republican beliefs. New members (full) may be admitted by the committee on the proposal of two full members, and such admissions by the committee shall be for a probationary period of three months during which period he or she shall not be entitled to vote at the Annual General Meeting.

The rules of the Republican Felons Club on the Falls Road, Belfast. Even though she is leader of Sinn Féin, Mary Lou does not qualify for full membership, which is only open to former prisoners who have been imprisoned or interned for their Irish Republican beliefs.

of eleven o'clock. There was no one to meet him. He is said to have lost his famous composure.

The story may be apocryphal, but the constituency was Bertie's obsession. He had demonstrated his total control over the Fianna Fáil local party organisation early in his career in 1983. At that time, there were three contenders for the Fianna Fáil nomination for a by-election after the death of one of the party elders, George Colley. It was a certain Fianna Fáil seat, so there was fierce competition to be the party's chosen one. There were two very strong candidates – George Colley's widow, Mary, an immensely popular local undertaker, John Stafford, and a councillor, Tommy Leonard. Taoiseach Charlie Haughey was determined that his oldest adversary George Colley's widow would not get the nod. Bertie was equally determined that neither she nor Stafford should be on the ticket; he did not want a strong running mate alongside him at the next election. He organised that Tommy Leonard, the weakest candidate, would win at the convention. Leonard, no threat to Bertie, was nominated and sailed into the Dáil. Bertie's grip on every convention vote was unbreakable. For years afterwards, admirers in Fianna Fáil would illustrate his control with the tale of that convention when Bertie's machinations had 'screwed the widow, buried the undertaker and selected the corpse'.

And Bertie's was not the only unassailable seat in Dublin Central. The legendary Tony Gregory, who had struck the famous 'Gregory deal' with Charlie Haughey in 1982, ran as an Independent; his reputation as a rival republican signalled danger to Sinn Féin. Gregory had won huge local support for his work against drug addiction.

Both Ahern and Gregory were local parish-pump politicians par excellence. So was sitting TD Joe Costello of Labour, who had pounded the pavements of the inner city for two decades. He was in the shake-up. So was a young Fine Gael councillor, Paschal Donohoe, who was already a formidable constituency force, working just as hard as others but in a more measured way. Paschal was a native of the constituency, representing the Cabra–Glasnevin area, and a long-time resident of the middle-class suburb of Phibsborough. He had observed the winning formula of the more experienced local TDs and was determined to keep his feet equally firmly on the ground. Many years later, his comments about his colleagues are still illuminating. He recently told me, 'I served with Nicky Kehoe on Dublin City Council between 2004 and 2007. He was extremely effective and committed, commanding huge loyalty from his voters, particularly in Cabra.' That is high praise from a Fine Gael minister for finance about a Sinn Féin councillor who was once an IRA terrorist. Paschal Donohoe's admiration was obviously limited to Kehoe's on-the-ground, grass-root skills, not his earlier history.

Mary Lou, the outsider, was pitted against four highly professional local politicians. In addition, she had to confront Bertie's surplus, the joker in the pack. Bertie Ahern had habitually not only topped the poll with an enormous surplus, he had also squeezed every last drop of added value out of his excess votes. His personal machine was so strong that he had become accustomed to bringing a party running mate into the Dáil on his coat tails. In the 2002 election he had lifted a local doctor, the late Dermot Fitzpatrick, over the line with his second preferences. It was Bertie's surplus that had deprived Sinn Féin's Nicky Kehoe of victory in 2002 and had delivered the last seat to Fitzpatrick by a whisker.

Fianna Fáil responded rapidly to the gauntlet Sinn Féin had thrown down. They recognised that Mary Lou posed a threat to Bertie's grip on the constituency. They countered by holding their own early convention and nominating two candidates to accompany the Taoiseach on the ticket. Senator Cyprian Brady and Dermot Fitzpatrick's daughter, Mary, were selected on 4 March 2006, over a year before the election was due. The decision to nominate three candidates, rather than two, raised a few eyebrows, but was an effort to satisfy two warring camps within Fianna Fáil. There was no love lost between Bertie and Mary Fitzpatrick, now seen as a serious contender in hot pursuit of her father's seat. Mary was no puppet of Bertie's. The Sinn Féin team took comfort in the certain knowledge that Bertie would not be steering his second preferences in her direction. Besides, although Cyprian Brady had been Bertie's trusted constituency organiser for many years, he was considered pitifully weak as a Dáil candidate. Without Bertie, Cyprian was dead meat.

Mary Lou had landed in a bear pit. Her early nomination had bounced others into holding their own conventions. One day after Bertie and his two running mates had been selected, her main rival from the 2004 European election resurfaced. Former Green Party MEP Patricia McKenna declared for the Greens in Dublin Central. McKenna would be fishing in the same pool as McDonald.

Dublin Central is a four-seater. It runs close to the Liffey on the northside of the city. It is regarded as one of the most socially mixed and ethnically diverse constituencies in Ireland. It includes Dublin's main shopping district, the General Post Office on O'Connell Street and the big retail outlets on Henry Street, the historic Moore Street with its famous street sellers and the International Financial Services Centre. It consists of largely traditionally working-class areas, such as East Wall, North Strand, Summerhill, Ballybough, Sheriff Street and Cabra, with more suburban middle-class Glasnevin and Lower Drumcondra on the northern fringes. According to 2016 Central Statistics Office census figures, its population is increasing far faster than the rest of the country's. It has a much higher number of non-Irish residents than elsewhere in the country, mostly accounted for by 12.1 per cent from other EU member states and 12.3 per cent from 'Rest of the World' nations. Overall, according to the Houses of the Oireachtas constituency profile, using CSO figures, only 65.7 per cent of residents of Dublin Central stated their nationality as Irish. In the rest of Ireland, the figure stands at 87 per cent. The number of people classified as 'At work' comes in at 59.3 per cent, as opposed to 53.5 per cent nationally. There are fewer retired people (9.9 per cent) living in the area than the national average of 14.5 per cent.

Dublin Central is flatland: 46 per cent is flats/apartments, as opposed to 11.8 per cent nationally, while it has a much lower level of houses/bungalows (49.5 per cent, compared to 86 per cent nationally). Rented housing from private landlords is high; outright ownership is low. Rented accommodation from local authorities is higher than it is nationwide.

The constituency is mixed. There are identifiable groups with specific problems, tailor-made for a pork-barrel politician to mine for votes. Cabra, which was Councillor Nicky Kehoe's power base, had a significant share of local authority housing. Phibsborough and Glasnevin offered fodder for Fine Gael's Paschal Donohoe; the inner city was Tony Gregory's fortress; while Bertie Ahern, based in Drumcondra, drew votes from everywhere. Unrelenting door-knocking, a highly professional local team and a constituency service in almost every street had guaranteed the Fianna Fáil Taoiseach a poll-topping position for life. Or so it seemed.

When Mary Lou eyed the constituency and the task ahead of her in November 2005, even she probably suffered from the odd moment of self-doubt. It was not a sentiment associated with her, but Dublin Central was not a typical political patch. She must have felt a nagging fear that a high proportion of votes was unavailable, already nailed down by existing Dáil deputies like Ahern, Gregory and Costello. And also by Councillor Paschal Donohoe.

Nevertheless, she had an unmatched media profile. Everybody knew her without having to meet her. She was instantly likeable. She possibly felt that Nicky Kehoe's 4,972 first-preference votes from the 2002 general election were already in the bag. She had two of the area's most popular local chieftains, Christy from the north inner city and Nicky from Cabra, escorting her around the streets. Sinn Féin would be funding her for eighteen months. Money would be no problem. She could bus in teams of supporters from Northern Ireland to back up the Sinn Féin Dublin team, who were already good to go. And, importantly, she was a woman in a constituency without a female TD.

After her nomination on 1 December 2005, the demands on Mary Lou's time looked crippling. Chairperson of Sinn Féin, MEP, Dáil candidate for Dublin Central, member of the party's peace talks team, wife of Martin and mother of Iseult, she looked as though she might be shouldering an unbearable burden. And there was one other, less than minor, development. As she embarked on her mission to capture Dublin Central, she was more than six months pregnant.

Nothing fazed her. This was the second time that Mary Lou had taken on a daunting election while expecting a baby. Nearly three years earlier she had accepted the party's nomination for the European Parliament when expecting her first child. Despite the heavy demands on her time and affections, she had gone on to win a famous victory. This time, with similar support on the home front from her husband and her mother, she aimed to repeat the European victory by getting elected to Dáil Éireann.

Europe would have to take a back seat. Happily, she was entitled to maternity leave. In December 2005 she made her last speech for the next nine months to the European Parliament. While delivering it in Strasbourg, she was cut off by the president of the parliament for running over time. She headed home, determined to take maternity leave, but equally eager to carry the battle for Dublin Central to the enemy.

Mary Lou's Achilles heel was her lack of roots in the constituency. She resolved to redress such a gaping chink in her armoury. According to media reports at the time, after her nomination she had suddenly taken to the streets with 'a full schedule of commitments'. Within eight weeks, by the beginning of February 2006, she had covered the districts of Montpelier, Arbour Hill, Cabra, East

Wall and Sheriff Street. She had attended local meetings, including a Mass for drug addicts in the inner city. However, at the end of January she had decided to call a halt to her frenzied canvass as the estimated date of her baby's birth was perilously close. Councillor Christy Burke, one of her campaign managers, was heard to jest that her husband 'was worried that the Burke face was the first that the baby would see'.

It was not. On 20 February 2006, Mary Lou gave birth to Gerard Lanigan-McDonald. Gerard was named after Martin's father, Gerard Lanigan, not after her political patron, Gerry Adams, as many mischievous wags suggested!

Mary Lou took maternity leave. She missed all the European Parliament's plenary sessions from December 2005 until September 2006. Similarly, during her maternity leave, she was less active in Ireland, although she did not neglect the new constituency or the party's interests. She put her family first. Her rivals, mostly the sitting Dublin Central TDs, gleefully took note of her new commitments, doubling their efforts to defend their patch while she was busy with the new baby and his older sister.

Mary Lou kept her hand in. She was obviously aware that her opponents were already in full battle mode, working the parish pump. Surfacing in May, she launched Sinn Féin's new all-Ireland 'free healthcare' policy. In the same month she had a spat with the Fianna Fáil defence minister, Willie O'Dea, about whether Irish troops would be under British command when they joined an EU battle group. In June, she attended the funeral of former Taoiseach Charles J. Haughey. In July, she addressed a protest meeting in support of Palestine; later in the month she visited Cloverhill prison in Dublin. In August, she resumed her role as a member of Sinn Féin's peace team at the ongoing talks in Northern Ireland. Towards the year end, she moved back into full election gear ahead of the general election, which everyone rightly expected would be held the following May.

Expectations were high for Mary Lou. Not only was she Sinn Féin's greatest hope of a gain countrywide, but the media had named her as a probable winner of one of the seats in Dublin Central. Sinn Féin was confident that, despite her unavoidable maternity absence, the combination of Nicky Kehoe delivering his vote in Cabra and Christy Burke's support base in the north inner city would carry her comfortably over the line. Their spirits had been raised by the improved Sinn Féin vote in the 2004 local election; the party believed it was on an upward trajectory.

Other insiders shared their confidence. Maureen O'Sullivan, later to succeed her mentor Tony Gregory as a TD, told me that she was 'enjoying a drink with Tony's supporters in an Amiens Street pub one night after a heavy canvass. We were almost unanimous, from the feedback we had got on the doors, that Mary Lou would be elected.' After earlier doubts, Mark Hennessy, the *Irish Times*'s political correspondent – in an eve-of-poll prediction – gave a seat to Mary Lou. He expected her to thwart Bertie Ahern's machinations to bring in a running mate, with the four seats going to Bertie, Joe Costello, Tony Gregory and Mary Lou.

Just as happened in her European election battle, Mary Lou's campaign was media-led. Journalists took to the streets with her, reporting that she was receiving a warm reception at the doors. Following the same winning template, Sinn Féin started election year with an ard fheis at which, once again, Mary Lou played a leading role. She enjoyed further soft media coverage as a negotiator at the March 2007 pre-election round of Northern Ireland talks in Stormont. She was prominent among the dignitaries attending the restoration of the Northern Ireland Assembly on 8 May, only 16 days before the election. Mary Lou was very visible and on a roll.

However, a few punters detected her political shortcuts. A vigilant observer wrote to *The Irish Times* with an astute observation:

HELLO MARY LOU

Madam:

I was taken aback to read that Sinn Féin could not find a ministerial role for Mary Lou McDonald in the new Northern Assembly.

Surely she was entitled to, at least, a junior ministry of bilocation, as she seems to pop up everywhere. She was last spotted sitting between Gerry Adams and Martin McGuinness at last week's historic meeting at Stormont.

I would respectfully suggest that President McAleese should be careful not to be upstaged by the lovely Mary Lou when Queen Elizabeth comes to call, as no doubt she will, now that sanity has returned to our country.

Yours etc.

Brendan M. Redmond

Shades of the cameras outside 10 Downing Street just before the European election three years earlier. Some people had rumbled the standard Sinn Féin sleight of hand.

Would the saturation press coverage of Mary Lou work for a second time?

The experts, the pundits and the media had greatly under-estimated Bertie Ahern. When election day dawned, rumours were rife that he had organised a so-called 'milk run' – a blanket leaflet drop in the early hours of the morning on election day, asking Fianna Fáil voters to give their number twos to his constituency organiser, Senator Cyprian Brady. The objective was two-fold: to win a few votes from Sinn Féin and, equally importantly, to shaft Mary Fitzpatrick and direct Bertie's surplus and a second Fianna Fáil seat to Brady.

Paschal Donohoe tells a fascinating tale about the Dublin Central constituency shenanigans on election day 2007. Canvassing on polling day itself is normally frowned upon. Paschal himself says he was 'doing a walkabout in Cabra on election day when large teams of canvassers suddenly appeared on the streets knocking on doors, thus defying the traditional "no canvassing" code.'

On first sight, he says, 'I guessed that they were probably a crowd of Sinn Féin members disregarding normal delicate conventions, on a mission, making a last-minute effort to elect Mary Lou. They were nothing of the sort. They were part of Bertie's Fianna Fáil crack hit squad, cleaning out Cabra, Nicky Kehoe's heartland, aiming to swing a few hundred last-minute votes away from Mary Lou to Bertie and his favoured running mate, Cyprian Brady.'

Bertie had counted the votes to the last household. He picked Cabra because it had been Nicky Kehoe's personal heartland but – as he inevitably knew – it was wobbling wildly at the prospect of an unfamiliar Mary Lou. Bertie was intent on teaching both Mary Lou and Mary Fitzpatrick a lesson.

The final result was sensational. Bertie topped the poll with 12,734 votes, nearly two quotas. In second place came Tony Gregory with 4,649, followed by Labour's Joe Costello on 4,353 and Fine Gael's Paschal Donohoe with 3,302. Mary Lou received 3,182 first preferences. The second Fianna Fáil candidate, Mary Fitzpatrick, managed just 1,725 votes, followed by the party's distant third runner, Cyprian Brady, holding up the rear with a paltry 939 votes.

The destination of the first three seats to Bertie Ahern, Tony Gregory and Joe Costello was obvious, although Gregory and Costello had to wait a long time for transfers. The fourth and final seat was in the balance all the way. Bertie's surplus proved to be the deciding factor. The seat went, not to Paschal Donohoe, who was runner-up, not to Mary Lou, who came in a dismal sixth place, but to the second Fianna Fáil candidate. Bertie had directed a vast proportion of his surplus to Cyprian Brady and hammered a stake through the heart of Mary Fitzpatrick. The deadly canvass Paschal

Donohoe had witnessed on election day had paid off. Cyprian Brady overtook Mary Fitzpatrick, Bertie's bête noire. It was an incredible act of electoral gymnastics by the most astute political acrobat in Ireland's history. He had pulled off the double. Bertie buried Sinn Féin's Mary Lou and scuppered his Fianna Fáil colleague.

The 2007 general election result was devastating for Mary Lou McDonald, but she was not on her own. Sinn Féin suffered a serious setback everywhere. Their onward march was halted. Instead of doubling their numbers to ten seats, as was widely expected, they lost one, returning only four TDs to Dáil Éireann. Seán Crowe, the hard-working incumbent in Dublin South-West, failed to be re-elected. They were reduced to Martin Ferris, Arthur Morgan, Caoimhghín Ó Caoláin and Aengus Ó Snodaigh. But the humiliation of Mary Lou was a body blow. Her widely predicted victory in Dublin Central had been listed as a 'must-win' seat for the party. She had not only lost, she had lost badly, trailing behind the pack in sixth place. Her transfers from other candidates were woeful. Once again, Sinn Féin was the second or subsequent choice of very few voters.

The reasons were quickly identified. The hubris in Sinn Féin had led them to believe that they could insert a complete outsider into a constituency where the writ of Bertie Ahern had run since 1981.

Worse still was Mary Lou's lack of local knowledge and her only recent familiarity with the area. She didn't live in the constituency, while the four successful Dáil candidates and the runner-up, Paschal Donohoe, were residents. All had been councillors. Mary Lou McDonald was a blow-in: she had no track record, no base.

The party's decision to oust Nicky Kehoe in her favour was fatal. Arrogantly, Sinn Féin expected that Kehoe would simply be able to hand her his votes from the last election. Results from the Cabra ballot boxes showed that Mary Lou had not polled well in

Kehoe's fiefdom. His followers were Kehoe voters, not Sinn Féin voters. She managed only 3,182 first preferences against 4,972 for Kehoe the last time out. Her tally was dismal.

There were other reasons. Gerry Adams had badly damaged the Sinn Féin vote nationally with a dreadful leaders' debate performance on television. He was exposed as floundering when discussing economic, financial and even certain social issues.

Sinn Féin needed to regroup. Mary Lou had to ask herself some hard questions. Was she going to defend her seat in Europe in two years' time? Should she redouble her efforts in Dublin Central, or was the constituency an impregnable Bertie bastion? Should she cut her losses and look at another Dublin constituency? Project Mary Lou was down, but it was certainly not out. Adams, her mentor, was under pressure. Her past – and now her future – were dependent on her loyalty to him and on his own survival.

Adams was going nowhere, despite the election reversal; but an even more significant political giant, both nationally and locally, was heading for the departure lounge. Bertie Ahern's election triumph in 2007 was his last hurrah. As 2007 moved on, the Taoiseach came under increasing pressure over his personal financial affairs at the Mahon Tribunal, which was probing planning and payments. Mary Lou eagerly watched his agonised explanations for the chaotic state of his personal finances. On 2 April 2008 Ahern announced that he would be resigning.

The Taoiseach's exit had national implications for the peace talks in Northern Ireland, for the economy and for other big issues; but for Mary Lou, his fall from grace had a more parochial importance: it was game on again in Dublin Central.

The mighty had fallen. It was the end of Bertie's battle to keep Mary Lou out of his patch.

When I spoke to Bertie Ahern about Mary Lou in 2022, he was generous with his words. He obviously still has a high personal regard for her: 'I first met Mary Lou on my election trail. She struck me as friendly and a very capable person. Later we were constituency rivals, after she became a Sinn Féin candidate, but we always had a cordial friendship.

'My great friends, Chris and Myra Wall, were Mary Lou and Martin's neighbours. They had a good relationship over the years and attended family gatherings. Chris and Myra always spoke about how they were brilliant neighbours.'

Bertie, as ever, was measured about her future prospects, but did not rule her out as a contender for the Taoiseach's office, saying: 'The next election is still in the distance, but I have no doubt Mary Lou will be a formidable opponent for the top slot.'

Bertie's retirement as Taoiseach and TD meant that there would be two Fianna Fáil seats up for grabs in Dublin Central. Bertie had, in reality, controlled the destination of his running mate's and his own seat. In addition, Fianna Fáil was tanking in the polls. Political luck was on Mary Lou's side. There was no one of Bertie's stature in the constituency, no obvious successor. Bertie's famous 'Drumcondra mafia' would melt away with his own decline. A general election was not due until the summer of 2012. Mary Lou had plenty of time to remedy her own low local work output.

Decision made. Mary Lou doubled down. A house was sought in the constituency. She, Martin, Iseult and Gerard moved from 10 Riverwood Green in Castleknock in the constituency of Dublin West into a rented house nearby in Villa Park Road, off the Navan Road, in the Dublin Central constituency. It was a blatantly political migration and a brazen declaration of intent. Simultaneously, they went in search of a permanent home in the neighborhood, preferably in Cabra.

After a long wait, they sold their house in Castleknock. The buyers never met them, but knew who the sellers were from pictures left in a cupboard. Martin and Mary Lou made a gratuitous gesture of kindness to strangers, leaving a bottle of champagne for the new owners with a card wishing them good luck. Neighbours say they never got to know Mary Lou because 'she was in Europe and Martin was out and about with the children'. Another said that 'Mary Lou's mother looked after the kids a lot too'.

Mary Lou had to settle for a fall-back position after her defeat in the summer of 2007. She still had her seat in the European Parliament, the place where she did not want to be. Her loss in Dublin Central made it practically certain she would be forced to defend her European seat in 2009 for fear of holding no democratic mandate. The European contest was a battle she did not want to fight. The political path back from Europe to Dublin was proving far more difficult than she had imagined. She could be stuck overseas in Brussels for several more years – that is if she was even going to hold on to her European seat in 2009.

Mary Lou's diary again became frantically overcrowded. Even more so when another door opened in 2008. The referendum ordered on the Lisbon Treaty was a perfect opportunity for articulate opponents to shine in the media debate. Nobody filled political gaps better than Mary Lou. She seized the lead position against the EU treaty nationally and campaigned relentlessly for a No vote right up to polling day on 12 June 2008. She was back in a key position after her crushing general election experience. She rose from the ashes as one of the loudest anti-establishment voices against the tightening grip of the Brussels bureaucrats. The result was a personal triumph for her, for Socialist Joe Higgins and for Independent Tony Gregory. Ireland's conservative political parties took a bath. The No side won by 53.4 per cent to 46.6 per cent. Mary Lou had grasped a national issue and restored her national profile. She was back on the winning side, reassuring Sinn Féin doubters that when it came to improving the brand nationally or fighting a media campaign, they could not do better than her.

It was a short-term victory. Within six months, the European governments and Ireland had agreed to hold a second referendum to reverse the decision. There would be some changes to the agreement, many cosmetic, to appease a few of the Irish groups that had opposed the treaty.

Mary Lou relished the prospect of a second treaty war. It began six weeks after the first referendum vote. On 21 July, President Nicolas Sarkozy arrived in the French Embassy in Dublin to give opponents of Lisbon a lofty lecture on the benefits of the treaty. It was an arrogant manoeuvre that played into the hands of those who insisted that France and Germany were bullying small countries like Ireland. This was meat and drink to Mary Lou, Sinn Féin and other fringe parties.

Mary Lou flexed her muscles, gearing up for a second referendum in late 2009 and, more importantly, for European Parliament elections in June 2009. She had taken ownership of a major European issue and held a lead position on it. She was once again attracting media coverage, the envy of her fellow candidates for re-election.

Suddenly, as the bleak new year opened on 2 January 2009, tragedy intervened. Tony Gregory died. The Independent TD for Dublin Central had been suffering from cancer for a year. His death at the age of sixty-one shocked and saddened the political world. He was a popular and principled Dáil deputy. He had been a good friend of mine for many years, despite our different political outlooks. I came to know him well on a trip to South Africa in 1994 when, as election observers, we both took leave of our senses in Johannesburg. We defied all the unbreakable security advice, broke with our group, went AWOL and headed for a monster ANC rally immediately on our arrival. I still have photographs of Tony with a trademark mischievous grin at the rally, which I treasure. We came to no harm, but breached all the ground rules.

The reverberations of Tony's death sent a political earthquake through the inner city and the entire Dublin Central constituency. A by-election was immediately on the minds of the hard-nosed professionals in Leinster House.

Inevitably, the death of a politician, however sad, prompts instant speculation, often respectfully unspoken, about a successor. The process is cruel, cold and lacks compassion. Protocol demands that the ambitions of aspiring successors are paused for a few days of mourning. Politicking is officially frozen. In reality, it begins immediately.

In Tony Gregory's case, the succession race began before the funeral. The political tributes to Tony were dispatched to media from all sides on the day of his death. Every party wanted to grab a piece of his legacy to Dublin. Nearly all of them were careful to mention his unique work for his constituents.

The funeral at St Agatha's Church, North William Street, in Dublin's inner city, was attended by Taoiseach Brian Cowen, Green Party leader John Gormley, foreign affairs minister Micheál Martin, Fine Gael leader Enda Kenny, Labour leader Eamon Gilmore and Gerry Adams of Sinn Féin.

Fr Peter McVerry, the priest celebrating Tony's life, was the only one to mention the word 'by-election'. In his homily, he suggested that Tony's successor was 'on a hiding to nothing', so great were his achievements in the inner city. Several dignitaries and even more of the hopefuls in the congregation fidgeted nervously.

They positively froze when Tony's most loyal supporter and friend, Maureen O'Sullivan, rose to speak. The woman who had been entrusted by Tony himself to organise the funeral criticised those who gave little assistance to the man when he was alive. She went on to ask how Tony would have felt about 'certain politicians and their lavish tributes and praise over the last few days. And about those people speaking profusely about him in death, but during his life, when he came looking for help, never as much as put a leaflet in a letter box.'

There was a hush around the church. Most of us were hardened to a dose of funereal hypocrisy. Such honesty was stunning.

And then Maureen delivered the killer blow. Inviting only

family and good friends to the graveside at Old Balgriffin Cemetery, north Dublin, she calmly reminded others: 'His funeral is not a photo opportunity.'

There was loud applause in the church.[3]

One very close friend of Tony's who did attend the burial told me that the first people he spotted at the cemetery, perched in prominent positions beside the grave, were Gerry Adams and Mary Lou McDonald. The by-election was already being fought in the graveyard.

Sinn Féin had a big problem. Tony had been one in a million. Mary Lou was their standout, obvious candidate, but could they risk her losing yet another Dáil election?

Tony Gregory's tight organisation was set to meet and choose Maureen O'Sullivan, who would start as a huge favourite for the seat. Fine Gael's Paschal Donohoe would not win a by-election, but was a strong candidate. Ivana Bacik's relative youth was certain to add value to Joe Costello's Labour pot. She would compete with Mary Lou for the feminist vote. Fianna Fáil was probably going to nominate Bertie's brother, Maurice, to shore up the declining Ahern vote, suddenly in free fall because of Bertie's tribunal travails.

Mary Lou was staring into the abyss. She must have realised that she might sink as low as a dismal fifth in a by-election because there was only one vacant seat. It would have been a humiliation, possibly even curtains. She would have looked unelectable and there would be little merit in Sinn Féin running her again. It would damage any chance she had of being re-elected to Europe.

As it happened, Sinn Féin was gifted a ready-made face-saving

---

3   I took Maureen's words as a clear message that only those very close to Tony should head off to the cemetery. I did not feel close enough to be included in his inner circle, although Tony had been to my house many times for parties, right back to my stockbroking days. I used to enjoy introducing him to other guests with the line that I was the republican socialist's stockbroker! He took it with good humour, but, despite the banter, I was never a bosom friend or comrade.

by-election exit. Fianna Fáil, the main government party, decided that the by-election should be held on the same day as Mary Lou's original big date with destiny, the June 2009 European elections. Fianna Fáil would force her to make a choice of one or the other. She would not be given two bites of the cherry. They saw their ploy of holding both elections on the same day as a way of putting her out of politics, leaving her no fall-back position if she failed at the first fence. They were wrong. It gave her an out.

No doubt Sinn Féin and Mary Lou had been doing some intensive opinion polling. It was clear that there was no chance she would win the by-election, in particular because her record on transfers was dire. Furthermore, the two vacant Fianna Fáil seats destined to emerge for the next contest, following Bertie's demise, suddenly made Dublin Central one of the most fluid constituencies in the country. Mary Lou would live to fight a general election when there were four seats up for grabs. Every observer knew that the by-election seat had the name 'Maureen O'Sullivan' written all over it. Maureen was not the classic political relation inheriting the seat. She was the dead hero's chosen successor.

Sinn Féin had the luck of the devil. In reserve, it had one of its most loyal servants. Councillor Christy Burke was the noblest IRA man ever to have walked the streets of the inner city. Christy had twice served time in Portlaoise prison in the 1970s for IRA membership, an activity he had long left behind him. He had fought six Dáil elections for Sinn Féin, never yet having captured a seat. As first and foremost a Sinn Féin stalwart, he had swallowed his pride and backed Nicky Kehoe in 2002 and Mary Lou in the 2007 general election. This time he saw himself as the natural successor to Gregory. He and Tony had stood shoulder to shoulder against the drugs barons, the scourges and the heroin pushers in the inner city. He and Tony had both been jailed for two weeks in 1986 after campaigning for the rights of Dublin's Moore Street traders to sell their wares. Christy felt his hour had come.

Christy Burke was no fan of Mary Lou. He saw her as the ultimate interloper – a power-mad opportunist – and he deeply distrusted her Fianna Fáil background. He saw naked ambition, but lack of compassion, from the woman from Rathgar. Christy willingly took up the cudgel for Sinn Féin where she feared to tread.

Burke was in for a nasty surprise. Sinn Féin was running him, but to lose. They still had the seat earmarked for Mary Lou. They needed a candidate who was prepared to take one for the team. Christy was personally popular, but no Sinn Féin candidate could win a seat in this by-election because the party brand was so transfer-toxic. Transfers were essential in a by-election where only one seat was available. In the middle of the campaign, Christy realised that Sinn Féin was not giving him the necessary resources; the support from headquarters was half-hearted. They needed him to do enough to keep the seat warm for Mary Lou in 2011. They needed Christy Burke to lose. He did.

Maureen O'Sullivan was a runaway winner. Gregory's old team, including Deputy Finian McGrath, worked themselves around the clock for her. After topping the poll on the first count with 26.9 per cent of the number ones, she gradually moved further ahead of runner-up Paschal Donohoe (initially 22.7 per cent) on later preferences. Ivana Bacik came in third with 17.3 per cent, followed by Christy, on 13.3 per cent, who pipped Bertie's brother, Maurice Ahern (12.3 per cent) by a few hundred votes.

There were two winners: Maureen O'Sullivan and Mary Lou McDonald. Maureen won the seat; Mary Lou dodged the bullet.

Christy Burke was a fall guy. Sinn Féin sacrificed a north Dublin working-class hero to save the seat for a south Dublin middle-class intruder.

The by-election was held on 5 June. Four days later, Christy Burke resigned from Sinn Féin. He was disgusted at the way the party, which he had served all his life, had exploited him. Happily, his career was not at an end. He has successfully defended his council seat as an Independent at every election since and became Lord Mayor of Dublin in 2014.

Meanwhile, Mary Lou McDonald had been watching the by-election campaign with more than a passing interest. Having opted to defend her European seat instead, she faced an uphill struggle. She had her own problems, not least that Dublin had lost one of its four seats for the European Parliament. It was down to three, instead of four. All four incumbents, Fine Gael's Gay Mitchell, Labour's Proinsias de Rossa, Fianna Fáil's Eoin Ryan and Mary Lou were defending their seats. Four into three does not go and, besides, Socialist Joe Higgins was breathing down their necks.

Mary Lou had been preparing carefully. Far from being a spent force following her disaster in the 2007 general election, she remained in favour with Adams and McGuinness. In January 2009 they had clearly demonstrated their continued confidence in her, despite her election setbacks. She was picked to succeed former IRA member Pat Doherty as vice-president of the party, becoming second only to Adams in Sinn Féin in the South. The appointment was subject to rubber-stamping at the February ard fheis. It was probably Adams's calculated decision to install her in high party office long before the European Parliament election. If she were to lose again, it would be far harder to justify. It was typical of Adams's strategic foresight.

Mary Lou had a good chance of retaining her seat – on paper, at least. She had been a vocal performer in the Lisbon Treaty debate and was recognised as a leading voice in that treaty's defeat at the polls. The other Dublin MEPs – Gay Mitchell, Eoin Ryan and Proinsias de Rossa – had been in the losing Yes camp. But Joe Higgins was threatening Mary Lou on her so-called radical flank. Higgins, an immensely popular national figure, was going into this election as her equal and as an advocate for defeating the Lisbon Treaty for a second time.

Mary Lou's high profile was expected to benefit her enormously, as it had done in 2004. Over the five-year term, she had been photographed at practically every meeting of Northern Ireland negotiators. She was a member of the Sinn Féin peace talks team and by far the most photogenic one. Her contributions behind closed doors were not reported to have been weighty, but she was invariably present when the cameras arrived. She was still tearing herself apart between three or four demanding locations. Europe had fallen down the pecking order. And that was part of her problem. Her attempts at bilocation, if not trilocation, over the previous five years had been damaging. Opponents had begun to examine her attendance record in Brussels and Strasbourg. What they found was a major embarrassment to her.

Whispers about Mary Lou's poor attendance had been circulating in political circles for several years. Her rivals spoke openly about her no-shows to anyone who would listen. It was a delicate subject, not least because she was obviously entitled to maternity leave after she had given birth to Gerard in February 2006. At the time, she did not appear at any of the plenary sessions between December 2005 and September 2006.

Nobody was going to criticise her for taking her entitlement to maternity leave. The official statistics from the European Union website show that her attendance at plenary sessions throughout the period of the entire parliament from 2004 to 2009 was only 56 per cent, one of the worst of the entire parliament. Out of 288 sessions she had managed to make it to only 162 meetings. Bairbre de Brún, her Sinn Féin colleague, attended 81 per cent, making it to 234 meetings, 44 per cent more than her missing colleague. Crueller critics began to say that Mary Lou McDonald was extending Sinn Féin's policy of principled abstentionism from Westminster to Strasbourg and Brussels.

Mary Lou rightly claims that many of her absences were due to her maternity leave in 2006, but only a minority of them qualify under this category. The raw figures do not take sickness and maternity leave into account, so she is entitled to maintain that her opponents were not comparing like with like. However, objective commentators who did their own surveys came up with figures indicating that, regardless of her legitimate maternity leave, her attendance in Brussels and Strasbourg was deplorable.

In August 2008 Mary Regan, political reporter of the *Irish Examiner*, published some highly embarrassing figures covering Ireland's MEPs' attendance at sessions of the European Parliament. The figures start eighteen months after Mary Lou had her baby, her maternity leave by then a distant memory. Listing MEPs' attendance in the period September 2007 to August 2008, Regan found that 'Sinn Féin's Mary Lou McDonald, who headed the No campaign in the Lisbon Treaty referendum, has the lowest attendance record among the Irish representation.' The piece continued: 'The Dublin MEP was present for an average of just three out of five days in the past year, ranking her among the lowest of all 767 MEPs from 27 countries.'

The *Irish Examiner*'s report must have made grim reading for Mary Lou, ten months before the election. All the other Dublin MEPs had a far better attendance record than hers. Gay Mitchell scored 84 per cent for attendance and had made 92 speeches. Eoin Ryan had attended 76 per cent of meetings and made 74 speeches. Proinsias de Rossa was similarly at 76 per cent of the meetings but had made 172 speeches. Mary Lou managed only 61 per cent attendance and 62 speeches.

Naturally, because of her low attendance her travel and subsistence expenses were lighter than Bairbre de Brún's. Mary Lou clocked up only €163,000 over the five-year term, as against de Brún's €241,000. But her costs under other categories showed a marked difference, with Mary Lou claiming far higher allowances than her Northern Ireland colleague. Mary Lou received €216,000 in office-cost allowances, compared to de Brún's €144,000. On the other big item – MEP staff allowances – de Brún incurred costs of

€555,000, while Mary Lou charged up €807,000 for this claim.

All in all, over the life of the parliament, Mary Lou's declared expenses amounted to €1,186,000; de Brún's total claim was for €940,000.

Mary Lou's Irish fellow MEPs were not slow to notice her low attendance, nor were they reluctant to point it out to journalists, but none was prepared to go on the record about it. At least not until the elections were in full swing. Sinn Féin disputed the five-year figures, somehow maintaining that Mary Lou had attended 75 per cent of meetings, and underlined that she had been on maternity leave in 2006.

Her Dublin fellow MEPs, even to this day, are incensed at her casual treatment of the European Parliament, one insisting that she 'found it boring'. Another said that she was linked to a group of 'headbangers' in the GUE/NGL group. A third remarked, approvingly, that she had brought her tiny infant to Strasbourg and was nursing the baby out there. Another said that she rarely saw Mary Lou there on Thursdays. At one point during the election, when the row about her no-shows in Europe was getting hot and heavy, Gay Mitchell went on the RTÉ *Six One* news. Asked what made a good MEP, he remarked pointedly: 'The first thing you need to do is turn up.'

The election itself took a controversial turn when Progressive Democrat Minister for Health, Mary Harney, waded into the fray to hammer away at Mary Lou's poor attendance record. Mary Lou responded that Mary Harney was prejudiced against her as a female politician taking maternity leave, saying: 'It is utterly despicable that a politician such as myself, one of the very few women in Irish political life, one of even fewer with young children, would be maliciously attacked for having the temerity to take maternity leave to which I was entitled.'

According to *The Irish Times*, Harney rejected Mary Lou's comments outright. 'It is ridiculous,' she retorted, 'for Mary Lou to suggest that I am attacking her because she is a woman. My comments regarding Mary Lou have nothing to do with gender. The reality is that her poor record in the European Parliament has nothing whatsoever to do with maternity leave.' And then Harney put the boot in: 'Last year, over two years after her maternity leave finished, she missed 55 per cent of the votes in the parliament. In September she even missed a full day of voting in order to go to the Sinn Féin tent at the ploughing championships. The proof of this is on Sinn Féin's own website.'

Mary Lou responded that she went to the ploughing champ-ionships every year. It was her 'duty to be in touch with the farmers of north Dublin who help us to feed the rest of the country'. Perhaps.

And then, having initially told Mary Harney not to hit her when she had the baby in her arms, she insisted that campaigning against the Lisbon Treaty had kept her away from her European tasks!

It was an uncomfortable end to a campaign for someone who had scored such a remarkable success in leading the charge against the Lisbon Treaty just a year earlier. Mary Lou had tried to keep too many balls in the air for five long years. She had been chairperson of Sinn Féin, an MEP, a mother, a wife and an aspiring TD, all together. She had bitten off more than most politicians could chew. Her lack of attention to Europe had been a hostage to fortune, but in reality she had never expected to be defending the seat.

The result on election day reflected Dubliners' sense that she was cutting too many corners, that they were still not sure of her. The accusations about her absences had landed. Was she a real republican or an outright opportunist? She was an engaging person on the surface, but how did that fit with her close alliance with the less charming Gerry Adams and the convicted gunmen in Sinn Féin? The electorate were hesitant about endorsing her.

On election day, Mary Lou imploded. She was fifth on the first count and never improved. Gay Mitchell, Proinsias de Rossa and

Eoin Ryan were the front runners on number ones. In later counts Joe Higgins overtook Ryan to win the third seat. Higgins cleaned up on the left-wing vote, easily outpolling Mary Lou among this cohort. The voters clearly trusted him.

Mary Lou, the great white hope, had failed in three elections out of four. The loss of her seat left her without a public platform. The future of Project Mary Lou was in jeopardy. Now aged forty, if she survived the fallout, it was back to the drawing board.

CHAPTER 6

THE MANSION IN CABRA

On 20 May 2010 Dublin City Council received an intriguing planning application. It was made in the name of a man called Martin Lanigan. A few days earlier, the planning notice had appeared in the *Sunday Business Post*, followed by a site notice at 186 New Cabra Road, Cabra, Dublin 7.

The notice didn't cause a ripple, probably because no one had ever heard of Martin Lanigan and because the *Sunday Business Post* had a small circulation. The paper is unlikely to have sold many copies in Cabra or in the constituency of Dublin Central.

The bungalow on the site was vacant. It was, however, still technically owned by a successful Mayo solicitor, Brendan Flanagan. He was the legal personal representative of the former owner, the late Mary Stafford, a member of the local Fianna Fáil Stafford family. Flanagan, a partner in the solicitors Higgins, Chambers and Flanagan, was a well-known Fianna Fáil activist.

Martin Lanigan, who had a 'contract to purchase' the property, was not yet the legal owner, despite being the applicant for planning permission. Brendan Flanagan sent a letter to Dublin City Council saying that he had no objection to Martin Lanigan applying for this permission and was giving his consent to the application.

No one objected. Not surprisingly, because the application aimed to convert a drab bungalow into a mini-mansion. The tone of the entire neighbourhood would be lifted by such a dramatic conversion. The value of neighbours' houses would probably increase. The site was in the posh part of Cabra.

Martin Lanigan had done everything by the book. He had attended a pre-planning consultation with Area Planning Officer Margaret Coyle in March 2010. He had employed professional architects, Fitzgibbon McGinley, with offices in Naas, County Kildare, to design and deliver on his elaborate plans. According to their website, Fitzgibbon McGinley have also done work for Ulster Bank, the EBS, the departments of both defence and education and the Health Service Executive. The architects' website opens with a promotion labelled 'an overview of the type of projects we have worked on'. Today, over a decade later, the pride of place, first property to appear, is none other than 186 New Cabra Road in all its new-found splendour. There is no mention of any of their private clients' names, but it is crystal clear from the list of commercial customers that Fitzgibbon McGinley do not come cheap.

Nor do the builders chosen by Martin Lanigan. Weslin Construction, of Damastown, Dublin 15, has a blue-chip client base to rival Fitzgibbon McGinley's well-heeled commercial customer list. Its website has the same formula of naming the great and the good as purchasers of the firm's services. Weslin Construction reveals that it has done work for Iarnród Éireann, Henkel, Bank of Ireland, Dublin Port and the Department of Education. It doesn't mention Martin Lanigan or other private clients.

The name of Mary Lou McDonald, wife of the applicant, was nowhere to be seen on Martin Lanigan's application, nor was anybody reading the notice ever likely to connect her with it. In 2010 very few people would have recognised the name of Mary

Lou's husband. He rarely, if ever, appeared anywhere with her in public, not even at election counts. Politicians and the media knew there was a 'Mr McDonald' somewhere in the background, but that was as far as it went. The application managed to keep below the radar and to escape the attention of the sleepy national media.

It was a staggering proposal, professionally prepared and presented.

The planners set multiple conditions, including that the applicant should pay a local levy of €11,433.26 to Dublin City Council, even before the work began on the bungalow.

The scale of the proposed increase in the size of the house was mind-boggling. It would be unrecognisable – effectively a new dwelling – when it was finished. It would no longer be a bungalow. It was going to have two storeys, five bedrooms (four of them new), bathrooms to match, a living room, a dining hall, a family room, a kitchen, a study/meeting room and a playroom. It would need a completely new roof and it would be largely gutted internally to make way for the lucky family of four who were moving in.

Initially, no one, not even the media, seemed to notice the affluent new arrivals. On 22 May 2011, three months after Mary Lou's election to the Dáil, the *Irish Mail on Sunday* carried a piece on Martin and Mary Lou's good fortune. There was little follow-up. Eventually, many years later, the media zoned in on the development. In 2015, journalist Sam Smyth, again in the *Irish Mail on Sunday*, wrote of the couple's 'luxurious 11 room detached villa' as 'like the sort of opulent pile where soap opera stars pose in celebrity magazines'. He was right. It was a home that could comfortably make the grade for a feature in *Hello!* magazine. Covering 254 square metres, it was almost three times the size of the average Irish house.

The planning permission positively flew through the hoops. The last day for observations was 23 June 2010. There were none. The decision to grant permission was given on 8 July.

Exactly a week before the formal planning decision date, on 1 July, according to Property Price Register Ireland, 186 New Cabra Road changed hands for €517,000. According to documents in the Land Registry, the property then passed from Brendan Flanagan, as administrator of the estate, to Martin Lanigan and Mary Lou McDonald. There is a Bank of Ireland mortgage on the house.

Martin and Mary Lou had moved house several times since their marriage in 1996. There was little doubt that it was her political ambitions that determined the area where they were living. By 2011 it looked as though she had opted to settle permanently within the Dublin constituency which she saw as her political home. She had lived in a modest semi-detached house in Riverwood, Castleknock, in Dublin West when she contested that constituency in 2002 and continued to live there until she and Martin sold it in November 2008. They then stayed strictly within the boundaries of her new hunting ground, Dublin Central. First, they rented 23 Ashington Heath, off the Navan Road, followed by another nearby property, 22A Villa Park Road, both in the Cabra area. Cabra was the base for her career aspirations.

Martin Lanigan did all the wheeling and dealing necessary to secure the little bungalow in Cabra, but the timing of its purchase was awkward and could have been electorally sensitive if the couple's names became public knowledge. If Martin and Mary Lou had been spotted embarking on such a lavish planning project just before the 2011 general election, there might have been a mighty media frenzy and a left-wing backlash from Éirígí and others. It could have torpedoed her election bid. Imagine the tabloid headlines about the 'Sinn Féin millionairess'. Her already faltering hopes of winning the working-class vote could have sunk without a trace.

In defence of the couple, however, there might have been dozens of malicious, politically motivated objections. There would certainly have been deeply critical comment. Indeed, when the true identity of the new residents eventually became known, an alarmed neighbour rang Bertie Ahern's office to complain that the IRA had moved into 186 New Cabra Road. The neighbour, claiming that new foundations had been dug, insisted that the new owners were building a bunker!

Perhaps it was the first time in their marriage that Martin was the front-of-house man. For once, his wife was willingly standing in his shadow.

Martin and Mary Lou were lucky. Nobody seems to have twigged Martin's name. The rebuilding works carried on during the countdown to the general election, but the family did not settle permanently in the mansion until Mary Lou was safely ensconced as a TD.

Very few people, apart from the *Irish Mail on Sunday*, asked questions. Journalist Sam Smyth was prompted to raise the issue only because, many years later, in 2015, he heard Mary Lou demanding personal accountability from others. Under parliamentary privilege, she had read into the Dáil record the names of politicians allegedly holding illegal Ansbacher accounts. She was mistaken. None of them had held them. Smyth's article taking her to task was headed: 'JUST HOW DOES MARY LOU AFFORD HER LUXURY HOME?'

Smyth first colourfully referred to Mary Lou's family house as having the potential to be 'categorized as what anti-austerity campaigners now call "property porn"'. Then he asked rhetorically: 'How could anyone earning the average industrial wage and a spouse in the public utility afford to build such a luxurious home? I'm still none the wiser. Maybe Ms. McDonald and her husband Martin have wealthy and generous relatives; perhaps they asked for anonymity after a big win on the Lotto.'

Smyth was touching a raw nerve, but he was asking a fair question. When public figures suddenly reveal vast sums of money, it is only right that they should give a plausible explanation of their origin.

Most politicians are led into temptation from time to time. Some have yielded to it, as we saw in the planning scandals, when Fianna Fáil and Fine Gael councillors abused their positions in the rezoning rows of the 1990s. After the controversies surrounding the unexplained housing extravagances of both former Taoiseach Charlie Haughey and ex-Fine Gael minister Michael Lowry, we should be wary of politicians suddenly living in mansions. Ministers have fallen by the wayside for financial misdemeanours. As recently as October 2020, a Sinn Féin senator, Elisha McCallion, was forced to resign her seat because of her failure to return a £10,000 sterling business grant wrongly sent into her bank account. To her credit, Mary Lou McDonald acted swiftly and firmly to remedy this wrongdoing and required the senator's immediate resignation.

No doubt, from time to time Sinn Féin councillors and other representatives have been tempted by ill-gotten gains. There is nothing to suggest that Mary Lou has ever been involved in anything untoward or has been other than a person of impeccable financial integrity, but she ruthlessly demands transparency of others. So Smyth's question was fair. Where did Martin and Mary Lou find the loot for the house?

There has been a deafening silence on the topic. The answer is far from sticking out a mile. Mary Lou has never had bucketloads of money. As we have seen in previous chapters, her father was a spendthrift, her mother a responsible, but – out of necessity – prudent person, who does not own her own residence.

Mary Lou's annual declaration of interests as a TD has always produced a 'nil' return, meaning that she has no declarable assets and no meaningful income beyond her Dáil deputy's salary. Cash in a TD or senator's bank account is, strangely, not a declarable interest.

The incessant accusations about the IRA's continued involvement in organised crime long after the Northern Bank heist, however unfair, makes it even more important that its public apologists in Sinn Féin are 'squeaky clean'.

We know a little about the couple's financial transactions, their incomes and their climb up the housing ladder. It is difficult to see any evidence of the sort of six-figure windfall needed to convert a small bungalow into a grand residence on New Cabra Road. Neither Martin nor Mary Lou has ever earned more than a modest income. When she was in the European Parliament, according to herself, Mary Lou insisted that during her five-year term she never received more than the average industrial wage. Speaking on the Sinn Féin website at the end of her time in Brussels, she was specific: 'I, like all Sinn Féin elected representatives and workers, am paid the average industrial wage from my salary, after which a small amount goes back into the party and the remainder to provide constituency services. This is a principle I am immensely proud of. Sinn Féin is not in politics for monetary gain; we are in it to bring about progressive political change.'

Her statement is helpful. Mary Lou had never been paid above the average industrial wage during her period in the European Parliament or when working for Sinn Féin. Her refusal to accept above the average wage was an admirably ethical position, albeit unlikely to persuade a bank manager to ramp up her mortgage. At the time of the house purchase, her political future was precarious. Her job was far from permanent. She was not even a TD, so she did not need to declare annual interests. And she was hardly a good risk for a big mortgage. Indeed, when Martin and Mary Lou bought the house in 2010, she had no public office, having lost her seat in the European Parliament in June 2009. If she was an employee of the party, consistency demanded that, again, her salary was not above the average wage.

Even the number of financial donors Mary Lou returned over this period was surprisingly small. Many of them could be covered by the famous biblical term as 'publicans and sinners'. Corporate donations were non-existent. While individual supporters were sometimes generous, they often proved an embarrassment. The maximum donation she ever declared was €2500, the lowest €500.

Possibly the most controversial donor was former Sinn Féin councillor, Jonathan Dowdall, who gave her €1000 in a single cheque in 2011. Three years after his donation, Dowdall was elected a Sinn Féin councillor within Mary Lou's constituency, but he didn't last long. Four months after his May 2014 election, pleading ill health, he suddenly left Sinn Féin, but not the council itself. Mary Lou was immensely disappointed. He had been a strong supporter. 'It is with much regret,' she said, 'that we accept Jonathan's decision to step down.'

A month later Dowdall rejoined the party, claiming that he had the 'total support of Mary Lou McDonald', but in February 2015 he resigned from the council itself. His was an erratic baptism into politics and was to prove his first and last one. In June 2017 Dowdall was sentenced to twelve years in jail for falsely imprisoning and threatening to kill a convicted fraudster, Alexander Hurley, in gruesome circumstances that included waterboarding. The offence happened while he was still a councillor. During his waterboarding of Hurley, Dowdall claimed to be a member of the IRA and bragged that he was a friend of Gerry Adams and Mary Lou McDonald. His father, Patrick, received an eight-year sentence for his role in the same crime. Both punishments were slightly reduced on appeal.

Mary Lou welcomed the conviction but she added a sting in the tail, attempting to disown Dowdall by asserting that he 'subsequently worked with and supported a political opponent of Sinn Féin in the Dublin Central Constituency'. She was pointing the finger at her former friend, but later adversary, Councillor Christy Burke. She even tweeted a photograph of Dowdall with Christy at Christy's general election headquarters during the 2016 general election. Burke blew a fuse. He insisted that Dowdall had turned up for only one meeting, but that 'after that we never seen or heard of him.' He lambasted Mary Lou, declaring that she had 'stooped to a new low' by posting the picture of him with Dowdall.

But Maeve Sheehan in the *Sunday Independent* wrote that Burke had known Dowdall well enough to go to his daughter's Holy Communion before the trouble broke. In 2021 Dowdall – after it emerged that he was a friend of well-known criminal gang leader Gerry 'the Monk' Hutch – was charged with the murder of David Byrne in Dublin's Regency Hotel. Byrne was an associate of the infamous rival Kinahan gang.

Other donors to Mary Lou had fallen foul of the law, but their offences were far more political and less violent in nature. Dermot Teeling, who has been a lifelong member of Sinn Féin, gave Mary Lou a donation of €1000 for the 2007 general election.

Teeling was caught up in the helicopter escape of three top IRA men from Mountjoy Prison back in 1973. According to former IRA commander Brendan Hughes in *Up Like a Bird*, his book about the escape, Dermot was incredibly unlucky. As Hughes tells it, Dermot, a seller of *An Phoblacht*, just 'happened to be walking past' when a taxi commandeered by the IRA had broken down. The two occupants, recognising him, asked Dermot for a push. He obliged but left his fingerprints on the car. He was sentenced to three years penal servitude for being part of the conspiracy that successfully sprang former IRA chief of staff, Seamus Twomey, with two other prisoners, Kevin Mallon and Joe 'J.B.' O'Hagan, from Mountjoy.

In early May 2022 I talked about Mary Lou to Dermot and Vera, his wife of more than fifty years, over coffee in the garden of their detached house in leafy Portmarnock, County Dublin.

Today Teeling is a healthy eighty-year-old who still canvasses for Sinn Féin. He is a member of the party's Thomas Ashe cumann in Mary Lou's Cabra base. Outside election time he knocks on doors for her for an hour every Friday. He says he is 'the youngest of four canvassers'. On Mondays he does the same for Sinn Féin TD Louise O'Reilly in Dublin Fingal.

A very large tricolour is flown outside the Teelings' house on appropriate occasions, including the republican Easter commemorations. On the Saturday morning when I visited the Teelings' house, the flag was flying high to celebrate Sinn Féin's (and Mary Lou's) historic victories in the Northern Ireland Assembly elections. Inside the house, the 1916 Proclamation hangs on the walls.

Teeling was described by the *New York Times* as 'a senior manager of Mary Lou's campaign' in 2007, the year that he gave her the €1000 donation. He becomes animated when talking about canvassing with her. 'I am a capitalist,' he says with a twinkle in his eye, revealing that he is a first cousin of Irish entrepreneur and Cooley Whiskey owner John Teeling. 'I drove her around in a big Merc at election time.' He adds that 'She is a nightmare to canvass with, because everybody wants to shake her hand. She's very popular with women. And she is absolutely classless.'

Dermot has canvassed at elections with Mary Lou's husband, Martin, and with her mother, Joan. He speaks highly of both, saying that 'Martin canvasses but he's not involved.'

He said that Mary Lou is 'very thoughtful, very human. Recently one of our group [local supporters] died. She took at least two hours off to spend with us and sympathise with us when it happened. We really appreciated that. She'll do anything that's required for Cabra. She's always on the bridge in Cabra for the Easter Sunday commemoration.'

Teeling's journey from republican activist to Sinn Féin supporter began in the year of Mary Lou's birth – in 1969 – when he collected money for the nationalist community in Belfast, giving it to the people he calls 'the defenders'. He despised what he calls the 'injustice of partition'. He says that Vera 'allowed him to join Sinn Féin but drew the line at the IRA'. When he was in prison, she was alone with their three children but visited him almost every day. She never admonished him for what he had done. He had no family attachment to republicanism. His father was in the Dublin Metropolitan Police and his uncle was in the British Navy.

He doesn't dwell too comfortably on the past or his own republican activities. He recalls how he used to paint graffiti like 'No to EEC' or 'No to Extradition' on walls, observing that 'it seems funny now.' Nor does he volunteer too much information about the helicopter escape, though he's grateful that no one was hurt. He was originally accused of 'being in possession of arms with intent to endanger life', a charge that was dropped at appeal stage; but the conviction of 'conspiring to rescue prisoners' was upheld. He says it was very important that the IRA leaders escaped because the morale of the republican movement got a huge boost.

Another donor with a republican past is Paul Clarke, now a successful businessman. He gave €500 in 2007, but hasn't donated anything since that date. He canvassed with Mary Lou's predecessor, Nicky Kehoe.

Publican John Browne, owner of Joxer Daly's pub in Dorset Street, in the heart of Dublin Central, has been a consistently generous donor to Mary Lou's cause. In 2007 her office reported that the Kerry native gave €1500 to her unsuccessful efforts to be elected a TD. In 2011 he gave her another €1000, this time to a victorious campaign. Joxer Daly's is spoken of locally as a 'Sinn Féin house'. In 1994 Gerry Adams celebrated his famous meeting on the steps of Government Buildings with Albert Reynolds and John Hume in Joxer Daly's.

When I called into a packed Joxer Daly's on a summer Saturday afternoon in 2022, a friendly middle-aged Kerryman greeted me: 'You're out of your neighbourhood?' queried Browne with a smile. I told him that I was looking to talk to himself about Mary Lou. We had a few brief words about the book and the likelihood of her becoming Taoiseach. He wanted to know which party she would go in with. He took my number and promised to ring on the following

Tuesday evening. Not surprisingly, he never rang. After a couple of days I texted him. He replied that he was 'not interested in the interview'. I had a final try, asking if he could give me a bit of colour. 'Not interested. Full and final,' he responded.

Browne has enjoyed a colourful career in the pub business. He is one of two directors and is secretary of Cornhill Circle Limited, the company that owns the pub. A judgement mortgage was granted against the company in favour of Gerard Harrahill of the Revenue Commissioners for €367,534.55 in 2009. A receiver from Grant Thornton accountants was put into the company in 2013. Documents lodged in the Companies Office reveal that an apartment in nearby Mountjoy Street owned by Cornhill Circle was sold for €257,500 in 2019 to discharge part of the amount owed to the Revenue Commissioners. Browne's generosity to Mary Lou, at a time when his pub was under such pressure from the taxman, is particularly noteworthy.

Greg Conroy from Cabra was a smaller donor to Mary Lou's coffers. When I contacted him, he first denied that he had supported Sinn Féin, but then remembered the donation that was registered by Mary Lou's office. His contribution of €500 was made to her 2007 election campaign. Local residents who know him say he was the beneficiary of a sudden windfall in the mid-noughties. Several of them insist that Greg won the Lotto, although he denies it; some say that he won it twice. His generosity extended beyond Sinn Féin to several local good causes, including the Gaelscoil. A former employee of Telecom Éireann, he is immensely popular in McGrath's pub in Cabra where I initially tracked him down. When I rang him back to ask him to talk to me about Mary Lou and his support for her, he said he was seeking legal advice. Afterwards, however, we met in McGrath's. He was unwilling to disclose why he supported Mary Lou, saying he meant the donation to go to Sinn Féin, but confirmed that he had helped local football clubs.

There were one or two less controversial donors. Publicans, but hardly sinners, the late Frank Quinn and Noel Tynan both donated €2000 in 2007. Quinn owned the Lansdowne Hotel in Dublin 4. Originally from County Tyrone, he also owned the Waterloo Bar, the 51 Bar and Toners, all in the Baggot Street area of Dublin. Tynan, a native of County Offaly, owned the Celtic Lodge in Dublin's Talbot Street.

Although she received several donations from publicans, there was never any indication that Mary Lou yielded to the demands of the strong vintners' lobby.

One donor who possibly could ill afford her €2000 donation was a woman who lives in a council house in north Dublin. Anne Taaffe gave Mary Lou €2000 in 2007. She respects Sinn Féin's leader as a 'really strong Irish woman' and says she was disillusioned with all the other parties. She wanted to give Sinn Féin a chance to sort out the housing problem where others had failed. She canvassed with Gerry Adams and Mary Lou in Ballybough in the inner city in 2007 and is deeply disappointed that they have never held the levers of power. Today Anne Taaffe lives alone, surviving on social welfare in Cromcastle, Coolock, a less advantaged area of north Dublin. In her sitting room sits a teddy bear with an 'Up the IRA' necklace around its neck.

All in all, Mary Lou declared only ten donations, valued at €14,000, over her first nine-year period of contesting elections between 2002 and 2011. More recently, it appears that the financial strength of the party's coffers has reduced the necessity for her to solicit personal funding from supporters.

Martin Lanigan's position was as solid as a rock. When the couple bought the house in Cabra, he had been an employee of Gas Networks Ireland (GNI), a state-sponsored body, or its original incarnation, Bord Gáis Éireann, for over thirty years. His job was permanent and pensionable. Few employees in Ireland were safer than Martin. However, his take-home pay was far from spectacular.

He did not sample the sort of spoils enjoyed by those at the top of state-sponsored bodies because he had never reached those dizzy heights. Martin was on the clerical side. He was a settled employee, a gas emergency controller. He worked shifts, sending out staff from the NGI control room, which has its own department. He was not a high-flier, and after thirty years in the company and possibly ten years away from retirement, he was unlikely ever to break through to the overpaid magic circle.

Some Sinn Féin sources have recently hinted that Martin received a big windfall from the sale of Bord Gáis Energy, the state-owned company that employed him. When the company was restructured and its energy arm sold, qualifying employees received a lump sum payout. However, the *Irish Independent* reported that the maximum amount available to any employee was €66,500, which would hardly have provided a small fraction of the cost of their house rebuilding. Besides, the sale of Bord Gáis Energy did not take place until 2014, at least three years after Martin and Mary Lou had completed the mansion.

There is no sign of any large capital sum available to either spouse, no windfall. Their own trading in houses had been limited. After their marriage, they purchased the compact dwelling in Dublin's Stoneybatter, before buying the Riverwood Green house in a quiet cul-de-sac in Castleknock. Like many buyers in those days, the young couple might have received very limited help from their parents. Martin's father, Gerard, might have managed to sell enough small pockets of land in the Strawberry Beds to raise a deposit to launch the couple on the ladder. In January 2008 they put 10 Riverwood Green on the market at around €530,000 and sold it for a lower price in a private November sale, probably for a price in the region of €485,000. That would give them a base, but no more, to buy a modest bungalow in Cabra. Behind the scenes, they were preparing to make a giant leap into the top of the property market, a level hitherto way above their pay grade.

While the couple waited for their palatial home to be ready, they rented a house in Villa Park Road, off the Navan Road.

The next part of their narrative is puzzling. They paid €517,000 to administrator Brendan Flanagan for the bungalow before partially demolishing it. They took out a mortgage. Their top-class architects had already designed their dream house. The big-ticket builders, Weslin Construction, moved on to the site.

No doubt the couple were able to meet the difference between the selling price of Riverwood, at around €485,000, and the buying price of the Cabra Road bungalow at €517,000 with an increased mortgage. Perhaps their mortgage from the Bank of Ireland would cover the stamp duty, the solicitors' fees and other miscellaneous moving costs. Their mortgage repayments might be heavy, but, even with two young children, they could probably afford them, at a stretch.

The real riddle is how Martin and Mary Lou funded the dramatic transformation of the building from bungalow into what the *Irish Mail on Sunday* had originally called the 'mansion fit for a queen'. Indeed, the newspaper had headed its 2011 piece 'How Mary Lou built her own White House'.

Perhaps they got a great deal? It was 2010, a time when business had slowed down in the construction industry. Architects were having a torrid time. If the couple could purchase at a deep discount for cash, maybe the hard-pressed builders and architects had given them a bargain.

To acquire an expert estimate of the cost of what the *Irish Mail on Sunday* had called 'a revolutionary change in the Sinn Féin TD's modest Cabra bungalow', I discreetly asked three experienced builder/developers for a ballpark estimate of the cost of the venture. None consulted with the other two; all insisted on anonymity. The first estimated that, at 2010 building-cost levels, the price of the works would be a minimum of €600,000. The second estimate was €900,000, including interiors. The third, a more modest €500,000.

Perhaps Martin's father, Gerard Lanigan, simply struck it lucky? It is difficult to see how he could have made a serious killing out of smallholdings in the Strawberry Beds. In any land transaction of this sort, a sale would have been subject to capital gains tax and to gifts tax on the transfer of any proceeds to any of his three children.

If Gerard, in theory, had gifted €500,000 to each of his four living offspring, he would probably need to have made over €2 million profit from the sale of small pockets of land. It is possible he paid nothing for parts of his land, since he acquired several smallholdings as a 'squatter', having obtained them initially as 'possessory title' before converting them into absolute title.

Nevertheless, the possible profits he might have gained from any small disposals he made are highly unlikely to have reached a fraction of the value needed to make any large distribution to one child, let alone to others.

Gerard Lanigan was not a rich man. In response to a request for a valuation of agricultural land in the Strawberry Beds in the 2000–2010 period, Lisney Sotheby's International Realty estimate that it changed hands at an average price of only €25,000 per acre. Gerard Lanigan probably never held more than a maximum of 7 acres. When he died in July 2011, he left only €168,000 (net) in his will, which was not administered until 2013. Martin was bequeathed 'the field at the rear of my premises', with the rest of his small estate being divided between Bernadette, Martin and Carmel.

All three developers' estimates may be wide of the mark, but the cost was undoubtedly deep in the six-figure stratosphere. One builder looked at the photographs and commented on the high quality of the windowsills, the expensive imported Scandinavian windows and the building's exquisite style.

If Mary Lou is to become Taoiseach, it is highly desirable that she sets out clearly the source of her sudden stroke of good fortune. It would put an end to the inevitable speculation about how the couple funded the dramatic conversions to the house. In September 2021, the *Irish Independent* ranked Mary Lou as the twenty-ninth wealthiest person in Dáil Éireann. Her net worth was estimated at €1.9 million, with the house valued at around €1 million.

Mary Lou and Martin bought and transformed 186 New Cabra Road at a time when she was on her political uppers. If the couple were taking on an albatross of debt in their uncertain financial situation, it was a particularly courageous punt. At the time, Mary Lou was in political limbo, while Sinn Féin had serious problems winning additional Dáil seats. Some jubilant critics had even suggested that, after reaching a high point in the local elections in late 2004, Sinn Féin's Southern section was in terminal decline, as was Mary Lou.

In 2010, Sinn Féin's fortunes in the North were flying, but in the South there had been a steady slide since 2005. Project Mary Lou, so strongly identified with Sinn Féin's entire Southern strategy, was in tatters. She had lost three elections out of four. The question being asked in the party, not so quietly, was whether the anointed one was really the true messiah. In a shamelessly partitionist strategy, she had been chosen as the face of Sinn Féin south of the border. Was she unelectable as a TD?

Worse still, the confidence that the party had enjoyed after the 1998 Good Friday Agreement 'bounce' had faltered in the South. In 2002 Sinn Féin had increased the number of its deputies in Leinster House from one to five. Caoimhghín Ó Caoláin, the border-county republican, was no longer a solitary voice. In the 2004 local elections the party had gained thirty-three seats and Mary Lou had won a stunning victory in the European Parliament battle.

By 2010 all the euphoria had been dissipated by a series of reversals, sporadic bouts of navel-gazing, mutterings of despair and plenty of hard questions. Sinn Féin South resented the domination of Sinn Féin North. Key Dáil seats had been lost, including Seán Crowe's in Dublin South-West in 2007, reducing the Sinn Féin tally to a meagre four TDs. Then, in 2009, Mary Lou had failed in her re-election bid for Europe, while the party's advances in local election seats stalled.

Worse still, the wildly differing agendas of Sinn Féin north and south of the border caused fierce tensions in a party unaccustomed to internal dissent. Perhaps the most obvious example of the contrasting fortunes was in the 2009 European elections. In Northern Ireland, Bairbre de Brún topped the poll; in Dublin, Mary Lou McDonald bit the dust. Dublin was a particular blackspot, where Aengus Ó Snodaigh's position as the only Sinn Féin TD elected in the capital in 2007 flashed yellow warnings.

In Northern Ireland, Sinn Féin's advance seemed unstoppable. In the 2007 Northern Ireland Assembly elections, a year when its Southern comrades were losing ground, it lifted its vote to 26 per cent, against the front-running DUP's 30 per cent.

In the 2010 Westminster elections, Sinn Féin took the biggest vote in Northern Ireland, pipping the DUP by 25.5 per cent to 25 per cent. Its advance was spectacular. It had relegated the SDLP, the party of the late John Hume, into a poor second place in the nationalist heartlands. Sinn Féin was in government. A former IRA chief of staff, Martin McGuinness, was now deputy first minister. He and Adams swept the boards. They were far more popular figures among Northern nationalists than they were among the citizens of the South. What had gone wrong?

Journalist Harry McGee, writing in *The Irish Times* in 2010, traced the origins of Sinn Féin's political setbacks in the South to two incidents in Belfast, back in 2004 and 2005. The first, the Northern Bank robbery in December 2004, was probably the most sensational bank heist in the United Kingdom's history. Raiders stole £26.5 million sterling in cash from the Belfast branch of the Northern Bank. The crime was carried out with military precision. The gang held the families of two keyholders hostage for twenty-four hours. Only one man, Cork financial adviser Ted Cunningham, has ever been convicted for connected offences, but he was later released by Dublin's Court of Appeal. At a retrial, he pleaded guilty to money laundering and received a suspended sentence. The discipline of the perpetrators and the findings of investigators pointed conclusively at the IRA. At a press conference in January 2005, the chief constable of the Police Service of Northern Ireland (PSNI), Hugh Orde, unequivocally held the Provisional IRA responsible for the robbery.

The IRA denied any involvement. Very few people believed them. Indeed, an IRA enforcer, the late Bobby Storey, is widely credited with being the brains behind the operation. The proceeds remain mostly unrecovered, possibly undistributed. Many reports suggest that the robbery was carried out with the specific purpose of providing 'pensions' for IRA veterans, who had been short of income ever since the terrorists' regular robberies had ceased. Others believe that it is a general slush fund to compensate or reward those who have been loyal to the republican cause. Some of the ill-gotten gains were traced across the border within forty-eight hours of the robbery. PSNI sources believe that the bulk of the stolen money is now held outside Northern Ireland.

The Northern Bank robbery strongly indicated that the IRA was still active at a time when all terrorist and criminal activities were supposed to have ceased under the terms of the Good Friday Agreement.

The second incident – the savage murder of Robert McCartney a month later in January 2005 – sent out a similarly ominous message. McCartney, a Roman Catholic nationalist, was murdered by the IRA in Magennis's Bar, a pub in the Short Strand nationalist area of Belfast. The incident began as a bar brawl, when McCartney was first beaten with metal bars and then stabbed to death. His offence was that he had defended a friend who was being viciously attacked by fellow customers. PSNI officers were originally driven out of the area when they arrived to investigate, and a wall of silence followed after they sought statements from seventy-one possible witnesses, who all pleaded that they were in the tiny lavatories at the same time. Before the PSNI arrived, CCTV tapes on the premises were removed, a very careful clean-up was carried out and clothes were burned to remove all evidence.

Robert McCartney's five sisters and his partner, Bridgeen Hagans, previously Sinn Féin supporters, campaigned to discover the truth of Robert's murder and to expose the subsequent cover-up. They brought the case to US President George W. Bush, British Prime Minister Tony Blair and politicians in the South, insisting that a named IRA man, Jock Davison, was responsible for the murder and that Sinn Féin was not doing all it could to help bring the culprits to justice. In March, the IRA, feeling the heat, issued a statement volunteering to shoot the people involved in the murder. Ten years later, in 2015, Jock Davison was shot dead as he left home for work. The sisters announced that their campaign for justice was over. They would have preferred to have seen Davison in the dock.

Harry McGee rightly claimed that these two events 'proved to be lasting setbacks in the South, much more damaging for the party than North of the border'.

Such unsavoury activities north of the border certainly spooked potential Sinn Féin voters in the South. They sent out a message of continued IRA activity, lawlessness, crime and murder happening on their doorstep. A vote for Sinn Féin risked spreading the virus of violence on to the streets of Dublin, Cork, Limerick and Galway.

Gerry Adams, too, was a problem in the eyes of many Southern voters. A Northerner, the president of Sinn Féin was widely assumed to be the IRA commander-in-chief (if not officially chief of staff). In Northern Ireland, the nationalist population increasingly saw him and Martin McGuinness as guarantors of their protection and peace. One person's protector can be another person's antagonist. The huge North–South gulf was being reflected in Sinn Féin's differing geographical voting successes and failures. Adams and McGuinness were Northerners from the military wing. In the South, the failure of Mary Lou McDonald to be elected in 2007 meant that Sinn Féin had no acceptable Southern face to lead in the Dáil and soften up the sometimes fearsome sight of Adams on television screens.

Meanwhile Sinn Féin's socialist wing had been growing impatient. The breakaway left-wing group Éirígí, which included Mary Lou's sister Joanne, had been formed in 2006. Many Éirígí members were from Dublin, where Sinn Féin had been haemorrhaging votes. Sinn Féin's move towards the political centre had disillusioned members on the republican socialist wing. Significant numbers walked.

Elsewhere, republican royalty was in rebellion. Martin Ferris's daughter, Toiréasa, voiced the fears of many party members in the South. In an unusually critical article in *An Phoblacht*, she claimed that the party was in crisis. Echoing the sentiments of some who had joined Éirígí, she wrote that voters in the South regarded Sinn Féin as a 'Northern-based party, irrelevant to the everyday concerns of people in the 26 counties'. The fact that her article was published in *An Phoblacht* suggested that the leadership had a degree of sympathy with her analysis. Sinn Féin was splitting into North–South factions with different ideologies, either republican or socialist.

The 2007 general election reverses were bad. A gesture had been made towards party reorganisation when Mary Lou was appointed vice-president in 2009, but her loss of any democratic mandate after the European elections hugely weakened her position, not only inside the party but also with the general public. Rumours circulated in political circles about her being relegated to a smaller office on the top floor, or even in the attic, of Sinn Féin's headquarters at 44 Parnell Square, Dublin. Some even hinted that Project Mary Lou should become Project Pearse. At least Senator Pearse Doherty had held a public platform in Leinster House since 2007. He was the first ever Sinn Féin senator, and now had a fighting chance of winning a Dáil seat in Donegal South-West at the next election. He was young, articulate, numerate and loyal. Unfortunately for him, he was not a woman. Sinn Féin was in search of a female leader, preferably from the Dublin middle class.

Sinn Féin's Dublin disarray had been fuelled by defections from its own local representatives. Even before the shock resignation of Sinn Féin's longest-serving councillor, Christy Burke, in 2009, the rot had set in among others. Again, Dublin was the problem. After the 2007 general election, a particularly hard-working Sinn Féin councillor, Tony Smithers, from the Ballyfermot/Drimnagh area, resigned, citing the Sinn Féin trademark excuse of 'family' reasons. The resignation had echoes of the reasons so unconvincingly offered by Councillor Nicky Kehoe for his withdrawal as a Dáil candidate in favour of Mary Lou McDonald. Sinn Féin 'families' were beginning to sound peculiarly useful when an exit plot was being hatched.

Tony Smithers was succeeded by the co-option to Dublin City Council of Louise Minihan, one of the younger breed of Sinn Féin left-wingers. Two years later, in 2009, Louise herself left. She gave no such gentle 'family' reasons for her resignation. Louise loudly denounced Sinn Féin, since she 'no longer' believed that it remained 'committed to its stated objective of ending British rule in Ireland and the establishment of an Irish democratic socialist republic'. She warned that 'many genuine activists' would follow her out the door. Louise joined Éirígí. Her exodus was another blow, but the next resignation was a bombshell. The man who had been Mary Lou's political assistant when in Brussels, her nominated replacement for the European Parliament and a Sinn Féin councillor earmarked for greater things, had suffered enough.

Killian Forde had joined Sinn Féin in 2001. He was well educated. Like Mary Lou, he was at Trinity College Dublin but, unlike her, he joined the TCD branch of Sinn Féin while studying for a master's in philosophy. He was left-wing, but not a socialist zealot. He was elected as a Dublin City councillor for Donaghmede in 2004 and was recognised as an upwardly mobile member of the party. He had been an aid worker in the Balkans before becoming a councillor and was talent-spotted by the Sinn Féin hierarchy soon after his arrival in the party. His big break came when, before the 2004 European election, he was appointed as Mary Lou's political assistant. When it became clear that the priority was to get Mary Lou back into the Dáil, Forde was appointed as her first substitute. He needed to learn the ropes of the European Parliament. If Mary Lou had achieved her objective of returning to Dublin with indecent haste, Killian Forde would have automatically succeeded her as an MEP. A rising star in the party, he was similarly middle class. The *Sunday Independent* once dubbed him 'the male Mary Lou'. He had even been the skiing correspondent for *The Irish Times* and had covered this upmarket sport for Newstalk. Just the ticket for the new Sinn Féin.

Killian Forde had given the party plenty of warning of his discontent. In June 2009, before the local and European elections, he had sent a detailed proposal about Sinn Féin's future Dublin strategy to an internal party review that was promised but never happened. He became disillusioned with his own lack of influence on the policies and procedures of the party he had joined. He was particularly concerned about the state of Sinn Féin in Dublin.

Killian Forde's analysis made grim reading. He didn't mince his words, warning of the party's 'critical decline in Dublin'. Sinn Féin was short of electable candidates in the capital. The membership was 'frustrated and tired'. His analysis warned that Sinn Féin would make little progress in the 2011 general election and forecast that Mary Lou herself would not win a seat in Dublin Central. He suggested that Sinn Féin should not even contest her chosen constituency. Little did he know that she and Martin had already sunk a huge amount of political and financial capital into a house in the area.

Forde's proposal that the party should abandon Dublin Central must have gone down like a lead balloon with the Sinn Féin hierarchy. They were reorganising and planning to put huge resources behind Mary Lou once again, despite her dismal performance in Dublin Central in 2007.

Forde advocated that a strong Sinn Féin candidate for the important post of Lord Mayor of Dublin should be fielded and should move into action early. He suggested candidate training for all Sinn Féin hopefuls, believing that the party's structures were designed to smother constructive initiatives, such as his own. He highlighted how the appointment of some people to key positions was bizarre. For example, the person appointed to manage Mary Lou's European re-election campaign, Ross Carmody, a barman who had returned to Ireland from Canada, had no experience in the field. On policy, Forde blasted the party's response to the economic crisis as 'glacial'. He spelled it out warts and all: the party did not tolerate dissent and was governed by a culture of fear. His submission was ignored. Sinn Féin, a party in deep trouble, seemed frozen in time, in denial of all problems, imprisoned by its inability to reconcile the needs of Sinn Féin North and Sinn Féin South.

The man who had observed Mary Lou at close quarters for ten years in Ireland, Northern Ireland and in Strasbourg had become disenchanted. I asked Killian Forde about working with Mary Lou McDonald, as he looked back twelve years later.

Despite differences with her on his departure as her political assistant following his exit from the party in 2010, he says that he felt 'relief' rather than anger. Mary Lou could bring herself to refer to him only as 'that person' at the time. Despite feeling disillusioned and frustrated, Forde was upfront and fair in his assessment. I asked him what Mary Lou was like to work with as an MEP or as an officer of Sinn Féin. He said that she was 'hard-working. She would go anywhere in Ireland to speak to branches of the party.'

In a much earlier interview with Kim Bielenberg of the *Irish Independent* in 2014, Forde had said that 'It was a bit of a nightmare for her when she was running for the European Parliament, because she had small children, and she was also heavily involved in running Sinn Féin.' He had added that 'She probably rose too fast in Sinn Féin. Because she hadn't worked too much at grass roots level, she didn't initially have a great deal of understanding of how politics worked. She was always a very good media performer, but didn't have more than a basic knowledge of economics.'

When I queried the depth of her European ambitions, Forde confirmed Mary Lou's lack of long-term interest: 'Yes, the intention had been for her to move home to Ireland, cutting short her term in Europe and that I would take her place. We tried to keep her here at home as much as possible. She was even considered by the party as a candidate for the Seanad in 2007, after she had failed to win the Dublin Central seat, in order to give her a national platform in Leinster House. In the end we couldn't risk her running, because there was a danger that Sinn Féin might not win the seat.'

Senator Mary Lou was shelved in favour of Senator Pearse Doherty. Sinn Féin didn't want their brightest prospect to be a three-time loser. So they ran Doherty, who comfortably captured a Seanad seat on the Agricultural Panel in 2007 on the first count, following a voting pact with the Labour Party.

Asked if he believed Mary Lou's yarn about the hunger strikers, specifically the death of Bobby Sands, being a convincing source of her republicanism, considering that it had happened nearly twenty years before she joined Sinn Féin, Killian Forde rebuffed my scepticism. 'Actually, I feel the same as her about the hunger strikers. They made a lasting impression on me. I was almost exactly the same age as Mary Lou. I cried when I heard of the death of Bobby Sands. And I didn't join Sinn Féin until I was thirty-two.'

Asked if Mary Lou was really a socialist, Forde said she might be better described as an 'equalitist', a whole new political philosophy and a phrase that I suspect he coined on the spot specifically for her. He was on the money. She is fond of talking about her commitment to equality, but skilfully avoids confirming that she is a disciple of any socialist doctrine.

Forde was complimentary about his former colleague's media savvy. 'She had none of that "the press is out to get us" attitude. She was never afraid to go out to face them. She didn't always take much notice of her brief and was often intellectually lazy. She wasn't interested in detail and regularly ignored seven out of ten of the speaking points she was given.'

Forde says she stayed aloof from the internal argument about the future of Sinn Féin raging in the noughties, especially the problems in the party's Dublin cumainn at the time. Some of the Dublin foot soldiers were disturbed that she didn't side with them. According to Forde, the well-known Glasnevin historian, the late Shane MacThomais, a member of Sinn Féin until he too left the party in 2010, was heard to say disparagingly that she was a WONO, shorthand for a 'woman of no opinion'.

I asked Forde if he had ever felt the long arm of the IRA when he was a Sinn Féin councillor or working with Mary Lou McDonald. 'Only once,' he said. He recalled a radio programme when he had mentioned the so-called 'Green Book', the IRA training and induction manual. Afterwards, a Sinn Féin press officer told him never again to talk about the Green Book on the air. Forde asked: 'Who told you to tell me that?' The press officer pointed to his epaulettes and muttered the word 'army'.

Responding to repeated criticism that Mary Lou was an opportunist with no strong political convictions, Forde defended her, asserting that in his experience she was always uncompromising on both racism and sexism. 'She took both of them seriously and stamped on a few Sinn Féin canvassers who were believed to be playing footsie with the racist agenda in pursuit of votes.' In another example of his former colleague's deeply held beliefs, Forde recalled accompanying her to a private meeting with the Israeli ambassador in Dublin. It was meant to be a below-the-radar exchange of views, no fireworks, no cameras, no press statement afterwards. Over tea and biscuits, she suddenly exploded about Israel's behaviour, its inhuman treatment of the Palestinians and the Israeli army's brutality. The ambassador was shell-shocked by her passionate, spontaneous outburst. It was not a piece of theatricality for the cameras, at which she normally excelled; there were none. Unannounced and unexpectedly, she simply tore into the man.

Forde provided many insights into the way Mary Lou thought and worked. He parted company with Sinn Féin in January 2010. Three days later he joined the Labour Party. Of his farewell, he says, 'I met Eoin Ó Broin in a café to tell him I was leaving. A very civil meeting. When it was announced in the media, I received a number of calls from Sinn Féin asking me to reconsider. I didn't hear from Mary Lou, but I didn't expect to.'

When Forde left Sinn Féin, he had correctly diagnosed some fundamental problems. He was fearful of a catastrophic general election result in 2011, followed by the party's terminal decline.

Forde's concerns were well founded. Mary Lou's general election flop in 2007, followed by her 2009 European re-election loss, required a rethink in Sinn Féin. There was little sign of it. The leadership appeared to be digging in. In August, fully two months after the party's serious electoral defeats and following a wave of councillor resignations, a meeting – dubbed a 'party think-in' – was held in the Ardboyne Hotel in Navan.

It was a post-mortem dressed up as a hive of activity. The consequence was business as usual. The leadership appeared to be still in denial. Gerry Adams flatly refused to accept that there was any rift between Northern and Southern Sinn Féin. Martin McGuinness blamed the media for exaggerating the importance of the loss of councillors. In a significant move, they appointed Mary Lou McDonald as party spokesperson against the second Lisbon Treaty referendum. According to media reports at the time, party insiders raised questions about the wisdom of appointing her, a vice-president of the party without a democratic mandate, to such a pivotal role. The *Irish Examiner* revealed that she 'rejected the suggestion that she should step aside and again blamed the media for the way her position was portrayed'.

Mary Lou's star was in the twilight zone, but Adams and McGuinness were still backing her. Just seven days after her European election defeat, she had been entrusted with establishing a 'Task Force for Unity'. At the press launch she was joined by Senator Pearse Doherty, a man who had leapfrogged her in the parliamentary pecking order. He was a senator; she was a citizen with the title of Sinn Féin vice-president, but with no popular endorsement.

In a surprise message after the Ardboyne meeting, the leadership was defiant. There would be no change in the party's dismissive attitude towards its Dáil deputies. They would not be given a greater role in Sinn Féin's operations. The existing system – of allowing unelected officers to dominate its policies and its decision-making – would continue.

Mary Lou must have breathed a sigh of relief. She had been granted a reprieve. She retained the number two spot and she would lead on Lisbon; the TDs would remain puppets of the party officers. She knew that she would now need to stick closer than ever to Adams and McGuinness or else she would become yesterday's woman.

Perhaps the picture on the front page of the next edition of *An Phoblacht* told the true story. It came straight from the Ardboyne think-in. The top four people were still in favour: Gerry Adams, Martin McGuinness, Bairbre de Brún and Caoimhghín Ó Caoláin. Clinging on by her fingertips was Mary Lou McDonald. A sixth figure appeared in the picture; tucked in at the back was the flavour of the month, the man who was appearing at the top table with increasing frequency, Senator Pearse Doherty.

The message on the front page, beside the picture, read: 'Sinn Féin must be rooted, relevant and republican.' And then, in smaller print: 'Activists discuss future political strategy.' Two stale clichés, but, decoded, they revealed that Sinn Féin in the South was in trouble; loyal readers must trust the same team with the same agenda to pull them out of it. It was a tall order.

Mary Lou, the leading voice against the Lisbon Treaty, was damaged goods. A letter to the *Irish Examiner* from Erin McGreehan of Dundalk, later to become a Fianna Fáil senator, summed up the views of many commentators at the time. Headed 'SF loses face in struggle to elect Mary Lou', it pulled no punches:

> In 2007 she failed in her bid to become a TD and has now failed to become an MEP. It seems the Sinn Féin leadership is intent on her acquiring an elected post regardless of the cost to its hardworking councillors.
>
> When will the Sinn Féin leadership realise that a policy of 'all style and no substance with regard to Ms. McDonald' will not wash with the public and is clearly not washing any more with their own councillors?
>
> SF desperately wants her in some elected position in the Republic. If she doesn't achieve this, she won't have any authority as the party's 'voice of opposition' on the Lisbon Treaty referendum rerun. The reality is that she no longer has a mandate to speak on important political issues. The sooner SF realizes this, the better for everyone.

The knives were out for Mary Lou. External critics and internal loyalists alike were asking why Gerry Adams was so politically infatuated by a woman with such a poor election record. Some of the press began to ask if Adams himself was the real problem. Maurice Hayes, a former Independent senator and the Northern Ireland Ombudsman, asked in an *Irish Independent* article if Adams was now a handicap? Andrew Lynch in the *Evening Herald*, predicting that Mary Lou might be past her sell-by date, openly sought Adams's retirement.

Inside Sinn Féin, there was not a murmur. Both politicians stood firm. If they were going to swing, they would swing together. Adams was going nowhere. Nor was Mary Lou.

She was fast out of the traps following the Ardboyne Hotel powwow of Sinn Féin insiders. A press statement from her hit the news desks immediately, announcing that Sinn Féin would be fighting a 'vigorous campaign' for a second No to the Lisbon Treaty. Her statement denounced the government's failure to broker a better deal with Europe after the defeat of the first referendum just sixteen months earlier. She condemned Brian Cowen's refusal to implement the mandate he had been given for changes to the treaty. The script was big into rhetoric about right-wing economic policies, low into argument about the treaty itself. The real message was subliminal: Mary Lou, despite everything, remained the party's standard-bearer in the South.

By opposing the treaty, Mary Lou was on another loser. The No side had pulled off a mighty coup in June 2008 with a 53.4 per cent to 46.6 per cent win. Nobody expected a repeat. The situation in 2009 was dramatically different. Europe and the world had plunged deeper into an economic crisis following the collapse of the banking system. People were fearful for their futures and preferred what they saw as the relative safety of a larger Europe over possible isolation. Ireland's national self-confidence was shot. The shadow of the infamous bank guarantee of September 2008 hung over the financial system. The European Union was suddenly a safer haven than the unknown. The mood was downbeat; the citizens were rattled.

Mary Lou launched Sinn Féin's doomed campaign. As with so many European contests, it was not fought on specifically European issues; personalities and national matters surfaced. Mary Lou took a fair amount of flak. She was mocked for her poor attendance when she was an MEP. She was ridiculed for her strange right-wing allies against Lisbon, including the United Kingdom Independence Party (UKIP), an assortment of British right-wingers led by Nigel Farage, a man who had actually opposed the Northern Ireland peace process. Three years later, in 2012, Mary Lou and Farage actually appeared together on a Today FM programme chaired by Matt Cooper, both calling for a No vote against the EU Fiscal Treaty. Matt Cooper recalls a bit of pre-programme reluctance from Mary Lou: 'In fairness to her, she was very uncomfortable at being seated next to him – my producer at the time had some persuading to do.'

In 2019 Farage used clips of Mary Lou's speeches in the European Parliament to support UKIP's European election campaign in the UK. It seems that he found the common ground politically useful. She was embarrassed by any association with him.

Sinn Féin was even reunited for the No campaign with some of its own defectors to the republican socialist group Éirígí. All the mainstream parties, including Labour, were on the Yes side. Sinn Féin benefited as the only party against the treaty, fishing alone in a large pool where a significant mixture of citizens were still against further integration with Europe. Serious argument was lacking, but Mary Lou did battle in some high-profile personal exchanges. Most notably, former European Parliament president Pat Cox called Sinn Féin 'vulgar hypocrites' for refusing to accept guarantees from Europe under a process that the party had welcomed at the time of the Good Friday Agreement. Mary Lou hit back, declaring that the attacks from Cox were 'ironic, particularly coming from a vulgar lobbyist'.

It was a low-life, bog-standard campaign, highly personalised.

Micheál Martin, Fianna Fáil's foreign minister, was not afraid to mix it with Gerry Adams, accusing him of 'playing poker' with the nation's future. Sinn Féin put intimidating pickets on some Fianna Fáil local campaign launches. There were even scuffles, notably at the ploughing championships in Athy, County Kildare.

On polling day, 2 October, the result was a resounding victory for the Yes side. They overturned the first Lisbon triumph of 53.4 per cent to 46.6 per cent in favour of the No side, converting it into a landslide 67.1 per cent to 32.9 per cent for the Yes supporters. Mary Lou will have nervously noticed that Pearse Doherty's county of Donegal was the only one to vote No. Another feather in the golden boy's cap. But she did not take the Lisbon loss lying down. Typically, she came out fighting, accusing the big parties of success-ful scaremongering: 'You had a situation,' she declared, 'where not just the government but the opposition parties too and others sent a very clear message to people which was as follows: "If you're unemployed, there will be no jobs if Lisbon goes down. And if you're fearful about your job or about your economic future, you've no option but to vote this treaty through." And I think not alone was that an inaccurate message. I believe that it was a very dishonourable message to deliver to people who feel very vulnerable. But it seems to have worked.'

She was on the button about the reasons for the spectacular U-turn in public opinion, but the sour grapes were unbecoming. She had her back to the wall throughout the campaign. The big battalions, the entire Irish establishment, including the employers' group IBEC and the Irish Congress of Trade Unions, had all backed the Yes side, although a few trade unions dissented. Nonetheless, the size of the defeat, by a margin of just over two to one, was another blow to Mary Lou's standing. Yet she had stamina in plenty. Unfazed and unbowed, her eyes immediately refocused on the next hurdle.

The bear pit beckoned. Dublin Central, the source of so much pain in the last three years, came back into Mary Lou McDonald's sights. The year 2009 had been her *annus horribilis*; she had failed to retain her European seat; now she had lost Lisbon and she was not even certain where she would fit into the Sinn Féin organisation when she reported for duty. She was the highest office holder in the South and the party's vice-president, but if she could not win a popular vote, she might be surplus to requirements. In the meantime, she rallied to the side of her patron and protector, Gerry Adams, suddenly facing a potentially fatal challenge.

In early December 2009, UTV's *Insight* programme alleged that Gerry Adams's younger brother, Liam, had sexually abused his own daughter, Áine, for a decade. Áine told *Insight* that the abuse had begun when she was only four years old.

Gerry Adams told *Insight* that he had known about these serious allegations for twenty-two years. He believed them. In the intervening period Liam Adams had been an active member of Sinn Féin in Louth. It was even reported in the *Dundalk Democrat* that he had unsuccessfully sought the Sinn Féin nomination for the Louth constituency in 1997. Gerry Adams says he prevented the nomination from going ahead. He also says that he removed his brother from Sinn Féin when he discovered that he was an active member. He never told anyone in Sinn Féin about the allegations against his brother.

Gerry Adams maintained that he had become estranged from his brother for about fifteen years after he learned of the allegations in 1987. There is plenty of evidence that they met during those years, including Gerry's attendance at Liam's wedding to his second wife (he and Áine's mother were separated) in the middle of this supposed estrangement.

In December 2009 Liam Adams was on the run from the PSNI to avoid twenty-three sex abuse charges. Gerry Adams appealed to Liam to give himself up to the police.

Gerry Adams had serious questions to answer. How did he

allow Liam to continue as an active member of Sinn Féin when he knew him to be a paedophile? If, as he told *Insight*, he had been estranged from Liam for fifteen years, how then did he attend Liam's second wedding in Bellingham Castle Hotel in County Louth ten years after they were supposedly 'estranged'? He claimed that he had 'dumped' his brother out of the Louth Sinn Féin operation as soon as he had learned about the abuse of his daughter. How then did Liam subsequently – in 1997– chair the fortieth anniversary commemoration for five IRA men killed by their own bomb in Edentubber, County Louth? Liam even later became involved in Sinn Féin party activities in the Felons Club, Andersonstown, west Belfast – Gerry's constituency – without formally joining the party. Gerry Adams said he didn't know about these activities at the time, but found out about them only in December 2009. He also knew that his brother was involved in various youth projects in west Belfast, hardly a pursuit suitable for a paedophile. After taking refuge in the South, Liam was finally extradited to Northern Ireland in 2011 and was sentenced to prison in 2013 for sixteen years for raping his daughter. He died in custody in 2019.

Suzanne Breen of the *Belfast Telegraph* summed up the feelings of most politicians throughout the island. In a powerful opinion piece on Gerry Adams's behaviour following Liam Adams's final conviction in 2013, she proclaimed: 'The Louth TD [which Gerry Adams then was] continues to cling on to the reins of power, but it is impossible to believe that any other political leader on this island would survive such a damning history.'

How did he survive?

Where was Mary Lou McDonald in late 2009 when the party needed a courageous voice to demand explanations of the leader? Where were Martin McGuinness, Bairbre de Brún, Caoimhghín Ó Caoláin, Pearse Doherty, but, above all, Adams's vice-president? Where was the custodian of Sinn Féin's moral conscience? No such person existed.

It was a measure of Adams's power over the party that there was not a hint of a challenge to his leadership. The wagons were circled, even in the face of a poisonous sex abuse scandal.

On 20 December, Gerry Adams revealed on RTÉ television that his late father had 'emotionally, physically and sexually abused' members of their large family. On the same day, a statement was issued from the 'Adams family' confirming their father's abuse.

On Christmas Eve, Mary Lou stepped in and defended her leader, sponsor, patron and protector. She claimed that he had acted correctly in dealing with the allegations of abuse against his brother. 'I'm absolutely satisfied,' she insisted grandly, 'that Gerry acted to the very best of his abilities throughout all of this. I know that Gerry cares about Áine and that he acted in her interest as her uncle. I am satisfied that, as a public figure, any of the questions that have arisen – and legitimately arisen – have been answered by him fully and frankly.'

Such a generous pardon. Mary Lou had chosen to forget a speech she herself had made barely one month earlier. Following publication of the Murphy Report into clerical child sex abuse, she concentrated her anger on those who had failed to show willingness to uncover the scandal: 'It is especially damning,' she had thundered, 'that the State authorities facilitated the cover-up and allowed the Church to be beyond the reach of the law. Senior gardaí, up to and including the level of commissioner, repeatedly turned a blind eye to crimes of clerical sexual abuse.' And then, with a phrase that might have made even the shameless Gerry Adams wince, she had protested with passion, 'Anyone, including gardaí, found to be complicit in the cover-up of child abuse must be arrested and made to face the full rigours of the law.'

Where did that leave Gerry?

Imagine if the boot had been on the other foot. If it had been a Fianna Fáil or Fine Gael Taoiseach in the same bind, Mary Lou would have been rightly causing uproar, demanding an immediate resignation. Even if she had wanted to raise questions, she was in no position to do so. Politically, she was a busted flush, depending on Adams to keep her afloat. It was not the last time that she would be prepared to defend the devil's work.

Sinn Féin was behaving like a cult. It demanded blind allegiance to the leader; it required secrecy. It had a chief who was president of the party, North and South, with influence over its supposedly defunct private army. He was consequently omnipotent. *An Phoblacht*'s next edition, on 7 January 2010, issued a sturdy defence of its party's president. A piece appeared headed 'Tragic Tale of Sexual Abuse'. It spun a narrative of a media witch-hunt against Adams. It sought justice for Áine and looked forward to the issue being dealt with through the courts. Below the official Sinn Féin message there was the 'Statement issued by the Adams family' already carried elsewhere. The general media may have given Sinn Féin and Adams a roasting, but the party stood loyal, down to the last volunteer.

Meanwhile Mary Lou McDonald took up an administrative position in Sinn Féin, carrying the party's united Ireland message across Ireland, to Northern Ireland and to the UK. She doubled down on the constituency work, determined to make a final assault on her Cabra base and on Dublin Central. In early 2010 her opponents noticed that her personal appearances in the constituency were increasing at a remarkable speed. She was making sure she was noticed. According to one of her rivals, she specialised in grand entrances into local residents' association meetings, as though making a 'Here I am' announcement each time. She was keeping her new mansion under wraps, living in her humbler local rented house for more than two years, up until polling day in the general election.

In March 2010, once again it was Mary Lou, not Pearse Doherty, who led off at the Sinn Féin ard fheis. Despite her setbacks, she was still given the prime media spot. Adams's strategy was unchanged long term. He was unshaken in his conviction that she was still the ideal face of a Southern Sinn Féin leader. The non-believers held their tongues, just as they had done over Liam Adams's paedophilia.

Many Sinn Féin members silently favoured Pearse Doherty in the looming succession stakes. One former Sinn Féin TD told me that Pearse was way ahead of Mary Lou in popularity among the troops, but added ominously that such matters were not decided by the ordinary members. Besides that, he asserted that while Mary Lou was regarded as an election agent's nightmare in Cabra, Pearse was seen as a certainty in Donegal.

Pearse Doherty was about to be tested. A by-election in his home territory of Donegal South-West had been delayed for many months by a Fianna Fáil/Green government that was anticipating a defeat. Agitation for the writ to be moved in the Dáil in May had been thwarted by the coalition, but in July Doherty took them to the High Court. He was granted a judicial review. On 2 November the court ruled that the delay was unprecedented and unreasonable. As a constituent, Doherty's constitutional rights had been breached. Judge Nicholas Kearns ordered that the by-election should be held 'soon'.

The High Court win was a boost for Sinn Féin and a triumph for Pearse Doherty. The by-election was called for 25 November. The conditions for an opposition walk in the park were ideal. On 18 November, just a week before polling day, the delegation from the International Monetary Fund arrived in Ireland with an austerity programme in its back pocket. Ireland was humiliated. On polling day, the Fianna Fáil vote in Donegal South-West collapsed from 50.53 per cent in the 2007 general election to 21.33 per cent in 2010, partly in response to the nation's shame. Pearse Doherty coasted home with nearly 40 per cent of the first-preference vote. The former councillor and former senator was now Deputy Pearse Doherty. Mary Lou, a loser for the European Parliament and the Dáil, was citizen Mary Lou.

Two days before polling, Taoiseach Brian Cowen had announced that he would call a general election early in 2011. His government was on its last legs.

The general election was a couple of months away. Pearse Doherty was a red-hot certainty. Mary Lou was, at best, an even money shot. Sinn Féin insiders were fearful that she would lose again. If Pearse was elected and Mary Lou lost, he would be the outstanding candidate to lead them in the next Dáil. He was only thirty-four, but none of the sitting Sinn Féin TDs matched his eloquence, his fluency or his familiarity with the nation's crippled finances. However, there was another surprising twist in the Sinn Féin story to be sprung.

Ten days before the Donegal South-West by-election, Arthur Morgan, Sinn Féin's sitting TD for Louth, announced that he was stepping down at the next election. On RTÉ's *Morning Ireland* programme he waffled on about the Dáil being a 'very stuffy and very restrictive place'.

I choked on my cornflakes. Anyone who had any contact with Arthur would know that he loved the entire Dáil set-up. He was no superstar in the chamber, but he relished the camaraderie and the craic. He was possibly the only Sinn Féin TD, except for Waterford's David Cullinane, who regularly appeared in the members' bar. He broke the Sinn Féin boycott on the Holy of Holies at will. I spent many hours in the bar discussing Arthur's escapades with him. In return, I would tell him about my mother, an unapologetic English monarchist, and about her work in Bletchley Park as a decoder, helping the British war effort against the Nazis. He would regale Finian McGrath and me with the hilarious, but friendly, exchanges he had enjoyed with British Conservatives since his election to the Dáil. Arthur humanised Sinn Féin.

I didn't for a second believe Arthur's sudden story of how he had never intended to stay long in the Dáil. Then I heard him tell the media how he was going back to the 'family' business. There was an echo of other Sinn Féin stalwarts, like Nicky Kehoe and Councillor Tony Smithers, who offered 'family' reasons for their exits. I smelled a rat. Arthur held one of Sinn Féin's only four safe seats in the Dáil. He was a very sprightly fifty-six.

Less than a week later the penny dropped. Sinn Féin announced that it had found a new candidate to replace Arthur Morgan in Louth. Arthur had made way for Gerry Adams. Sinn Féin do not make big moves without meticulous preparation. Why Adams?

At first sight the decision seemed strange. Everyone knew that Sinn Féin's TDs were already puppets of Adams. He had been the controller of the entire republican movement for over thirty years. He moved Sinn Féin and IRA members around the island like pieces on a chessboard. He didn't need to be in the Dáil to control the deputies. He would have to give up his seats at Westminster and in the Stormont Assembly. There was always the danger that he might not hold Arthur Morgan's seat. Gerry might be a cult figure, but Arthur had put in the hard graft as a councillor before finally winning his passage to the Dáil. And there was still the unsavoury stink of Liam Adams's child abuse scandal and its effect on Gerry's standing. But Sinn Féin had undoubtedly carried out extensive polling in Louth. Gerry Adams would have been topping the poll by a distance in their research, far outstripping Arthur Morgan's tally. He was a hero in republican border counties. He was home and hosed.

On 15 November, when announcing his decision to enter the fray, Adams gave economic policy as the reason for his candidacy. It was unconvincing. Economics was never his strongest suit. He was a plodder on the dismal science. There was a far bigger game at play. The Sinn Féin Dáil team desperately needed strengthening. Pearse Doherty was not the right face for the posters in the South. He was able, but border county. He was neither Dublin, nor female, both characteristics being sought by the leadership. Nor was Gerry, but he could keep the seat warm for someone who answered that description. Sinn Féin insiders were seriously apprehensive about Mary Lou's future. If she was to lose once again in Dublin Central and Pearse Doherty was to win once more in Donegal, he would be unstoppable as the face of Southern Sinn Féin. He would be on the box every night from the Dáil chamber.

Flushed with Doherty's by-election success, there was enthusiasm for him among the euphoric ranks of many Sinn Féin loyalists, accompanied by excitement in the media. Mary Lou was an uncomfortable spectator in the weeks after his triumph. When Adams launched his election campaign in Louth, it was Pearse Doherty who was chosen as the first speaker to introduce his leader. Mary Lou followed.

Just before Christmas, on 19 December, journalist Eamon Keane put his finger in the wound. In his *Sunday Independent* column, he referred to 'The new world of the clean-cut, articulate Sinn Féin, as embodied by Donegal TD Pearse Doherty'. He went on to spell it out, writing that 'Pearse Doherty is the new Mary Lou McDonald. Personable, sellable and articulate, Mary Lou was mooted to be the new head of the party at one stage. Pearse would do well to remember how Mary Lou's career stalled.' Keane was practically writing her off, a lesson to Pearse Doherty of how Sinn Féin superstars could be history if they faltered.

But Adams kept the faith. The grand strategy and the political infatuation remained intact. He had stepped into the breach. He was one of the few big names in the party who was known north and south. His presence as party leader in the Dáil would ensure that Doherty's career, not Mary Lou's, would be put on hold if she was not elected. Everyone recognised Doherty's immense talents, but he did not fit in with the long-term Adams vision. And Adams knew that if he himself was the leader in Leinster House, he would have absolute power over day-to-day matters, like who took the top media spots. More importantly, he would control the succession.

Mary Lou could only watch and wonder, work her obstinate

constituency, appear at the press conferences alongside Doherty and write a regular, but uninspiring, column in *An Phoblacht*. She lived in the shadow of Pearse Doherty throughout the period leading up to the February election. She was diminished as a national figure. As Deaglán de Bréadún had already written a few months earlier, 'Just at the point when this minority party most needs a voice and a talking head to put its case and win over middle-ground voters, there is nobody on the scene. McDonald does her best but lacks the credibility and confidence that elected office brings.' He goes on to comment on Pearse Doherty: 'intelligent and articulate as he is, Doherty lacks that crucial "Middle Ireland" appeal that Sinn Féin needs'.

Gerry Adams TD was the interim solution. When Brian Cowen announced in December that he would be seeking a dissolution early in the new year, the campaign had begun early. He headed for Áras an Uachtaráin on 1 February, when President Higgins formally dissolved the Dáil and named 25 February as election day.

The only serious question about the election was which combination of parties would replace Fianna Fáil and the Greens. The economic collapse and the associated ignominy was set to crush the coalition. Fianna Fáil was running third behind Fine Gael and Labour in most public opinion polls.

Some polls had even put Sinn Féin ahead of Fianna Fáil, but the campaign started badly for Gerry Adams. Wikileaks disclosures in early December revealed that both Adams and the Sinn Féin leadership knew about the Northern Bank robbery before it happened in 2004. Fianna Fáil threw the book at Sinn Féin, reminding them and the voters of the IRA's murder of Robert McCartney. Adams was constantly on the back foot, denying any foreknowledge of the Northern Bank heist and repeating that he had never been a member of the IRA. Almost nobody believed either assertion.

Sinn Féin had hoped that these murky memories were fading. They issued a manifesto that hardly mentioned Northern Ireland, aiming to fight the election as the voice of the underdog, opposing all possible austerity measures enforced by the IMF. They wanted to be seen as the alternative to Labour on the left.

All parties in opposition to the Fianna Fáil–Green coalition were destined to make healthy gains. The real question was whether Fine Gael would win an overall majority on its own or be forced to enter coalition with Labour. Sinn Féin had only an outside chance of being in the shake-up for government formation, but the number of seats they gained would be important. All the major parties said they were hell-bent against any coalition deal with Adams.

Sinn Féin remained political pariahs. More significant to them was the fate of Mary Lou, as pivotal to their future direction. If she lost in this election, it would be her third defeat in a Dáil contest. Even Gerry Adams might have found it hard to rescue her.

While Mary Lou kept out of many of the controversies, her own position was the focus of much attention. Kathy Sheridan in *The Irish Times* suggested that she had been marginalised at a Sinn Féin campaign press conference. Describing the media event when the hustings had only two and a half weeks to go, she wrote that 'Gerry Adams was flanked by new fair-haired boy Pearse Doherty and Caoimhghín Ó Caoláin. On the cold side of the three – on the fringe to Doherty's right – stands Mary Lou McDonald, the party's vice-president, carrying off the cool, elegant, grande dame look with a well-coiffed head and glittery, multi-stranded necklace. It's forty minutes into the press conference before she gets a word in, which may or may not mean something.'

It did. At the same press conference, Pearse Doherty received a round of applause from all forty-one Sinn Féin candidates present when Gerry Adams sang his praises for his competence on financial issues.

The Dublin Central electorate should have proved easier prey for Mary Lou than in 2007. Bertie Ahern had retired, leaving his efficient machine disabled. There was definitely one, possibly two, seats up for grabs. Paschal Donohoe's strong by-election performance (when he was runner-up) almost guaranteed him one of the seats. Joe Costello of Labour was thought to be certain, reflecting the soaring Labour vote nationally. The 'Tony Gregory' candidate, Maureen O'Sullivan, was expected to romp home after her by-election victory. The last seat was between three women: Mary Lou, Fianna Fáil's articulate anti-Bertie Fianna Fáil candidate, Mary Fitzpatrick, and Labour's second candidate, Áine Clancy. Mary Lou was destined for the fight of her life. She was still a relative blow-in to the area; she was still not transfer-friendly. She had passed the 2009 by-election poisoned chalice to Christy Burke, now an Independent and certain to take precious republican first preferences from her; she would lose votes to Cieran Perry, the Independent from her own Cabra home territory. At least she would have a valuable mansion to retire to if all failed.

On the other hand, her workload in the constituency had increased, helped by her enforced presence in Ireland. She needed the Sinn Féin vote to rise nationally to carry her over the line.

It was a long count. Fine Gael's Paschal Donohoe topped the poll just short of a quota with 6,903, followed by Labour's Joe Costello with 6,273. Mary Lou came in third on the first count with 4,526 votes, well behind the two leading runners, with Maureen O'Sullivan fourth on 4,139 and Mary Fitzpatrick in fifth place with 3,504. The Fianna Fáil vote – now without Bertie – had fallen by 30 per cent. Labour had picked up half of it, while Paschal had attracted 10 per cent. Mary Lou had gained only 4 per cent of it. On subsequent counts she was overtaken by Maureen O'Sullivan. On the final count she was the last person elected without reaching the quota, 844 votes ahead of Fianna Fáil's Mary Fitzpatrick.

A sigh of relief must have been heard in Louth. In Dundalk, Gerry Adams, vilified by the press, barely out of his recent quagmire with his paedophile brother, the man who was a constant reminder of the Northern Troubles to the Southern electorate, had topped the poll, with the third highest vote in the country. Apart from Mary Lou's success, Sinn Féin had won an extra nine seats to return a total of fourteen, a net gain of ten.

This was a new high point of Mary Lou's career. She had been in pursuit of a Dáil seat for over ten years. She had shown persistence, stamina and courage. And cowardice too. At times during that decade, there were rumours of despair in the McDonald camp as all looked lost. At the first sitting of the new Dáil, she was accompanied to Leinster House by her happy mother and her husband. She had Gerry Adams, above all, to thank for not abandoning her after so many serious setbacks. She was deeply in his debt. In the coming years she was to repay that loyalty, shamelessly defending the indefensible.

On the surface it looked like a very good result for Sinn Féin. Professor Yvonne Galligan of Queen's University Belfast, writing a report and analysis for the Electoral Reform Society, generously called it 'a triumph for a party that had faced the electorate with just four TDs, one of whom stood aside to enable party leader Gerry Adams to contest in the border constituency of Louth. Party deputy leader Mary Lou McDonald finally won a seat in the competitive Dublin Central constituency.'

On the surface, Professor Galligan's positive verdict on Sinn Féin's achievement is numerically correct, but it may be a trifle simplistic. It was possibly the easiest Irish election ever fought by any opposition party. The Greens were wiped out, losing all six seats. Fianna Fáil dropped fifty-seven seats, down to just twenty, while Labour picked up seventeen and Fine Gael added twenty-five. Even the loosely grouped 'Others' gobbled up more seats than Sinn Féin, adding fourteen seats to their total of nineteen.

While Fianna Fáil and the Greens lost 27 per cent of the vote between them, Sinn Féin picked up only 3 per cent, to finish at just under 10 per cent. Labour jumped from 10 per cent to 19.5 per cent, Independents added 6.9 per cent to 12.1 per cent, and Fine Gael increased by 9 per cent to 36 per cent. The story of the election was of the massacre of Fianna Fáil and the wipeout of the Greens. Their downfall provided easy pickings for any party in opposition. Professor Galligan rightly pointed out that Sinn Féin remained transfer-toxic. They were the least successful group in extracting flesh from the coalition's carcass.

For the nation, long term, the most significant result was when Mary Lou squeezed into the Dáil on the final count in Dublin Central. If she had failed again, Irish history might have needed to be rewritten. Project Mary Lou had received the kiss of life.

CHAPTER 7

A STAR TAKES THE
DÁIL BY STORM

Mary Lou's election to the Dáil in 2011, along with thirteen other Sinn Féin deputies, did not fill many longer-serving TDs with undiluted joy. However, most sitting politicians had overcome any ingrained prejudices against newcomers whose parties were only recent converts to democracy.

We just had to suck it up. Sinn Féin were there to stay in Leinster House, albeit still in small numbers. Those elected had a mandate from the people. They may not have fulfilled their opponents' worst fears in the general election, but they could no longer all be dismissed as apologists for terrorism. A personal liking for Arthur Morgan on all sides of the chamber and a grudging respect for Pearse Doherty's abilities after his four years in the Seanad had helped to reduce hostilities. Shinner or not, Pearse had talent aplenty and was easy enough to get along with. The new Sinn Féin intake didn't have horns and were not all former IRA volunteers. Sinn Féin's fourteen TDs were enough to give them critical mass, speaking rights and, crucially, places on key Dáil and Seanad committees.

Mary Lou and I were elected to the Dáil on the same day. I

remember meeting her at its first sitting and exchanging warm congratulations. Like many others, I had a sneaking regard for her, not because she was a rebel from Rathgar, but because I had followed her career from a distance ever since she had won her seat in the European Parliament in 2004. It had been all downhill for her since then. She had lost her European seat and failed to win a Dáil contest in the intervening years. But she was admirably dogged – she never gave up. I did not know enough about the inner manoeuvres of Sinn Féin to be aware of the benefits she had reaped from Adams's unswerving political patronage; but still, she had finally arrived. She was a fact of life, a fixture in Leinster House.

As far back as 2000, Mary Lou had been earmarked for greatness, was then nearly written off as a loser, but was now finally in the citadel of power. Europe, the scene of her only previous triumph, was a story of five lost years. In 2011 she was starting again where she had hoped to be nine years earlier, when she had fought a hopeless fight for a seat in Dublin West.

Even before Mary Lou arrived in the Dáil, my own icy relationship with Sinn Féin had thawed. Apart from the friendly fire with Arthur Morgan and Pearse Doherty, I had met Caoimhghín Ó Caoláin as a colleague on the British–Irish Parliamentary Body (a talking shop for Irish and British parliamentarians) and – to my surprise – I discovered I liked Aengus Ó Snodaigh. Martin Ferris, the IRA Army Council member now a TD, had always been disarmingly delightful. They had been understandably suspicious of a British public school 'Prod' who had once wanted to lock them all up, but sporadic dialogue meant that the mutual distrust had been breaking down.

Emboldened by this better relationship and knowing that Sinn Féin and my Independent Dáil group were both destined for opposition to the Fine Gael and Labour coalition, I approached Aengus Ó Snodaigh with a proposal. Modesty not being my strongest suit, I asked him if Sinn Féin would propose my name for the chair of the

Dáil's most influential body, the Public Accounts Committee (PAC), when it kicked off a few weeks later. By tradition, the chair of the PAC, which is mandated to examine public spending and hold powerful mandarins to account, has always been given by governments to a member of the largest opposition party. In 2011, that meant that Fine Gael and Labour would probably support a Fianna Fáil nominee.

I had already been fortunate enough to secure my own Independent group's only place on the PAC. Aengus looked a bit surprised at the request. Sinn Féin had one seat on the committee as well, which they had allocated to Mary Lou. My request signalled that I would need her to propose me for the chair. The Fine Gael–Labour coalition would nominate a Fianna Fáil candidate. John McGuinness was the chosen one, because Micheál Martin wanted to keep him sweet, busy and out of his hair. Aengus Ó Snodaigh said he would come back to me with an answer. I knew what he was thinking: why not the other way round? Why should I not nominate Mary Lou for the chair?

A few days before the first meeting of the PAC, I met Pearse Doherty. He brought good news: Mary Lou would be proposing me for the chair of the committee. We knew we could not win because every other TD present would be a member of one of the three big parties – Fianna Fáil, Fine Gael or Labour. All their deputies would be whipped into line to support McGuinness. It was simply worth making the point that the larger parties divvied up the spoils. Traditionally, the PAC worked under the pretence that members were above politics. The committee was sniffy about divisions and never had votes. We resolved to force a vote so that people would realise how the job, with its €10,000 a year allowance, had been stitched up between the three main parties.

The PAC held its first meeting on 15 June 2011, nearly four months after the general election. The event had been well flagged. I had quietly alerted members of the media that there would be two candidates, John McGuinness and me. Everyone had arrived on time, except Mary Lou. I looked around, a trifle nervous. Where was the famous Sinn Féin military discipline? The meeting had not begun, yet it was already well past the scheduled starting time.

Ted McEnery, the clerk to the committee, decided to fire ahead because there was no requirement that all members should be present. I began to stress a little. I would look like a proper idiot without a proposer. Where *was* Mary Lou? The three big parties' TDs were all present. They sensed a bloodless triumph and an opponent with egg all over his face.

The clock was ticking. I could not make an SOS phone call to Mary Lou since there was no mobile coverage from the meeting room in the dungeons of Leinster House. I could not leave the room because the nomination of McGuinness would then be passed unopposed in seconds, in the absence of both Mary Lou and me. I wondered if I had been betrayed by Sinn Féin, in revenge for all those years of political abuse that I had heaped all over them in the 1980s and '90s?

Ted McEnery looked around and opened the proceedings. I could feel a cold sweat: still no sign of Mary Lou.

The clerk sought nominations. I hesitated, paralysed by my isolation. Fianna Fáil's Michael McGrath proposed McGuinness. I relaxed a little because he would probably take a few minutes to sing the praises of his candidate. A breathing space beckoned.

Fianna Fáil are no innocents. McGrath began: 'I propose the name of John McGuinness to be chairman of the committee.'

I waited for the eulogy. McGrath stopped in his tracks. End of proposal. He wanted to go straight to the vote. And still there was no Mary Lou.

McEnery looked around again. He asked innocently, 'Are there any other nominees?' The all-party group of TDs turned towards me, some smirking with visible pleasure at my discomfort. Had Mary Lou hung me out to dry?

Mortified, I decided to start a row, hoping for a diversion to buy a little more time for her to turn up. I sheepishly declared that 'I was waiting for somebody to propose me but I will now put my name forward myself'. I confidently expected McEnery to rule my proposal as inadmissible by insisting that no member could nominate himself or herself, giving me an opening to launch a time-wasting legal argument about Standing Orders.

McEnery didn't. He instantly ruled: 'That is in order.' He would not allow discussion. I had been more than ready, as always, to sing my own praises, but he decided to put the question without delay. I was goosed. He put the nomination of John McGuinness, as the first name proposed, to the committee. I cursed Mary Lou.

Deputy John Deasy, a Fine Gael TD, suddenly perked up. In an effort to achieve my total humiliation, he asked: 'Are there seconders or is there . . . ?' He wanted his good friend McGuinness to win a walkover without even a vote. He knew that Mary Lou was missing and he was teeing up the media for my failure even to secure a seconder.

An impatient McEnery declared, 'There is no requirement under Standing Orders for a seconder. I am required to put the question.'

'On a point of order,' I interjected in desperation, trying to think of some utterly spurious point to prolong the proceedings. It was a last throw of the dice.

The door of the committee room swung open. An elegant lady, cool as a cucumber, casually ambled into the room, passed the media and the ushers and walked towards her seat. She was grinning.

I stuttered and stumbled. Sinn Féin salvation had arrived. 'Deputy Mary Lou McDonald might propose me, now that she is here,' I suggested, trying not to betray the panic in my voice.

She put one word on the record: 'Yes.' Her face was a picture of innocence.

The division bells rang. McGuinness's name was put to the vote. He won by ten votes to two.

The real winner was Mary Lou McDonald. She had put manners on me. She had delivered on Sinn Féin's promise. In the PAC's coming term, she would put manners on many far more significant people.

It was Mary Lou's first appearance on the committee she was destined to dominate for several years. It was the vehicle that gave her the profile that eventually lifted her into the leadership of Sinn Féin.

It also marked a time when she, chairman John McGuinness and I formed an informal inter-party alliance. During that period, I observed Mary Lou at close quarters. We all three combined in an effort to call some of Ireland's most powerful vested interests to account. Mary Lou was professional, eminently likeable and happy to be part of a unique chemistry, a cross-party mix that often worked.

The extraordinary ease with which she instantly slotted into the Dáil procedures, its adversarial nature and the unarmed combat of the PAC were a revelation. Unlike Pearse Doherty, she had never been a county councillor or a senator. She had served her apprenticeship in the European Parliament, where plenary sessions tend to be exceptionally tame, brief set pieces, dominated by colourless statements of party positions, with few interruptions, let alone fiery duels. Mary Lou was a natural for the PAC. Her father had told *Magill* magazine twenty-five years earlier that she wanted to be a lawyer. She had told Rodney Edwards, in her June 2020 interview for the *Impartial Reporter*, that she would probably study law if she ever returned to Trinity College. She starred at the PAC because her natural skills as an orator were closer to those of a sharp prosecuting barrister than to the meanderings of a long-winded politician.

Mary Lou McDonald's arrival in the Dáil was part of a giant improvement in Sinn Féin's performance in the lower house. There was a change in the guard. Caoimhghín Ó Caoláin, the man who had kept the Sinn Féin flag flying in Leinster House since 1997, was ruthlessly sidelined. Two political veterans, but Dáil novices, seized the reins. Sinn Féin president Gerry Adams, a man whose party had for many years refused to contest Dáil seats, had now assumed leadership of the fourteen TDs in Leinster House. He had no knowledge of, or respect for, its traditions or its procedures, but, uncontestably, he had an overbearing presence in the house. Beside him in the chamber sat the party's deputy leader, Mary Lou. The president and vice-president of Sinn Féin, strangers to the ways of Irish democratic bodies, had been elected by the people and floated straight into key positions in the Dáil and its committees.

A third Sinn Féin star player togged out in the chamber: Pearse Doherty completed the troika. He held a few weeks' start over his two senior colleagues because of his by-election victory. The composition and calibre of Sinn Féin TDs in 2011 were many moons away from Sinn Féin 2007-style. After the 2007 election, the team – of only four – had consisted of Ó Caoláin, Morgan, Ferris and Ó Snodaigh. Following the 2011 battle, it was Adams, McDonald and Doherty overshadowing eleven others sitting on the subs bench. The 'A' team had landed.

Mary Lou was assigned the PAC, the highest profile committee. She grabbed it with open arms, despite her lack of accountancy expertise. Pearse, whose financial knowledge surpassed hers by a distance, took the Finance Committee, distinctly a second best. Mary Lou was now being reanointed. She was back in pole position, but she still needed to prove herself.

She cut her teeth at the PAC in unarmed combat with top dogs in the civil service. She quickly mastered controversies on the salaries, corporate governance excesses and failings of the mandarins facing her across the committee room. Initially, she appeared to be hitting the easy targets, grabbing attention from the discomfort of the usual suspects; but that conclusion would be doing her a disservice. In July 2011 she mixed it with the secretary general of the Department of Finance, Kevin Cardiff, about junk bonds and fiscal adjustments, with which she displayed a surprising familiarity. In September, it was chairperson of the Revenue Commissioners Josephine Feehily's turn to face a polite Mary Lou, who set about probing her about Revenue's accounts, while in October she showed no respect for the National Treasury Management Agency's self-important chief executive, John Corrigan, when tackling him about the lack of transparency surrounding appointments and vast salaries at the body he managed. She closed her first year at the PAC with a tour de force, challenging National Asset Management Agency (NAMA) chair Frank Daly and chief executive Brendan McDonagh about the NAMA tender process. More pointedly, she asked McDonagh up front about his own €430,000 salary at a time of bleak austerity. She brilliantly exposed the sense of entitlement to their bloated pay packets felt by public-service plutocrats when McDonagh brazenly made a virtue of refusing a bonus of an extra 30 per cent top-up to his already unacceptably high salary.

In 2011 Mary Lou McDonald proved a revelation in the PAC. No one familiar with her consummate media performances in various elections could have doubted that she was box office. Nobody who had witnessed her rabble-rousing speeches to large crowds or to Sinn Féin ard fheiseanna doubted that she knew which buttons to press when the mob was baying for blood. Nobody who had heard her addressing the Dáil in her first months in Leinster House doubted her powerful presence. Yet the Mary Lou of the PAC was formal and penetrating. She came to PAC meetings superbly briefed. I often sat beside her at its sessions and squinted over her shoulder at her briefing notes. They were detailed, showing impressive signs of painstaking preparation. Her contributions reflected the handiwork of back-room tutors who were well versed in statistics and the nuances of politics. She was undoubtedly a showboater, but so was I. So was the less theatrical John McGuinness in his more dignified way. We gave each other support in the name of transparency and the pursuit of answers and, eventually, we landed in the height of trouble together, often the glue of a good relationship.

John McGuinness was the vital vehicle in the PAC's voyage into uncharted territory. John was a semi-detached Fianna Fáil deputy whose disillusionment with the party leadership was well known. His leader, Micheál Martin, wrongly felt that a demanding, but rewarding, position might keep John gainfully employed. It did, but his insatiable appetite for challenging the establishment, in particular the mandarins, caused untold panic in certain sections of the civil service. His chairmanship of the PAC spooked them. In the past, sometimes with the help of a more benign chairperson than McGuinness, they had managed to duck the political bullets flying in their direction.

McGuinness is a maverick. Far from suppressing Mary Lou's enthusiasm and energy, he primed the pumps for both her and me. And when we had emptied our arsenals, he often came in himself with all guns blazing. He let us run over time if we were in hot pursuit. He allowed discussion on matters where public money was involved to wander into aspects that had never before been included. He broadened the interest and the remit of the PAC to put in the frame the mandarins, overpaid semi-state chiefs, the garda commissioner, the Central Remedial Clinic, Rehab and other charities in receipt of state largesse. Not surprisingly, Official Ireland closed ranks against us.

John's views of Mary Lou were generous and positive, despite their membership of rival political parties. Nearly ten years later, asked what Mary Lou had achieved on his watch as the chair of the PAC, John McGuinness says: 'She was able to prove every single Thursday that the state had a lot to answer for. She never minded what other TDs felt.' She would not have done it without a degree of latitude from an obliging chairman. McGuinness says that he 'liked her personally and liked her style at the PAC. Her arguments were well founded in facts.'

Some critics have rubbished Mary Lou for being weak on detail but brilliant at rhetorical flourishes. Such criticism may be true of her scripted contributions in other fora, but in the PAC she confounded those doubters. She does rhetoric. She does rabble-rousing. She doesn't do dull and boring. She did detail when necessary.

By far the most insightful observation John McGuinness made when I interviewed him for this book was that Mary Lou's membership of the PAC 'separated her from Sinn Féin'. It was meant as a compliment. He reckoned that 'In the PAC she became Mary Lou McDonald.'

His point was perceptive. The PAC was not about republicanism or socialism, the twin ideologies to which Sinn Féin and Mary Lou McDonald paid lip service. There was never any mention at its sessions of a united Ireland, nor of her beloved Basque separatists, nor of the social injustices of capitalism. It was primarily about accounting for state money and unearthing wayward governance. Inevitably, in pursuit of transparency, it uprooted greed and uncovered scandals. In this environment Mary Lou found her métier. She was a questioner par excellence, fearless but fair. The PAC gave her a platform for important matters that were not ideological. She was not flanked at PAC meetings by the long shadow of Gerry Adams or Martin McGuinness with their military records. Nor was she delivering speeches at lecterns decorated with Armalites, as she was elsewhere. The PAC was attacking waste, inefficiency and financial sleight of hand, targets with which a wide middle-class Southern audience could identify. Her role in its activities moved public opinion in Sinn Féin's direction.

Mary Lou was dragging her party into the mainstream. Her sometimes nightly appearances on the airwaves about PAC issues attracted the approval of some who had always considered Sinn Féin beyond redemption.

Despite our common purpose and political alliance on the committee, neither John McGuinness nor I formed a strong personal friendship with Mary Lou. We both liked her immensely. She was good company, but she was not an inter-party mixer. According to him, 'she didn't mix much, but worked hard'. I enjoyed plenty of collegial, friendly, sometimes funny conversations with her, but these never took place in the members' bar, the Leinster House café or the restaurant. Nor was she seen there with others. Gone were her old pre-Sinn Féin days when Finian McGrath and the Irish National Congress gang would enjoy a drink with her in the Teachers' Club.

John McGuinness says he thinks 'she was sincere, a genuine believer in the importance of holding officers of the state accountable'. He pays tribute to her by saying that her presence and 'commitment at the PAC made it possible to carry out the investigations that would otherwise have been blocked by government TDs'.

Mary Lou's early PAC skirmishes in 2011/12 were only the warm-ups for more momentous confrontations to come. Among the most sensational in 2013, 2014 and 2015 were the conflicts between two garda whistle-blowers and the garda commissioner Martin Callinan, the grilling of former chief executive of the Central Remedial Clinic Brian Conlan and the long saga with Rehab boss Angela Kerins. John McGuinness and I joined forces with Mary Lou in all three instances.

Perhaps Mary Lou's finest hour at the PAC was during her exchanges with Garda Commissioner Martin Callinan in January 2014. Two whistle-blowers, serving Sergeant Maurice McCabe and retired garda John Wilson, had claimed that senior gardaí had inappropriately wiped the penalty points off the driving licences of favoured offenders. Commissioner Callinan had come to the PAC in a bullish mood, determined that the two whistle-blowers should not be allowed to make their complaints to a hearing of the committee. He insisted that an internal garda investigation was adequate.

On that day, Mary Lou followed me in questioning the

commissioner. He had just answered a query I had put to him about the limited value of internal garda probes by declaring, 'I do respect the notion that the gardaí, in certain circumstances, should not be investigating one another. There is not a whisper anywhere else, or from any other member of the Garda Síochána, however, about the corruption, malpractice and other charges levelled against their fellow officers.' And then, on the whistle-blowing of Sergeant McCabe and Garda Wilson, he uttered the fatal words: 'Frankly, on a personal level, I think it is quite disgusting.'

It was my last question. On that note, there was nobody better than Mary Lou to pick up the baton for the whistle-blowers. She excelled herself.

She had been waiting patiently for me to finish. I headed for my office, where I watched the exchanges on the monitor. Opposite the lonely, diminutive figure of Mary Lou sat the formidable garda commissioner, Martin Callinan. He was flanked by garda heavy-weights: in uniform, by his side, sat Assistant Commissioner John O'Mahony from the crime and security branch, Deputy Commissioner Nóirín O'Sullivan and Assistant Commissioner John Twomey, in charge of the Dublin Metropolitan region. Their head of legal affairs, Kenneth Ruane, and their director of finance, Assistant Commissioner Michael Culhane, sat and stared. Facing them across the room was Mary Lou McDonald, alone with her laptop.

On the surface, it was an uneven contest. Six people, four in uniform, eyeballing one lone woman in mufti; but Mary Lou took complete command. The gardaí could have done with reinforcements.

She welcomed them all, as if they had just come into her drawing room at her grand new home in Cabra. The sight of a Sinn Féin chief grilling the country's top law enforcers must have prompted symbolic shudders among gardaí who remembered that, only two decades earlier, their respective armed wings were exchanging bullets. Indeed, it had not been long since the gardaí had used their own interrogating skills to interview friends of Mary Lou. Now, the boot was on the other foot.

I had expected an explosion from Mary Lou after Callinan's 'disgusting' remark.

On the contrary, the dialogue was almost chummy at the start. The commissioner tried to reduce the tension in the room. When Mary Lou had suggested, almost apologetically, that one of her queries might have required him to be a mind reader, she quipped 'that would be beyond his pay grade'.

The commissioner replied jocularly, 'Which is not enough, as one knows.' There were loud chuckles, an outburst of bonhomie on the garda benches.

Mary Lou rapidly hauled them all back into the sober mood of the meeting, quietly seeking information on garda officers acting outside their jurisdiction. When McGuinness suggested a lunch break, Callinan tried to lower the temperature by responding good-humouredly that he would be delighted to keep answering questions 'provided the Deputy is not too hard on me!'

McGuinness explained that he was 'getting notes from the outside', [meaning mandarins], who were worried about the witnesses not having a break. But 'If Mr Callinan is happy to go on,' he offered, 'that is fine. I was just asking the question.'

Callinan tried another joke: 'I hope it is not a whistle-blower.'

It fell flat. Mary Lou ignored him, immediately demanding a precise figure for the number of garda officers acting outside their jurisdiction when writing off penalty points.

The exchanges settled into a more formal vein. The commissioner resisted the idea of the whistle-blowers appearing before the PAC. He did not think it the appropriate forum for a discussion about penalty points. He tried to move on. Mary Lou dug in and refused to allow him off the hook. In reply to further questions – not about individual cases, but about the investigative process – he hid behind confidentiality. He could not explain why it had taken eight months to investigate four complaints. Mary Lou slowly pinned him against the ropes. The commissioner became openly irritated by the line of questioning. He was exasperated, protesting that 'We went through all this on the last occasion.'

Mary Lou responded, 'We will go through it again.'

Callinan was not used to being spoken to like that. He became increasingly brief, replying unhelpfully to a question about the Department of Justice's possession of documents with the curt response: 'I have no idea.'

Mary Lou challenged his version of events. The pair were on a collision course.

Finally, she came to following up his 'disgusting' remark about the whistle-blowers, made in reply to my final question. Callinan stuck to his guns. He would reserve his views for an impending High Court action. Mary Lou could take a hike.

She nailed him to the cross on the 'disgusting' gaffe. He responded in monosyllables. He would take legal advice on the committee's decision to invite the whistle-blowers to give evidence. It sounded like a threat. We anticipated a possible injunction.

She exposed him, especially his dismissive attitude to those he had contemptuously dubbed 'so-called whistle-blowers'. No wonder they had brought their complaints to the Houses of the Oireachtas. They had no confidence in the commissioner and his complaints process.

Finally, Mary Lou forced him to repeat his earlier refusal to disclose the number of reports made to the garda confidential recipient over the previous twelve to eighteen months. He wouldn't budge.

Mary Lou had torn a garda commissioner to shreds at an open public meeting in Leinster House. She had blown wide open the flaws in An Garda Síochána's system for dealing with whistle-blowers' complaints. She had given hope to two gardaí, hitherto hopelessly overwhelmed, frustrated and finally stymied by garda procedures. She had done it politely, not once raising her voice.

Events moved quickly after the PAC clash with the com-missioner. Despite threats to his job from inside the garda force, whistle-blower Sergeant Maurice McCabe appeared before the PAC within a week. A row within the committee about whether the hearing should be held in public or private threatened to blow us off course. It was diplomatically resolved by the intervention of Deputy Kieran O'Donnell, Fine Gael's most clear-headed, calm PAC member.

Despite opposition to the hearing from Minister for Justice Alan Shatter and from Commissioner Callinan, Sergeant McCabe appeared in garda uniform at a private sitting on 29 January.

The committee found Maurice McCabe's evidence to be true. On 13 March a second report, by an independent garda inspectorate, confirmed consistent breaches of policy by the gardaí in administering the penalty points system. It also found that Sergeant McCabe's narrative was credible. Garda whistle-blower John Wilson claimed that he and Maurice McCabe had been 'totally vindicated'. He added that in any other police force in the world the commissioner would have been forced to resign.

Wilson hadn't long to wait. Less than two weeks later, on 25 March 2014, Commissioner Martin Callinan threw in the towel and resigned. The PAC had captured a scalp. The persistence of the committee and chairman John McGuinness in stretching its remit to the limits had allowed two brave men to air their grievances. Despite the opposition of the minister for justice and the garda commissioner, the determination of Mary Lou and others had secured the presence of two groundbreaking gardaí in front of a Dáil and Seanad committee.

After the penalty points problem was finally resolved, on 26 September 2014 Fiach Kelly, deputy political editor of *The Irish Times*, acknowledged the role of the PAC in the downfall of a commissioner. He wrote that 'its hearings into the penalty points

affair rank among its finest moments in a year which has seen the
Committee take centre stage within the Oireachtas'. Kelly picked
out the appearance and questioning of Commissioner Callinan as
crucial to 'bringing to a head the many criticisms of the force'. He
stopped short of giving individuals credit, but Mary Lou could take
a bow.

Kelly did not mention another PAC 'special' in which Mary
Lou had also played a leading part. In November 2013, during a
routine examination of the Health Service Executive at the PAC, it
had emerged that the Central Remedial Clinic (CRC), a much-loved
charity for the care, treatment and development of people with
physical and multiple disabilities, had been topping up its executives'
ballooning salaries and padded pensions out of voluntary donations.
It was revealed at the PAC that the clinic's former chief executive
Paul Kiely had received not only a top-up of €135,000 – added to
his basic €116,000 salary – but also a pay-off of €742,000. We
invited the CRC in for questioning. The result was the resignation
of the entire board and the chief executive, Brian Conlan. Mary
Lou had, again, calmly dissected the witnesses. The CRC directors
folded their tent. A completely new board was installed. After the
clean-out, the charity's reputation was slowly restored and its
donors' generosity gradually resumed.

Both John McGuinness and I found Mary Lou a highly
professional colleague. We were all accused of grandstanding,
which was a fair charge, yet Mary Lou never pulled political stunts
to steal a march on other members of the PAC in order to grab a
media spot. She took her turn, put her questions and accepted the
media slots when they were offered. It probably helped our cause
that all three of us were lone rangers. She had no other Sinn Féin
TDs breathing down her neck at the committee, I was an Independent
deputy reporting to no party, and the last person on God's earth
whom John McGuinness would have consulted with about the
PAC was his party leader, Micheál Martin.

Meanwhile powerful forces outside the PAC were muttering about how some members of the committee were out of control. We were treading on too many delicate corns not to provoke attempts to clip our wings. The sight of Mary Lou, in particular, a member of Sinn Féin, holding many of Ireland's great and good to account was a bridge too far for many establishment interests. Despite the undoubted successes recorded in curbing wrongdoing in both the Central Remedial Clinic and An Garda Síochána, many top civil servants, lawyers and charity chiefs were uneasy. The Fine Gael members on the committee came under pressure to cool its aggressive style of approach.

The CRC fiasco prompted the PAC to shine a brighter torch on the entire charity industry and the excessive rewards paid to some of the top brass, especially those with government contracts.

Next on the PAC's list was another disability services provider, the Rehab Group, and its chief executive, Angela Kerins, who was discovered to be earning a salary of €240,000 a year. The PAC was curious about her pay package, her stewardship and the entire corporate governance structure of Rehab. We invited Angela Kerins into the committee to enlighten us. She agreed to attend.

On 27 February 2014 we had a tortuous seven-hour session with her and other Rehab executives. Members of the committee put her under pressure. The meeting was highly adversarial. It marked the beginning of a five-year legal wrangle between the PAC and Rehab, finishing in the Supreme Court in 2019.

Barely one month after the controversial meeting, on 2 April 2014, Angela Kerins resigned her position in Rehab, citing as the reason 'the toll that public controversy has taken on the Rehab Group and my own family'. In July 2014, following a period of legal and political bickering, the politically controlled Committee on Procedure and Privileges refused to give the PAC the compulsory powers it needed to ensure that Angela Kerins would return to give further evidence and that former Rehab chief executive and Fine

Gael strategist Frank Flannery would answer questions about his own earlier stewardship.

One week later, Angela Kerins sued the PAC in the High Court. She pleaded that it had overstepped its remit with our line of questioning. Her doctors supplied a letter saying that, as a result, she had suffered from various serious ailments. She sought significant damages. Two years later, in July 2016, she lost the case in the High Court, but by then the work of the PAC had already been blunted, since it was rendered toothless by the earlier decision from the Committee on Procedure and Privileges refusing to give us powers to compel witnesses to attend. High Court President Peter Kelly ruled that 'the separation of powers meant that Oireachtas respondents cannot be made amenable to the jurisdiction of the court'.

Kerins appealed to the Supreme Court and won. In 2019 the seven Supreme Court judges overruled the High Court decision. According to Chief Justice Frank Clarke, the PAC had condoned the significant departure by at least three deputies from the terms of the invitation to Ms Kerins, extended to include reference to her salary. On that basis, he said, it was appropriate to make a declaration that the committee had acted unlawfully.

Their lordships named no names, but nor did they offer any prizes for guessing which three offending TDs they had so coyly failed to identify.

Leaving aside the questionable merits of the Supreme Court judgement, Mary Lou's initial successes in the PAC were an honourable chapter in her first term in the Dáil. She rattled cages that shook an Irish establishment which detested accountability. She helped to extend the remit of the PAC members, demanding transparency from Ireland's privileged and powerful. Without her determination, the gardaí might not have been reformed and charities might have remained easy pickings for greedy insiders who saw them as a soft source of excessive remuneration. Mary Lou McDonald was a force for good.

The attempts from on high to muzzle the PAC did not deter others from approaching us with less bulletproof causes of complaint. We resolved to investigate them when we could.

In early November 2014, a dramatic dossier arrived in the hands of PAC members. Another whistle-blower was claiming that a spectacular scandal had been suppressed. No lesser person than Gerard Ryan, the official appointed in 1998 as authorised officer to investigate the infamous Ansbacher accounts – illegal offshore tax evasion schemes used by Ireland's elite – had become a whistle-blower. He was accusing ten politicians and other public figures of exploiting these tax dodges. He further alleged in his dossier to PAC members that Mary Harney, Tánaiste at the time, had asked him to 'terminate' his probe in June 2004 after her party colleague Des O'Malley had been implicated. Mary Harney strenuously denied this accusation.

While Mary Lou and I immediately expressed concern at these allegations, Fianna Fáil and Fine Gael voices insisted that they had already been 'fully investigated' by numerous state bodies, including the Revenue Commissioners, the Garda Bureau of Fraud Investigation and the Office of the Director of Corporate Enforcement. Mary Lou was disturbed by the way the authorised officer's complaints had been handled. I was particularly concerned that he should be given the same access to a PAC hearing as Sergeant Maurice McCabe had already enjoyed. Otherwise, we would be charged with protecting politicians while eagerly probing the wrongdoings of gardaí.

The PAC decided to listen to the Revenue Commissioners' response to Ryan's story before making a final decision on whether or not to hear his submission. Mary Lou, John McGuinness and I favoured giving Mr Ryan a hearing, but the six Fine Gael members were characteristically jumpy about it because the committee had received legal advice that an investigation was beyond its remit. Cautious opinions from in-house Oireachtas lawyers invariably provided a crutch for opponents of openness. Some of us, unimpressed by the plethora of legal expertise always available to those opposed to transparency, wished to go ahead with a private hearing, which Maurice McCabe had been accorded.

On 4 December, Josephine Feehily, chair of the Revenue Commissioners, gave evidence that the commissioners had already investigated Mr Ryan's allegations and that there had been 'no political interference' in their work, as he had alleged. On the same day, John McGuinness announced that whistle-blower Ryan would receive a copy of Josephine Feehily's evidence and be asked, in response, to give oral evidence at the committee. That seemed like a sensible and fair way of proceeding.

Unfortunately, Mary Lou had broken cover a day earlier. In her most dramatic intervention since her election to the Dáil nearly four years earlier, Mary Lou went nuclear.

It was midday on 3 December 2014: Leaders' Questions in the Dáil. Gerry Adams had yielded his live television leader's slot to his deputy, Mary Lou. She rose to her feet, flanked by Caoimhghín Ó Caoláin and Aengus Ó Snodaigh. Behind her sat Cork deputies Sandra McLellan and Jonathan O'Brien.

Taoiseach Enda Kenny was taking her questions. Behind him sat five Blueshirts, led by chief whip Paul Kehoe, alongside Tipperary's Noel Coonan, Ray Butler from Meath, Dan Neville from Limerick and 'Dinny' McGinley from Donegal. All middle-aged rural TDs. All men. They scowled at the woman across the chamber preparing to harangue them. They were no lovers of Sinn Féin.

In the chair was Seán Barrett of Fine Gael, no lover of Sinn Féin either. Nor was there any love lost between him and Mary Lou. He called on her to put her first question to the Taoiseach.

Mary Lou began with her well-practised, casual tone, supported by unthreatening mannerisms, a technique she had perfected for occasions when she was preparing her most lethal ambushes. Her volume was low key, but her words were dynamite. Her topic was the Ansbacher Cayman Island accounts. No warning of the questioner's topic is given at Leaders' Questions.

Ceann Comhairle Seán Barrett was in relaxed mood. When she kicked off about the Ansbacher accounts, he remained passive, until she mentioned that an investigation had been 'terminated by then minister Mary Harney in 2004, once Mr. Desmond O'Malley was discovered to be one of the holders of these accounts'. Barrett's ears pricked up enough for him to intervene with mild disapproval: 'The Deputy,' he asserted calmly, 'cannot make allegations of that nature in the chamber.'

She had just made them. She looked at him wide-eyed, but unapologetic. She simply carried on in the same vein, outlining further allegations made by the whistle-blower, not by her, of course. She fingered the late banker Des Traynor and 'a Mr. Padraig Colleary, formerly of Guinness & Mahon' as administrators of the accounts. She was throwing names around the chamber like snuff at a wake. She forgot to mention that Traynor was known as the late Taoiseach Charlie Haughey's 'bagman'.

Barrett didn't seem to be too stressed about her naming the non-politicians. She rabbited on about tax evasion. Barrett suggested that she actually ask a question.

Mary Lou framed a question. In reality, she was teeing up an incendiary allegation under the cover of Leaders' Questions. As Enda Kenny was offering a standard answer to defuse her opening salvo, she was removing the pin from the grenade that she had been preparing for several minutes.

Kenny's reply was of little moment.

Mary Lou stood up again, this time to lob her grenade at the Taoiseach. 'It is not a case of me making allegations against anyone,' she riposted. 'I emphasise that they are allegations, but they come from a credible source.'

And then the grenade exploded. 'The whistle-blower,' she emphasised to ensure that everyone knew they were not her allegations, 'alleges Des O'Malley, Ray MacSharry . . .'

Around the chamber the sound of jaws dropping could almost be heard. Both men, very much still in the land of the living, had recently retired as senior ministers with good reputations. Those of us watching expected Ceann Comhairle Barrett to implode. No doubt, so did Mary Lou. But he hesitated. She kept going. She added two further senior ex-ministers: 'Gerard Collins, Máire Geoghegan-Quinn . . .'

Not a murmur from the chair. There was a hush in the chamber. Barrett was allowing her to run amok.

And then, with a glint in her eye, she delivered the killer punch, 'an S. Barrett [pause], Richie Ryan – a former Minister for Finance – and others . . .'

Sinn Féin deputies sitting behind her covered their grins. Mary Lou had released her entire Ansbacher arsenal unchecked all over the sacred chamber. The Exocet was the name 'S. Barrett'.

The sound of his own surname and his own 'S' initial had suddenly stirred the Ceann Comhairle into an almost incoherent intervention.

'Sorry,' he said, visibly flustered. 'Is the Deputy making these allegations here in the chamber?' As though Mary Lou's outburst was the voice of a disembodied demon invading his sanctuary from on high.

Mary Lou looked at him quizzically. 'Pardon me,' she muttered insincerely; she was almost taunting him. She knew she had just got away with murder. The Ansbacher names were out in the public arena. And the Barrett name would cause consternation.

Seán Barrett came to life, suddenly realising the extraordinary scene that he had allowed to develop. He was at sixes and sevens. She had slipped into the Dáil record half a dozen names against whom there were serious, but totally unproved, allegations, under privilege, unchecked by the chair. One name even sounded alarmingly like his own.

'Did the Deputy,' Barrett asked inanely, 'make allegations in the chamber regarding—?'

Mary Lou interrupted him. It was an ambush, but he had been painfully unready. 'I am echoing,' she pleaded unconvincingly, 'the serious allegations that have been brought forward by the whistle-blower. That is the allegation.'

Barrett was slowly beginning to grasp the gravity of the situation: 'The Deputy knows quite clearly, if she bothers to check the record and take advice from the clerk of the Dáil, that she cannot name names of people who are defenceless to contradict her. There is a long-established principle in this chamber. I know you are only new in the Dáil, but I ask you to brief yourself clearly on what you can and cannot do in a democratically elected chamber.'

Mary Lou looked hopelessly happy. Barrett was losing the plot. She was by no means 'new in the Dáil', as he had suggested. She was a veteran of Leaders' Questions. It was 2014. She had been in the lower house for nearly four years. The Ceann Comhairle was asleep at the wheel.

Mary Lou simply ignored Barrett's ramblings. She turned to the Taoiseach and explained to him: 'The difficulty, Taoiseach, is this . . .'

Barrett hit the outrage button. He was particularly incensed about the 'S. Barrett' reference, mischievously included in that format to raise his hackles. The reference in the whistle-blower's dossier to 'S' Barrett was not to Seán Barrett, but to a former Fianna Fáil minister, Sylvester Barrett, who had died in 2002. The ambiguity was Mary Lou's delicious *coup de grâce*.

Seán Barrett was angry. She had made a monkey of him while simultaneously defaming six former ministers. He boomed out at the assembled TDs, 'I wish to state quite categorically, in case anybody is under any doubts when the Deputy says "S. Barrett," it does not apply to me.' He looked as if he might burst a blood vessel. He knew that there would be hell to pay for this.

And there was. Mary Lou had done a solo run. She had not told either John McGuinness or me or, indeed, any other member of the PAC about her plan to use parliamentary privilege to name the former politicians as Ansbacher account holders.

The former politicians named by Mary Lou were shaken. They threatened legal action. All vehemently denied the veracity of the charges. While I was eager for the PAC to call in the whistle-blower to justify his claims, equally it seemed imperative that the targets of his dossier should be given a fair hearing to prove their innocence. Especially now that their names were out in the open. They had no real redress, because privilege in the Dáil is absolute. No deputy can be sued for defamation for anything said in the chamber. If abused, this protection can become a weapon of character assassination.

The day after Mary Lou had dumbfounded the Dáil, she attended a meeting of the PAC. Her colleagues on the committee showed no tolerance for her previous day's behaviour. Fine Gael's John Deasy was incensed. 'You think you can use this committee any way you feel like it, but you can't,' he said, in a personal attack unusual in the PAC. Later on, other PAC colleagues were openly hostile, including Labour's mild-mannered Robert Dowds, who denounced Mary Lou's actions as a 'cheap political stunt which served no purpose other than grabbing headlines'. Another Labour TD, Joe Costello, from her own constituency, questioned Mary Lou's suitability to remain on the PAC. Even John McGuinness could not support her, having said on RTÉ's *Morning Ireland* that naming the politicians in question could discourage others from coming forward. Nor did I, for once, back what Mary Lou had done. I still favoured an inquiry that would offer Gerard Ryan the same access as Maurice McCabe had been given, while believing that all politicians or citizens under fire were entitled to a right of rebuttal to protect their good names.

Mary Lou, typically, stood her ground. She insisted that there was a growing pattern of political obstruction to an opening of

Ryan's dossier. She had sought legal advice before naming the politicians in the Dáil. Who, she asked, would examine the allegations if not the PAC?

A month later the PAC dropped the idea of an inquiry. Mary Lou and I still wanted to give both the whistle-blower and the politicians a hearing, but the battle was lost. Fine Gael, Labour and Fianna Fáil members, and now even John McGuinness and I, had parted ways with Mary Lou over her unilateral decision to take advantage of parliamentary protection to stain the reputations of retired politicians. She had done mighty work in the PAC, but giving oxygen to unsubstantiated allegations made in the Dáil under the shelter of privilege was beyond reckless. It was indefensible.

Four of the six ministers named by Mary Lou wrote to the Dáil Committee on Procedure and Privileges, seeking redress. Former Progressive Democrat leader Des O'Malley, former EU commissioner and finance minister Ray MacSharry, former minister for justice and EU commissioner Máire Geoghegan-Quinn and another former Progressive Democrat leader and Tánaiste, Mary Harney, demanded that the Committee on Procedure and Privileges amend the record of the House and that the remarks made by Mary Lou McDonald be withdrawn. The first three angrily denied that they had ever held Ansbacher accounts. Mary Harney strenuously repudiated any suggestion that she had terminated an inquiry into them, as the whistle-blower had alleged.

Former foreign minister Gerard Collins and former finance minister Richie Ryan did not make formal complaints.

The Committee on Procedure and Privileges, chaired by the living S. (Seán) Barrett, produced a report in April 2015. It found that Mary Lou McDonald had abused her parliamentary privilege. Her accusations were judged 'in the nature of being defamatory'. It reported that she had shown no intention of withdrawing her remarks. She was defiant. Despite an outcry from many TDs, she refused to retreat an inch. Government chief whip Paul Kehoe said that he would be seeking to bring a motion censuring her before the Dáil. She was unimpressed, asserting that 'I absolutely refute the suggestion that I abused Dáil privilege.' She insisted that there was 'no merit or reason' for any motion of censure against her.

Mary Lou, at least temporarily, lost the middle ground, the people whom she had been recruited to attract; but Sinn Féin supporters were ecstatic. Gerry Adams, the man whom she had backed when his brother Liam was being sought for paedophile charges, the man whom she had supported over his account of the murder of Jean McConville, the man who was never in the IRA, said that the party stood 'shoulder to shoulder' with Mary Lou over her behaviour in the Ansbacher row. He praised her as being a 'very, very good parliamentarian' and asserted that she was 'not guilty of any abuse of privilege'.

Adams was partly right. She had been a PAC superstar, but she had gone way over the top on Ansbacher. She had given enemies of the PAC ammunition to prove how reckless we all had been. The Committee on Procedure and Privileges, spooked by Angela Kerins's court action and by a few mandarins with an agenda against inquiries, managed to put the lid on any further extension of our remit.

Since that battle over the Ansbacher whistle-blower's evidence, the PAC has never reached such heights in pursuit of accountability. After the 2016 general election, when John McGuinness asked his party leader, Micheál Martin, if he could return to the chair of the PAC, he was dispatched to preside over the less politically fertile Committee on Finance. McGuinness was a maverick who had long been a thorn in the leader's side.

Adams's assertion that Mary Lou was such a 'very, very good parliamentarian' was probably premature in 2014. Her high-profile record in the PAC shows that she was fearless, refreshingly probing and unimpressed by vested interests. But how about the Dáil chamber, the centre of Irish democracy? How did she rate there?

Her critics say that she was big into bombast, but brutal on detail.

Mary Lou's record in her first Dáil from 2011 to 2016 was a mixed bag. As Sinn Féin's spokesperson on public expenditure, she contributed on the second stage of many bills. She frequently led off for her party in 'Statements only' sessions, votes of no confidence and constitutional amendments. Numerically (excluding questions and committee stage), she spoke over 150 times in the chamber, a formidable tally, although most of these speeches were rigidly scripted for her in the well-manned Sinn Féin back offices. She delivered the scripts to the letter, with effortless displays of passion. She was not restricted to her limited public expenditure portfolio, but asserted party policy on issues ranging from industrial relations to abortion. During those five years, when the Fine Gael–Labour coalition was constantly making cuts, particularly in the public expenditure portfolio which she was shadowing, there were easy pickings for the opposition. The man she was marking in the Dáil at the time, the minister for public expenditure, Labour's Brendan Howlin, today surprisingly acknowledges her commitment to progressive measures. 'She genuinely supported Freedom of In-formation changes,' he volunteers generously. 'For her, the Dáil was not merely a theatre for a dramatic performance; she backed reforms if she believed in them. She was perfectly capable of taking pragmatic positions.'

Howlin is equally magnanimous about her attitude to his Registration of Lobbying Bill 2014, when he accepted many of her amendments at committee stage. She supported the bill, and their exchanges during the debate over the nitty-gritty parts of this important piece of legislation read like a political love-in. Away from the glare of the cameras, Mary Lou was capable of adopting a more conciliatory public stance to government measures.

However, Howlin has no recollection of her interest in the minutiae of other bills. She was not really into the nuts and bolts. Mary Lou, he says, 'was nearly all scripted on the set pieces. I am a

The candidate stands beside her campaign bus for the European elections in 2004.

Newly elected MEP Mary Lou carries former IRA chief Joe Cahill's coffin towards St John's Church on the Falls Road in July 2004.

Patron and protégée: Gerry Adams and Mary Lou at a press conference in the run-up to the 2004 European elections.

Sinn Féin's first two Members of the European Parliament North and South – Bairbre de Brún and Mary Lou – at a conference in Dublin in 2005.

Sinn Féin parliamentarians in 2008. Party chairperson and MEP Mary Lou McDonald (centre) with (left to right) Dáil deputies Arthur Morgan, Martin Ferris, Aengus Ó Snodaigh, Caoimhghín Ó Caoláin and Senator Pearse Doherty at the party's annual think-in.

A Dáil seat, at last. Mary Lou embraces former IRA man and Sinn Féin councillor Nicky Kehoe after her victory in the 2011 general election.

The family: Mary Lou with her husband Martin, daughter Iseult (6) and son Gerard (3) after voting at St John Bosco Primary School on the Navan Road, Dublin in the 2009 European elections.

Mary Lou, deputy leader of Sinn Féin, with Sandra McLellan, the TD who left Sinn Féin within a year of this 2015 picture, alleging bullying by local party members.

Committee of Public Accounts

Payments made to Rehab and the operation of the Charitable Lotterie
Scheme

Houses of the Oireachtas

A star is born: Mary Lou at the Public Accounts Committee (PAC) with the author in 2014.

© PA Images/Alamy Stock Photo

The anointment of Mary Lou by Gerry Adams and Martin McGuinness at the 2016
Sinn Féin ard fheis.

Sinn Féin's Conor Murphy, Mary Lou McDonald, Gerry Kelly and Michelle O'Neill speaking to the media at Stormont in June 2021.

How the mighty are fallen! Mary Lou and Michelle O'Neill celebrating Martina Anderson's (centre) re-election to the European Parliament in 2019. In 2020, after her European seat was abolished by Brexit, Martina was co-opted to the Sinn Féin seat for Foyle as an MLA in Stormont. In 2021, the leadership forced her to resign her Stormont seat and make way for new blood.

Mary Lou, flanked by Tipperary relations her Uncle Jimmy and Aunt Breda Hayes, at Sinn Féin's 2019 commemoration of the cemetery of the Soloheadbeg ambush in Tipp. Mary Lou ended her oration with the words 'Where Tipperary leads, Ireland follows. Tiocfaidh ár lá.'

© Fitzpatrick Printers, Tipperary

Mary Lou with councillors, locals and relations of her great-uncle, the late James O'Connor, at his memorial headstone in Kilmoyler churchyard in Tipperary. O'Connor, on the anti-treaty side, was executed in the civil war.

Old rivals, new friends? Mary Lou warmly greets her former constituency opponent, ex-Taoiseach Bertie Ahern, at the funeral of her neighbour and Bertie's good friend Chris Wall in January 2022.

Victory in the Northern Ireland Assembly elections, May 2022. Mary Lou and Michelle O'Neill arrive at the Titanic Counting Centre in Belfast as Sinn Féin becomes the biggest party in Northern Ireland.

detail person, but I did not detect similar enthusiasm from her at the teasing-out stage of legislation. Nor did I see any meaningful financial analysis from her, but she compared well with Adams, who was so weak on economics.'

Pat Rabbitte, minister for communications, energy and natural resources during that 2011–16 Fine Gael–Labour coalition, had many jousts with Mary Lou. He says, 'I didn't know Mary Lou before 2011, although I thought I did. She was intriguing because she wasn't your typical Sinn Féin TD – it does not appear to be a hereditary thing – moving from a conventional middle-class family, educated at Trinity and having cut her political teeth in Fianna Fáil.' On her parliamentary performance, Rabbitte distinguishes between her role in the PAC and in the Dáil chamber itself. 'She came to national prominence as a member of the PAC, who pushed out the boundaries of the Dáil's oldest committee. In consort with the Author and the acquiescence of the Chair, the committee morphed into a star chamber feared by senior mandarins and anyone else the committee could get their hands on. The Supreme Court called a halt, but not before Mary Lou had become a national figure.'

Moving to the Dáil itself, Pat Rabbitte had this to say: 'Her theatrical approach on the floor of the House has been very effective, especially on Leaders' Questions. Her rhetoric is relentless, media-focused and well prepared. The economy is probably her Achilles heel, but she knows when to lay it off to others. Undoubtedly, in her single-minded daily attacks on government performance, she has left hostages to fortune on the record of the Dáil. She is probably strong enough to tough it out when and if government beckons.'

Former minister Rabbitte was speaking from personal experience. In one notable debate he felt the need to heckle Mary Lou at least a dozen times in a heated exchange during her second stage speech on the Electricity Supply Board. He managed to dub her as both 'the tooth fairy' and 'Little Red Riding Hood' in the same speech. He also indicates that she did not carry political rancour outside the Dáil itself. After lively exchanges between them during a debate in 2011, he gallantly held the door open for her as they were both leaving the chamber. She hesitated, giving way to the minister. He held on to the open door, quoting former President Eamon de Valera that 'Labour must wait'. She smiled broadly. 'You'd better believe it,' she declared as she swept past him.

Mary Lou's relationships with other Labour ministers were not all as good as she had sometimes enjoyed with Howlin and Rabbitte. Her most anarchic move of the 2011–16 Dáil was, surprisingly, not the Ansbacher breach of parliamentary privilege, but a 'spontaneous' sit-in which she had organised in the Dáil chamber in November 2014. The issue of water charges was causing political mayhem, with parties of the left competing fiercely for leadership of the popular opposition to them. A month earlier, on 10 October, Sinn Féin had lost the by-election in Dublin West its leadership had expected to win. Outflanked by Paul Murphy of the Anti-Austerity Alliance, who had left Sinn Féin flat-footed on the water charges issue, the party badly needed to regain the ground it had hoped to hold following excellent local election results in May.

Mary Lou had been taking an increasingly militant role on Leaders' Questions in the Dáil, persecuting Tánaiste Joan Burton at every opportunity, specifically on the water charges controversy. On 13 November at approximately 12.30 p.m. she asked the Tánaiste whether people who had not paid their water charges would see their wages or social welfare payments deducted accordingly. Burton replied that she did not know because the water charges decisions would be made the following week.

Mary Lou blew a gasket, or at least appears to have done. She protested loudly that she was tired of the Tánaiste refusing to answer questions in the Dáil, hardly an original complaint. Although she had left the chamber after another row with Ceann Comhairle Seán Barrett a few weeks earlier, this time she defied him when he told her to sit down. She was ordered to leave. She refused. A vote was called to suspend her. It was passed.

Normally, when a motion suspending a TD is passed, that ends the kerfuffle; Dáil business resumes after the offending TD leaves the chamber, having attracted publicity for a protest. Not Mary Lou. She refused to depart. She turned down requests from the Captain of the Guard for her to leave the premises.

Barrett adjourned the Dáil for a short recess, awaiting her departure. She still politely declined to exit. She stayed in her seat with other Sinn Féin colleagues, occupying the chamber for four long hours. Eventually, the Ceann Comhairle re-entered the House at 4.30 p.m. and adjourned the business until the following Tuesday at 2 p.m.

The media had been speculating all afternoon about how long Mary Lou could last without a call of nature forcing her to leave. If she had left, she would not have been readmitted and proceedings could have been resumed. When the house was finally adjourned, a gaggle of Shinners sprinted for the loos. I was in the house when that point came and decided to head in the same direction. As I arrived at the gents', situated just outside the chamber, I was greeted by a tall man with a beard and glasses blocking my entrance, guarding the door. 'You can't go in there,' said the man who had never joined the IRA. 'Mary Lou's in there.'

She had broken yet another rule.

In the eyes of Sinn Féin, the episode was a triumph for Mary Lou. Her stock in the party soared. She had, almost alone, brought the Dáil to a standstill in the fight against water charges. An old-fashioned sit-in had worked.

Her opponents were horrified. The wrath of the Blueshirts came crashing down all over her. Frances Fitzgerald, a genuine Fine Gael feminist and a cabinet colleague of Joan Burton, was furious, denouncing the whole escapade as a 'diversionary stunt'. Seán Barrett issued a statement to the media saying that Mary Lou

McDonald had interrupted business and would not resume her seat when asked, so he had no option other than the course of action he had taken. It was an admission that she, not he, was dictating the pace of proceedings and that he was powerless to stop her.

Mary Lou wore many hats in her first term in Dáil Éireann. There was the disciplined orator who delivered second-stage speeches without departing from the script. There was the lawyer manqué who quietly and effectively quizzed witnesses in the PAC. There was the theatrical performer at Leaders' Questions, armed with the sound bite, landing punches on government ministers day after day. There was the conciliatory, constructive legislator improving a bill at committee stage. There was the anarchist who broke all the rules and occupied the chamber, the heart of Irish democracy. There was the charmer whom everybody, irrespective of party, liked as a person. There were big blemishes, but her balance sheet as a Dáil deputy was already heavily in credit.

Yet in late 2014 her growing number of destructive parliamentary exploits was disturbing. Many observers put them down to Gerry Adams, the monkey on her back, breathing down her neck, whispering in her ear wherever she turned. Others gave a more devious explanation for her sudden enthusiasm for smashing parliamentary rules as the thirty-first Dáil came to a close. Sinn Féin was being forced to defend itself on various serious scandals. The party of protest was itself being cornered, forced to deal with poisonous events from the past haunting it in the present. The cover-up of paedophilia had already raised its ugly head when Mary Lou was forced to defend Gerry Adams's behaviour following the discovery of his brother Liam's abuse of his daughter. Accusations of bullying of female members of Sinn Féin were breaking with an ominous frequency. Worst of all, cover-up of rape by Sinn Féin members was surfacing, with dark tales of IRA kangaroo courts damaging the party. The day before Mary Lou's sensational occupation of the Dáil in protest at Joan Burton's unwillingness to answer questions, Sinn Féin had been forced to face a full debate on its evil treatment of rape victim Máiría Cahill. The party was on the ropes.

Were the barbaric actions of those men who had controlled the IRA and Sinn Féin – before her time – forcing Mary Lou to embark on desperate 'spectaculars' to distract media attention from the menacing tales that were slowly emerging? Was that the thinking behind her Ansbacher outburst and her occupation of the Dáil? Was she capable of dealing with the unravelling Sinn Féin atrocities, denouncing them, apologising and cleaning them up, or was she going to duck, dive, divert attention and back Adams whatever the cost? The case of Máiría Cahill, slowly gathering momentum, coming into the open, and how Mary Lou dealt with it would be a defining moment in her claim to have escaped from the clutches of the old IRA.

CHAPTER 8

ADAMS CALLS THE SHOTS

Máiría Cahill's great-uncle Joe Cahill died on 23 July 2004, aged eighty-four. His funeral was held four days later. It was the largest republican burial ceremony since the death of hunger striker Bobby Sands in the Maze prison in May 1981. Thousands of people attended, following the cortège from Cahill's home in Andersonstown down to St John's Church at the bottom of Whiterock Road on the Falls.

Joe Cahill was a republican legend. As a young man of twenty-two in 1942, he was given the death penalty for the murder of a Roman Catholic policeman, Constable Patrick Murphy. His sentence was commuted to life imprisonment after the intervention of Pope Pius XII, and he was freed in 1949 after seven years. Following his release, he rejoined the republican movement, only to be interned in 1957 after the IRA had resumed its campaign of violence. In 1961, Cahill was one of the last internees released, a few months before the guerrilla campaign was abandoned in February 1962. He took a back seat in the 1960s, losing interest when the republican movement forsook violence to concentrate on social agitation. After the sectarian riots and the arrival of the

British Army on the streets of Belfast in 1969, Cahill was a prime mover in the creation of the new Provisional IRA, becoming a member of the IRA Army Council and commander of the Belfast Brigade.

On 9 August 1971 Cahill, not a natural media showman, pulled off a 'spectacular'. It was the day that internment without trial was introduced in Northern Ireland. This draconian security measure was specifically designed to round up IRA leaders like Cahill and the growing number of gunmen on the streets of Belfast and Derry. Cahill had been in hiding, apparently tipped off about the imminence of internment, when the security forces came calling. Despite the arrest of over 400 suspects on that fateful day, despite the presence of hundreds of soldiers patrolling west Belfast in hot pursuit of any elusive IRA members, he managed to hold a snap press conference in a school in Ballymurphy, right under the noses of the British Army. Forewarned of the approach of a British armoured car, the media event was rapidly cut short, but Cahill had made his point: the IRA leadership was intact, well organised and had given the British Army the slip. Pictures of the commander of the IRA's Belfast Brigade wiping the eye of the mighty British flashed around the world. From that day Cahill was a household name, an eternal presence in republican folklore.

Joe Cahill was an unapologetic advocate of violence. Heroics or not on the day of internment, he had blood on his hands. Apart from his role in the murder of Constable Murphy, he had openly declared in 1971 that 'our aim is to kill as many British soldiers as possible. I am a gunman. Talking will get us nowhere.' He lived up to his commitment, authorising the IRA's bombing campaign, with attacks on both the army and the RUC, resulting in dozens of deaths.

After becoming chief of staff of the IRA in 1972, Cahill took charge of importing arms from abroad, mainly from Libya and the United States. In March 1973 he was arrested off the coast of

Waterford aboard the *Claudia*, a ship carrying five tons of weapons courtesy of Libyan dictator Colonel Muammar al-Gaddafi. He received a three-year prison sentence. Over the course of the Troubles, Cahill was involved in other, more successful importations of arms – from Libya with the help of Gaddafi and from the United States with the help of NORAID.

In his later years, Cahill signed up for the peace process, becoming a messenger for the IRA, sent across the Atlantic to persuade militant US republicans to embrace the Good Friday Agreement.

Peace process or not, Cahill's funeral was a paramilitary affair. Not all those present had been in the IRA, but they came from far and wide to pay homage to an unrepentant advocate of violence. The appearance of former Taoiseach Albert Reynolds caused a stir and was greeted as a propaganda success by the republican movement, but, apart from Reynolds, there were few present who had not supported the terrorist campaign. Many of them had participated in it.

Generations of hard-line republicans – some IRA killers and bombers – lined the streets. Convicted terrorists carried the coffin. The congregation included IRA London bomber Brian Keenan, who had organised the cold-blooded murder of several people; former IRA leader in the Maze prison Padraic Wilson; Shankill Road bomber Seán Kelly; Brighton bomber Patrick Magee; and IRA 'enforcer' Bobby Storey. The predictable duo of Martin McGuinness and Gerry Adams played prominent roles, as did another retired gunrunner, Martin Ferris.

Wreaths were sent from the general headquarters of the IRA and from the Belfast Brigade. A piper led the cortège; the coffin was covered in a tricolour. A republican guard of honour flanked the hearse, four on the right side and three on the left. They wore black berets and white shirts, with regulation dark suits and ties. The guard of honour, including former IRA man Councillor Christy

Burke and MEP Bairbre de Brún, marched in military-style step. At the Cahill residence, where Joe Cahill's body was being waked, he was given a round-the-clock IRA four-person vigil. In the bedroom upstairs, at all times, there were four republican volunteers, ready to rotate the watch over the deceased. All that was missing at the funeral was a volley of shots over the coffin.

Máiría Cahill, a young woman of twenty-three who had been raped by a senior IRA member seven years earlier, sat in one of the pews of the church, honouring her great-uncle. As a member of the Cahill family, she had been personally close to him, but she was no longer a fully committed member of the republican family that had protected her IRA abuser. She had distanced herself from Sinn Féin three years earlier in 2001.

As Máiría Cahill left the church, following the coffin and the large crowd, a few yards away from her stood Sinn Féin's rising parliamentary star, MEP Mary Lou McDonald, elected to the European Parliament only six weeks earlier. Mary Lou had no hesitation in eagerly endorsing the paramilitary trappings. The woman from Rathgar had never been a member of the IRA. She was not born into the republican ritual that dominated the funeral in Northern Ireland. Nevertheless, she took her place as a coffin carrier. Mary Lou had joined others, including McGuinness, Adams and singer Frances Black, in lifting Joe Cahill's coffin from his Andersonstown home down the road to the church and towards his final resting place. Mary Lou's gesture that day attracted attention and approval, exactly as she had intended.

She was making a statement. Not only was she attending the funeral – she was going the whole hog in honouring Joe Cahill. She was not a lifelong friend of his, but a leading presence in the same party as the now departed republican giant, the man who had authorised unspeakable acts of violence. It was understandable that she should attend the obsequies, but, by carrying the coffin, she became a player in a military-style production. She was sending out an early signal that she was buying into Joe Cahill's legacy. And it is not a pretty one.

Mary Lou McDonald was seamlessly insinuating herself into the affections of the more militant mourners. The funeral was a family service but also a political occasion, an IRA celebration, honouring a man with a legacy steeped in blood and bombing. Joe Cahill may have belatedly joined the Gerry Adams journey of peace, but he had done untold damage on the way. Many of the men (and they were mostly men) at that Christian funeral had approved of the IRA campaign of murdering and maiming their fellow human beings. Mary Lou was letting them know not only that she shared their grief, but also that she understood Cahill's violent legacy. It was a perfect occasion to further her ambitions, to earn acceptance and respect from the hard men in the North. At the graveside, she positioned herself near the burial plot, close to Gerry Adams when he delivered his eulogy to Joe Cahill. Mary Lou was playing cemetery politics to perfection. She was learning from Adams, the master of this ghoulish art, who had buried IRA men by the barrowful, each time using the IRA 'martyr's' funeral as a weapon in his relentless propaganda war.

Adams flagrantly exploited his graveside homily to promote the living, namely Mary Lou and Bairbre de Brún. Citing Cahill as a supporter of the peace process, Adams claimed that the deceased had observed – just a few weeks before his death – that the 'cream on the cake of the growth of our party north and south was Mary Lou and Bairbre's election to the European Parliament'. It was a soft sell, but a subtle one. Gerry Adams was marketing the Southern woman, the well-groomed, very Dublin MEP who had carried the coffin, to the sceptical hard men from the North who were listening in the crowd.

Frances Black, the singer, whose family were friends of Joe and his widow, Annie Cahill, sang 'The Bold Fenian Men' at the graveside.

Similarly, sixteen years later in 2020, the funeral of IRA chief Bobby Storey was turned into another rallying cry to the faithful veterans in Belfast. Mary Lou sped up to Belfast on that day to walk behind Storey's cortège. She didn't look comfortable, but she was there.

Her gesture of carrying the coffin at Cahill's funeral was meant for Northern consumption. It was undoubtedly inspired by Adams and appreciated by the citizens of west Belfast. It was not an action that served her best interests in the suburbs of Dublin. A letter to *The Irish Times* the following week from Brian Moran of Balrothery, County Dublin, highlighted the dangers of playing such graveyard games.

FUNERAL OF JOE CAHILL

Madam,

I have been duped by Mary Lou McDonald. For the first time ever and against my better judgment, I voted for Sinn Féin in the European elections under the misguided impression that the party was positively striving towards a mainstream political entity and leaving its bloodied past behind. My vote was out of recognition for Sinn Féin's efforts in the peace process.

Then, to my horror, I see that they haven't changed at all. How stupid am I? Pictures of Mary Lou McDonald carrying the coffin of that monster Joe Cahill shocked me to the bone. You fraudster – I want my vote back!

Joe Cahill's grand-niece Máiría Cahill wouldn't have endorsed those sentiments about the character of her great-uncle. She was burying a blood relation, not a terrorist.

Máiría Cahill carried a deep personal wound, permanently nursing a horrific trauma perpetrated by a high-ranking member of the republican movement who had raped her when she was only sixteen. The IRA, spooked by Máiría Cahill's royal republican blood, had held a kangaroo court of senior members to sort out her allegations. She had been forced to meet her assailant face to face. She had been petrified. The IRA inquiry had been, conveniently, inconclusive. Máiría had been traumatised, seeking refuge in psychiatric therapy.

Gerry Adams, a friend of the Cahill family and the most powerful republican on the island, had been involved in bungled attempts to respond to Máiría's agony. Top IRA people who had served on the 'kangaroo court' – set up to sweep her grievance under the carpet – were seated at Joe Cahill's funeral service.

Máiría Cahill had discussed her case with her great-uncle Joe. He had sat in the car and wept with her while she told him of her plight. According to Máiría, he insisted that if he had known about it, he would have advised her to go to the RUC. He was raging, telling her that there had been a 'fuck-up' in the IRA. It sounded as though he was split between disgust at the rape of his blood relation, a kangaroo court set up by his fellow IRA members to intimidate Máiría, and loyalty to the violent movement to which he had given his life.

Máiría remembers a bit of 'chit-chat' between Mary Lou, former Sinn Féin general secretary Lucilita Bhreatnach and herself at the funeral. She says she felt 'uncomfortable' at the service, 'seeing some of the ones involved in my case'. The 'chit-chat' did not include any mention of Máiría's rape case on that day, although it is inconceivable that two senior republicans, like Lucilita and Mary Lou, were unaware of it. It was a below-the-radar running sore, common knowledge in west Belfast, certainly in republican circles. Even though she bore the family name 'Cahill' – impeccable republican nobility – she received no words of comfort from her republican sisters on that day.

Mary Lou's and Máiría's paths seldom crossed over the next ten years. There was a chance meeting in 2007 at a get-together to address the Northern Ireland policing hot potato. Otherwise, Máiría kept her head down, but the impact of her rape had overwhelmed her life. She was hospitalised in a psychiatric unit in 2005. She lost two close members of her family, her cousin Siobhán O'Hanlon in 2006 and her paternal grandmother in 2007. From 2005 to 2010 she attended twice-weekly counselling sessions. She worked on a cross-community project on Belfast's Lenadoon Estate before becoming pregnant in January 2010.

In the Christmas–New Year period 2009/10, Máiría saw a programme on Ulster Television about Gerry Adams's support for his brother Liam and the allegations of Liam's child abuse. It finally prompted her to make a complaint to the police about the abuse she had suffered in 1997/98. It was a brave decision for anyone from west Belfast to point a finger at the IRA, especially if accompanied by a demand for PSNI action. She spoke to the police in January and made a formal complaint in April. The birth of her daughter, Saorlaith, in September 2010 brought joy to her life, which she says, 'changed everything and gave me focus'.

After Máiría had given an officially anonymous, but easily identifiable, interview about her rape to the *Sunday Tribune* in January 2010 and had made her complaint to the police in April, it took until 2014 for charges of IRA membership and other offences to be brought against five well-known republicans, named as Martin Morris, Padraic Wilson, Seamus Finucane, Agnes McCrory and Briege Wright. Morris was charged with rape and IRA membership, while the other four were arraigned for IRA involvement in the kangaroo court. All charges against the defendants were dropped after Máiría Cahill withdrew evidence and refused to testify, saying that she had lost all confidence in the state's prosecution service.

In October 2014 the BBC's *Spotlight* programme broadcast a sensational investigation into Máiría Cahill's case entitled 'A Woman Alone with the IRA'. She had bravely waived her right to anonymity, repeating on air her allegations of rape by Martin

Morris, and of senior IRA members setting up a kangaroo court before forcing her to meet her alleged rapist face to face. They had then ordered her to keep silent in order to protect the republican movement.

The *Spotlight* programme caused a political earthquake. Northern Ireland's prosecution service responded to Máiría Cahill's revelations by setting up an independent review of three cases linked to her alleged rape. Sir Keir Starmer, a former director of public prosecutions for England and Wales and later leader of the Labour Party, was appointed to conduct it. Separately, Máiría herself made a complaint to the Police Ombudsman about the PSNI's conduct in her case. The two reviews were up and running.

These events prompted instant political reaction North and South. First Minister Peter Robinson and Taoiseach Enda Kenny both praised Máiría's courage after hastily agreeing to meet her in Belfast and Dublin respectively. Politicians everywhere began to joust for position after the *Spotlight* programme had given Máiría Cahill serious credibility. Sinn Féin was on the back foot. The momentum and demand for action built up. The controversy reached the floor of the Dáil and the Northern Ireland Assembly. In the Assembly, a motion calling for a full inquiry into the Cahill case and the role of Sinn Féin junior minister Jennifer McCann, whose responsibilities included victims of the Troubles, was passed by sixty-eight votes to twenty-seven. The DUP demanded McCann's resignation. She was a former member of the IRA who had served ten years in jail for the attempted murder of an RUC officer.

In the Dáil, all eyes turned to Mary Lou McDonald and Gerry Adams. The other political parties united, eagerly seizing the opportunity to put the president and vice-president of Sinn Féin in the dock. Normally scarce Dáil time was found for a full five hours of 'Statements on Allegations Regarding Sexual Abuse by Members of the Provisional Republican Movement'. Taoiseach Enda Kenny, Fianna Fáil party leader Micheál Martin and Labour's Joan Burton seized the moral high ground. They took the opportunity to nail Gerry Adams to the child abuse cross and to crucify Mary Lou McDonald alongside him.

Máiría Cahill turned up for the Dáil debate on 12 November 2014. Those sitting at her side in the public gallery included three formidable supporters, Labour senator Mary Moran, former Labour minister Liz McManus and Máiría's cousin, journalist Éilis O'Hanlon.

The relationship between Mary Lou and Máiría was icy. Máiría says that she bumped into Mary Lou just before the debate. According to Senan Molony in the *Daily Mail*, the two adversaries exchanged harsh words at the chance meeting. He reported that Fine Gael's Regina Doherty first raised the encounter on an RTÉ programme, while Mary Moran asserted that McDonald had smirked and grimaced at Máiría, adding 'her eyes were glaring'. Mary Moran went on: 'Máiría said, "I hope you are going to tell the truth, Mary Lou," and she [McDonald] stared her out of it. Her mouth was smiling, but her eyes were definitely not. The whole thing was extremely uncomfortable for Máiría. I don't know if it was designed to intimidate, but it would have promoted a definite discomfort. It was more the manner. She did not smile, absolutely not.' Witnesses said that Mary Lou replied: 'Máiría, I always tell the truth.'

The scene was set for a thoroughly poisonous afternoon.

The debate lived up to expectations. Taoiseach Enda Kenny pulled no punches, tearing into the republicans sitting in the chamber. Launching into both Sinn Féin and the IRA, he insisted that they had put their own movement's interests above Máiría Cahill's. 'They covered up the abuse,' the Taoiseach declared, 'and moved the perpetrators around in order that the untouchables would remain untouchable.' And in a damning indictment of the IRA's loathsome habit of settling their offenders south of the border, he thundered, 'I refer to republicans who thought so much of this

Republic that they would honour us with their rapists and gift us their child abusers . . . The children of the Republic should not be obliged to live with the risk posed by the IRA's misfits.'

Kenny hurled Adams into the frame, while giving Mary Lou no quarter. Turning to her own frequent condemnations of child abuse in other cases, he spoke of her 'seismic rage and righteousness about victims now'. He denounced her 'pathological loyalty' to Adams and her 'compulsive denial of a cover up' in the Cahill case. It was as though he had hoped for better from Mary Lou McDonald, but expected less from her leader.

Kenny was only teeing up the debate for the next speaker. His party colleague Regina Doherty followed him, in the full knowledge that it was open season on Adams and Mary Lou. Doherty, with a reputation as a Fine Gael rottweiler as far as Sinn Féin was concerned, but a fearlessly principled politician, did not let down her leader. She shredded Adams for his earlier conduct in bringing another victim, his own niece Áine Tyrell (Adams), to suffer a similar face-to-face meeting with her abusive father, his own brother, Liam. Doherty was adamant that we should not forget Áine. There were others. She dismissed Gerry Adams's version of events with the words : 'I would not believe the Lord's Prayer from his mouth.'

Then, woman to woman, she turned her anger on Mary Lou. 'Let me address Deputy McDonald . . . Today I feel disgusted by Deputy Mary Lou McDonald's response to Máiría Cahill and all the other victims of Sinn Féin and IRA sexual abusers. I am disappointed beyond belief that she would so cheaply sell her integrity for political positioning, that her naked political ambition would cause her to fail the children of our nation, fail families and fail victims, all in the name of a cheap power grab . . . For all her rhetoric about women's rights, she did not know how to respond appropriately to Máiría Cahill's allegations because to respond or react like a woman, a human being, would have meant telling the truth.'

And finally, the *coup de grâce*, staring across the chamber at

Mary Lou, she fingered Adams. 'It actually would have meant criticising that chap beside her. Maybe I am being too harsh because perhaps, like the rest, she is probably afraid of the real Belfast leadership. I ask her sincerely to step outside the groupthink that obviously characterises Sinn Féin and stand up for victims with sincerity, not in the mealy-mouthed way she has done in recent weeks by saying she believes Máiría Cahill while undermining her at the same time.'

Doherty had animated the chamber. Even today she remembers being very nervous before that debate, and told me: 'Mary Lou just sat beside him [Adams] and tut-tutted and nodded in all the right places. She would have said black was white for him. She treated Máiría Cahill despicably. After that, I was on the Sinn Féin radar and subject to particular scrutiny and reduction, but I think it made me bolder.'

When I recently asked Regina Doherty about Mary Lou's demeanour in the debate, she replied, 'The only emotion we saw was her contempt for us – steely stares etc. Particularly to Máiría personally – poor behaviour towards her, a victim of the kind of people Mary Lou McDonald celebrates annually.'

Labour leader and Tánaiste Joan Burton was the next to speak. She took careful aim at the woman who had been her recent tormentor on the floor of the Dáil, reminding the house of Mary Lou's stance on the issue of child abuse five years earlier: after the abuses of children by Roman Catholic priests had been exposed, Mary Lou had loudly demanded that anyone found to be complicit in the cover-up of child abuse 'must be arrested and made to face the full rigours of the law'. The vice-president of Sinn Féin was hoist with her own petard. 'I agree fully,' Joan Burton uttered gleefully, 'with Deputy McDonald's sentiments and I ask her to apply these same standards to Sinn Féin and the IRA. In particular, does Deputy McDonald apply this standard to the powerful man who leads her own party?'

And in case anyone was in any doubt, she branded Adams's reaction to Máiría Cahill's case as one of 'denial, evasion and seeking to protect the IRA'. Mary Lou was painted as complicit. Joan Burton appealed to both Mary Lou and later to Pearse Doherty to 'challenge the powerful men in their own movement'.

Labour junior minister Ged Nash – a constituency rival of Gerry Adams in Louth – was next to speak. He challenged 'the women of Sinn Féin' head-on, accusing them of being 'uncharacteristically silent on these grave matters. Where,' he asked, 'are Mary Lou McDonald and Sandra McLellan? Where do the Sinn Féin Senator [Kathryn Reilly from Cavan] and female councillors stand on the matter?'

Ged Nash was right. Sandra McLellan, the only other female Sinn Féin TD, did not speak in the debate. Unknown to many at the time, she was another lonely woman fighting her own losing battles within the party.

Fianna Fáil's Micheál Martin repeated many of the earlier speakers' charges about the knowledge, hypocrisy and duplicity of Adams and McDonald. There was unanimity of revulsion from all the main parties at the responses of Adams and McDonald. It remained only for the Dáil to hear what they had to say in their own defence.

Adams was unyielding. He conceded that Cahill had been raped, even admitting that the IRA response had been inadequate. He rejected charges that there had been a cover-up by Sinn Féin and insisted that his concern had been for Máiría's welfare, as had been the motivation of 'those republicans who played any part in speaking to Máiría' – a somewhat benign description of a kangaroo court. He condemned Sinn Féin's trial by media on the BBC *Spotlight* programme, asserting that the defendants had been smeared and were acquitted by a court of law, a fact ignored by all speakers in the Dáil. Adams knew nothing about the Taoiseach's accusations that sex offenders had been moved across the border from Northern Ireland to Dublin, Donegal and Louth. Referring to the statements made about the child abuse case of his brother Liam Adams, he and his family 'deeply rejected the taunts and offensive commentary by some here about what was for our family a deeply traumatic episode in our family life'. Adams was trying to grab a slice of the victimhood floating around the chamber. Whatever emotions Adams provokes, sympathy is hardly the most immediate.

Adams never had a chance of an ounce of sympathy from his audience of hostile TDs, but many deputies awaited the words of Mary Lou McDonald. She was a woman who would surely identify with Máiría Cahill's ordeal? The two women had spent at least one convivial evening in each other's company in Glór na nGael on the Falls Road in happier times. Did that never pass through McDonald's mind before she rose to speak? If there was ever going to be a time to divert from the Adams line of defence, this was it. Mary Lou had been the target of unprecedented, blunt and stinging criticism. Had the words of other female TDs – Frances Fitzgerald, Joan Burton, Maureen O'Sullivan, Joanna Tuffy, Ruth Coppinger, Áine Collins, Ciara Conway and Regina Doherty – landed? Was she rattled?

Mary Lou never flinched. She had a script and she stuck to it. She gave a metaphorical two fingers to the women from all other parties. She issued a general condemnation of rape and a cold analysis of its occurrence. She threw back the other TDs' allegations in their faces, attacking the state's record on child abuse and the institutions of the state's failures to redress it over the years. She outlined the background in Northern Ireland, where victims in the past had found nowhere to turn because they did not trust the RUC. She denied Máiría Cahill's claims that the investigation by the IRA was 'coercive', insisting that the investigators were not interrogators. She repeated her condemnation of the child abuses and cover-ups by priests in the Roman Catholic Church. She, like Adams, denied any cover-up of Máiría Cahill's case by Sinn Féin.

And then the trademark sound bite: 'I am the mother of two

young children and, like any mother, I would walk the hot coals
of hell to protect my children.' Mary Lou answered none of the
specific questions posed to her in the debate. She brazened it out.
Her feminist credentials may have been terminally damaged, but
Gerry Adams will have been mightily pleased. True to form, Mary
Lou was repaying him for all the patronage he had lavished on her
in the past.

After the emotional debates in Stormont and Leinster House, a
lot of credibility rested on the reviews being carried out by Sir Keir
Starmer on behalf of the director of public prosecutions and by the
Northern Ireland Police Ombudsman. Lingering doubts, sown by
Sinn Féin about Máiría Cahill's failure to give evidence against all
five defendants, needed to be resolved. Her withdrawal from the
case had been spun by her Sinn Féin detractors as evidence that her
story did not stand up. They constantly pointed out that all five
defendants had been acquitted by a court.

In May 2015, Sir Keir reported that the Public Prosecution
Service had failed Máiría Cahill. The director of public prosecutions
for Northern Ireland, Barra McGrory, publicly apologised to her,
making an unequivocal statement: 'I wish to make it clear that no
fault or blame attaches to Máiría Cahill. The Director of Public
Prosecution Service let you down, and for that I am sorry.'

She was vindicated.

A few months later, in November 2015, Joan Burton proposed
Máiría Cahill as Labour's candidate in a by-election for a vacant
Senate seat on the Industrial and Commercial Panel. She enjoyed a
landslide victory in an election where voting is restricted to members
of the Houses of the Oireachtas. She was only 'Senator Cahill' for
five months because she did not defend the Senate seat in the contest
following the 2016 general election.

Her final vindication had to wait until September 2018 when
the Police Ombudsman for Northern Ireland, Dr Michael Maguire,
released his review of her complaint about the PSNI's behaviour in

her case. In a statement, his office revealed that, in 2000, intelligence received by the Criminal Investigation Department (CID) and RUC Special Branch about the abuse of Máiría Cahill and others was not properly acted upon. She had been 'failed' by the police. The Ombudsman recommended that four officers should be disciplined. The chief constable, George Hamilton, apologised to Máiría and two other victims of the same man. Three of the officers were disciplined; the fourth had already retired.

After the publication of the Ombudsman's report, Mary Lou also apologised, but in a half-hearted manner. She said sorry for the way the allegations of rape were handled, but she ducked responsibility for the republican movement's consistently disgraceful behaviour about instances of sexual abuse over a long period. She still failed to admit that there was an IRA investigation followed by a cover-up. She made bizarre comments, pleading that she was not a 'spook or a spy', so could not comment on the findings of the CID that Martin Morris, the defendant in the rape case, had been suspended from Sinn Féin because he was a suspected child abuser. She pleaded feebly that Sinn Féin records were not as good in 2000 as they were in 2018. An *Irish Times* editorial was not impressed, calling the police response a 'proper apology' and noting that 'the same cannot be said of Sinn Féin and its leader Mary Lou McDonald'.

Máiría Cahill rejected Mary Lou's apology as 'woefully inadequate'. The two women met at Máiría's request in Leinster House shortly afterwards. There was no meeting of minds.

In July 2018 Máiría was co-opted as a councillor for Lisburn and Castlereagh Council by the Social Democratic and Labour Party. It was again a short-lived public position. She withdrew from the local elections in 2019 because of a law requiring candidates to publish their home addresses. Fearful of threats to her safety, Cahill refused to defend her seat under that sort of pressure. The British government later apologised and changed the law.

Máiría Cahill was treated barbarically. She, at least, was a

woman who could fight back. She was articulate and could speak
out. She was republican royalty wronged, but had an unerring will
to win and protect others from the same savage treatment she had
received from the IRA.

Unfortunately, Jean McConville had no such opportunities to
expose her assailants. McConville was another female victim of the
IRA. She was not from a republican family. She could not speak
out. In 2014 Jean McConville had been dead for forty-two years.
She had not been raped. She had been murdered.

Jean McConville, a widowed mother of ten children, was
kidnapped, shot as an 'informer' and buried by the IRA in 1972.
She was born a Protestant, married a Roman Catholic and was
driven out of a Protestant area to live in Belfast's Divis Flats, an
IRA fortress. Her body was secretly buried across the border on
Templeton Beach, County Louth, on the Cooley Peninsula. It was
found thirty-one years later in 2003 with a bullet in the back of
her head. In 1999 the IRA had admitted to her murder, claiming
that she had been paid for passing on information about its activities to the British Army. Some Sinn Féin sources spin that a
transmitter had been found in her apartment, that she had been
warned but that she repeated the offence. A later report by Northern
Ireland's first Police Ombudsman, Nuala O'Loan, found no evidence
for this assertion.

Jean McConville's murder was not properly investigated until
1995, when the RUC carried out a very limited probe. Rumours
were rife about who in the IRA was responsible, but witnesses, as
ever, went missing. Identifying McConville's killers appeared to
have been a lost cause until an initiative known as the Boston
College Belfast Project was launched in 2001. The brainchild of
author Ed Moloney and former Provisional IRA volunteer and
historian Anthony McIntyre, the Belfast Project aimed to record an
accurate history of elements of the Troubles that had proved
opaque. The tapes contained confessions. Moloney and McIntyre

persuaded key terrorist figures from both sides of the divide to speak on tape, provided that none of their contributions were published until after their deaths. The murder of Jean McConville was a key component.

Brendan Hughes, a leading republican, a one-time great friend, but later sworn enemy, of Gerry Adams, died in 2008 at the age of fifty-nine. After his death, some of his statements to the Boston Project appeared in a book by Moloney called *Voices from the Grave*. Hughes admitted that he had participated in McConville's kidnapping and that she had confessed to being an informer. He insisted that Gerry Adams had ordered her death. His account was later separately backed up by a newspaper interview with another senior republican and Old Bailey bomber, Dolours Price. She revealed that Adams had ordered her to take part in the kidnapping and murder of McConville. Adams denied all the allegations made against him, pointing out that both Price and Hughes were opposed to the peace process.

In 2011 the PSNI began a legal action in the US to gain access to the tapes. Boston College initially opposed handing them over, but the Northern Ireland police force was eventually granted the transcripts of Hughes's and Price's statements. (Price died in 2013 at the age of sixty-two.) In March 2014 this new material gave the PSNI enough evidence to arrest several people over the murder of Jean McConville, including Ivor Bell, a former IRA chief of staff. On 30 April, Adams pre-empted his own predictable arrest by volunteering to submit himself for questioning. He was arrested and questioned about Jean McConville's murder for four days in Antrim police station.

Once again, Mary Lou came under pressure to defend Adams. The spectre of her mentor being quizzed about one of the worst atrocities of the Troubles was a political nightmare for her, but she rose to the task. She tried to turn the tables, transitioning into 'attack dog' mode, claiming that since there were elections going on (both European and local) the arrest was timed perfectly to hurt republicans. She let rip at the PSNI, saying, 'I believe the timing of this latest decision by the PSNI is politically motivated and designed to damage Gerry Adams and Sinn Féin.' She threw 'unionist elements' into the mix, combining them with the 'old guard' in the PSNI as the culprits behind Adams's arrest.

Mary Lou was hounded by the media during Adams's period in custody. She yielded no ground, repeating her attack on the PSNI at every opportunity, a sudden departure from Sinn Féin's more recent policy of claiming credit for the reform of Northern Ireland's police force. She said the arrest followed a 'concerted and malicious effort to link Gerry Adams to this case for a considerable time'.

Gerry Adams was released without charge after four days. It took five years for Ivor Bell to be charged and acquitted of all accusations relating to the murder of Jean McConville.

Repeatedly, Mary Lou had opted to defend Adams for unspeakable horrors linked to him. His past was haunting her. In the public mind he had become forever linked with the murder of Jean McConville, possibly the darkest atrocity of the entire Troubles. Mary Lou's credibility had already been badly dented by her continual protestations that she believed Adams's declarations that he had never been a member of the IRA. In a year that had started so well with her stellar performance on RTÉ's *Late Late Show* and consistent successes in the Dáil and the PAC, she was simultaneously dogged by a string of scandals surrounding her patron. Sinn Féin's outstanding parliamentarian was no longer being exposed as Adams's protégée, but as his house-trained poodle.

Mary Lou's determination to ingratiate herself with the hard men in the North was constantly landing her in deep political water. She had carried former IRA chief Joe Cahill's coffin; she had defended Gerry Adams's behaviour over his paedophile brother, Liam; she had positioned herself in Gerry's corner in the case of the violation of Máiría Cahill; she had supported and swallowed his story in the Jean McConville killing. It was a pattern: the brutality and sexual crimes of the IRA in the North were jumping up to bite her. Perhaps as part of a new generation she could plausibly plead that she had not been directly involved in any of the old scandals, that she was only a three-year-old child when Jean McConville was murdered and that she had no direct involvement in any IRA crimes. Unfortunately, she was a consistent apologist. She invariably backed Gerry Adams's fairy tales.

The case of Paul Quinn was different. In 2007, nine years after the Good Friday Agreement, deep in south Armagh, one of the cruellest crimes ever recorded in Northern Ireland was being plotted.

Paul Quinn, a twenty-one-year-old lorry driver, living with his parents, Stephen and Breege, was murdered in cold blood on 20 October. A 'friend' lured him from his home to a cowshed in a farm over the border in County Monaghan. After he was trapped in the shed by a gang of around fifteen men, he was beaten to death with iron and nail-studded bars. According to his parents, every bone in his body was broken before he died in hospital later that evening.

In March 2022 I visited Paul Quinn's still heartbroken parents in their home in Cullyhanna, close to Crossmaglen, a hotbed of IRA activity in the Troubles. Stephen and Breege still live in the house where they brought up Paul. They are adamant that he was killed by the Provisional IRA because he had bested one of their number in an altercation.

No one has ever been charged with Paul Quinn's murder. South Armagh is not an area where witnesses come forward to give evidence against their neighbours, especially if they have been members of the IRA. Throughout the Troubles, the British Army was incapable of breaking the grip held by the Provisional IRA over south Armagh residents.

When I arrived in Crossmaglen on 28 March 2022, it was not long before Assembly election time. I spotted several election posters of the local Sinn Féin candidate, long-time republican Conor

Murphy, the outgoing minister for finance in the Northern Ireland executive. Murphy, who was born and bred in south Armagh, played a prominent, but dishonourable, role in the Quinns' tragic story. A former activist in the IRA, Murphy began a five-year prison sentence for IRA membership and possession of explosives in 1982.

After his release from prison, Murphy climbed his way up the Sinn Féin ladder. In October 2007, when Paul Quinn was murdered, he was minister for regional development in the Northern Ireland executive. More importantly, he was MLA for the Newry and Armagh constituency, where the Quinns lived. A month after the murder, Conor Murphy had given an extraordinary interview to the BBC *Spotlight* programme, claiming – without a shred of supporting evidence – that 'Paul Quinn was involved in smuggling and criminality and I think that everyone accepts that'. It was a low smear of unparalleled proportions.

It was almost as if, had Paul Quinn been a convicted smuggler – which he wasn't – it would somehow explain away his fate. Murphy also said that he had spoken to IRA members about the murder. They had told him that the IRA was not involved. The ex-IRA minister believed his comrades.

Conor Murphy's line was simple: Paul Quinn was a criminal. Murphy's friends in the IRA were not involved in Quinn's murder. Case closed.

Not quite. Writer and former Labour Party minister Liz McManus, in a piece for *Legacy Matters* magazine, recalls a public meeting a year after Paul Quinn's murder in the heartland of militant republicans, Crossmaglen. McManus relates the mood of the community and the hopelessness of those seeking justice for Paul Quinn following Conor Murphy's smear.

His parents, Breege and Stephen Quinn, had garnered support from the local community. And they were reaching out to members of Dáil Éireann in the hope of deepening that groundswell of support. There were Christmas lights in the main street of

Crossmaglen when I arrived, and the community hall was full to capacity. The atmosphere was solemn, respectful and determined. People who may not have ever spoken publicly before, spoke out in support of the Quinn family. The chairman reinforced their message. He was a local farmer who recalled how the British Army raided his farmyard on a regular basis, how they had tied his hands with baling twine and how he had always stood firm against them. According to Liz McManus:

> It was an electrifying moment. I never expected to hear such sentiments expressed and certainly never in Crossmaglen. Then Paul Quinn's mother spoke with extraordinary dignity and courage. There were TDs present for the main parties at the time and we promised her that we would pursue the case. And we did by securing a formal debate in Dáil Éireann shortly afterwards. That day, every party spokesperson spoke in the chamber. It was a fitting tribute to the Quinn family and to the community solidarity that had been shown on that dark evening in Crossmaglen.
>
> It was a fitting tribute but a futile one.
>
> No one has been brought to justice for the killing of Paul Quinn. The sorrow of the family has not lessened. The support expressed by a community that night still goes unrecognised.

McManus's words resonate today. Fifteen years later, when I visited the Quinns, no one had been brought to justice. Conor Murphy has never taken back his description of Paul Quinn as a criminal, so the agony goes on for Stephen and Breege Quinn. They are not giving up. For years, they have demanded that Murphy withdraw his statement that their son was a criminal. For years, they have demanded that Murphy release the names of the IRA men who told him it was not they who killed their son. For years he kept his head down and hoped the Quinns would disappear.

They didn't. For thirteen years they kept the torch burning

while the false narrative that Paul was a criminal was being whispered loudly in republican circles. From time to time, they were given airtime to plead their case that neighbours of theirs knew all about the murder. The Quinns appealed to them to go to the PSNI or the gardaí. Arrests were made, sometimes of known IRA members, but no charges were ever brought. Omertà held firm. However, in the 2020 general election the murder of Paul Quinn broke out as a major controversy.

Mary Lou was president of Sinn Féin. Gerry Adams had retired. Conor Murphy was minister for finance in Stormont. He came under severe pressure to withdraw his 2007 remarks branding Paul Quinn as a criminal. He refused to do so.

All hell broke loose. The controversy reopened. Mary Lou told RTÉ's Bryan Dobson that she had spoken to Murphy and that he was 'very clear that he never said' that Quinn was involved in criminality. 'And that is not his view.'

Unfortunately for Conor and Mary Lou, there was a tape. There was no ambiguity. Murphy had said that Paul Quinn was a criminal. Mary Lou had accepted Murphy's solemn word that he hadn't made such an accusation.

It was clear as daylight that someone was telling lies. It was Mary Lou's, the new leader's, heaven-sent chance to put her stamp on the Northern military wing, to show that the Northern tail did not wag the Southern dog.

But it did. Instead of sacking Murphy on the spot for misleading her, she bottled it. She floundered, pleading that it was an 'honest mistake' by herself. She had misunderstood the Northern Ireland finance minister. She had thought he was talking about criminality and smuggling around the border region, and she did not know that his remarks were 'quite so pointed about Quinn'. A patently incoherent excuse. Not to worry – she had spoken to him and he was apologising and retracting his comments.

Conor Murphy apologised all right, but he used the oldest

empty formula in the political world. He apologised for the 'hurt' he 'might have caused' to the grieving family, but only for saying it. He admitted to Tommie Gorman on RTÉ that he had no evidence for his allegation, but he specifically wouldn't say that Paul Quinn was not a criminal. Mary Lou had already said that Quinn was not a criminal, but Murphy wouldn't say it. He defied her.

Mary Lou, now the Sinn Féin leader, supposedly no longer Adams's poodle, had bowed the knee to the Old Guard in the North. Conor Murphy had been 'army'. He had eyeballed his new leader, and she had blinked. She looked foolish and weak.

Or was there another reason for her cowardice? A more sinister skeleton was dug up; it suggested that the Sinn Féin party's answer to questions following Paul Quinn's murder had probably been cooked up over a decade earlier by Conor Murphy and none other than Gerry Adams himself. The BBC *Spotlight* team had discovered a second inconvenient tape, this time of an interview with Sinn Féin president Adams on 22 October 2007, just two days after Paul Quinn's murder and three weeks before Conor Murphy had made his false accusation. Adams was quite specific. Denial was his trademark, just as it was with Jean McConville. 'There is no republican involvement in this man's murder. The people involved,' he said, 'are criminals. They need to be brought to justice. It's fairly obvious to me this is linked to fuel smuggling and to criminal activity.' A devilishly clever red herring, a possible scenario in south Armagh where smugglers fuel a black economy. Many of them combined smuggling with being members of the IRA. Adams had cleared the decks for Murphy's smear.

Mary Lou was in a worse spot. After extracting an insincere apology of sorts from Murphy, the next question was if she would now require the same from her former leader and patron. Asked by Virgin Media whether Adams should now join his former comrade in apologising and should state that Paul Quinn was not a criminal, she backed off. Mary Lou said that she didn't feel an apology was needed from Adams because Breege and Stephen Quinn had taken issue only with Conor Murphy's comments, not because Murphy accused Paul Quinn of criminal activity, but because of the explicitness of his comments. Her excuse for not asking Adams was again painfully weak.

First, she had let Murphy off the hook. Second, nominal Sinn Féin leader as she was, she had capitulated to Adams. Unfortunately for Mary Lou, Breege and Stephen Quinn instantly demanded from Gerry Adams the same admission that their son was not a criminal. Her defence was exposed as unconvincing.

The Quinn family firmly believe that an IRA gang carried out the savage attack on their son, that Conor Murphy is peddling a line that protects his old comrades and discredits their murdered son. They say they know that it was Sinn Féin. They told me over tea and sandwiches in their house that they did not receive any visit of sympathy from the Sinn Féin party, whereas all the other parties sent mourners with messages of sorrow to the house when Paul died. They say they know the names of the killers, who live nearby.

Before I left, Breege Quinn took me to the window. She pointed out various houses visible from her bungalow. She was identifying the home of the man who had made the phone call to her son to lure him to the shed to meet his killers. She and Stephen remain as residents in a community where they believe the murderers of her child are living untouchable. It is a neighbourhood where murderers are being protected. It is a locality where a native minister brands innocent people as criminals and accepts the word of members of an illegal terrorist organisation. 'It isn't easy,' Breege Quinn said.

The IRA may no longer formally exist, but its successors, the gangs with the culture of omertà, flourish and dispense justice, just like the IRA kangaroo courts did in Belfast. As leader of the party sheltering many of the successors of the IRA, Mary Lou had a chance of confronting them in 2020. She flunked it.

Perhaps even today Mary Lou remains out of her depth in south Armagh. For her, the lawless district always had the potential to become a political graveyard. In late 2015 another long-serving IRA godfather from the same border area had come to the attention of the tax authorities in the Republic.

Thomas 'Slab' Murphy had run a multi-million-pound smuggling racket across the North–South border for decades. In 2004, according to the BBC's 'Underworld Rich List', he was the wealthiest smuggler in the UK, having amassed a €40 million fortune from trafficking in oil, cigarettes, pigs and grain. He is alleged to have been a former chief of staff of the Provisionals and a supporter of Gerry Adams. He had a house that was perfect for smuggling because the building actually straddled the Louth–Armagh border. He had been linked with the deaths of eighteen British soldiers at Warrenpoint in 1979 and was believed to have played a leading part in the death of Lord Mountbatten and three family members in Mullaghmore, County Sligo, on the same day. His role in smuggling weapons from Libya was widely believed to have prolonged the Troubles in the 1980s. Neither the RUC nor the gardaí had ever been able to bring charges against him, so hard was it to find any witnesses for crime in the area. In 1987 Slab Murphy overstepped the mark, suing *The Sunday Times* for libel for saying that he had run an IRA bombing campaign in London. Slab lost. The jury ruled that he was both an IRA man and a smuggler.

It proved hard for the gardaí or the PSNI to make criminal charges stick; but tax, reminiscent of Al Capone, was the route chosen to nail Slab Murphy.

In March 2006 a large-scale dawn raid was launched on his house and other suspected smugglers in the south Armagh–Louth area. Tankers, computers, shotguns, cigarettes, over half a million euro worth of sterling and vast quantities of euro were discovered. Four diesel-laundering operations with a widespread network of storage tanks were unearthed. Later that month the Criminal Assets Bureau was granted orders to seize cash, cheques and drafts totalling over €1 million euro discovered in this raid.

Over the next decade, Murphy defended himself in a series of tax evasion cases. He faced the Special Criminal Court, a non-jury trial, because the director of public prosecutions feared the intimidation of witnesses and jurors. A man who testified against Slab was later bludgeoned to death. Eventually, on 17 December 2015, Slab Murphy was found guilty of tax evasion.

Gerry Adams rode to the rescue in response, straining to reassure his ally that he would not be deserted. 'Tom Murphy,' Adams insisted, 'is not a criminal. He's a good republican and I believe what he says and, very importantly, he's a key supporter of Sinn Féin's peace strategy and has been for a long time.' He went on: 'I want to deal with what is an effort to portray Tom Murphy as a criminal, as a bandit, as a gang boss, as someone who is exploiting the republican struggle for his own ends, as a multimillionaire. There is no evidence to support any of that.'

Adams was sending out a clear, but deeply cynical, message. First, to both Irish and British governments, that harassing or arresting Slab endangered the peace process. Second, to the republican faithful, a signal that the republican movement stood shoulder to shoulder with Slab Murphy, 'the good republican' from south Armagh.

Mary Lou certainly got the message. She was soon parroting Adams's mantra.

The court's verdict sent shock waves through Sinn Féin. There seemed to be a controlled silence. Were they going to dump Slab?

Mary Lou was under the most pressure. She even delayed a few days. Did she back Gerry Adams's assertion that 'Slab' was a 'good republican'?

On 22 December 2015 Mary Lou emerged. She stood by her man. 'Everybody,' she told the *Irish Independent*, 'has a duty to pay their taxes in full. That includes good republicans like Mr Thomas Murphy.'

Adams's 'good republican' endorsement was repeated, but Mary Lou went one better. The next day she was folksy and composed. She described Murphy as 'a typical rural man' and 'very nice'. She admitted to having met him 'perhaps twice or three times' and had found him 'approachable'. She did not elaborate where and under what circumstances she had met the south Armagh republican smuggler.

In typical Mary Lou diversionary mood, she attacked the format of Slab Murphy's trial, trying instead to make the central issue the pursuit of Murphy in the non-jury Special Criminal Court. Once again aping Adams, she said, 'I have said and I think Gerry and others have said that that is not the norm.'

In early February, three weeks before Slab Murphy received a jail sentence, Mary Lou was launching a Sinn Féin election demand for the Moore Street Dublin 1916 site to be saved. A BBC *Spotlight* programme had just broadcast a former British intelligence officer, Colonel Richard Kemp, alleging that Slab Murphy was a 'mass murderer' who 'sent those people out to commit murder on behalf of the Provisional IRA'. Asked about Kemp's claim, Mary Lou declined to comment. She even failed to repeat her statement that Slab was 'a good republican'.

Slab had no previous convictions. On 26 February 2016 he received an eighteen-month prison sentence. He could comfort himself that he still commanded the support of the president and vice-president of Sinn Féin. His writ still ran in south Armagh. All that had been pinned on him was a tax offence.

Senator Máiría Cahill commented, 'Justice has finally caught up with this notorious individual.'

Less than two years later, south Armagh again reared its unwelcome head in the politics of the South. It was to bite a final chunk out of Mary Lou's credibility.

Forty-two years earlier, on 5 January 1976, the south Armagh brigade of the IRA had stopped a minibus carrying eleven Protestant textile workers near the village of Kingsmill in south Armagh. It was a tit-for-tat revenge killing. Ten of them were shot dead. The eleventh, Alan Black, survived, although he was shot eighteen times. A Catholic worker was spared because of his religion.

On 5 January 2018 Barry McElduff, the Sinn Féin Westminster MP for West Tyrone, marked the forty-second anniversary of the Kingsmill massacre in an obscene way. He uploaded a video of himself on Twitter balancing a loaf of Kingsmill bread on his head. He played the fool for the camera, later writing below the clip: 'I'm in the Classic Service Station here, but I'm wondering – where does McCullough's keep the bread?'

There was uproar from victims' groups, relatives of the dead and from unionists. The pain of the Kingsmill murders remained raw, not least because, as happens so often in south Armagh, no one has ever been convicted for any of the ten murders.

Sinn Féin responded by summoning McElduff to a meeting on 8 January in its Belfast headquarters where he was met by, among others, Gerry Adams and Michelle O'Neill. He was suspended from party activities for three months. Michelle O'Neill, keen to assert herself, declared, 'I have suspended Barry with immediate effect for a period of three months.' She added that his tweet was 'ill-judged and indefensible' but that she did not believe his actions were 'malicious'. Worse still, McElduff remained on full pay. It was a major misjudgement. The public reaction was universally hostile. It was hardly a punishment at all.

The next day Mary Lou came out puffing and blowing. With characteristic bombast, she branded McElduff's behaviour 'very crass, very stupid and unforgivable'. She insisted on RTÉ's *News at One* programme that 'It is very clear that we do not tolerate behaviour like that.'

It was far from clear. The opposite appeared to be the case. It was a token punishment. Mary Lou was relying on her loud bluster and anger to camouflage the leniency of the penalty. She went on to say that McElduff 'takes full responsibility and accepts that it caused great offence to the grieving families. It was most regrettable behaviour and it was not acceptable to cause that kind of hurt.' Nevertheless, she defended his punishment, tritely describing the three-month suspension on full pay as 'appropriate and proportionate and a significant disciplinary action'.

It was neither. It was another sign that McElduff, like all former members of the IRA, especially in south Armagh, was a protected species.

An avalanche of media criticism followed. Alan Black, the sole survivor of the Kingsmill massacre, surfaced. He was outraged with the offhand way Mary Lou McDonald and others had striven to downgrade McElduff's offence. Black gave a highly emotional television interview, accusing Sinn Féin of 'dancing on the graves' of his dead colleagues. Public opinion and politicians from all parts of Ireland with widely different views were appalled. Even some of Sinn Féin's own supporters in the North were incandescent with anger, demanding a more appropriate penalty.

Mary Lou had stooped too far in her craven attitude to the hard-liners. It couldn't have happened at a worse time for her. She was Sinn Féin's leader-in-waiting, with her coronation due just four weeks later on 10 February. Sinn Féin for once yielded to public opinion.

Barry McElduff was forced to resign his seat in Westminster, a position he had never taken up because of the republican doctrine of abstentionism. He explained to deaf ears that it had never occurred to him that his stunt had been offensive. He had never known what was written on the paper wrapping the bread. His explanation was ridiculed, but his forced resignation softened the demands of the injured victims, even though it was late in the day.

Sinn Féin was forced by public opinion to extract a greater

price than ever before from an old IRA member from south Armagh. For Mary Lou, it was a humiliation. Her approval of an initially light, almost meaningless, penalty for such a monstrous deed was probably a parting gift from her to Adams. She wasn't going to start taking a tougher line with the hard men at the very moment when the prize was within her grasp. She had worked to win the leadership for nearly twenty years. Why would she risk all and challenge him at the eleventh hour?

An ominous pattern was now established. The woman on the brink of taking over Sinn Féin was a new broom with a bad record of deferring to the old guard. In 2004 she had carried Joe Cahill's coffin. In 2014 she had defended Adams's corner on the execution of Jean McConville. In the same year she had taken the Adams line on the rape of Máiría Cahill. After the 2007 murder of Paul Quinn, she had refused to countenance the Quinn family's case and failed to take action against former IRA convict Sinn Féin minister Conor Murphy for blackening the Quinns' name. For over a decade she had been passive and silent in the face of the foul deeds of Gerry Adams's pal Slab Murphy in south Armagh, lamely following her leader in calling the former IRA chief a 'good republican'. And finally, in accordance with the leadership's wishes in 2018, she had opted to insult the memory of ten dead innocent victims by giving former IRA volunteer McElduff what amounted to a fool's pardon. All these actions would have pleased her mentor, patron and leader Gerry Adams. But in a matter of weeks he was due to retire. The question should soon be answered. Would all those years waiting have been in vain? Or was she a true believer in the Adams doctrine of biting her tongue and heeding the bidding of the men in the shadows from Northern Ireland?

CHAPTER 9

PLAYING THE CEMETERY GAME

Since 1997, when Caoimhghín Ó Caoláin had won Sinn Féin's first seat in the Dáil, the party had been making slow, but steady, electoral progress in the South. Constant reminders of past IRA atrocities in the North had slowed its advance. The 2011 general election had been an anti-climax because Sinn Féin's hopes had been higher than its ultimate tally of fourteen Dáil seats. Nevertheless, it had scored totemic victories in that contest, not only with Mary Lou's final arrival in the Dáil, but, perhaps, even more significantly, with Gerry Adams's runaway win in the border county of Louth. Sinn Féin was proving its potential as an all-Ireland party. Adams's 15,072 first-preference votes showed that, despite the Northern Troubles, candidates from across the border were not always toxic.

Emboldened by Adams's triumph in February, Sinn Féin eyed the October 2011 presidential election. Although its nationwide vote had landed at only 9.9 per cent in the February poll, presidential contests were more personality driven. Ideology mattered, but charisma counted. If Sinn Féin was ever to play senior hurling, it was time to take the plunge. Unfortunately, there were only two

republican giants of presidential stature among its number: Gerry
Adams and Martin McGuinness.

On the charisma count, on a scale of one to ten, McGuinness
had a healthy surplus, while Adams had a deep deficit. Adams was
popular in Northern Ireland and the border counties, but, with his
more sinister, dour manner, he had alienated many voters farther
south, particularly in urban areas. His dark paramilitary side always
seemed to be lurking just beneath the surface. He had little obvious
humour. It had long been rumoured that he eyed Áras an Uachtaráin
as his final destination, but this was a pipe dream.

Martin McGuinness was a more magnetic figure in the South.
He openly admitted that he had been in the IRA. Those of us who
had met him had to park our prejudices and concede that he was
congenial company. We had heard, of course, that, like Adams, he
had been involved in some despicable acts, but many saw him as a
source of healing, a man who could convert his murky past into a
positive catalyst for peace. McGuinness had a disarming sense of
humour. His well-publicised surprise friendship with his former
arch-enemy, DUP leader Ian Paisley, had revealed a side of both
men's personalities hitherto unseen. They crossed the sectarian
divide, becoming widely, almost affectionately, known as the
'Chuckle Brothers'. It made sense for Sinn Féin to run the younger,
humanised 'Chuckle Brother' for President of Ireland.

First, the party needed the signatures of twenty members of the
Dáil or Seanad to put McGuinness's name on the ballot paper. They
had only fourteen TDs and three senators. They quickly collected
an additional four: deputies Finian McGrath (Dublin North-
Central), Luke 'Ming' Flanagan (Roscommon–South Leitrim) and
two Kerry South TDs, Tom Fleming and Michael Healy-Rae. The
'Chuckle Brother' was out of the traps.

The entry of McGuinness into the presidential campaign radic-
ally changed its dynamic. The former IRA chief was dogged by
constant, but legitimate, questions about his past. On the hustings

in Athlone, he was confronted by the son of an army private killed by the IRA in 1983. David Kelly's father, Patrick, had been shot dead by an IRA gunman while he was trying to rescue the kidnapped businessman Don Tidey from captivity. Twenty-eight years later, in full view of an eager media, David Kelly thrust a picture of his deceased father in front of McGuinness, demanding to know the name of his killers. The candidate protested that he didn't know, to which David replied 'Liar'.

Despite such reminders of his past, McGuinness's performance was respectable. On polling day, he received 13.7 per cent of the popular vote, finishing in third place behind Michael D. Higgins (Labour) and Seán Gallagher (Independent). McGuinness relegated Fine Gael hopeful Gay Mitchell into the 'also-rans'. The early front runner, Senator David Norris, pro-lifer 'Dana' Rosemary Scallon and Special Olympics chief Mary Davis trailed far behind.

More significantly for Sinn Féin, McGuinness's vote was nearly 4 per cent more than the Sinn Féin tally (9.9 per cent) at the general election eight months earlier. Incrementally, the party was improving at every hurdle. The McGuinness gamble had given them another lift.

The austerity measures being implemented by the Fine Gael–Labour coalition probably aided the swing to Sinn Féin, but a longer-term trend was now appearing. Since Fianna Fáil had decided not to contest the presidential election for fear of a derisory vote, Sinn Féin had proved that if it fielded a good candidate, he or she could overshadow both the main parties in a national election. Sinn Féin more than doubled the vote of Fine Gael's Gay Mitchell. The party was now well positioned for the next challenge, the local and European battles in May 2014.

Meanwhile, in 2012 and 2013, Mary Lou was making a favourable impression on the national stage, in the media and in the PAC. And the party was growing rapidly at grass roots level. Fianna Fáil remained on the ropes.

As the austerity imposed by the troika of the International Monetary Fund, the European Central Bank and the European Commission began to bite deeper nationwide, the drift to the left continued. At the next hurdle, on 23 May 2014, Sinn Féin won 19.5 per cent of the vote and three seats in the European Parliament, up 8.3 per cent from the 2009 reverse when Mary Lou had lost her seat in Europe. Lynn Boylan (Dublin), Liadh Ní Riada (South) and Matt Carthy (Midlands–North-West) all recorded Sinn Féin wins.

In the local elections on the same day, the party gained 7.8 per cent above its 2009 total to finish on 15.2 per cent, bagging 105 additional council seats, mostly from the battered government parties. Labour bombed, losing eighty-one local contests and all three of its MEPs. Leader and Tánaiste Eamon Gilmore resigned, to be replaced by Joan Burton.

Sinn Féin had crossed a Rubicon. They had captured the lion's share of the left-wing protest vote that had deserted Labour. They had claimed a major scalp in toppling Eamon Gilmore. They had won seats nationally and locally. They looked poised to lead the opposition after the next general election, due in less than two years, before the end of February 2016.

It was an easy time to be in opposition. The coalition was deeply unpopular, especially on the issues of water charges and the local property tax, two measures introduced to satisfy the troika. The political winds offered plain sailing for a shamelessly populist Sinn Féin. However, the Dublin South-West by-election held in the autumn of 2014, only six months after the party's local and European election successes, threw up a shock result.

Sinn Féin was expected to win the empty Dáil seat, vacated by Fine Gael's Brian Hayes, who had just become an MEP. Water charges were the main issue and Sinn Féin had been opposed to them from the start. The Sinn Féin candidate, Cathal King, topped the poll on first preferences but was edged out on the last count by the hard-left socialist, former MEP Paul Murphy, running under the Anti-Austerity Alliance banner.

Sinn Féin had promised to abolish water charges if they were voted into power but baulked at the idea of breaking the law by refusing to pay them. They were on the defensive on an issue where they might have expected to reap dividends. Gerry Adams was forced to explain why he was paying the charges himself while urging abolition. The Anti-Austerity Alliance called on its supporters not to pay the charges and launched a non-payment campaign. A bitter left-wing bidding war between Sinn Féin and the more radical Anti-Austerity Alliance, backing Murphy, followed. At one point Mary Lou and others in Sinn Féin shared a fake Facebook comment by Murphy, prompting accusations of dirty tricks. Murphy won by 566 votes on the final count. Sinn Féin had been outflanked by an even more populist left-wing candidate. Once again, weak preferences, fatal for the party in past elections, had proved to be Cathal King's downfall.

True to form, Sinn Féin immediately changed its tack on water charges. In future, like the winning Anti-Austerity Alliance, Sinn Féin's leadership would not pay their own personal water bills. Seeing the danger suddenly appearing from the left-wing parties, they did a U-turn, standing alongside all others in a nationwide boycott. The competition for the anti-austerity protest vote had intensified.

Nevertheless, as Gerry Adams and Mary Lou McDonald approached the February 2016 general election, they looked set for the breakthrough that had been predicted for so long. In October 2014, opinion polls had shown the party with as much as 26 per cent of the votes, and holding at the same level in February 2015. Many polls put them ahead of Fianna Fáil, a party still suffering from the charge that it had nearly bankrupted the country in 2008/09. In an average of all polls between the 2011 and 2016 elections, Sinn Féin recorded 19 per cent support, suggesting that a historic change was on the cards. The duopoly, comprising the two parties, one of which had always held power since the state's foundation, was in peril. Sinn Féin's by-election setback in Dublin South-West was generally dismissed as a blip.

The 2016 election campaign shaped up as a battle between the establishment parties of Fine Gael, Fianna Fáil and Labour on the one side, against the only cohesive alternative, Sinn Féin. The latter's leadership underlined the divisions between the two camps by signalling in advance that they would not go into coalition with any of the three traditional parties.

Sinn Féin had outshone most others in the Dáil throughout the 2011–16 parliamentary term. The eloquent delivery of Mary Lou's oratory in the chamber and her role in the PAC had given the party an added dimension; but there was one big problem increasingly mentioned in the media, yet hardly even whispered by anyone within the party: Gerry Adams.

Adams was irreplaceable as a unifier of Sinn Féin North and South. He was (with the possible exception of Martin McGuinness) the party's unique internal asset. His mere presence quelled all dissent. He was respected, but also feared, by insiders. He ensured that the party – North and South – normally spoke with one voice. As a Northerner with a paramilitary pedigree, he controlled the IRA veterans in Belfast and elsewhere. As a Louth TD and party leader in the Dáil, he ruled the passive Sinn Féin deputies with a rod of iron. He was a big-ticket item in media terms, partly because he smelled of sulphur, but he was an acquired taste outside border areas. The number of Adams's skeletons that were consistently popping out of the IRA's cupboard of horrors was having a negative impact in the public mind on the standing of his chosen successor. Mary Lou, his hand-picked heir apparent, was suffering from the consequences of constantly being forced to defend Adams's less than believable denials of various charges levelled against him. So was the party. Adams's demons held Sinn Féin back in the 2016 general election campaign. He was always certain to hold his seat in the republican fortress of Louth, but his persona was a vote loser elsewhere. He knew pitifully little about domestic politics south of the border, less about economics or the public finances. He was a brilliant strategist but, as a spokesman in televised media debates, a woeful embarrassment. As the 2016 election approached, the party leader became the elephant in the room.

Sinn Féin had a bad campaign. The conditions were perfect for a populist party fighting against the deeply unpopular coalition of Fine Gael and Labour. Labour, the traditional voice of the underdog, was paralysed by its five years of imposing austerity on its supporters. They felt betrayed.

Labour lost thirty seats, returning with just seven. Their casualties should have provided easy pickings for the new force on the left, Sinn Féin. Fine Gael lost twenty-six, meaning that between the two outgoing coalition partners, there were at least fifty-six vacancies to share among the other parties. Surprisingly, the lost seats scattered far and wide, evidenced by a sharp Fianna Fáil recovery – from twenty-four to forty-four seats – with a rise in the number of 'Independents and Others' from fourteen to twenty-three. The fledgling Social Democrats held three seats and the Greens raised their number from zero to two.

Sinn Féin salvaged only nine new seats out of the wreckage of the coalition, increasing their total of TDs from fourteen to twenty-three. They received just 13.85 per cent of the vote, far less than Fianna Fáil's 24.35 per cent, despite the earlier opinion polls' findings that the party would overtake Fianna Fáil.

Sinn Féin's advance had faltered. At the 2011 election they had received 9.94 per cent of the popular vote. Eight months later, in October 2011, Martin McGuinness had lifted it to 13.7 per cent. After three years of austerity, in May 2014, Sinn Féin achieved 15.2 per cent in the local elections and a record 19.5 per cent in the European Parliament battles on the same day. They seemed to be on a steady upward trajectory. Immediately before the 2016 general election, opinion polls put their numbers at between 15 and 20 per cent. Suddenly, as the campaign moved into gear, the party began to tumble. On polling day, they hit a low point, retreating back to 13.85 per cent, almost exactly the same vote that Martin McGuinness had won three years earlier in the presidential election. The result was far below their expectations. Something was wrong. The 2014 by-election loss to Paul Murphy had not, after all, been a blip.

Gerry Adams had been the face on the posters. He had also been the face appearing in the leadership debates on television. He had a very poor campaign, proving time and again that he was not only uncomfortable, but even incompetent, in the economic arguments that dominated an election in the South. All the policy papers on taxation, austerity, housing and unemployment produced by Sinn Féin for the election had been in vain because the man promoting them was out of his depth.

In the first televised leaders' debate, the three main party chiefs, Fine Gael's Enda Kenny, Labour's Joan Burton and Fianna Fáil's Micheál Martin, showed a rare display of unity. They seized the opportunity to unite against Adams and savage him about Jean McConville, Máiría Cahill, the Sinn Féin attack on the Special Criminal Court that tries terrorists and the murder of Garda Jerry McCabe. Adams himself, not the economy, was the principal centre of attention.

The second debate was nearly as bad for Adams. This time, there was less concentration on his IRA record. Instead, according to the *Irish Independent*, he 'mixed up his numbers'. A few days later, just a week before polling day, Adams hit rock bottom. In an interview with RTÉ's Seán O'Rourke he was all at sea. He was unable to answer questions about the economy, the health system, his own Sinn Féin finance policies, taxing the rich, subsidies or water charges. His replies about the need for 'patriotic regeneration' and how Fine Gael had 'cooked the books' failed to camouflage his inability to master the nation's finances in any detail. At one point he protested to O'Rourke, 'Don't shout me down,' to which the RTÉ man responded, 'I won't shout you down if you don't waffle.'

The exchange was a car-crash interview for Adams, forcing Sinn Féin's finance spokesman Pearse Doherty to defend his leader in a press briefing later that day. In the same interview, Doherty said that becoming leader of Sinn Féin was not his ambition, but that he would 'be willing to step up to the challenge'. It sounded as close as he had ever come to a rare piece of impertinence.

Not a vote had even been cast and the media were already zoning in on Adams's leadership.

On 24 February, forty-eight hours before polling day, Harry McGee of *The Irish Times* penned an article entitled 'Is Gerry Adams an asset or a liability for Sinn Féin?' It was a rhetorical question. Everybody knew the answer. Gerry Adams's appeal was limited to Sinn Féin's core base. Beyond that, he was a negative. He was sixty-seven years of age, almost thirty-three of them already spent as leader of the party, and was increasingly an obstruction to growth in the South.

After the 2016 battle, Sinn Féin could take comfort from the arrival in the Dáil of talented, younger, articulate TDs like Eoin Ó Broin and Louise O'Reilly from Dublin, Donnchadh Ó Laoghaire, a law graduate from University College Cork, and the long-time-waiting David Cullinane from Waterford, elevated from his five-year stint in the Seanad. None of them had been in the IRA. Mary Lou had finally reinvented herself from being a narrow winner – after taking the final seat in 2011 – into a poll topper in 2016. Her status as Adams's preferred successor remained intact, but arguably it had been too long delayed. If she or Pearse Doherty had been Sinn Féin leader for the 2016 election, neither would have been humiliated, as Adams had been, by media gaffes about the economy. Doherty was fluent with figures and utterly comfortable with budget balances. Either would have been able to assert that they carried no terrorist baggage. Unlike Adams, Mary Lou was a competent bluffer, but, more importantly, she would have been capable of distancing herself and Sinn Féin from the murder and mayhem of the Northern Ireland paramilitaries. The message would have been different, with austerity topping her list. And probably even more different, because she was a woman who liked to champion social issues.

The election result sealed Adams's fate. There would, however, be no putsch against the leader, who was still a cult figure for the faithful. The mediocre result of a match that should have been a series of penalty kicks for the opposition ensured that Adams would not lead them into another contest. He knew it. Mary Lou knew it. And Pearse Doherty knew it too. It was time to settle the succession.

The Sinn Féin leadership tussle turned out to be similar in its execution to all other actions of the party: deeply secret. Nothing exposes the difference between Sinn Féin and its rivals more clearly than the transfer of power at the top. The others hold publicly visible campaigns. A leader is usually toppled following open challenges by at least one pretender to the throne. Senior party figures endorse candidates. A vote is called with TDs, senators and councillors often having a significant input. Contests are common. In Sinn Féin they did it Gerry's way, and at a time to be decided by Gerry. And they selected a candidate selected by Gerry.

In Sinn Féin it would have been political death to have challenged Gerry Adams about anything during his eventual thirty-five-year reign. In Fianna Fáil, Fine Gael and Labour, dissent sometimes signals unwelcome, but healthy, ambition. Well-timed internal argument is often rewarded with a path to the top to pacify dissident elements. In leadership elections or even internal heaves, there is often razzmatazz. Candidates are required to make their views on the party's direction known to its TDs and senators. In Sinn Féin, the deputies are passive observers, even during leadership changes. The key to preferment is blind loyalty to the leader.

In 2016 Mary Lou had already been running for the leadership for a dozen years. She had never once wavered in public from the Gerry Adams line. Insiders say they had never seen her do it at party meetings either. Nor had Pearse Doherty. Even when pressed by the media, both contenders were ultra-careful not to indicate to Adams that they were even squinting sideways at his job. Mary Lou's long campaign was limited to feigning a vague interest in the position. In reality, it was her life's ambition, a position that she craved. As early as 2013, when the murmurings about Adams losing his touch were emerging, she said, 'If at some stage, there was a vacancy, I would certainly consider it.' In Sinn Féin-speak that is tantamount to sedition. In Mary Lou's case it *was* sedition, but sedition with the leader's imprimatur. She was protected.

Normally she responded to the succession query by declaring that there was no vacancy, full stop. From time to time she went a little further, expressing an interest, but far away into the future when the great leader wished to hand over the baton. Her bogus 'vague interest' narrative was a message targeted at Pearse Doherty and anyone else like Conor Murphy or Aengus Ó Snodaigh, both of whom might have nurtured hopes. Decoded, it meant not just that she wanted the job but, more importantly, that she had the support of Adams to say so. Others need not waste their time.

On the same day in 2013 that Mary Lou expressed interest – but only if there was a vacancy – Pearse Doherty was asked the same question and ruled himself out. He cited family reasons, the time-honoured Sinn Féin face-saver for volunteers or ambitious members accepting an unwelcome decision the leadership had already made about their future.

Gerry Adams always parried the succession question with the reply that the next leader would be chosen by the ard fheis. The membership would pick his successor. That, of course, was a flight of fancy. And Adams was still in no hurry. He wanted to be the leader who saw the 1916 centenary celebrations through to the finish. He wanted to be certain that Mary Lou would win the prize without dissension in the ranks.

After the 2016 election, Sinn Féin affected aloofness from inter-party talks aimed at forming a government, but, in reality, they were political pariahs. None of the major parties would talk to Gerry Adams. Nevertheless, political isolation suited Sinn Féin's longer-term strategy. Although they now wanted to be in government soon, they were happy to allow Fine Gael and the Independent Alliance to form a coalition, which no party expected to last for long. They were even happier to see Fianna Fáil signing a 'confidence and supply' agreement with the government. Fianna Fáil agreed to support the Fine Gael-led minority government from the opposition benches on votes of confidence. Sinn Féin was left as the only significant party in outright opposition, enjoying the freedom of unconditional manoeuvre. Micheál Martin might have been the nominal leader of the opposition, but he had volunteered to be handcuffed to the governing coalition. For Mary Lou, the political fallout and the outcome of coalition talks was ideal. She became the dominant figure in the Dáil, even before she assumed the leadership of Sinn Féin.

Sinn Féin was happy to regroup, sort out the succession and oust Fianna Fáil in the public mind as the main opponents of Fine Gael. Their strategists saw the next general election in 2021 – or earlier – as their big opportunity. The civil-war parties were moving closer and closer together. A historic breakthrough was in the party's sights.

Sinn Féin's steady expansion had not come without inevit-able problems. The extra nine Dáil seats captured in the 2016 election followed an increase in councillors, MEPs and senators. Back-room workers, advisers and office personnel had grown accordingly. The party remained rigidly directed from the top, but its culture of control and secrecy was difficult to reconcile with the demands of larger numbers of talented and ambitious younger members. The new recruits had no military-style culture of unquestioning obedience. Centralised authority did not come naturally to them.

One particularly embarrassing problem kept surfacing. There were constant accusations of internal bullying from Sinn Féin members. Many, but not all, came from councillors around the country; embarrassingly, most of them were voiced by women. The highest profile, most problematic of these allegations arose in 2015 from the sitting TD for Cork East, Sandra McLellan.

Apart from Mary Lou, Sandra McLellan was the only female Sinn Féin deputy elected in the class of February 2011. She was fifty years old, a lively deputy, educated at the Loreto Convent in Cork. A former SIPTU trade union representative in an electronics factory, she was eloquent and intelligent, exactly the type of recruit the party needed. Sandra McLellan had contested the 2007 general election unsuccessfully, but her hard work as a Cork county councillor and as mayor of Youghal since 2009 saw her comfortably elected to the Dáil in 2011. As a TD of roughly the same vintage as Mary Lou and a mother of three children, it might have been expected that the two female newcomers would have bonded. They didn't.

Mary Lou was destined for greatness. Sandra was not one of the chosen ones, but just another of those Sinn Féin TDs designated to be seen in the Dáil at certain times, to vote, to read speeches prepared by back-room researchers, to accept the personal staff allocated to her from on high and generally to make up the numbers. A presentable loyalist. Sandra McLellan was not a member of Mary Lou's and Gerry's inner circle.

One day in the summer of 2015, my colleague in the Independent Alliance and in government, John Halligan, told me that he was friendly with Sandra and her husband, Liam. He sometimes met her in the Leinster House café. Sandra was distressed. She had been complaining to him that she was being 'bullied' by local Sinn Féin members down in Youghal, County Cork. She was 'under pressure and being intimidated in her constituency'. John Halligan was proposing that we should invite Sandra to join us in the Independent Alliance. He felt that she was 'a good TD and she has a lot to offer'.

Just like Sinn Féin, we would have welcomed a bright female TD to our ranks, as well as the joys of wiping Gerry Adams's eye. But, more importantly, if Sandra McLellan was being bullied, she certainly deserved a new political home. John spoke to her and left her with an open offer. A few months later Sandra went public. She posted on Facebook that her work as a TD had consistently been undermined by a small number of Sinn Féin party members locally. She was pulling out of politics.

A day later, *The Journal* ran with a story entitled 'Sinn Féin selects Cork East candidate, as TD at centre of bullying storm confirms she won't run'. Sinn Féin in Cork East had been in turmoil throughout 2015. One Sinn Féin councillor had been suspended and another expelled as a result of fallout from the allegations that Sandra McLellan had been bullied. Countless party members had resigned. Another female councillor, June Murphy, a close ally of McLellan, left the party, dubbing her spell in Sinn Féin as 'an increasingly negative experience'.

Sandra McLellan, downbeat and unsupported by the higher echelons of Sinn Féin, left the party utterly disillusioned. She told Hugh O'Connell of *The Journal* that 'I am now unemployed. So why would anyone who loves their job so much give it up voluntarily? I wanted to go another five years. Efforts to defame and undermine me were particularly vicious and I had a decision to make regarding my family.'

It was strange that Mary Lou, the feminist deputy leader, did not intervene and mediate on behalf of the only other Sinn Féin woman in the Dáil. She did sit down and listen to Sandra's woes, but nothing seemed to happen. Jonathan O'Brien, another Cork

TD, later a full-time Sinn Féin employee, was brought in to sort out Cork East.

Today, sources close to Sandra McLellan insist that at the time Mary Lou did not seem to have any power to offer more than a sympathetic ear. Sandra had had enough. So had her family. She gave up a political career that could have blossomed in any other party. In October 2021, I visited Sandra McLellan in her house in Youghal. It was an amicable encounter, but she did not want to speak about her experience. She wishes to put this unhappy chapter in her life behind her. Sinn Féin is a painful memory.

Sandra McLellan was only one of many women to feel driven out of Sinn Féin at the time. When June Murphy, her councillor colleague in Cork East, left the party at around the same time, she too said little. Two years later she broke her silence, claiming that there was a 'bullying culture' in Sinn Féin and that the party demeaned women. June went on to point her finger at the Dublin leadership and was particularly scathing of Mary Lou McDonald. 'No one is stopping them,' she insisted. She spoke of 'systemic abuse' within Sinn Féin. 'It is a culture of men. It gives the illusion that they support women. They do not; they tell women what to do.' Mary Lou, she declared, was no exception: 'She does what she is told.' There was a widespread view in the ranks that Mary Lou had let women down.

In April 2017, Kildare Councillor Sorcha O'Neill resigned from Sinn Féin, claiming that she had experienced 'bullying, hostility and aggression'. The pattern worsened. Councillor Melissa O'Neill, a single mother from Kilkenny, was expelled from Sinn Féin in 2016 after video footage of a row she had had with her neighbours went viral. She said that the party had sent her to 'Coventry', alleging that it had imposed isolation, deliberate psychological abuse.

A particularly sensitive case appeared in Mary Lou's backyard in north Dublin. Councillor Noeleen Reilly first made her claim of bullying in 2014. She said that every time she went to the party about being bullied, she was ignored or sidetracked. Her case dragged on for four years. Noeleen Reilly's eventual resignation came in 2018. She alleged an 'orchestrated bullying campaign by a number of people in Dublin North-West', including physical assaults, verbal abuse, isolation and other offences. She insisted that she had been the victim of the infamous army of Sinn Féin trolls, mostly from 'a barrage of fake accounts on social media'.

Noeleen resigned from the party, but held on to her council seat. Sinn Féin demanded its 'return' to them since she had been elected on a Sinn Féin platform. She refused.

The initial wave of bullying exposed by Sandra McLellan had become an avalanche. The list lengthened every month. It was not only women. There were men making similar claims. In 2017 a significant figure, Councillor Séamie Morris, a long-time, hard-working Sinn Féin loyalist who had stood for the party in the 2016 general election in Tipperary, lodged a complaint. He was supporting Sinn Féin's youngest councillor, Lisa Marie Sheehy from Limerick, after she had quit the party alleging bullying by other party members. She said she had been 'undermined, bullied and humiliated'. Morris, a man who fought for his community as a councillor, said he had been 'a victim of an intense, nine-month campaign of harassment and slander' after a local disagreement with other Sinn Féin members. There had been a nasty whispering campaign against him, a hate crusade. It was ugly. An odious leaflet was circulated suggesting that Morris was a paedophile. He had been in a 'dark place'. He had even considered taking his own life.

Both Lisa Marie Sheehy and Séamie Morris insisted that the investigations launched by the party into these matters were a 'joke'. Others say that the investigators are nearly always old IRA 'army', now members of Sinn Féin, doing the bidding of party headquarters, with little interest in the rights or suffering of the individual complainant. Morris and Sheehy said that at least 20 of Sinn Féin's

159 councillors were affected. In November 2017 Morris resigned from Sinn Féin. He was handsomely re-elected as an independent councillor in 2019.

The loss of councillors was bad enough, but the resignation of Senator Trevor Ó Clochartaigh in November 2017 was a move that rocked the party. His departure was in a different league altogether. Ó Clochartaigh was a political heavyweight with a national profile. He had been a senator since 2011 and as a runner-up in the 2016 general election, finishing with over 8000 votes, was clearly in pole position to win a seat on his home turf in Galway West.

However, he was not in favour with the party leadership. It is believed that Adams and his followers wanted Ó Clochartaigh off the pitch to ease a path into the Dáil for a local rival, Mairéad Farrell. Farrell happened to be a niece of the IRA volunteer carrying the same name killed by the SAS in Gibraltar in 1988. Local politicians say that Sinn Féin 'made life hell' for Trevor. Some say he was 'hounded out' of the party.

Ó Clochartaigh's resignation statement pinpointed what he called 'serious unpunished breaches of the Sinn Féin code of conduct in Galway West'. He accused those involved of 'ruthless, unscrupulous and ambitious behaviour'. It was a local shafting, a specialist area for Sinn Féin. His biography was removed from the Sinn Féin website within an hour of departure. He was utterly disillusioned, saying that the party was supporting 'wrongdoers, ignoring misconduct and ploughing ahead with a [selection] convention with a predetermined outcome . . .' He pointed the finger at Adams when he said that he had taken issues 'as high as the President'. He stayed on as an Independent in the Seanad, before later applying successfully for the post of Communications Manager of TG4, the Irish language public service television network. He has been in the station ever since and was promoted to Director of Operations and Human Resources in 2019. He was a loss to Sinn Féin.

When Ó Clochartaigh spoke to me, although he had serious

issues with the party, he was complimentary about Mary Lou personally. He says that 'On a personal level, I have a huge regard for her. She is very vivacious, even very funny one-to-one. She has incredibly strong emotional intelligence and a good touch with ordinary people.' He added a familiar lament: 'She was very much in Gerry's shadow when I was there.'

When I asked him about Pearse Doherty's challenge for the leadership he said that there was always 'in theory going to be an open vote if it came to a contest, but everything was kept under wraps. People were not told how to vote but knew the right thing to do.' Crucially, he added that 'conversations happened and Pearse did not stand.'

The former senator, who saw the party's modus operandi over six years from the inside, called Sinn Féin an 'authoritarian leadership', meaning it was very centralised. Interestingly, he said that he believed that 'a very strategic decision had been made to feminise the party. The core vote inside Sinn Féin had been primarily Northern and republican, but it now needed leadership that was not connected with the Troubles. The party sought a Dublin demographic to support it. Mary Lou had done her apprenticeship and was an obvious choice. She lived up to her potential. There is real substance in her.'

On Mary Lou's support levels in Northern Ireland, he says that he believed that 'initially there was reticence north of the border, but the leadership brought her to places, like Downing Street, to boost her profile. It took a long time for them to get her accepted. She was socially confident and her warm, likeable nature helped. She gives out the same likeability vibe as Nicola Sturgeon.'

When questions were raised with Sinn Féin and Gerry Adams about bullying, they took the usual road of outright denial: there was no bullying culture in Sinn Féin, just perfectly normal local spats.

Mary Lou provided little comfort to anyone. Her eyes were

focused elsewhere. After the 2016 election she knew that the day of Gerry Adams's departure could not be postponed for much longer. It is widely accepted that she was privy to his timetable. Indeed, she may have been a major influence on the chosen date for his exit. She certainly would not have wished to become embroiled in arguments on behalf of women who were victims of decisions made by former IRA volunteers acting as arbitrators in bullying disputes. That was a minefield, a distraction from the real business in hand.

Mary Lou's Achilles heel in the party remained the same: Doubting Thomases on the military wing, especially the Northern Ireland veterans. She had been working the Ulster chicken-and-chips circuit for donkey's years. She would head to Belfast and Derry at the drop of a hat. In 2016 the big prize was hers to lose. She was in the driving seat, but Pearse Doherty was popular, particularly in the border areas. She might have been Gerry's chosen one, but the Northern brigades could probably have quietly vetoed her accession if they found her to be too detached from their violent tradition. There had been rumours that Martin McGuinness might be interested in taking the party president's post, short term, following his relatively successful presidential outing in 2011, but a vacant Dáil seat would probably have been needed. Former IRA member Conor Murphy, the MLA for Newry and Armagh, was even believed to have fancied his chances against Mary Lou. As a non-combatant woman, Mary Lou was exposed. She travelled tirelessly to Northern Ireland, working the commemorations, the party meetings, the dinners and the smoke-filled rooms. She even knocked on Northern doors for Sinn Féin candidates at election time. It was game on!

On 12 November 2016 Mary Lou was the guest speaker at the Derry Volunteers dinner. It was billed as the last major event of the centenary year of 1916. The invitation reminded members of 'fallen comrades' and of the ceremony on Easter Sunday earlier in the year when 'tens of thousands of people took to the streets of Derry to commemorate the sacrifice of those who took on the British Empire in 1916'.

More than 500 people attended the dinner, including many of the former IRA activists who had been members of the Derry Brigade. During the Troubles, the Derry Brigade was one of the most unsavoury of all the IRA units in Northern Ireland. It practised vile acts, including proxy bombing with a human bomb as the weapon of death. This involved chaining so-called 'collaborators' to the steering wheel of a vehicle with a bomb on board. The collaborator was then forced to drive to the target where the IRA, often holding the driver's family captive, detonated the bomb by remote control. On some occasions, but not all, the driver escaped.

Patsy Gillespie was strapped into a van and forced to drive a bomb into a British Army checkpoint on the Derry–Donegal border in 1990. He died in the explosion alongside five soldiers. His shouted warning saved many lives. He was forty-three, with a wife and three children. Sinn Féin described him as a 'legitimate target' because he worked in the British Army's canteen. The IRA's Derry Brigade was responsible for the death of dozens of other innocent civilians.

Nothing deterred Mary Lou in her mission. At the Derry dinner she delivered a rousing speech, recalling the great 'sacrifices' made by the IRA. She spoke from a lectern decorated with a crossed rifles poster. Underneath the rifles were the words 'Óglaigh na hÉireann', a term used by Sinn Féin to refer to the Provisional IRA. It was a chilling sight.

Mary Lou went down a treat that evening. She knew that the key to the leadership lay in winning the hearts and minds of the former volunteers in Derry, not in the malcontents seeking justice and an end to offences, like bullying, south of the border.

As she spoke that night, Martin McGuinness sat at the dinner listening approvingly. So did Martina Anderson, the former IRA bomber who had been elected to the European Parliament. Co-chairing the event was Andrew McCartney. They represented three of the six powerful families that controlled Derry Sinn Féin. At the end of Mary Lou's speech, McCartney and McGuinness raised her arms to thunderous applause. It was a benediction, an anointment. The dinner was the biggest republican gathering in Derry for many months. The next one would be just four months later for Martin McGuinness's funeral.

A terminally ill Martin McGuinness resigned as deputy first minister on 9 January 2017 in protest against the government's Renewable Heating Incentive Scheme, known as the 'Cash for Ash' project. Sinn Féin was making serious allegations of fraud against its unionist opponents. The scandal brought down the Northern Ireland Executive. Ten days later, a visibly weak McGuinness announced that, on health grounds, he would not be standing for re-election. He had been diagnosed with a rare illness known as amyloidosis, a terminal disease that attacked the organs. Martin McGuinness died in Altnagelvin Hospital, Derry, on 21 March 2017.

His funeral, two days later, was probably the largest ever held in Derry. I attended it along with my colleague Finian McGrath – we were both ministers in the South at the time. We were seated in the pew just behind former US President Bill Clinton. He, of course, not having a clue who we were, engaged us in friendly conversation, somewhat indiscreetly telling us that he had travelled to the funeral with 'Bertie' on 'Denis[O'Brien]'s' private jet. Perhaps he did not realise that in Ireland at the time 'Denis' was a lightning rod for unfavourable publicity and was seen as having other less noble qualities than being a supporter of Clinton's philanthropic global foundation.

McGuinness's obsequies had the potential to bring the communities together. The high point was not the eloquent eulogy from Clinton, nor the presence of President Michael D. Higgins or the Taoiseach, Enda Kenny. The arrival of Arlene Foster, First

Minister and leader of the DUP, into the church was greeted with spontaneous applause by the mainly nationalist congregation. Foster had reason to despise McGuinness: the IRA had attempted to kill her father, shooting him in the head and blowing up her school bus when she was a child. Her attendance at the service was seen as a generous gesture of forgiveness.

The low point in the service was when Gerry Adams took hold of Clinton and very publicly escorted him to the McGuinness family to sympathise with the bereaved. Taoiseach Enda Kenny trotted along behind them, almost elbowed out of the picture by the Sinn Féin leader. Adams milked the funeral of his friend to the last drop for the Sinn Féin cause. The party, as always, took ownership of the ceremony. Adams delivered the oration at the graveside. Mary Lou stood close to him. The cameras clicked and sent their pictures around the world.

Mary Lou was now a past master of republican funerals, where she naturally deferred to Adams. She greeted me in the church, expressing appreciation that I had attended. Then she headed off to do her well-practised coffin-carrying duties. She was joined in the same duties by none other than Michelle O'Neill, the woman who had so recently been chosen to take on the mantle of McGuinness to become Sinn Féin's 'party leader in the North' following his resignation. Michelle carried the coffin of their fallen comrade alongside Mary Lou and Gerry Adams.

The imagery was striking. A gradual political changeover was happening in the cemetery before our eyes. Adams was easing himself out. The two women to whom he planned to pass the baton – North and South – carried the coffin of the former IRA chief in Derry alongside him. Both women were non-combatants, or not 'army', as republicans called them. McGuinness's death had accelerated the arrival of the next generation.

Michelle O'Neill's selection to be McGuinness's successor as the next leader in Northern Ireland was a game changer. She had impeccable Irish republican credentials. Her father, Brendan Doris, had been an IRA prisoner and a Sinn Féin councillor. Her cousin, Tony Doris, had been killed in an ambush of three IRA men by the SAS twenty-six years earlier. She herself, although from an IRA family, was, crucially, without terrorist traces. Her earlier political career had been overshadowed by several luminaries from the higher profile paramilitary wing, who had turned away from the balaclava to the ballot box. She had been elected as an MLA for Mid-Ulster in the 2007 Assembly elections. In 2011 she had become Minister for Agriculture and Rural Development, followed by Minister for Health in 2016. Her selection to succeed McGuinness was a rebuff to Conor Murphy, the IRA veteran from south Armagh. Women of the next generation were moving into position, replacing older men of the IRA, North and South.

Michelle O'Neill had all the credentials that Mary Lou lacked. Her family had an IRA record, even if she had none herself. She was part of the tribe that had felt the pain. She came from the war zone.

Mary Lou had consequently spent much more of the previous decade than is realised energetically, but quietly, compensating for her lack of an IRA pedigree. Her preparation for the leadership was long and meticulously measured. Her high-profile part in the funeral of Joe Cahill in 2004, when she had been a Sinn Féin MEP for only a few weeks, and her prominent part in the last journey of Martin McGuinness in 2016 were not unique events. Her willingness to accompany former IRA chief of staff Brian Keenan to commemorate Nazi sympathiser Seán Russell in 2004 was in the same vein, an early signal to the hardest of the hard men that she too was a 'good republican'. It was not a one-off test of her loyalty, as some have suggested, but more probably a signal that, if she had been born in different circumstances, she would have stood shoulder to shoulder with activists Martina Anderson and Rita O'Hare and other women warriors on the front line. Her high-profile appearance at all three events was part of a far-sighted, well-planned process to win the leadership in the killing fields, in the cemeteries of Northern Ireland and at the commemorations of those she unfailingly recognised as the 'patriot dead'. Some of the veterans had initially been sceptical of her, suggesting that the Mary Lou story simply didn't add up. Nevertheless, she convinced others. Her charm and her dedication were relentless. Perhaps the reason it took the Southern electorate so long to warm to her was related to her attendance at such events, although most of them conveniently took place beyond their gaze, in Northern Ireland. Her appearance with Keenan to pay tribute to Russell in Dublin's Fairview Park was a step too far for some and still sickens others to this day. Keenan was possibly the most gruesomely ruthless of all IRA bosses. He organised the Balcombe Street gang in London, the terrorist group responsible for bombings and shootings and credited with thirty-five gory deaths in the 1970s.

Nevertheless, she persisted. Mary Lou was far from coy about any further association with Keenan or others with blood on their hands. Keenan himself died of cancer in May 2008. Once again, the cemetery beckoned. At his funeral, amid all the usual para-military trappings, Mary Lou popped up carrying the coffin. She never missed an opportunity. Alongside her on that day, helping to shoulder Keenan's casket wrapped in the tricolour was Martina Anderson, the veteran ex-prisoner. Beside them walked men in black berets. The last 'lift' of Keenan's coffin was made by the four fearsome members of the Balcombe Street gang. Speeches were given by former Army Council member Armagh's Seán ('The Surgeon') Hughes, MLA Martina Anderson and by Adams himself.

Mary Lou's appetite for Northern Ireland visits was consistent throughout her years as Adams's devoted disciple, but it intensified as the leader's departure loomed. It was not confined to funerals, but extended to party events, debates and endless commemorations, all offering her frequent opportunities to press the flesh of those bereaved by the death of an IRA volunteer. In 2013 she gave the keynote speech at the Belfast Easter commemorations. Speaking in yet another cemetery, Belfast's Milltown, she reminded her audience of 'RUC brutality', of 'internment', and paid tribute to the IRA's courage. Her words on that day would probably never have been uttered south of the border. In June later that year, she was at the Crossmaglen Rangers Gaelic Athletic Club in south Armagh, the heart of militant republicanism, participating in a debate on a united Ireland.

While she had attended many events in Northern Ireland that were not commemorations, Mary Lou never lost sight of the families and followers of the republican dead. After she was elected to Dáil Éireann she appears to have stepped up a gear. In 2014 she was the keynote speaker at Derry's Easter commemoration at the city's republican plot, an occasion that allowed her to not only remember the heroes of the 1916 Rising, but also to mark the hundredth anniversary of the founding of Cumann na mBan, this time in Derry City Cemetery. One hundred and twenty women, many former prisoners, led the parade. Once again, tailoring her speech to her audience, Mary Lou lashed out against unionists and the British government. As always, she paid tribute to all republicans who had died, including the recent IRA fighters. On 22 October 2015, she ventured into Armagh, where she delivered the Peter Corrigan political lecture on 'One Hundred Years of the Republican Struggle'. Corrigan was a Sinn Féin election worker murdered in the street by an Ulster Volunteer Force death squad in 1982.

As the 2016 general election approached and it became obvious that there would be no immediate Sinn Féin leadership change, Mary Lou's main focus switched temporarily to republicans from her home base, fulfilling remembrance commitments in various southern locations, including Dublin, Donegal and the annual Bodenstown commemoration. On one rare occasion in 2013, she was even accompanied to Bodenstown by her husband Martin and both her children.

In December 2015, Mary Lou chaired a night of 'celebration and remembrance' at Dublin's Gresham Hotel for Jim Monaghan, a friend of Adams and one of the infamous Colombia Three, who was convicted of training Colombian FARC guerrillas and travelling to the country on a false passport. Monaghan was on the run after fleeing Colombia and arriving back in Ireland. In his memoir *Up Like a Bird*, IRA man Brendan Hughes describes Monaghan as 'the best engineer the IRA ever had'. Nicknamed 'Mortar' Monaghan for his explosives expertise, he had skipped bail in Colombia and dodged a seventeen-year custodial sentence. There was no extradition agreement between Ireland and Colombia. Mary Lou's decision to take the chair for the evening will have further raised her stock among the paramilitary wing. Among those in attendance was Bridget Rose Dugdale, the British heiress turned IRA bomber who had been sentenced to nine years' imprisonment (and served six) for her terrorist activities.

After Sinn Féin's disappointing February 2016 general election result, Adams's retirement was only a matter of time. Mary Lou further increased her efforts to ensure the approval of his hardcore Northern Ireland base. There is no doubt that she was working for the ultimate prize with Adams's collusion, but she still needed to complete all the spadework for him to be certain that Northern republicans would accept her bona fide republican convictions and confirm his plans for her coronation as his successor.

The general election in February 2016 was followed by a Northern Assembly election in May. Mary Lou took full advantage of the opportunity to make multiple appearances in the North supporting Sinn Féin candidates. She attended campaign launches in Gerry Adams's West Belfast constituency and in Martin McGuinness's Derry Foyle patch, among others. She busted a gut for the Sinn Féin candidates, building up further goodwill from Sinn Féin sceptics in the North.

After the 2016 election campaign, she was back in the

cemeteries. On 29 July she spoke at a commemoration in south Armagh for republican heroes Peadar McElvanna and Michael McVerry. McElvanna had died in 1979 when preparing an IRA ambush of British Army Royal Green Jackets in Keady, County Armagh. A year earlier he had been unsuccessfully prosecuted on a charge of gunning down an off-duty British soldier on his wedding day. Lieutenant Gary Cass was shot while walking away from the Trim, County Meath, church with his bride. Cass somehow survived. Acquitted alongside McElvanna was Dessie O'Hare, known as 'the Border Fox', a man later convicted for many of the most grisly acts of the Troubles.

Michael McVerry, the other man being revered by Mary Lou on that day, was a former officer commanding the First Battalion of the IRA south Armagh Brigade. McVerry died during an IRA attack on Keady Barracks in 1973.

Mary Lou was back in the fertile leadership-campaigning territory of south Armagh in October, this time to mark the fortieth anniversary of the death of Máire Drumm, the militant republican hero murdered by loyalists while recovering from an eye operation in Belfast's Mater Hospital in 1976. Mary Lou led local representatives and family members in a wreath-laying ceremony.

Next stop was the Derry Volunteers dinner in the following month, then the funeral of Martin McGuinness in March 2017, followed a month later by a separate ceremony in Derry City Cemetery for the Easter 1916 commemoration, where a new headstone was unveiled at McGuinness's grave. The occasion gave her a platform, once again, to make her low-key, unspoken pitch for the leadership to the Derry faithful.

She even managed to further claim the McGuinness mantle in August 2017 when, at the Belfast Féile an Phobail, she shared a panel with Belfast republican Danny Morrison and former MLA Mitchel McLaughlin on the topic 'An Outstanding Leader: The Life and Times of Martin McGuinness'.

As Adams prepared to announce his departure date, no stone was being left unturned in Mary Lou's pursuit of the prize. She had been on the trail between Belfast, south Armagh and Derry, but she was not going to neglect any other former IRA strongholds. In September, she headed for the Tyrone Volunteers' annual commemoration in Strabane. She addressed the crowd that had assembled in the Diamond in Lifford, County Donegal, before parading across the bridge straddling the border to the republican plot in Strabane cemetery in the North. Fifty-nine IRA activists from County Tyrone had died in the Troubles. The Tyrone Brigade was notorious for its sectarian nature. It was responsible for many merciless deaths.

Victims' groups were outraged at Mary Lou's presence. Kenny Donaldson, a prominent victims' campaigner for the South-East Fermanagh Foundation, was furious, asserting that Mary Lou 'had associated herself with a number of commemorative events to those within the republican movement, many of whom were serial killers who murdered their own neighbours because of sectarian and ethnic-motivated hatreds. This is certainly the case,' Donaldson added, 'with a considerable number of those commemorated at the Strabane event where she acted as keynote speaker.'

Mary Lou ploughed on. She was completing a long campaign fiercely committed to honouring IRA volunteers whatever the cost, irrespective of the depths to which some had stooped. She was ticking boxes, moving from dinners to cemeteries, to memorials, to parades, even to canvassing on nationalist doors. The survivors, the dead IRA men's successors and the bereaved relatives of the 'patriot dead' would remember her attendance and her eulogies. She had probably covered every IRA brigade that had lost members in the Troubles. She had done her master's bidding, following his footsteps and promising continuity. She would never abandon the memories of those who died. Many of her activities were largely unknown and deliberately unpublicised in the less republican South, but delivered and targeted at the eyes and ears of those in the North who mattered, those who undoubtedly held sway over the choice of Sinn Féin's next leader.

The fifteen-year campaign was almost over. It was time for Gerry Adams to begin his farewell journey. The Sinn Féin ard fheis was due in November 2017. Inspired articles began to appear in the media, reporting that Adams would use the party's annual get-together to announce his future plans. Even as Mary Lou attended the commemoration for the IRA's Tyrone Brigade in September, Gerry Adams was putting the finishing touches to his exit plan.

No one doubts that Adams had kept Mary Lou in the loop about his every step and the precise timing he planned for the handover. Sinn Féin's president and vice-president appeared to be working in tandem. On 18 November he revealed a badly kept secret, telling the 2017 Sinn Féin ard fheis that he would be stepping down after thirty-five years. It would be his last time to address the faithful. Nor would he be defending his Louth seat at the next election. He disclosed that he and the late Martin McGuinness had agreed a year earlier that it was time for an orderly transition, with both of them handing over to the next generation. Sadly, Martin had died, but Adams would keep his part of the agreement. The delegates decided that an extraordinary ard fheis would be held to pick his successor.

Nominations for president of Sinn Féin were opened on 8 January and closed on 19 January 2018. The media attempted to drum up an atmosphere of excitement about the contest. Adams promoted the pretence that an open democratic process was beginning. Alternative names to Mary Lou's were bandied about. In reality, all other possible runners were already off the pitch. On the Monday morning after the Saturday ard fheis, Pearse Doherty went on RTÉ's *Morning Ireland* to silence all speculation. He confirmed that he would not be a candidate, pointing out that he had young children and needed to balance his time between fatherhood and

politics. No one was unhelpful enough to mention to him that Mary
Lou's children were aged fourteen and eleven, or that she seemed to
think she and Martin could manage fine.

Michelle O'Neill said that she too would not be a runner. She
had 'enough to do' in her current role. She would have to deal with
'problems in the North'.

Conor Murphy, the man from south Armagh with the 'army'
background, kept his powder dry and his mouth shut. However, if
he nurtured further ambitions as a candidate from the old 'army',
they were fanciful. He had already been overlooked for leadership
of the party in the North in favour of Michelle O'Neill. His hopes
were dead in the water. Other names floating around included Matt
Carthy, the MEP for Midlands–North-West and Deputy Eoin Ó
Broin, but they were never at the races.

Adams told RTÉ's *The Week in Politics* – with his tongue stuck
in his cheek – that 'any member of Sinn Féin can be nominated for
any of our leadership positions. Our ard fheis – and not our parliamentary group or any of the little elites that are in other parties –
our ard fheis will appoint the next leader through a democratic
process of free election.'

There was only one flaw in his continued disingenuous protestations of a free and democratic election: when nominations
closed on 19 January, there was only one candidate.

Of course, Mary Lou's unchallenged status was not an accident.
In Sinn Féin they know how to organise 'democracy'. The thirty-
five-year period when Adams was re-elected president annually was
not being replaced by a healthy democratic contest. The decision to
hand over the reins to Mary Lou had been arranged behind closed
doors. The parliamentary party, puppets as always, had no say in a
key decision. Sinn Féin was still being led by a few unaccountable,
unelected figures. The rubber stamps followed. Even the 2000
delegates at the ard fheis were deprived of the option of voting for
an alternative. Opponents of Mary Lou insist that the Sinn Féin

hierarchy was determined not to risk a contest. Despite all the campaigning, the years of plotting and planning the succession, and the undoubted appeal of Mary Lou to the wider electorate, they would not take any chances.

Many Sinn Féin delegates felt that, despite his protests, Pearse Doherty had been nobbled. He dismissed such suggestions as 'ridiculous'. I spoke to several former members of the Ard Chomhairle, to TDs past and present, about Doherty's prospects of a win if he had challenged Mary Lou. A current TD admitted that 'Pearse had his followers', but former party members were more adamant. One said that if there had been a free vote of party members, 'Pearse Doherty would have walked it' on ability alone. Another told me that Doherty – and others – had actually received nominations from Sinn Féin cumainn but they had all been subsequently withdrawn. Another former Sinn Féin TD made it clear that, in his experience, Pearse Doherty was far more popular than Mary Lou with the foot soldiers. 'Pearse,' he said pointedly, 'had come up through the ranks and was credible on the republican stuff.'

But Pearse Doherty was not the anointed one. When Adams was asked by Michael Reade of LMFM local radio, based in Louth, whether or not he believed there should be a challenger to Mary Lou, he answered with a straight face: 'That's a matter for the party.' He added that he had decided not to comment on whatever contest emerged. Then he did comment, with an effusive endorsement of Mary Lou, admitting that he was very close to the Dublin Central TD. 'I appreciate the work she does and she's an outstanding candidate, but I don't think it would be fair for me, or to Mary Lou McDonald or anybody else, if I was to go off and give my preference. Let the party decide.'

The party duly decided. At the special ard fheis on 10 February 2018, Mary Lou McDonald, the only candidate, became president of Sinn Féin. The woman who had been appointed a member of the Ard Chomhairle in 2001 (unopposed), chair of the party in 2005 (unopposed) and vice-president of the party in 2009 (unopposed) had now been chosen as president of the party in 2018 (unopposed). They know how to dispose of opponents in Sinn Féin. The new president's guardian angel had delivered four bloodless coups in a row.

On the same day, Michelle O'Neill was elected to succeed Mary Lou as vice-president (unopposed).

As Mary Lou rose to make her acceptance speech, a small, overjoyed woman sitting beside her clapped wildly. The new Sinn Féin president had brought her mother along to share her moment of triumph. Joan McDonald was making one of her rare public appearances. Seven years earlier she had accompanied her daughter on her first day in the Dáil. In 2014 she had been in the audience for Mary Lou's first RTÉ *Late Late Show* triumph, but otherwise she had remained in the background. Her life had not been easy, but today she was receiving her reward for her determination to support her children with a good education in the face of many early obstacles.

Mary Lou, whose affection for her mother is clearly evident, thanked Joan in her opening lines, mentioning that 'My husband Martin, my children Iseult and Gerard are forever patient, my mother Joan, my brothers, my sister and my wider family – all precious people in my life. Thank you all.'

There was no mention of her father, Paddy. Perhaps he was watching his daughter's triumph on television somewhere. He was well and truly airbrushed.

He was not alone. The speech was more notable for its omissions than for its content. Like all ard fheis speeches in all parties, it was strong on rhetoric, weak on detail. No leader in Irish political life does rhetoric better than Mary Lou McDonald; few do detail worse. And the troops on that day wanted to celebrate. They were not at a republican political think-in: they were cheering a rock star.

Predictably, Mary Lou invoked the ghosts of past republicans. She identified closely with Countess Constance Markievicz, 'the most unmanageable of revolutionaries. A woman who came from privilege but who lived and worked to end British rule in Ireland.'

She name-checked Máire Drumm, whom she had commemorated recently in south Armagh, and hunger striker Margaret Buckley, president of Sinn Féin from 1937 to 1950. All three women were very safe republican territory.

Mary Lou poured the mandatory praise on her predecessor Gerry Adams, her 'political mentor, inspirational leader and great friend'. She hauled the late Martin McGuinness into her narrative at least six times in a speech where she indulged herself in recalling that she stood on 'the shoulders of giants'. Even the SDLP legend (now the late) John Hume was included in her pantheon of republican heroes.

Professing a less convincing tolerance for others from diverse political backgrounds, she insisted that 'Everybody has that right – to remember their dead with dignity. I respect,' she asserted, 'the right of those from other traditions, with a different historical narrative, to do likewise.' (Two years later, during the heat of the 2020 general election campaign, she called on the government to cancel a commemoration of the Royal Irish Constabulary.)

Appealing to women, she addressed the battle looming on the termination of pregnancies. 'I trust women,' she thundered in her support for the proposed referendum removing the ban on abortion from the constitution.

But she appeared to show generosity to delegates with other views. 'Some people,' she said, 'will not share our analysis. I respect their right to hold that view. Some of those will be republicans, friends and family.' Within a few months, two of her finest TDs, Carol Nolan and Peadar Tóibín, had been forced out of the Sinn Féin party for voting according to their consciences on the issue of abortion. Other parties had allowed a free vote.

There was no room to mention many of the other anchors in her life. Not a word of tribute to Pearse Doherty, her unrecognised rival, nor even to Eoin Ó Broin, the party's guru. Nor to Nora Comiskey, the Fianna Fáil woman whom she once referred to as her 'shepherd', the republican matriarch who had launched her on her long journey to glory. Nor of the Irish National Congress which paved her way into republican politics. She did not thank her other mentors: the nuns from her private school in Dublin's southside, nor her Trinity College tutors. The faithful did not need to be troubled with her privileged past.

There was one further omission. There was no tribute to the recent, so-called 'patriot dead'. Was the new leader about to airbrush them from the narrative? Had cemetery politics been suddenly buried?

Right at the finishing post, Mary Lou departed from her prepared script. The media had received a copy of her speech containing the rousing parting words 'Let's get to work. Ar aghaidh linn le chéile! Up the Republic.'

She delivered something very different. Electrifying the delegates, she concluded, lifting her voice, 'So my friends of Sinn Féin, let's get to work. Up the Republic.' And then the bombshell, the slogan in Irish that made every IRA volunteer's heart miss a beat, 'Tiocfaidh ár lá' – the Provisional IRA's rallying cry, the signature words meaning 'our day will come'. Mary Lou raised her clenched fist. She was once again – in her moment of victory – playing footsie with the men and women who had carried the Armalites.

It was an extraordinary achievement for Mary Lou McDonald. Nothing would spoil it for her. She had achieved her life's ambition. She had pressed the necessary buttons to raise the roof and bring the audience to its feet.

Time, however, was not on her side. In less than eighteen months she would face a test of her leadership. European and local elections were due in 2019. A general election could not be far behind. The people would have an early opportunity to give a verdict on her presidency.

The riddle of Mary Lou was ready to unravel. She was now, at least in theory, for the first time in nearly twenty years, her own woman. Her actions would surely soon reveal whether the Adams monkey was off her back. She would have to challenge, not pander to, the IRA veterans in the North if she was to appeal to the electorate in the South. She was the first leader of Sinn Féin without a terrorist past. Her predecessors had been in jail. A brilliant polemicist, a magnificent orator would now have to ensure that the balance of power in Sinn Féin shifted from Belfast to Dublin. The inevitable scrutiny, hugely increased now that she was a political leader, even a potential Taoiseach, would surely reveal her as a unique visionary or expose her as a permanent prisoner of others.

CHAPTER 10

TO HELL AND BACK

Many poison pills lurked in the chalice that passed from Gerry Adams to Mary Lou McDonald. As the euphoria from her victory faded, the new leader of Sinn Féin must have wondered how she would heal long-suppressed divisions in the party. Officially, the leadership never acknowledged differences or splits, but Adams had left deep fault lines behind him. Northern Sinn Féin felt very differently from Southern Sinn Féin on many issues. Adams had managed to stifle them with his iron control, some would say tyranny. Bullying, particularly of women in the party, was a problem, but nowhere were the stresses more apparent than in the re-emergence of the incendiary political time bomb that hardly dared to speak its name: abortion.

Most politicians avoided the A word. Sinn Féin was no different, preferring to call it the more delicate 'termination of pregnancy'. The two larger parties were in equal disarray on abortion when Mary Lou took over as leader. Sinn Féin had avoided forming a policy for many years. In 2018, just as Mary Lou landed in the party presidency, crunch time had come. A referendum beckoned to amend Ireland's constitution to delete the ban on abortion. The government was moving slowly towards repealing the offending Eighth Amendment. Mary Lou would be forced to lead Sinn Féin off the fence.

In their day, both Adams and McGuinness had held traditional anti-abortion views. However, back in January 2013 the party had made an exception by supporting legislation to comply with the consequences of the famous X case, allowing for abortions where the life of the mother was threatened. There had been signs of further change coming in January 2015 when Martin McGuinness took issue with the anti-abortion stance of the Roman Catholic archbishop of Armagh, Eamon Martin. McGuinness, asserting that he tried to be 'the best Catholic I can be', remained against abortion on demand but believed that 'compassion' in hard cases of pregnancy terminations should be a guiding principle for legislators. He referred specifically to the 'heart-breaking' case of a Northern Irish woman, Sarah Ewart, who had to travel to England for an abortion following medical advice that the baby in her womb would not survive. She had a fatal foetal abnormality, a condition where doctors believe that an unborn child will die in the womb or shortly after birth.

A month after McGuinness's spat with the archbishop, in February 2015, United Left TD Clare Daly proposed a bill in the Dáil allowing abortion in the case of fatal foetal abnormalities. Sinn Féin, including Mary Lou, abstained. The party had been caught offside.

Sinn Féin's abstention must have been deeply embarrassing for Mary Lou and for Sandra McLellan, the only two women on its male-dominated Dáil team in 2015. Gerry Adams explained away the indecision, lamely apologising that Sinn Féin had no policy on fatal foetal abnormalities. He promised that a firm party position was imminent.

Within weeks, the party held its 2015 ard fheis. It passed a motion, enthusiastically backed by Mary Lou McDonald, supporting legislation to allow abortion in the case of fatal foetal abnormalities. She insisted that it was 'the absolute entitlement of those women, their partners and their families to full care . . . every support and, above all, choice'. After failing to join the radical feminist voices in the Dáil a month earlier, she suddenly discovered her convictions. It was one of the few occasions recorded where the McDonald tail may have been wagging the Adams dog. Adams parroted McGuinness's earlier appeal for 'compassion'.

It was the Fine Gael–Labour coalition's view that Clare Daly's bill was unconstitutional, that repeal of the Eighth Amendment of the constitution banning abortion would be needed before new laws allowing such terminations could be contemplated. The coalition felt compelled to edge towards repeal. Sinn Féin decided not to be left behind. Consequently, a motion favouring repeal was passed at the same ard fheis in March 2015. The party was playing catch-up.

Within Sinn Féin there were more than token pockets of resistance to the party's change in policy. A new pressure group, Cherish All the Children Equally, was founded on both sides of the border to give dissenting republicans a platform for their opposition to abortion.

Sinn Féin lost members, leaving in protest at the abortion volte-face. Among them in 2016 was a prominent republican called Anne Brolly, a former mayor of Limavady and a long-standing, loyal member of Sinn Féin. Anne, mother of Joe Brolly, RTÉ's well-known GAA pundit, and husband of the former Sinn Féin MLA Francie Brolly, was disillusioned by the party's U-turn. Initially, Francie decided to stand and fight the abortion battle within the party, but in February 2018 he followed his wife and resigned his membership. Francie died in February 2020.

Anne Brolly was not on her own. Several other prominent party members – North and South – were unable to stomach this break with Roman Catholic doctrine.

Meanwhile, the new Fine Gael-led government was setting out a programme for a referendum, after tortuously slow deliberations in 2016 and 2017 at the Oireachtas Health Committee and the

Citizens' Assembly. Eventually, both bodies recommended a liberal abortion regime. On 9 March 2018, Minister for Health Simon Harris introduced the long-awaited bill proposing that a referendum to lift the ban on abortion be held on 25 May. On 21 March it was passed at second stage by 110 votes to 32.

Sinn Féin supported the referendum, but two of its TDs, Peadar Tóibín (Meath West) and Carol Nolan (Offaly), publicly opposed it. Tóibín had been a consistent advocate of a free vote on the abortion issue. He had been disciplined for refusing to support a Sinn Féin Dáil motion seeking legislation following the X case, where the life of the mother was in danger. At the 2014 ard fheis he had failed to persuade party members to agree to a conscience vote. Mary Lou had opposed his proposal, insisting, ominously, that the party must take policy positions.

Tóibín was not for turning. He was opposed to the 2018 proposal to hold a referendum, but he was absent from the Dáil on that day for family reasons, and so avoided a showdown. Carol Nolan voted against a referendum and was suspended from the party for three months. Mary Lou, now leader, said she understood that Nolan 'held strong personal convictions on the matter', adding that 'the party has respected her views and her right to articulate them'.

However, Carol was for the hangman's noose. Mary Lou ruthlessly pulled the trapdoor, asserting that, 'As legislators, we have a responsibility to vote as mandated by long-standing Sinn Féin policy.'

On 25 May the referendum lifting the ban on abortion was passed by the people by 66 per cent to 34 per cent.

A month later, at the June 2018 Sinn Féin ard fheis, delegates voted to support draft legislation to introduce abortion. The party backed a leadership motion stating that women should have access to abortions 'within a limited gestational period'. It still needed to agree the exact details of the new laws. Carol Nolan, a member of the Love Both pro-life group, resigned from the party, adamant that it was wrong to force TDs who were strongly opposed to abortion to vote against their consciences. Although more than twenty Sinn Féin branches had called for a conscience vote, Mary Lou wouldn't budge.

Carol Nolan departed. She successfully defended her seat in 2020, but as an Independent. In August 2021, I asked her whether she had any regrets and for her views on Mary Lou's attitude over the abortion issue. She was unwilling to reopen the controversy, merely saying: 'I want to leave it behind me. I had little interaction with Mary Lou. It was unfair that we were not given a free vote. She took a harsh line, and it was unethical to force us to vote against our consciences.'

After Carol Nolan's exit in late 2018, all eyes turned towards Peadar Tóibín. The loss of a political heavyweight threatened. Although he had not been present during the Dáil vote in March, he had proceeded to oppose the referendum, campaigning against it in a 'personal' capacity. It was a clear challenge to Mary Lou.

The party leader looked – for a moment – as though she might blink. She told the *Irish Examiner* that she would prefer it if Peadar Tóibín did not oppose party positions in public, but signalled that if he voted against Sinn Féin policy in the Dáil he would be walking the same plank as Nolan. She appeared to be offering an olive branch, hoping that Tóibín would toe the line when detailed legislation was put to the vote, even though the party had already agreed to support abortion on demand within a limited period. She had led them into a position that would have been unthinkable a few years earlier. Sinn Féin was backing abortion, subject to a limited time period of gestation.

Detailed legislation was brought to the Dáil in October, allowing for unrestricted abortion during the first twelve weeks of pregnancy. At second stage it was passed by 102 votes to 12. Peadar Tóibín took the honourable course he had always outlined when he voted against the measure. He joined eleven others, including his former colleague Carol Nolan, in the opposition camp. He was suspended from Sinn Féin for six months. Mary Lou had issued a warning during the debate that there was no 'à la carte position' on the legislation.

Three weeks later, on 15 November, Peadar Tóibín took a giant step into the unknown. After submitting his resignation from the Sinn Féin party, he announced that he would be helping to build a new '32 County movement'. In his letter of resignation, he said that when he had voted against the party on the same issue in 2012, he had struck a deal with the leadership. He had been promised that he would 'not be marginalised due to my views on the right to life as long as I gave the party view'. He now accused the party of 'unilaterally binning' the deal. He had recently tried to raise the issue with the new leader, 'but with no success'. Mary Lou had not even replied to his emails.

The leader issued an almost nonchalant response, expressing 'regret' and wishing Tóibín and his family well for the future.

Mary Lou had lost two of her twenty-three TDs in her first year in office. Whatever her personal instincts, she needed to assert her authority by imposing strict discipline. Abortion was tough territory for her. She had received fierce criticism from women, North and South, because of her less than sympathetic attitude to the case of Máiría Cahill, reflecting her deference to the men who had been running the Sinn Féin show for decades. She had seemed detached in the face of bullying charges made by many women within the party. Her feminist credentials were deeply suspect, shallow compared to Clare Daly's, Frances Fitzgerald's or Joan Burton's. She needed to put her stamp on the abortion issue, albeit belatedly, if she was to convince the middle classes, the young and female voters that Sinn Féin was fighting their corner. She could have taken the road of a free vote, but such indiscipline would have opened the floodgates to demands for the same conscience clause on other topics. Although Fianna Fáil and Fine Gael had decided to allow their deputies to follow their consciences on abortion for the first time, such laxity was a stranger to the Sinn Féin ethos of rigid party control inherited from its paramilitary past.

Peadar Tóibín began holding well-attended meetings, targeting support from nationalists North and South whose republicanism was backed up by a strong religious faith. He organised rallies not only in his own Meath West patch and elsewhere in the South, but also north of the border. One, in the key republican pro-life stronghold of Derry, was attended by Anne and Francie Brolly, joined by a former councillor for Ballymena, Monica Digney, and Declan McGuinness, a brother of the late Sinn Féin deputy first minister. Former IRA prisoner and well-known pro-lifer Gerry McGeough also attended. Disaffected Sinn Féin pro-lifers stood ready to poach a small, but possibly significant, portion of the party vote in both parts of Ireland.

In January 2019 Peadar Tóibín launched his new party, named Aontú, meaning 'unity' or 'agreement' in English. It was unwelcome news for Sinn Féin. The local elections, due in both North and South in 2019, would show whether it had stolen any of Sinn Féin's clothes.

In the Dáil, abortion had overshadowed other parliamentary business in 2018. It put an end to Mary Lou's short honeymoon period. It had caused conflict within her Dáil team and exposed public divisions, as bad as any of those in other parties. Sinn Féin suffered losses where other parties papered over the cracks. Mary Lou was on the back foot, despite taking a strong line on the issue. Her early months in the leadership were marked by discord, not harmony.

Mary Lou's first ard fheis leader's speech in Belfast in June 2018 was typically well delivered, but uninspiring in content. She simply pressed the right buttons, raising the old reliables of Palestine, Gaza, the Irish language and a united Ireland. She invoked memories of Nelson Mandela, Martin McGuinness and Bobby Sands. She attacked the easy targets, like the Tory government in London and the Democratic Unionist Party. She clasped to her bosom Vicky

Phelan and Emma Mhic Mhathúna, victims of the tragic cervical cancer misdiagnosis scandal. She identified housing and health as the main problems in the South. Her solutions were clichés and meaningless slogans. 'Republicans', she thundered at the end of her speech, 'get things done.' On abortion, 'no woman will be left behind. Women will have space and a place in the new Ireland.' On the North, she insisted that 'unionists cannot hold back the tide' and that 'we will talk to everyone' when it comes to taking a stand on a united Ireland. And she resolved that 'we must find a home for unionists' when it comes to reunification. There was no mention of where she would house these inconvenient citizens of her new Ireland. Almost the entire speech was empty rhetoric, a cocktail of brilliantly delivered negatives. It might rally the audience of the converted in Belfast, but it would hardly impress the bewildered middle-of-the-road voters in search of solutions to the chronic health and housing crises in the South.

Mary Lou's ard fheis offerings were always crafted for the crowd, but her Dáil performances often lacked substance. As she was preparing for the leadership throughout 2017, she had vacated her place on the Public Accounts Committee, her most powerful platform. Sinn Féin and Mary Lou had developed a penchant for high-wire debates. They preferred motions of no confidence in unpopular ministers, grabbing headlines with manoeuvres that flourished on sound bites, shortcuts that personalised a problem, lacking the rigour of detailed legislation.

In September 2018, when the Dáil returned from holidays, Sinn Féin proposed a vote of no confidence in the embattled housing minister, Fine Gael's Eoghan Murphy. Such motions had the added benefit of putting Fianna Fáil on the spot. The main opposition party's deal with the Fine Gael-led government obliged Fianna Fáil not to support such votes of no confidence. If Fianna Fáil was to give the thumbs-down to a minister, the government would lose the vote and be forced to resign. On this occasion, the party's deputies sat on their hands and abstained. Eoghan Murphy survived.

Votes of no confidence had become Sinn Féin's typical modus operandi. However, a month after Eoghan Murphy escaped, a Sinn Féin chicken came home to roost.

A year earlier, one victim of this easy parliamentary tactic who had not survived a Sinn Féin vote of no confidence was Minister for Justice and Tánaiste Frances Fitzgerald. At the time, Sinn Féin had put down a motion of no confidence in the Tánaiste, alleging that she was fully aware of a nasty garda campaign to smear the whistle-blower Maurice McCabe and that she had done nothing about it. Mary Lou led the charge, demanding Frances Fitzgerald's head on a plate.

Fianna Fáil, petrified of being spectators at a Sinn Féin hanging, decided to put down its own motion of no confidence, despite its deal to support the government or abstain. Frances Fitzgerald was toast. Fine Gael played hardball until a few hours before the confidence motions were due for debate. If the debate went ahead, the government was certain to lose the vote. Frances Fitzgerald resigned, still pleading her innocence, but refusing, in the national interest, to be the cause of a general election.

Mary Lou had captured a political scalp, but she had to share the spoils with Fianna Fáil leader Micheál Martin.

The removal of Fitzgerald left a sour taste in the mouth of many politicians. The matter was referred to the Charleton Disclosures Tribunal, luckily already sitting to examine the garda treatment of whistle-blower Garda Maurice McCabe. Meanwhile, the former Tánaiste was banished to the backbenches.

On 11 October 2018 the Charleton Disclosures Tribunal reported. It vindicated Frances Fitzgerald's position, finding that her evidence had been truthful. Even Fianna Fáil admitted that she had been cleared of any wrongdoing.

Mary Lou was unimpressed. Refusing to apologise, despite a serious rebuff from the tribunal, she insisted that her calls for

Fitzgerald's resignation were not 'a personal attack'. She tried to shift the blame on to the 'system', stating that 'politics is about accountability, and the system had gone catastrophically wrong, failing Sergeant McCabe. The political system has to be answerable.' She added, 'Charleton wasn't asked to make political assessments. And the political assessment was that Frances Fitzgerald had lost the confidence of the Dáil.'

She tried to switch the topic back to the whistle-blower, to return to her own comfort zone, pushing out Maurice McCabe as her shield against criticism. 'Apologies,' she scoffed irrelevantly, 'were necessary to the injured party, Maurice and Lorraine McCabe and their family, and it is the Garda Síochána, the Department of Justice, the current Minister for Justice, Charlie Flanagan, and previous ministers for justice who owe an explanation and apology to that man and his family.' She was muddying the waters, spreading the blame, diverging from the victimisation of Frances Fitzgerald, who had been wrongly hounded out of office by Sinn Féin and Fianna Fáil.

Even by Sinn Féin's political double standards, Mary Lou's response was breathtaking. Yet there was no escaping the reality that an independent tribunal had found that an honest politician had been forced to fall on her sword. There was no political price to be paid by the executioners in this blood sport. Mary Lou and Micheál Martin would swan away scot-free from the political carnage and personal pain they had caused.

Or would they? Fifteen days after the Charleton tribunal reported that Frances Fitzgerald had been wronged, it was polling day in Ireland's presidential election. The result was a sobering outcome, a wake-up call for Mary Lou McDonald.

On 10 July 2018 Michael D. Higgins had announced that he would run for a second term as president of Ireland. He was believed to be unbeatable. Fianna Fáil, Fine Gael and Labour all promised to support his re-election, believing that standing a candidate against him was a lost cause, expensive and politically perilous. Mary Lou took the opposite view, seeing the election as an opportunity to mobilise more support for Sinn Féin in a contest without the three main parties. She wanted to announce Sinn Féin's early entry to deter others and to seize an opportunity to champion her 'change' mantra nationwide. She believed that Michael D was certain to win, but that Sinn Féin could come a good second. It would be an opening to establish the party as the principal alternative to Fine Gael. The campaign would need to tread carefully to avoid crossing swords with Michael D, whose stature had grown over his first term of office. Four days after Michael D's own declaration, Mary Lou confirmed that Sinn Féin would challenge for his post. Careful not to say anything critical of a popular president, she spoke of how it was right to 'give this generation the opportunity to be part of a wider conversation of what a better Ireland would look like'.

Sinn Féin was mindful of the good performance from Martin McGuinness back in the 2011 presidential race when he garnered 13.7 per cent of the votes in a field that included a Fine Gael hopeful. There was an opening for a party on the make. All they needed was a candidate of McGuinness's stature.

As always, their selection procedure was opaque. A commission to recommend a candidate was set up, chaired by David Cullinane, a staunch ally of Mary Lou McDonald's. Three days later, an inspired article appeared in Northern Ireland's leading nationalist newspaper. The *Irish News* reported that John Finucane 'has emerged as one of the contenders to be Sinn Féin's presidential candidate'. Finucane is the son of the late Pat Finucane, the nationalist human rights lawyer murdered by loyalist gunmen in 1989. The newspaper further reported that bookmakers Paddy Power 'yesterday said it had suspended betting on Mr Finucane following a "string of bets" backing him'. John Finucane wasn't available for comment, but perhaps he isn't a betting man.

The article was not music to Mary Lou's ears. When contacted by the *Irish News* about a possible Finucane candidacy, she replied that John Finucane was 'wonderful'. She didn't say he was a 'wonderful candidate'.

In support of its story, the *Irish News* cited RTÉ reports that John Finucane had been described by senior unnamed Sinn Féin figures as a 'strong contender' for the party's choice for president of Ireland. It looked as though a shadowy hand was trying to bounce the party into a Finucane candidacy.

Mary Lou had other ideas. The same inspired article surmised that, 'despite the president of Sinn Féin's complimentary response, most observers still expect the party to choose a woman who hails from south of the border'. The *Irish News* was on the money.

It appeared that a North–South split needed nipping in the bud.

On 27 July David Cullinane outlined the process for picking a candidate. A nomination process would open on 20 August and close on 10 September. The ard chomhairle would make a decision on 16 September. Cullinane said they wanted a candidate 'who will address the changes seen in the abortion referendum and the same-sex marriage referendum and will address the issue of changing a patriarchal society'. The job description didn't sound like it fitted a man over a woman. Cullinane said there would be no 'gender intervention', and while they 'would love to have a woman candidate, there will be no issue if there is a man'.

John Finucane was sunk. Decoded, the selection would be a Southern woman of stature who had participated in the referendums on same-sex marriage and abortion. That meant Mary Lou McDonald, Lynn Boylan or Liadh Ní Riada. Lynn Boylan had already ruled herself out. Mary Lou was leader of the party.

Sinn Féin was still in the same old mould. The ard chomhairle would consider only one name. The selection process would remain unseen. The decision would be unanimous. The name would be Liadh Ní Riada. Sinn Féin democracy, Mary Lou-style, was an exact replica of her mentor Gerry Adams's. Secrecy was sacrosanct.

On 16 September Liadh Ní Riada was named as one of the candidates to challenge Michael D. Higgins for the presidency.

At first glance, Mary Lou was probably right that Liadh Ní Riada was a strong candidate, well capable of expanding the party's base beyond the Martin McGuinness total of 13.7 per cent. She was the daughter of the late Seán Ó Riada, one of Ireland's best-loved, legendary music composers. Her father had died when she was only four. Like him, she spoke fluent Irish. She was fifty-two, married with three children and had been elected to the European Parliament for Ireland South in 2014. She had no history of flirting with IRA terrorism, having joined Sinn Féin in 2011 as its national Irish language officer. She looked powerful on paper.

Liadh was Mary Lou's choice. It was also her decision to contest the election. Unlike other parties, Sinn Féin had bucketloads of money. Mary Lou never expected to defeat Michael D, but she believed the absence of big-party candidates from the field offered an open goal, an opportunity to promote their united Ireland agenda and their vague programme for change.

A dull campaign was dominated by a rumbling row about the lack of transparency over Michael D's €300,000 allowance and anti-Traveller comments by Independent contender Peter Casey.

Liadh Ní Riada was a bystander in many of the controversies. However, she managed to create one or two of her own. Her statement that she would wear a poppy, if elected, caused consternation in the Sinn Féin ranks. Some party members even publicly criticised her. She had to haul in the cover of Martin McGuinness's meeting with Queen Elizabeth to support her poppy problem. Reports that she had stopped one of her daughters from having the HPV anti-cervical cancer vaccine left her struggling to profess that she had merely expressed 'concern'. She was stranded, unable to explain how she had told *Hot Press* magazine that she was taking only the average industrial wage as an MEP when she was actually receiving €47,000 per annum after tax. The other candidates – all Independents

– businessmen Gavin Duffy and Seán Gallagher and mental health activist Senator Joan Freeman, hardly featured.

On polling day, Michael D. Higgins triumphed on the first count with 55.8 per cent of the vote; Peter Casey came in second with 23.3 per cent, followed by Seán Gallagher (6.4 per cent), Liadh Ní Riada (6.4 per cent), Joan Freeman (6 per cent) and Gavin Duffy (2.2 per cent).

For Sinn Féin, it was little short of a catastrophe. RTÉ's political correspondent Martina Fitzgerald was unusually forthright, asserting that 'the real political story was the disastrous election for Sinn Féin, a serious blow for which party leader Mary Lou McDonald would have to take full responsibility'.

Sinn Féin's 2011 candidate, Martin McGuinness, had attracted double Liadh Ní Riada's vote in 2011 after facing far tougher opposition. It appeared not only that Mary Lou's decision to contest the election was wrong, but that her choice of candidate was a mistake.

Michael D. Higgins was unbeatable. Other party leaders, Micheál Martin and Enda Kenny, took a wise decision to stand aside and back the incumbent. They rightly avoided possible humiliation and unnecessary extravagance with scarce party funds. Sinn Féin admitted to spending €175,000 on its doomed campaign.

Moreover, the party had not chosen its candidate until 16 September, just six weeks before election day. The nominee was hardly known outside her Ireland South constituency. She was never going to raise her low national profile adequately in barely a month. Her father, Seán Ó Riada, was a household name, but he had died in 1971, aged forty. Her gaffes on the poppy, her confusion on her own salary and her past views on the HPV vaccine left her on the defensive. She had desperately tried to focus on a united Ireland, a subject that failed to inspire the electorate. Sinn Féin's odd decision to campaign in Northern Ireland on at least one occasion was probably symbolic, but questionable in a region where none of the citizens had a vote.

Mary Lou was typically unapologetic for her mistake. She insisted that it would have been a political failure on her part not to have contested the election. In characteristic rebuttal mode, she attacked the other parties for becoming 'spectators'. She even paradoxically declared that it had been 'a good campaign for us, albeit with a disappointing outcome on the day of polling'. And then she emitted a philosophical sigh, 'Sin an saol,' meaning 'That's life'. Her loyal lieutenant, David Cullinane, conceded that Michael D had been strong and, consequently, mobilising canvassers and supporters was difficult. He claimed that many Sinn Féin voters had stayed away, anticipating a coronation for Michael D.

Liadh Ní Riada blamed the low turnout and headed back to Brussels within days, no doubt solemnly reflecting on the reality that she had attracted 30,000 more votes in the much smaller European constituency of Ireland (South) in the 2014 elections than she had managed to gather in the entire twenty-six counties in October 2018.

Sinn Féin had food for thought. Mary Lou needed to nurse her wounds. And watch her back. Members of the media noticed that in November her mood became tetchy. Her exchanges with Leo Varadkar in the Dáil chamber were more personal. The Taoiseach taunted her, accusing her of 'rank hypocrisy' for missing not only the November armistice services, but also the painful occasion – for her – of Michael D's second inauguration. Instead, according to Leo, she had opted to 'hobnob with the super-rich' at a $400-dollar-a-head Sinn Féin fundraiser in Manhattan.

An incident, spotted by alert journalists at the time, involving Mary Lou during an event held to mark a hundred years of women's suffrage caused consternation among past and present female members of Dáil Éireann. A photo shoot had been arranged in the chamber to mark the occasion. According to journalist Senan Molony, writing for Extra.ie, the seating arrangements were made by the ushers, placing former ministers in the front row and others elsewhere in the chamber according to their rank.

Mary Lou, not an ex-minister, arrived at the last minute to find former Fianna Fáil minister Mary Hanafin sitting in the seat she always occupied during ordinary Dáil sittings. Normal seat places had been suspended for the photo opportunity. Mary Lou asked Mary Hanafin to tell her who had given her 'permission' to sit in her seat. The Fianna Fáil ex-minister replied that the ushers had shown her to her place. Molony told his readers how Mary Lou announced that she 'would not be sitting for any photograph until she was sitting in her own seat' and stormed off in search of the head usher. The unfortunate usher politely asked Mary Hanafin if she would mind surrendering her place to Mary Lou, a request with which Hanafin complied in order to avoid an awkward row. Afterwards, Hanafin accused McDonald of 'bullying pure and simple' but refused to comment further except to declare that 'As Michelle Obama says – when they go low, we go high.'

Mary Lou's behaviour provoked a bad reaction from colleagues. Former Tánaiste Joan Burton said it was ' a terrible incident . . . and it was unfortunate the Dáil staff had been dragged into it . . . they were put in a very invidious position. It was highly uncalled for. It was sheer petulance.' According to Molony's report, there was general disapproval among the sisterhood at a lunch afterwards, with an almost unanimous view that Mary Lou should cop on to herself.

Pieces began to appear in the media suggesting that Mary Lou was showing signs of the strains of leadership. Noel Whelan was particularly cutting in his influential *Irish Times* column. In an article entitled 'Pressure of Leadership Getting to McDonald', he pointed out that Sinn Féin had enjoyed no 'Mary Lou bounce' since her election ten months earlier and that stress was showing in her increasingly testy interviews. According to Whelan, her Dáil contributions were 'fixed at one high-pitched tone of outrage'.

Nevertheless, an internal review of the presidential election carried out by deputies Martin Ferris of IRA Army Council fame, McDonald ally Denise Mitchell from Dublin Bay North and Sam

Baker, chair of Belfast Sinn Féin, reported that the campaign had been below par, but that the leader was blameless.

Mary Lou badly needed a parliamentary or an electoral success. Neither was emerging. As Christmas 2018 approached, Micheál Martin and Leo Varadkar patched together a renewal of the 'confidence and supply' agreement, leaving few openings for the opposition to exploit.

The year 2018 had begun on a high note for Mary Lou. In February she had achieved a twenty-year ambition. Gerry Adams was gone, leaving her the chance to exorcise past ghosts and put her stamp on the party that he had ruthlessly controlled. She had seen the political gap. Instead, she sometimes seemed lost without her master and mentor. She started well, playing a prominent role in the abortion referendum campaign, despite internal difficulties on the issue. But she had not solved the party's long-running bullying row; she had lost two TDs, had seen councillors defecting on the same issue and a new party led by Peadar Tóibín on the verge of formation. She had insisted that Sinn Féin run a presidential candidate, who flopped on the hustings. Her Dáil performances were sounding more and more like the bombast of an empty vessel. The opinion poll ratings of the party were stagnant. And now, on 12 December 2018, the Fine Gael-led government had secured its own stability by agreeing an extension of the 'confidence and supply' deal with Fianna Fáil for another year. The big test for Mary Lou awaited six months down the line, in May 2019, when the local and European elections would be held. A general election was unlikely until 2020. There were mutterings in the media, but no sedition in the Sinn Féin ranks.

Mary Lou had ended 2018 on a low note, but she showed little sign of any change of direction. Unrepentant, she hardly paused to think. On 12 January she was back in her element, addressing the faithful in Dublin's Mansion House at a meeting for Sinn Féin activists to commemorate the centenary of the first Dáil in 1919.

The meeting was packed. Mary Lou did not mince her words. Far from moderating her republican rhetoric, she embellished it. She was introduced to the faithful by the Derry maverick Elisha McCallion, a Sinn Féin Westminster MP, soon to cause a bundle of trouble to the party. Mary Lou's speech was full of the old anti-British hostility reminiscent of pre-Good Friday Agreement days. She spoke passionately about the 'landlord classes', how women had been 'brutalised' and the terror of the Black and Tans. The source of all our ills was partition. This time she invoked the memory of a rare hero, James Connolly, and favourably uttered the even rarer words 'socialist republic' when praising his ambitions. Declaring triumphantly that 'the Orange state is gone', she namechecked Connolly, Pearse, Markievicz and 'our hero Bobby Sands'. Remembering the 'patriot dead', she insisted – to loud applause – that we should honour the 'men and women of the Irish Republican . . . movement who have given their all'. And she finished up slowly, hesitating, creating anticipation and drama, before raising her clenched fist and uttering the inflammatory slogan 'Tiocfaidh ár lá', so beloved of the IRA. The Round Room was rocked by the rhetoric.

Neither Elisha McCallion, the republican from Derry who gave the warm-up to her speech, nor Mary Lou's own words were going to win friends among the middle class whom she was wooing in the South. The meeting was not widely reported. She made a similar but much watered-down speech, again in the Mansion House, a few days later when the Dáil held a special session to celebrate its centenary. The Sinn Féin message of the 'failed state' was the same, but the rhetoric was far less provocative. The RTÉ cameras were at the official event.

There was nothing new in her oration. Nor was there any sign of rethinking or a fresh message in the wounded party's use of Dáil time. When the House resumed after the 2018 Christmas break, Sinn Féin resorted to yet another vote of no confidence, this time in Minister for Health Simon Harris. Business as usual.

Votes of confidence had now deteriorated almost solely into a Sinn Féin device to embarrass Fianna Fáil, rather than the Fine Gael–Independent coalition government of which I was a member. Micheál Martin's signature in December to a new agreement, binding him not to vote against the government in votes of confidence had encouraged Sinn Féin. The party immediately responded by putting down a motion targeting Harris, who had presided over an extremely awkward overrun in the cost of the National Children's Hospital.

In her contribution on the motion, Mary Lou spelled it out. Her target was Micheál Martin, not Harris. She criticised the Fianna Fáil leader for his continued commitment to the confidence and supply formula and for propping up the government. She hammered home the message that Martin's 'grubby' deal covered the blushes of the Fianna Fáil leader who, she insisted, was in a de facto coalition with Fine Gael.

Sinn Féin's spokesperson on health, Louise O'Reilly, threw the kitchen sink at Harris, including criticising him for claiming too much credit for the passage of the abortion referendum. Harris won by fifty-eight votes to fifty-three. Fianna Fáil saved the coalition's skins with their abstentions. Mary Lou had again made a good point, but it seemed to be lost on the electorate.

In March, Mary Lou stumbled into further tricky waters. This time it was the PSNI's appointment of a successor to retiring chief constable George Hamilton. She rashly declared that no one inside the force was fit for the top job. She had good cause to criticise the PSNI, albeit reformed, but even managed to embarrass her own Sinn Féin colleague, ex-IRA prisoner and Army Council member Gerry Kelly, with her outburst! Kelly happened to be a member of the police board choosing the new constable and had to lower his leader's tone. She received a rebuke from an *Irish Times* editorial.

In the same month, Mary Lou courted even more controversy when she headed to New York for the St Patrick's Day celebrations.

She joined a group on the march carrying a banner blazing out the message 'ENGLAND GET OUT OF IRELAND'. Criticism poured in, not just from the usual suspects of the DUP and the UUP. Simon Coveney described the banner as 'offensive, divisive and an embarrassment'. Coveney, three years her junior, exclaimed, 'Grow up, Mary Lou.'

More disconcerting was probably the reprimand from another nationalist, SDLP leader Colum Eastwood. 'Sinn Féin,' he declared, 'aren't capable of convincing unionists of anything. The rest of us will have a lot of heavy lifting to do.'

Worse still were the withering words of Alliance Party leader Naomi Long, who mercilessly patronised Mary Lou, saying that some politicians 'can get giddy on a kind of high of hanging around with people in the Irish-American lobby who perhaps don't see the subtle distinctions that we are aware of back home'. She went on: 'I think Anglophobia is one of the least permissible kinds of xenophobia that we accept. And I don't think it's good enough.' Long's words were crushing.

Mary Lou didn't budge – well, not until the next weekend when the *Sunday Business Post* published an opinion poll: less than two months before May's local and European elections, Sinn Féin's vote had plunged from 18 per cent to 13 per cent. Mary Lou hurriedly appeared on RTÉ and apologised for carrying the banner. She inexplicably said that its message was not directed at English people.

The background to the local and European elections was mixed. Mary Lou was determined to fight both contests on the government's poor record on health, housing and the environment. She expected to hoover up votes by constantly branding Fianna Fáil and Fine Gael as a coalition in all but name. Unfortunately for her, there was another issue that she probably did not anticipate. Her consistent involvement in damaging controversies meant that her own performance was also on trial.

The European elections, local elections and a referendum on divorce were ordered for 24 May 2019. Despite so many contests being held on the same day, the poll still barely broke 50 per cent (50.2 per cent in the locals and 49.7 per cent in the European elections). The campaigns focused mainly on national politics, with European issues once again taking a back seat, despite the continuing uncertainties surrounding Brexit at the time.

Climate change emerged as an important issue among voters, reflecting a pan-European Green wave. In Ireland, the Greens were the big winners. After holding no seats in the outgoing European Parliament, they captured two: Ciarán Cuffe in Dublin and Grace O'Sullivan in South. Fine Gael's Frances Fitzgerald took a seat in Dublin, helping the Fine Gael party to increase its vote by 7.3 per cent nationally on a good day for Leo Varadkar. Fianna Fáil's overall vote declined by 5.7 per cent, but the party managed to add a European seat after strong winning campaigns by Barry Andrews in Dublin and Billy Kelleher in South. The two major parties held their own in the local elections, slightly adding to their councillor numbers. The Greens increased their councillor count by thirty-seven, from a base of just twelve to a total of forty-nine.

But the bigger story was the shock reversal for Sinn Féin. They lost two of their three MEPs: namely, presidential candidate Liadh Ní Riada, despite her extensive exposure just seven months earlier, and Lynn Boylan, whose defeat in Dublin had never been anticipated. Matt Carthy alone hung on, scraping home for Sinn Féin in Midlands–North-West.

The local elections made even worse reading for Mary Lou. Both of the big parties could take some comfort from their small gains, and even Labour recouped six council seats after their 2014 debacle, but the sensation was the humiliation of Sinn Féin. Mary Lou's party lost 78 of its 159 councillors. The party's reverses were nationwide. It was a rout.

Mary Lou was stoical in defeat. Maybe surprisingly, she did not immediately emerge with a ready-made list of others to blame. Everywhere she looked, she faced calamity. The Dublin vote had collapsed. Even in her own Dublin Central constituency, Sinn Féin managed to land only a single seat. Nor was there any comfort offered by the European election result from Northern Ireland on the same day. Although Martina Anderson, the London bomber of the 1980s, had topped the poll with 126,951 votes, she had lost more than 30,000 votes from her total of 159,813 in 2014. Worse still for Mary Lou personally, in the South many of the Sinn Féin councillors who had left the party over bullying allegations sailed in as Independents. Noeleen Reilly took 1700 first preferences in Mary Lou's backyard of Ballymun Finglas. After his re-election as an Independent Tipperary councillor, Séamie Morris put the knife into his former party when he said that he was 'surprised that Mary Lou McDonald hadn't been able to turn the ship around'. Wicklow county councillor Gerry O'Neill, who had left the party in disgust after forty-seven years, was easily returned as an Independent with 1800 first preferences.

Mary Lou showed plenty of backbone in defeat. The litany of excuses, familiar to defeated politicians, did not emerge. She told the media that Sinn Féin were not 'cry-babies', even insisting that 'the buck stops with me'. It did. Sinn Féin's vote in the local elections was down to 9.5 per cent, a reduction of 5.7 per cent on its 2014 share of 15.2 per cent under Gerry Adams. The electorate had given a thumbs-down to Mary Lou. She had stumbled at the first fence. Gerry Adams, despite his links with terrorism, had been far more successful in 2014.

The media had a ball. Some of them tried to bury Mary Lou alive. Philip Ryan in the *Irish Independent* dubbed her leadership as 'utterly abysmal'. Elaine Loughlin in the *Irish Examiner* insisted that she had misjudged the mood of the nation. Suzanne Breen of the *Belfast Telegraph* reported that there was 'speculation of a quick goodbye to Mary Lou'.

But the leader made it crystal clear that she was going nowhere.

A review was ordered to report rapidly on where the party had gone wrong. Meaningful reviews are not the traditional parties' response to an election defeat. They are often thinly disguised delaying devices to save the losing leader's skin. Sinn Féin resolved to act decisively on its review.

A meeting of the ard chomhairle on 8 June became a post-mortem. A review body was ordered to report as a matter of urgency. Obsessive Sinn Féin secrecy has prevented full disclosure of the review group's recommendations, but reliable sources have confirmed that two sub-committees of three members were set up, one to consider the European elections, the other the local contests. Submissions were invited from individual members, cumainn and cúigí. At an early stage of the post-mortem, it became clear that there would be no change in policy direction. Sinn Féin had positioned itself as left-of-centre republican. That stance was not up for debate. Nor was Mary Lou's leadership, although there was plenty of implied criticism of her in the recommendations.

The review panels focused on the approaching general election and avoiding the mistakes of the past. They identified poor communication with the public as a significant reason for the party's decline in support. The review received internal submissions, asserting that the party was far too negative and rarely offered solutions; the overuse of votes of confidence as a Dáil tactic was questioned. Sinn Féin was seen by some as a party of endless protest that was not serious about government; it was perceived by others as permanently angry and far too lacking in positivity. There was a general acknowledgement that they had been fighting against a global Green wave. Sinn Féin was fortunate to have increased its seat numbers so dramatically in the 2014 elections because of the water charges rebellion at that time. There was little, if any, dwelling on the failure to exploit the housing or health issues, the bullying problems in the party, the arrival of Aontú or the dangers of a resurgence of Fianna Fáil.

Instead, Sinn Féin set about implementing the contents of the review. In August, Mary Lou gave a sombre 'state of the party' address to all members through the pages of *An Phoblacht*. It was almost humble. She emphasised how the results in the South were 'disappointing' and how 'we all needed to listen'. Her emphasis shifted to 'solutions'. She wrote of 'climate change' and of how it was necessary to 'reconnect'. The way the party operated would change to combat how it had 'failed' in the elections. It was a call to arms, without the Armalite. The next staging post would be the ard fheis, fixed for Derry in November. In the meantime, the party back-room staff were putting their noses to the grindstone to change the messaging, to move into solution mode and to communicate better. They knew that they had the money and the boots on the ground. They were back on course, confidently remedying their mistakes in a committed, methodical way. Then, suddenly, a bombshell exploded.

On 31 August one of the elders of the party broke ranks. John O'Dowd had been a minister at Stormont, even deputy first minister when Martin McGuinness took time off to run for the presidency of Ireland. He was respected, while not being one of the high-profile military men. The *Belfast Telegraph* revealed that he would be making a bid to oust Michelle O'Neill from the vice-presidency of Sinn Féin at the November ard fheis. O'Dowd confirmed the story in a tweet, saying that he 'looked forward to the debate across the party and island'. It had all the signs of a well-coordinated coup.

Sinn Féin don't do leadership challenges. As O'Dowd would soon find out, Sinn Féin don't do leadership 'debates' either.

The top brass in the party was shell-shocked and apparently angry that the challenge should come at such a vulnerable time. Michelle O'Neill was on holiday, but pluckily tweeted her 'welcome' for the oncoming debate. Most Sinn Féin members were caught off guard, wondering whether the challenge was a result of the party's move to more liberal abortion laws, a lack of faith in Michelle O'Neill or O'Dowd's despair at the dismal election results in the South.

O'Dowd was never given the chance to let them know. Within hours, Michelle's fighting tweet was retweeted by MEP Martina Anderson, Foyle MP Elisha McCallion and ex-culture minister and IRA ex-prisoner Carál Ní Chuilín. The old guard were circling the wagons. Only former Fermanagh–South Tyrone Westminster MP Michelle Gildernew rowed in behind O'Dowd. She pointedly told the BBC that 'after recent elections it is now time to ask questions about the party leadership'. Gildernew referred to 'disappointments across the island from electoral terms'. She was pointing the dagger in the direction of Mary Lou, not really at Michelle O'Neill. In reality, she was backing a challenge to Mary Lou via her soft underbelly. At this stage Mary Lou and Michelle O'Neill were joined at the hip.

True to its word, the party went through at least the formalities of a contest. It opened and closed nominations. There were two: O'Neill and O'Dowd. There would be no discussions, no debate, no hustings. John O'Dowd was perfectly entitled to stand but he would get no oxygen. Indeed, according to Mary Lou, speaking to the *Irish News*, he would not be 'punished' for the challenge. It was Sovietesque. The Sinn Féin hierarchy had closed down the contest. There would be a vote, but no platform would be entertained for the two candidates to explain their vision for the party. John O'Dowd suddenly clammed up and gave no interviews. His challenge was stillborn.

The outcome was announced on 16 November at the ard fheis in Derry. Michelle O'Neill was pronounced the winner. No figures were released. After a major dust-up, the numbers were made public. Michelle O'Neill had received 493 votes (67 per cent), John O'Dowd 241 (33 per cent). There was a substantial minority voting against the wishes of the hierarchy. It was far from a ringing endorsement of the two leaders.

Mary Lou badly needed an electoral success. No sooner had she finished at the party's ard fheis than she faced a further hurdle.

Four by-elections were looming south of the border on 29 November. The vacancies were caused by departed TDs who had won seats in the European Parliament. If Sinn Féin repeated its dismal local and European election performances, the leader was in even deeper trouble. Three of the four Dáil seats – Cork North-Central, Dublin Fingal and Wexford – had been held by opposition TDs. The fourth, Dublin Mid-West, had been vacated by Fine Gael's Frances Fitzgerald.

Sinn Féin had held none of the seats. They targeted Dublin Mid-West as a live prospect, partly because they had a hard-working grass-roots candidate in former mayor of South Dublin County Council, local councillor Mark Ward. More significantly, Sinn Féin's sitting TD in the four-seater, housing guru Eoin Ó Broin, ran a well-oiled election machine in the constituency. Ó Broin, who had topped the poll in 2016, is credited with single-handedly organising a maximum number of Sinn Féin-supporting working families turning out to vote. Ward took 24 per cent of the vote on the first count. Against all the odds, on the final count he snatched the seat by 525 votes from under the nose of Fine Gael candidate Councillor Emer Higgins.

The win was a mighty relief for Mary Lou. Asked what had changed since May, she admitted: 'I have learned a million lessons since then.' She said the result showed that the party was 'turning the ship'. Sinn Féin was back in the game.

Fine Gael failed to win any of the four seats. The Greens won Dublin Fingal while Fianna Fáil filled the other two vacancies. The loss of the Fine Gael seat to Sinn Féin made the already delicately poised Dáil arithmetic even more perilous for the government. A general election was unstoppable.

Mark Ward's first vote on his first day in the Dáil was on yet another vote of no confidence in Eoghan Murphy. Significantly, it was not Sinn Féin's, but the Social Democrats' motion. Sinn Féin was holding back from being the Dáil's rottweiler. Mary Lou devoted much of her speech to a denunciation of Fianna Fáil for abstaining.

The confidence motion was beaten by just three votes. Its defeat removed the threat of a Christmas general election, but within a week, the rural Independents, Labour and Sinn Féin were jockeying for position about who would wield the next dagger. The rural Independents were the most enthusiastic, threatening to put down another motion of no confidence in Simon Harris after the Christmas recess. Sinn Féin, in keeping with its determination to soften its negative image, was far less eager than heretofore, telling the media that they might even use their Dáil time to table key legislation of importance to its TDs' individual needs.

In the background, Leo Varadkar and Micheál Martin were trying in vain to agree an unforced election date. Another vote of no confidence in Simon Harris's handling of the continuing health crisis would put unbearable pressure on Martin to jump ship. On 9 January the rural Independents confirmed they would be putting down the no-confidence motion the following week.

If the motion had been forced to a Dáil vote, the government would almost certainly have lost. No Independent would have been persuaded to defend a deeply unpopular health service. On the morning of 14 January 2020, Leo told us in cabinet that he would be seeking a dissolution that afternoon. The election date would be Saturday, 8 February.

The mood among Fine Gael members of the cabinet that morning was surprisingly upbeat, despite the party's humiliation a week earlier. The government had been forced to cancel an insensitive and ill-advised decision to hold a commemoration for the Royal Irish Constabulary (RIC) in Dublin Castle in late January. Mary Lou had been handed an open goal. She never missed penalties and enjoyed a field day condemning the event and demanding its cancellation. 'In no other country,' she exploded with indignation, 'would those who facilitated the suppression of national freedom be celebrated by the state.' And then, on safe ground, she accused the state of commemorating 'the Black and Tans'. The Great Commemorator herself was in full flight. Selective commemorations were her forte.

Justice Minister Charlie Flanagan caved in and cancelled the event just seven days before the election campaign was formally launched.

The election may have been forced on the government by the unfavourable Dáil numbers, but Fine Gael's standing in the polls was steady. Throughout the autumn and winter months they had been scoring in the high twenties, marginally ahead of Fianna Fáil, leaving Sinn Féin trailing in third place, at least 10 per cent behind. The Greens had not picked up any further momentum following their local and European successes. Fine Gael naively expected the campaign to be fought on the issues of Brexit and the strong economy. The Northern Ireland Executive had been restored on 11 January, for which the party would claim credit. Simon Coveney and Paschal Donohoe were highly reassuring figures for a stressed public worried about an uncertain future for the island. Or so the coalition felt.

Such overconfidence was a measure of how out of touch Fine Gael was. Brexit and a generally good economic performance didn't butter many parsnips. Nor did the restoration of Stormont resonate with an electorate who didn't really seem to give a hoot about developments in Northern Ireland. The Fine Gael hierarchy saw themselves as saviours of the nation, thoroughly deserving of due rewards from grateful citizens. Sadly for them, the citizens were instead more deeply worried by the number of people without houses or on hospital trolleys.

Fortune failed to favour Fine Gael. Tragedy struck. Just as Leo left the cabinet to ask the president for a dissolution, a Waterways Ireland mechanical grabber on Dublin's Grand Canal badly injured a homeless man, still in a tent that the grabber had attempted to lift into a waste truck. The poor man suffered serious, life-changing injuries. The horrific scene prompted some ugly political exchanges about homelessness between Leo Varadkar and Fianna Fáil's Dublin Lord Mayor, Paul McAuliffe. Sinn Féin wheeled out their housing spokesman, Eoin Ó Broin, to comment on the homeless man's tragedy. The controversy ran for several days. A poster of the unlucky local Fine Gael candidate, Eoghan Murphy, who also happened to be minister for housing, was rapidly removed from a nearby lamp post by party workers.

Housing became the biggest issue. Fine Gael was seen as the guilty party. On 19 January, an opinion poll in the *Sunday Times'* Behaviour and Attitudes series put Fine Gael down 7 per cent to 20 per cent, while Fianna Fáil was the main beneficiary, gaining 5 per cent to 32 per cent to take a sensational lead of 12 per cent. Sinn Féin stood just 1 per cent behind Fine Gael on 19 per cent, while the Greens were on 7 per cent.

There was panic in the Fine Gael ranks, but cool heads pointed out that much of the polling had been done during the height of the RIC commemoration row. The next day, 20 January, the *Irish Times* Ipsos/MRBI poll brought solace. It had taken soundings more recently than its rival, sampling voters since the campaign had started. It confirmed Fine Gael's plunge, but found that Fianna Fáil was on 25 per cent, just 2 per cent ahead of Fine Gael on 23 per cent.

It had been a disastrous first week for the government party, but the polls were proving unusually volatile. However, there was one undeniable trend: Sinn Féin was consistently holding on to its position of shadowing the two leaders, but was now closer behind, in third place. In all the surveys, they were landing around the 20 per cent mark. Maybe even more ominous for the main parties was an increase in Mary Lou's satisfaction ratings, from 30 per cent to 34 per cent.

Something was stirring in the political undergrowth. In reality, it had been moving for months. Commentators, mostly supporters of the establishment, had tended to dismiss the by-election success of Sinn Féin's Mark Ward in November as a flash in the pan. It wasn't.

Behind the scenes, Mary Lou and her team had been implementing exactly what the review of the local and European setbacks had recommended. For several months Sinn Féin had concentrated on putting forward solutions, limiting endless negative outbursts. They held the moral high ground on housing, not just because of the unacceptable homeless figures but because they were proposing practical solutions. In 2019, Eoin Ó Broin had published a credible book called *Home: Why Public Housing Is the Answer*. More people knew of its existence than had read it, but that didn't matter. The party was seen to be in solution mode.

Ó Broin was only one of several younger politicians being put up front by Sinn Féin. Mary Lou was only fifty; but even younger, patently competent TDs were presented as a fresh team pitted against the tired old men of the other parties. Sinn Féin paraded Pearse Doherty, Eoin Ó Broin, Louise O'Reilly, Matt Carthy, Rose Conway-Walsh and Donnchadh Ó Laoghaire on the front line. Gerry Adams and Martin Ferris were retired. Dessie Ellis alone of the old military brigade was a TD, but was never allowed an outing in the media. Even loyal and able party stalwarts, like Seán Crowe and Aengus Ó Snodaigh, were kept on the sidelines.

Policy didn't change. Just messaging and tone. The team behaved like ministers-in-waiting. They were concerned, younger, well-educated politicians, not crusty old warhorses.

The broader policy message fitted in with the new, more responsible image. Sinn Féin made it clear that it was prepared to go into government, even as a junior partner if the party could negotiate a republican programme. The two major parties countered by competing with each other for the anti-Sinn Féin vote with shrill denunciations. Their object was not only to plunder the militant anti-Sinn Féin block of middle-class citizens, but also to persuade waverers that a vote for Mary Lou would be wasted because no one would touch her with a bargepole as a coalition partner.

Fianna Fáil and Fine Gael played straight into Mary Lou's hands. Her constant, but convincing, cry that Fianna Fáil and Fine Gael were almost identical twins – 'Tweedle-Dum and Tweedle-Dee' – resonated with voters far outside the normal Sinn Féin pool. Her repetitive demand for 'change' without full details of what it meant hit precisely the right note; so much so that in the later stages of the battle Fine Gael and Fianna Fáil woke up and aped her, frantically trying to pose as agents of change themselves.

Perhaps the operational edge that Sinn Féin perfected most skilfully was its utter dominance in the social media space. The party's professionalism here simply left the others standing. It boosted its appeal to the younger vote, where one out of three of the under-thirty-fives supported the party. Its overwhelming presence on the internet during the 2020 election was estimated at ten times that of other parties and, according to *The Irish Times*, its interaction with 'friends' on Facebook swamped its rivals: 567,000 for Sinn Féin, as opposed to 49,358 for Fianna Fáil and 55,152 for Fine Gael. According to Agnès Maillot in her recent book *Rebels in Government: Is Sinn Féin Ready for Power?*, the party had the most followers on Facebook, Twitter and Instagram. On YouTube, its engagement beat Fianna Fáil and Fine Gael by a distance.

Sinn Féin spent far less on advertising than either of the two main parties. In the last week of the campaign, Sinn Féin paid out €15,725 on adverts on Facebook and Instagram, against €32,000 for Fianna Fáil and €57,000 for Fine Gael. Sinn Féin targeted its messages, county by county, while the older parties threw money at a blanket nationwide campaign. The outcome: Sinn Féin were the subject of 60 per cent of the Facebook conversations against less than 10 per cent for either Fianna Fáil or Fine Gael. The Shinners understood how to use the internet.

The *Irish Times* Ipsos/MRBI poll on election day found that

Sinn Féin significantly increased its youth vote. Its far superior communications and social media strategy was bearing fruit. But its internet savvy had been getting results long before election day. All the polls during the campaign showed Sinn Féin competing with Fianna Fáil and Fine Gael to be the largest party. The change in its fortunes presented RTÉ, Ireland's national broadcaster, with a problem. They planned a leaders' debate with only two guests, Micheál Martin and Leo Varadkar. Mary Lou was excluded.

Secretly, she must have been delighted. Here was further fodder for her narrative. The media establishment – namely RTÉ – was ganging up with the political establishment – Fianna Fáil and Fine Gael – to keep her off the air. For over two weeks she railed at them, playing the role she loved: Mary Lou the underdog, Mary Lou the victim of the insiders, was in her element dubbing the projected media duel between the two men 'a farce'. RTÉ explained its criteria, including Sinn Féin's modest performance at previous elections. Sinn Féin pointed at the opinion polls. It was, they said, a three-horse race. And they were right: the polls offered compelling evidence.

Incredibly, RTÉ capitulated. The day before the big debate, Mary Lou accepted a surprise invitation to appear. It would be a three-way contest.

On 4 February, the promised spectacular took place. It was more interesting than it would have been without her, but all three leaders came under pressure. Mary Lou was the hardest pressed. Presenter Miriam O'Callaghan pinned her against the ropes about her Sinn Féin colleague, ex-IRA man Conor Murphy MLA, and his despicable behaviour over the death of Paul Quinn. She apologised, she wriggled, and she lost. When she left the RTÉ studio that night, she probably wondered if it would have been wiser to have remained on the margins while Micheál and Leo slugged it out.

The next three canvassing days leading up to polling day itself were nervous ones for Mary Lou. The harsh reminder of the

behaviour of Conor Murphy, her Sinn Féin colleague in Northern
Ireland, was reminiscent of Martin McGuinness being ambushed by
David Kelly in 2011 about the murder of his father, Private Paddy
Kelly, by the IRA. Both were nightmare moments, handled badly.

The episode made little difference. The result of the election
four days later gave Mary Lou's party more votes than Fianna Fáil
or Fine Gael. The nation was breathless. Sinn Féin received 535,595
votes (24.5 per cent), gaining fourteen deputies; Fianna Fáil was in
second place with 484,320 (22.2 per cent), losing seven; while Fine
Gael was down four, coming in third with 455,584 (20.9 per cent).
The Greens were fourth, a long way behind on 155,700 (7.1 per
cent), but added nine seats to finish with twelve deputies. Peadar
Tóibín's Aontú gathered 40,917 votes (1.87 per cent), with Peadar
himself alone returned, holding his own seat.

No one was more surprised with its success than Sinn Féin.
The party's strategy had been a defensive one, informed by the
nasty losses in the local and European elections. The Greens looked
as if they might be flavour of the month, but their onward march
was halted. Sinn Féin played to its strengths, including its social
media presence, its enormous number of foot soldiers, its superb
organisation which would get out the vote. But the result presented
a democratic conundrum: the biggest party with the largest vote
was a political pariah. Its forty-three deputies were untouchables,
with a mandate from the people to form a government. Micheál
Martin, Leo Varadkar and Eamon Ryan were to spend the next
four months plotting how to keep Mary Lou out of the Taoiseach's
office. Their ultimate success was a convincing confirmation of her
message that there had always been a conservative conspiracy,
disguised as a high moral principle, to block her road to power.

CHAPTER 11

A UNITED IRELAND OR BUST

No one was more shell-shocked by the 2020 general election result than Mary Lou McDonald. Sinn Féin had certainly considered themselves to be potential junior partners in a coalition on a good day, but they had been suddenly thrust into pole position. Mary Lou was the surprise, but decisive, election winner. Both Micheál Martin and Leo Varadkar took a bath. She rapidly declared victory and asked Fine Gael and Fianna Fáil to join her in talks about the formation of a government.

It looked momentarily as if Micheál Martin was on the same page. He performed his first post-election somersault within hours of crossing the finishing line. Asked about forming a government with Sinn Féin, he suddenly insisted that he was a democrat, telling the media, 'I've heard the people speak today. They have voted in number, and I respect that.' The next day's *Irish Independent* carried the headline 'Martin Opens Door to Coalition with Sinn Féin'.

Martin's response had been hasty; he was in the last chance saloon for Taoiseach. He could not afford to slam any doors in Mary Lou's face or be left out of talks. However, within hours, his concerned Fianna Fáil colleagues Michael McGrath, Jim

O'Callaghan and Dara Calleary had cooled his ardour for the Mary Lou route to 'democracy'. He was back in line, refusing to talk to the Shinners.

Leo Varadkar who, like Micheál, had suffered a bloody nose from the electorate, stuck to his pre-election position: Fine Gael would not be talking to Mary Lou. Sinn Féin remained, for him, a different sort of party.

As far as Fianna Fáil and Fine Gael were concerned, Mary Lou was still leading a pack of political pariahs. She, in turn, made overtures to the Greens, the Social Democrats, Labour and the far left, but the numbers needed to form a government of left-wingers fell short.

Mary Lou should have been in an even stronger position. Sinn Féin would have won further seats if they had run more candidates. Mary Lou herself had failed to take a running mate in Dublin Central, where she topped the poll with 11,223 votes, almost double the quota. Her surplus could have elected a second Sinn Féin candidate. It was a bad mistake, repeated in several other constituencies.

But the error may have been a blessing. The leader was soon to discover that her new recruits were a motley crew. Her fifteen fresh TDs were far from the battle-hardened Dessie Ellises, Martin Ferrises and Arthur Morgans. They were young, untested and wet behind the ears. Many of them had failed to win seats at the local elections a few months earlier, but had suddenly been propelled into the Dáil, riding an unexpected Sinn Féin wave. Several were unknowns, even within their own constituencies. The magic Sinn Féin brand was Mary Lou McDonald on the posters and a relentless message that the party would solve Ireland's chronic housing, rental and health problems. Brexit hardly featured in the election. Neither did a united Ireland, so beloved of the Sinn Féin leader. She had kept the shadowy men in hiding. Even she must have been spooked by her own success. But how was she going to rein in this collection of undisciplined TDs, some of whom had been nominated but were intended as token candidates with no apparent chance of success? Their election to the Dáil was never part of the grand plan. One candidate, Patricia Ryan in Kildare South, topped the poll after spending the final week of the campaign on holiday. Known as 'accidental TDs', they were going to surface at regular intervals as loose cannons in a party that exercises such tight control.

So there must have been a silent sigh of relief in Parnell Square when the big parties held their nerve and refused to entertain talks with Sinn Féin. When Micheál Martin, Leo Varadkar and Eamon Ryan of the Greens formed a government in June, Sinn Féin were off the hook. They were not ready and did not have the votes in the Dáil to lead a government.

Mary Lou made no such mistakes in the Seanad Éireann elections that followed in early April. Councillors and sitting members of the Houses of the Oireachtas, not ordinary citizens, elect most of Ireland's senators. It is an insiders' election where the number of seats won by each party is almost inevitably predetermined. Sinn Féin had enough votes to elect five senators, one on each of the five Seanad panels. The party leadership, not the party members, chose the runners. Consequently, those selected were almost certain of eventual election because Sinn Féin's councillors and Dáil deputies never waver from voting the party ticket. Sinn Féin's anointed candidates included two from Northern Ireland: Mary Lou, despite her now invincible position within the party, was still watching her back. The leadership had decided to look after Belfast and Derry. Two supposedly solid, reliable Northern republicans were nominated and duly elected to the Seanad as decreed from on high.

Senator Niall Ó Donnghaile had already been a Sinn Féin senator in the 2016–20 period. A native of Belfast, he had been a councillor for the Pottinger nationalist area in the east of the city from 2011 to 2016. He had served as Belfast's youngest ever lord mayor, aged twenty-five, in 2011. He was a safe selection, far too young to carry any IRA baggage, but nevertheless probably a popular choice with the members of the Felons Club.

Elisha McCallion was far less predictable. Her election to the Seanad in 2020 balanced the geographical demands of Sinn Féin's Northern cadre because she came from Derry. Aged thirty-eight, she had been elected a councillor on Derry City Council in 2005, the first mayor of Derry and Strabane in 2015, and an MLA at Stormont for Foyle in early 2017. She was an almost permanent fixture on the podium at Sinn Féin ard fheiseanna and a frequent favourite to do the warm-up speech before Mary Lou's arrival on the stage at party events. She scored a shock upset when she ousted SDLP leader Mark Durkan in the Foyle constituency in 2017, a particularly sweet victory since the seat had once been held by the SDLP leader John Hume.

In 2019 the SDLP recaptured Hume's old seat when party leader Colum Eastwood sent Elisha packing with a thumping majority of 17,110 votes. She was only out of a job for a few months before she was favoured by the Sinn Féin hierarchy to take a Seanad seat. Like Niall Ó Donnghaile, she was too young to have seen action, but she was the niece of Sinn Féin blueblood, MLA for Foyle and former bomber Martina Anderson. Her aunt Martina's position as respected republican royalty will not have harmed McCallion's career path.

The gift of one of Sinn Féin's five Seanad seats to McCallion in 2020 soothed the internal tensions between Derry and Belfast Sinn Féin. Both cities now had a nationalist voice in Dáil Éireann. Sinn Féin issued a press statement appointing Ó Donnghaile as the leader of its five senators, declaring that he would be the North's voice in the Seanad.

Covid severely restricted Seanad sittings during 2020, but this lack of activity did not stop Senator Elisha McCallion from hitting the headlines for all the wrong reasons in October.

BBC Radio Ulster's *Nolan Show* and other media outlets

revealed that £10,000 (€11,070) from a Covid-19 emergency fund – the Small Grant Scheme – had been mistakenly sent to a bank account in Elisha McCallion's name. Two other Sinn Féin officials, the chairperson of the party's Upper Bann Association and an official in its West Tyrone office, also received £10,000 in error and were forced to resign. The money remained in all three accounts for several months and was paid back only a few days before the story broke.

Mary Lou moved swiftly. She demanded McCallion's resignation, which was immediately delivered. The leader publicly apologised for the 'failures' of all three recipients of the funds who had not returned them. She added that the money had been paid back only the previous Monday or Tuesday (two days before McCallion's resignation), but months after the three individuals had received it. All those involved had been 'censured' by the Sinn Féin Ard Chomhairle.

Mary Lou was blunt: 'Last night I accepted the resignation of Senator Elisha McCallion. She accepts full responsibility for the failure to return the grant immediately.' Elisha McCallion apologised 'unreservedly', admitting that the money was paid into a joint account to which both she and her husband, Declan, were signatories.

It was an unequivocal assertion of Mary Lou's authority. On the surface, it appeared that she was sending out a clear message: any financial scandals, whether caused by republican royalty, North or South, male or female, would not be tolerated. She had taken swift, assertive action against a rising star from a republican family in the nationalist stronghold of Derry. She had been prepared to lose a Seanad seat and to risk the ire of the guilty party's aunt and ally Martina Anderson. It was possibly her finest hour since she had taken over the leadership.

But Derry would soon return to haunt her.

Mary Lou's willingness to confront financial shenanigans – from whatever quarter – contrasted sharply with a continual tolerance of indiscretions from the loose-lipped, nostalgic political murmurings of other members of Sinn Féin. After his election victory, her loyal Waterford TD David Cullinane celebrated with a cry of 'Up the 'RA, tiocfaidh ár lá' in his victory speech. He drew fire on himself. Cullinane responded to criticism of his use of IRA slogans by asserting that it was said 'during the excitement of the night', but added that he would never turn his back on the past. When Mary Lou was asked about his words, she replied that, as far as her TDs were concerned, 'I am not their Mammy.' She trivialised it. Across the border, Cullinane had provided further fodder for unionists. Similarly, Dessie Ellis escaped without any censure when, in the full flush of victory, he joined supporters singing 'Come Out, Ye Black and Tans', a song often performed by the Wolfe Tones, but regarded by some as an IRA ballad. Mary Lou could hardly object to it; Sinn Féin had used the song in one of its party political broadcasts.

Five months later, her own high-profile presence at IRA leader Bobby Storey's military-style funeral merely underlined Mary Lou's continued deference to the old guard. She walked behind the hearse, flanking her former boss, Gerry Adams, and other one-time IRA Army Council members. She played second fiddle to them that day, reading a lesson in the church but being excluded from the final coffin-carrying party, which was restricted to 'army'. Gerry Adams, not Mary Lou, gave the principal funeral oration. The breach of Covid rules by her and ministers in the Stormont executive drove unionists ballistic.

Later in the year, showing the same latitude she had awarded to Cullinane and Ellis, Mary Lou refused to demote another wayward Sinn Féin TD, Laois–Offaly's Brian Stanley, from the chair of the Public Accounts Committee after he had gleefully sent a deeply offensive tweet about two infamous IRA ambushes: one at Kilmichael, County Cork, during the War of Independence, when sixteen members of the RIC's auxiliary division were killed by the

IRA; the other at Narrow Water, County Down (otherwise known as Warrenpoint), in 1979, when the IRA's south Armagh brigade ambushed and killed eighteen members of the British Army. Narrow Water was a scene of utter carnage on the same day that Lord Mountbatten was murdered in County Sligo. Stanley left himself no leeway for clarification. His tweet was unequivocal: 'Kilmichael (1920) and Narrow Water (1979), the two operations that taught the elite of the British Army and the establishment the cost of occupying Ireland. Pity for everyone they were such slow learners.'

There was outrage in the Dáil. Mary Lou suggested that Stanley take a rest at home for a week but refused to punish him. On his return, Stanley made a statement in the Dáil apologising for the 'hurt and anger' he had caused; but he held on to his key position on the Public Accounts Committee, with its €10,000 annual allowance.

Unionists were incensed with Stanley. Arlene Foster reflected her community's fury in her own response, tweeting that 'I will be writing to the Ceann Comhairle of the Dáil about this shameless tweet. Although deleted, it is outrageous that someone with such warped views can hold a senior position in the Dáil. SF talk about respect and equality, but there's not much sign of respect for victims.'

Mary Lou could hardly complain. After the election, she herself had indulged in quasi-military parades, when she had marched – shoulder to shoulder – with the old IRA chiefs at Storey's funeral. She had herself several times selectively uttered the sulphurous words 'tiocfaidh ár lá'. Her stern stand against McCallion's lapses was courageous, but most of the hard men of the IRA would have been equally disapproving of such financial failings. She seemed to be stuck in a Gerry Adams time warp. Her opponents, North and South, wondered whether she was still taking her lead on the North from Adams himself. Was he still in the loop? Or, indeed, in control?

In an interview with Hugh O'Connell in the *Sunday Independent*

on 24 May 2020, three months after the general election, five weeks
before Storey's funeral and more than two years after she had
succeeded Adams as leader, O'Connell asked her about her
relationship with him. It emerged that she still talked to him 'every
week'. Mary Lou volunteered that 'Gerry is very wise'. Her words
read like someone who was perhaps a little too dependent, a little
defensive about the frequency of their contact. Typically, she never
said how many times 'every week' they spoke.

O'Connell went on to ask her if she knew Ted Howell, Adams's
controversial guru, reputedly a highly influential person in the
Provisional IRA.

'I do,' she responded.

'How often do you speak to him?' asked O'Connell.

'Not much,' she replied with characteristic vagueness. 'Ted is
retired.' And then, very awkwardly, she changed direction. Out of
the blue she volunteered: 'Ted's a great cook.' Then she proceeded
to safer waters, talking about the wonders of Bertie Ahern.

It was an uncomfortable moment for Mary Lou. She admitted
that she 'probably was a favourite of Adams' and 'it was nice to be
affirmed'.

Her respect for the 'wisdom' of Adams was a minority view,
but there was no doubt that the former Sinn Féin boss was still in
close touch about current issues. She portrayed him as a sort of
'elder', a senior consultant. Their conversations would certainly not
have centred on domestic politics. Adams had his strengths, but
mastery of internal Southern issues was not among them. In any
case, Sinn Féin had heavy-hitting front-benchers, Pearse Doherty on
finance, Eoin Ó Broin on housing and David Cullinane on health.
They didn't need, nor would these men have welcomed, advice from
Adams. But Mary Lou remained in awe of her mentor.

Adams's great strengths were twofold. He was unmatched in
power, knowledge and influence on the Northern front, and he was
an unchallenged strategist on internal party matters. Mary Lou had

almost certainly consulted him about Cullinane, Stanley, Ellis, Storey's funeral and Elisha McCallion's folly. While her amazing election success ensured that her leadership was now accepted, albeit grudgingly by the Northern diehards, she desperately needed someone from that region to keep her aware of the various tensions and rows that from time to time broke out within Sinn Féin. By far the closest relationship she enjoyed with any of the Sinn Féin chieftains from Northern Ireland was with Gerry Adams.

Mary Lou didn't need the wisdom of Adams to steer her path in the South. She had won the general election without him. No one believed that Sinn Féin would have scored the same success if Adams had still been in command. It was her victory. While the Dáil was her kingdom, the North was still her minefield. At the same time, Dáil politics were seriously restricted, now dictated almost totally by the onslaught of Covid. Sinn Féin played Covid clever, supporting public health advice from the National Public Health Emergency Team (NPHET) on nearly all occasions. Covid provided convenient cover in a political quagmire. Mary Lou made helpful suggestions about openings and closures – they usually coincided with public opinion – but she skilfully managed to appear responsible at the same time. Covid was difficult for Mary Lou because governments tend to attract public support in times of emergency.

But she had one advantage over nearly all her opponents when it came to being an authority on Covid: she had caught it herself.

On 28 March 2020, when government formation talks were still at an early stage, Mary Lou was tested for Covid. She had been feeling unwell for several days. Her definitive diagnosis was not confirmed until 13 April, but it was a bad dose at a time when Covid was rampant. No vaccine existed. Ireland was in lockdown. On 14 April Sinn Féin issued a statement confirming that the leader had contracted the virus. She was no longer infected, but she had developed post-viral pleurisy in her right lung. However, she was responding well to treatment and was expected to be back in action in a week. On Twitter, she urged people to 'stay home, stay apart, stay safe'.

Her illness was serious, maybe even dangerous. Her recovery was politically managed. As she prepared to surface, she sent a message to reassure the faithful gathering online on Easter Sunday, 12 April, to commemorate the 1916 Rising, reminding them that 'the deadly virus does not recognise borders', citing the pandemic as another reason for ending partition.

On 20 April, her first day back at work, she was out in the media speaking to Aoife Moore of the *Irish Examiner*, laying her illness bare. Readers were given a blow-by-blow account, from the beginnings of a 'head cold', followed by feeling 'incredibly ill', to the 'viral pleurisy in her lung'. She added that she was an asthma sufferer as well, an underlying condition which was a danger signal. And finally, Mary Lou felt 'lucky to have come through the whole thing'.

No one can blame Mary Lou McDonald for sharing her horrible experience with the citizens of Ireland. Whether she was doing a public service by showing that they too could conquer the virus or was scaring the wits out of them will never be known, but it did her no political harm to share a highly personal experience with a population hungry for solid news about how to conquer Covid. There was a subliminal message: Mary Lou was a fighter and a survivor. She took advantage of the situation to complain about the 'distress' she felt over the delay in receiving her test results. Countrywide, thousands of families identified with her.

Five days later she appeared as the top billing with Ryan Tubridy on RTÉ's *Late Late Show*. Intent on reaching the widest audience available, looking tired and puffy from the medication, she embellished her interview with Aoife Moore. 'My sockets ached, every part of my body hurt,' she explained; 'all my nerve endings were hypersensitive.' She even revealed that her husband, Martin, 'who doesn't panic, he's the calmest person on earth, but . . . he panicked'. She took advantage of the interview about Covid to take a swipe at Fianna Fáil and Fine Gael for uniting against Sinn Féin in their eagerness to form a government from the ongoing talks. She said that she still held out hopes of becoming Taoiseach, but at that stage such an immediate ambition was not a runner.

Sinn Féin's decision to be constructive on the Covid front fitted well with its switch to looking like a government-in-waiting, not opposed to everything, putting the national interest first; but it restricted Mary Lou's room for manoeuvre and her talent for scoring easy political points. Covid dominated everything. The Dáil's limited sittings suited the government well and gave less oxygen to the opposition, especially to Mary Lou, the chamber's leading star. The agenda was set by the coalition.

Mary Lou used her time strategically. She embarked on a series of media interviews, designed to soften her image. *The Late Late Show* was only the first of many. In mid-May she took time to talk to Hugh O'Connell in the *Sunday Independent*, but seemed uncomfortable with the penetrating nature of his questions. Immediately afterwards, she hurried from her grilling by O'Connell to journalist Rodney Edwards, doing a 'Human Nature' podcast for Northern Ireland's *Impartial Reporter*. She was an hour late because the O'Connell encounter overran, but she was far more relaxed with Edwards, who took advantage of her rare willingness to open up a little about her family and her childhood. She even allowed him to ask her about her first kiss without telling him the name of the beneficiary. It seems, though, that it was at a local rugby club dance – not GAA, please note. She spoke of love, loss, death, grief, saying goodbye to Martin McGuinness, her husband Martin, her mother, maternal grandmother, her children and happiness. The only political question posed was when Edwards asked her to reveal something that she liked about Arlene Foster. Mary Lou volunteered that she really 'liked' the DUP leader because she stood up for herself.

After the summer, she opted to accept an invitation to Joe Duffy's *The Meaning of Life* programme, a very personal series with prominent people being questioned about God, their religious beliefs, theology and why we are on the planet.

Mary Lou told Joe, 'I go to Mass. I am a Catholic. It's how I was raised.' She repeated a lot that was known about her family life from other interviews, but spoke of hers as 'a Catholic household, but not dogmatic'. She prays; her children go to Mass with her. But Joe Duffy became politically inquisitive. He wouldn't give her a free run, referring her back to a response to Hugh O'Connell's interview three months earlier. O'Connell had asked her whether, if she'd been old enough, she would have joined the IRA. She had responded, 'Yeah. I think there'd be every chance, every possibility.'

Joe Duffy asked her how in God's name she justified endorsing the violence of the IRA. She twisted and turned, explaining that she saw it differently. She was in politics to 'make sure we don't go back there'.

It rang hollow. The truth is Mary Lou *was* old enough. She could easily have joined the IRA if she had wanted to and if she really felt as strongly as she has maintained she always did. She was eighteen in 1987, a time when the so-called 'shoot-to-kill' policy was supposedly at its height. The IRA's campaign continued in full force – with an eighteen-month ceasefire in 1994, followed by a resumption of violence – until July 1997. If she had joined the IRA in 1987 at the age of eighteen, she could have given the military wing at least eight years of her life. Instead, understandably enough, she opted for Trinity College, the University of Limerick, marriage to Martin and a (later abandoned) doctorate in Dublin City University. During those years the 'volunteers' or the 'patriot dead', as she usually refers to them, gave up their lives for a cause in which she apparently now so passionately believes. She joined Sinn Féin in 2000 when the ceasefire was three years old. Critics ask where was the true believer when she was needed?

Three days later, Pearse Doherty was asked the same question by the *Irish News*. He was more sure-footed. Doherty, eight years Mary Lou's junior, could credibly claim that he was too young to join before hostilities ended. He was more wily than Mary Lou, humbly hoping that he would have had the 'courage' to oppose the British Army, but he was unsure if he would have joined the IRA.

Mary Lou seemed to be dogged by interviewers determined to pursue her about Northern Ireland and the contradictions in her past. She far preferred to deal with Southern problems, where she could savage the government.

On the few occasions that the Dáil sat after the February election, Mary Lou and her visibly competent crew had been playing a blinder. She was triumphantly taunting the two traditional parties to close ranks, prove her right and form a conservative coalition government.

She skilfully managed to defuse an annual Sinn Féin headache. Days before the new government was finally formed, the topic of whether to renew the Special Criminal Court's mandate raised its head in the Dáil. Sinn Féin agonised. For decades the party had denounced the non-jury court that had locked up IRA men and women. Sinn Féin's TDs abstained on the renewal vote, selling the U-turn to their unhappy hard-line republican base on the grounds that a non-jury court was needed for the drugs gangs. Otherwise, witnesses would be intimidated. Sinn Féin wriggled off the hook, but in reality the U-turn was a breakthrough. Sinn Féin was gradually shedding its subversive history. Such a reversal might have been harder under Adams's leadership.

When the new coalition government took office on 27 June 2020, Mary Lou became leader of the opposition. The polls showed that Sinn Féin's general election voters were holding steadfast behind her. In the period immediately following the general election and the onset of the Covid crisis, Fine Gael, as the symbol of stability in the Covid-stricken caretaker government, had soared in the polls. As the pandemic took a grip on the nation and deaths hit frightening levels, the rally to Fine Gael was dramatic. Its support leapt from a general election low of 20.9 per cent in February to 34 per cent in mid-March, when the number of Covid cases was accelerating and the daily count of mortality rates was rising rapidly. Caretaker Taoiseach Leo Varadkar and Minister for Health Simon Harris took personal charge of the emergency. Fear gripped the nation. Lockdown was introduced. The main political casualty was Fianna Fáil, waiting in the wings, powerless to affect events until a government that included them was formed. Fianna Fáil's vote plunged into the low to mid-teens. On 14 June an *Irish Times* Ipsos/ MRBI poll found that Fine Gael stood on 37 per cent, while Fianna Fáil, still waiting for a coalition deal, had tanked to 13 per cent. Normal politics was shelved.

The big surprise in the polls was Sinn Féin. The party that had won the February election on the issues of housing and health might have been sidelined as citizens, suddenly fearful of Covid, rallied to the Fine Gael flag and its perceived stability, but Sinn Féin stood as steady as a rock, actually marginally improving its vote. That pattern, where Fine Gael offered a refuge for frightened voters, Sinn Féin held its own and Fianna Fáil languished in the doldrums, continued until December 2020, when a new trend emerged. A *Sunday Times*/Behaviour & Attitudes poll signalled a changing pattern as Fianna Fáil – with Micheál Martin now Taoiseach – began to recover from its disastrous summer start when it had lost two cabinet ministers: Dara Calleary and Barry Cowen.

Slowly Micheál Martin steadied the ship. Fianna Fáil began to look more relevant in the Covid crisis. In June, when Micheál Martin replaced Leo Varadkar as Taoiseach, he suddenly became the man talking to the nation about Covid from the steps of Government Buildings. At the end of 2020, the gap began to close. Fianna Fáil's voting strength increased to 22 per cent, while Fine Gael dropped back to 27 per cent, but it was Sinn Féin that led the field with 28 per cent. The two traditional parties were fighting for a shrinking share of the middle classes, while Sinn Féin was gradually gaining ground.

As opposition leader, Mary Lou exploited the constant gifts of gaffes from coalition ministers, but she always carefully retained the party's position as critical, but constructive, on Covid.

She did not lack opportunities, often handed to her on a plate. In August she was granted the gift of 'Golfgate'. Government TDs, a Supreme Court judge, an EU commissioner and a cabinet minister were alleged to have breached Covid rules at a Houses of the Oireachtas golf outing, providing a ready-made opportunity for Mary Lou to ride a wave of public outrage. Instead, she was surprisingly low key. Probably mindful of her handlers' insistence that she tone down the polemics, she settled for sound bites, claiming that the Dáil 'is a parliament, not a club'. In the back of her mind may have lurked her own alleged breaches of Covid protocol the previous month at Bobby Storey's funeral.

She continued to star at Leaders' Questions, where she and Micheál Martin exchanged a distasteful amount of personal venom; but the most dramatic clash in the Dáil of 2020 was Sinn Féin's motion of no confidence in Tánaiste Leo Varadkar.

The revelation in *Village* magazine of Varadkar's decision, when Taoiseach in 2019, to leak the details of a confidential deal between the government and the Irish Medical Organisation to a friend of his in a rival medical outfit caused consternation. It left Mary Lou with little option. She led off for Sinn Féin, raging once again about the 'old boys' network' in the full knowledge that there was no hope of dislodging Leo once Micheál Martin had wheeled in his party behind the Fine Gael leader. Mary Lou took the moral high ground, but as before her real target was Micheál Martin, the man responsible for Leo's survival under the last government and the weak link in the coalition. Leo won the vote by ninety-two votes to sixty-five in November, but Sinn Féin rose above Fine Gael in

December's opinion polls. Throughout 2021 the pattern was similar, when most polls put Sinn Féin in the lead, followed by Fine Gael and Fianna Fáil in that order. Occasionally, the Behaviour & Attitudes poll in the *Sunday Times* put Fianna Fáil edging ahead of its old rival, but the most consistent finding throughout the year was that Sinn Féin was leading all three government parties, including the Greens.

In February 2021, Mary Lou achieved a personal milestone. In an Ireland Thinks/*Irish Mail on Sunday* poll she emerged as Ireland's most popular political leader for the first time, overtaking both Martin and Varadkar. The formula was working. She had stuck to the same message – housing, health and constructive solutions – regardless of how expensive they sounded. Increasing numbers of a disillusioned electorate believed that Sinn Féin would wave a magic wand, build the houses, reduce the rents and improve the health service. She kept up the pressure on the coalition, while ensuring that her own Achilles heel, the North and Northern Sinn Féin, stayed in the background. She was on a roll in the South, riding high in the polls and accepting the own goals that the coalition kept scoring.

It couldn't last. In May 2021, just as Southern Sinn Féin was beginning to settle into a winning rhythm, a long-running sore in the North erupted. Derry Sinn Féin was back on the boil. It was not just a routine personality clash, a policy difference or even a candidate selection battle, all difficulties that Sinn Féin habitually settled in deep secrecy. This time, it was more fundamental. Derry Sinn Féin was in rag order electorally, organisationally and maybe even ethically. A lot of finger-pointing had been going on. Complaints from Derry Sinn Féin members were rumoured to have been made to Sinn Féin's Connolly House headquarters in Belfast and to head office in Dublin. There were widespread allegations of jobs for the boys and girls, of Sinn Féin factions controlling the destination of community grants and of a consequent fallout among the wider electorate.

Derry Sinn Féin had long been controlled by a few republican families, the McGuinnesses, the McMonagles and the McCartneys being the most prominent. When Martin McGuinness was in command, the lid was kept on any incipient tensions. His death in 2017 had opened the gates to civil war between the local party factions.

In May 2021 Derry Sinn Féin was still in shock from the 2019 loss of Elisha McCallion's Foyle seat in Westminster to SDLP leader Colum Eastwood. In the same year's local elections, Sinn Féin's council support fell back from 36 per cent in the previous local election to 28 per cent. Five Sinn Féin councillors in Derry and Strabane had lost their seats. The party was in retreat in Martin McGuinness's heartland.

Derry had somehow become a Sinn Féin blackspot. With the Stormont Assembly elections looming just a year away in May 2022, the Dublin head office ordered a review to recommend sufficient surgery to ensure that Elisha McCallion's Westminster loss was not repeated. For both nationalist parties, Derry had a huge significance. It was the stronghold of two deceased icons: the SDLP's legendary leader John Hume and Sinn Féin's war hero Martin McGuinness. It was as though these two giants were engaged in a posthumous duel.

Sorting out Derry was, at least in theory, Mary Lou's baby. She fully understood the gravity of the unfolding drama. It would be difficult to tackle the loss of support and the allegations of jobbery, especially after the recent problems surrounding Elisha McCallion, niece of the local powerhouse Martina Anderson. But the big headache was no longer the niece. The headache was now the aunt.

Martina Anderson was the MLA for Foyle. Her long jail sentence, her loyalty to Martin McGuinness and her deep commitment to the united Ireland ideal all meant that she was almost untouchable. She bore the scars of battle, a hero who had suffered for her beliefs. She had been a woman on the front line. She had been an ally of Mary Lou's in the past, as had her niece, the now discredited ex-senator Elisha McCallion.

The initial review's findings, even the personnel involved, remain guarded by Sinn Féin secrecy to this day. The party denied a *Sunday World* story that three former Army Council members – Gerry Kelly, Seán 'The Surgeon' Hughes and Martin 'Duckster' Lynch – were asked to review, report and recommend; that they proposed a few superficial changes but no radical surgery; that the big shots in Dublin were dissatisfied with their lack of urgency and had dispatched a second team to recommend fundamental change, particularly of personnel, if necessary.

Whatever the truth of the identity of the first review team, Mary Lou sanctioned a second group of investigators. They took a far harder line and came back with sensational solutions. All versions of the story agree about the inclusion in the final outcome of no less a Sinn Féin grandee than Gerry Kelly, a man deliberately chosen because he had a military record to match Martina's. The findings were explicit: that Derry needed root and branch reform; that both the current MLAs, Martina Anderson and Karen Mullan, should be stood down; and that the entire Sinn Féin Foyle officer board must be replaced. The seats were in danger from an electorate disillusioned with the antics of Derry Sinn Féin, particularly the jobbery, the ruling families and the failure to deliver results to ordinary people. Many felt that only favoured factions of the party in Derry were reaping the benefits of the peace dividend.

Martina Anderson had, in the words of one insider, become 'too big for her boots'. Certainly, she was sometimes singing out of tune with the more moderate voices adopted since the peace process had taken hold. She was particularly prominent at Bobby Storey's funeral, part of a guard of honour outside the church after marching military-style in the cortège, wearing regulation black blazer, white shirt, black tie and dark trousers.

Unfortunately, Martina Anderson had put her foot in it once too often. On one occasion in the European Parliament in 2016, she had declared that the Israeli lobbyists 'are all over this place like a rash'. On another in 2017, she shocked even her own supporters when, directing her remarks on Brexit at British Prime Minister Theresa May, she said: 'Theresa, your notion of a border – hard or soft – stick it where the sun doesn't shine cos you're not putting it in Ireland.' Back in the Stormont Assembly, she caused consternation when she claimed that pensions for victims of the Troubles were 'for those who fought Britain's dirty war in Ireland and mainly for those involved in collusion'. She was forced to apologise unreservedly, not an action that came easily to her.

Mary Lou and others in the leadership had had enough. Martina and – to a lesser extent – Karen Mullan were damaging Sinn Féin's chances of holding two seats in Foyle in the May 2022 election. After they received the damning reports, Gerry Kelly and another high-ranking party official – according to some reports, the MLA for South Antrim, Declan Kearney – were dispatched to Derry to deliver the bad news to the two female MLAs. The party had decided that they would not be the Sinn Féin candidates at the 2022 election. Kelly's importance as the messenger was paramount. Insiders say that Martina Anderson was still so deeply embedded in the military culture of Sinn Féin of the past that she would accept her dismissal only from Kelly as a higher-ranking officer, and a fellow bomber to boot. Mary Lou's ranking in the military pecking order was zero.

Martina Anderson's reaction was explosive, as near to an outright rebellion as Sinn Féin had suffered. There had never been anything like it under Adams's leadership. While Anderson recorded a video accepting the decision, she said that it was 'a body blow'. She even went close to outright sedition when she revealed that she had 'received support from across Derry and beyond' urging her to stay. She was devastated, but she pulled back from the brink, confirming that she would not be a candidate at the May election.

Mary Lou McDonald and Michelle O'Neill issued statements paying tribute to Anderson and Mullan. Mary Lou insisted that Martina Anderson would 'continue to lead, as the prospect of a referendum on Irish unity comes ever closer'.

Both leaders hoped that their statements would put a painful issue to bed. They were in for a rude awakening. A week later, the Anderson family let Mary Lou have it with both barrels. In a statement that rocked the party nationally, they accused Sinn Féin of 'publicly humiliating' Martina Anderson.

The statement – issued by Martina's sister, Sharon Burke – was savage. It reflected the deep resentment of her family and many friends inside the party. It was the voice of Martina Anderson without her official stamp of approval. It was rebellious, appealing for support 'to correct what we believe is a massive miscarriage of justice'. It continued by asserting emotionally that 'The British could not do to our Martina what her comrades and friends have done.' The message invoked the name of Martin McGuinness, insisting, with some credibility, that if he had been alive, he would never have allowed the dismissals to happen.

Asserting that Martina Anderson had asked the family to say nothing, despite her humiliation, they declared that they could not stay silent. Sharon's exocet then added the final, most stinging rebuke: 'Indeed, our Martina gave everything to the Irish Republican struggle, including her biological clock. She is married to an ex-prisoner who served over eighteen years in prison, mainly in English jails. Both of them are not allowed to foster or adopt children.' The barely concealed target was obvious. Martina Anderson had been locked up in Armagh, Brixton, Durham and Maghaberry jails for the republican cause during most of her child-bearing years. She was released in 1998 under the Good Friday Agreement deal at the mature age of forty-six. During much of Martina's sentence, Mary Lou was sampling the pleasures of Trinity College, Limerick and

Dublin City University. Later on, Mary Lou gave birth to two beautiful children in the safe surroundings of Dublin. Unlike Martina, she was thirty before she settled for the Sinn Féin party. The idea of Mary Lou signing up for the IRA in her early twenties – when the 'struggle' was in full swing – never competed with the joys of an undergraduate experience.

Sharon Burke's statement was a thinly disguised call for a political insurrection within Sinn Féin. The gloves were off. Many republicans felt that the two MLAs had been shabbily treated, that Martina Anderson had been carrying out the orders of others in the movement when she planted bombs in London. Now she had been shafted by armchair republicans who had never even seen action.

Sympathy was one thing, but rebellion was something completely different. Mary Lou weathered the storm, but it was only the first instalment. On 24 August 2021, at the height of the silly season, Sinn Féin announced that Martina Anderson and Karen Mullan were resigning as MLAs before the new term began on 13 September. Mary Lou was giving no quarter. They were not even being allowed to serve out their terms. A Sinn Féin convention to select new MLAs to be co-opted to the Assembly would be held on 8 September. Nominations would close three days earlier. The selected Sinn Féin members would take their seats in the Assembly on 13 September.

Martina Anderson and Karen Mullan had been 'politically disappeared'. Their humiliation was total, their political assassination complete. Anderson was given a new international assignment for the party in Europe, promoting Irish unity. Mullan was granted a regional role, overseeing cross-border co-ordination between TDs, MLAs, MPs and council groups in the north-west. Neither post sounded too demanding nor looked likely to require clocking in at 9 a.m.

Mary Lou headed for Derry to take ownership of the solution. She gave a press conference on Derry's walls, the visuals sending out the message that it was she who was in command of Sinn Féin in the city that had endured Bloody Sunday. Martina Anderson and Karen Mullan snubbed her by their absence.

The Sinn Féin leader did the hatchet job perfectly, insisting that 'Martina and I, and Karen, are friends, we're activists together and we work in a common cause.' And she asked, 'Had it been a challenging period? Yes it has and that's evidently the case but have we gotten past that? Yes, we have.'

Flagging the coming convention to select candidates, the leader added: 'I await with interest the names that will come forward, and of course I have to pay a very great tribute to our friends and comrades Martina Anderson and Karen Mullan.' The two deposed MLAs should have shuddered. She was again calling them her 'friends', a deadly description she often used at her most unctuous when she spoke of her unionist 'friends' – namely her sworn opponents Jeffrey Donaldson and the DUP.

No one listening to Mary Lou believed that the identities of the new MLAs had not been decided months earlier. On 8 September two unknowns, Pádraig Delargy, a twenty-five-year-old primary teacher from Derry, and Ciara Ferguson, a community development worker from Strabane, were duly selected. After their anointment, even party insiders were asking Pádraig who? And Ciara who? Pearse Doherty popped over from Donegal to supervise the convention. Afterwards, he spoke to the delegates, while congratulating the two successful candidates. His presence sent a clear signal that Dublin was now in charge.

Sinn Féin conventions cut no ice with Derry's Dixie Elliott, a disillusioned former IRA H-Block prisoner, who has a dim view of them. When I met him in the Ex-Prisoners Outreach Programme (Ex-POP) centre in Derry he didn't mince his words about them: 'The way these Sinn Féin conventions work is that certain people, like Raymond McCartney, pick who they want to put up as a candidate, then they go through the charade of a convention with the party's choice known beforehand.' He says that Sinn Féin lines these guys, like Gerry Kelly and Duckster Lynch, along the back walls. They 'give you looks'. In short, he is saying that they are rigged.

Dixie knows a bit about modern republicanism in his native Derry and further afield. He shared a cell with Bobby Sands, went on the blanket for over four years and has the scars to prove it. He was convicted of hijacking, attempted murder and IRA membership in 1977. Today he feels betrayed by those republicans who somehow have emerged largely unscathed. He has strong views on Mary Lou.

'Mary Lou,' he says, 'is out to cleanse Sinn Féin of republicanism. Martina Anderson was a sacrificial lamb. Mary Lou was quickly elevated to Adams's side as vice president. Clearly, she was being groomed for the leadership. A clean pair of hands with no Republican background, military or otherwise. This was the beginning of Sinn Féin Nua.

'She was in Derry a few times,' he went on, as we devoured tea and biscuits in the Ex-POP centre, 'on her royal visits to show that the city was still a Sinn Féin stronghold, which it was . . . but only briefly until it crashed around them in recent years.' (He was speaking before the May 2022 elections.) He makes serious allegations about senior republicans living the high life. He says cronyism in Derry Sinn Féin has been rife.

Today Dixie feels totally betrayed. He is deeply sceptical of both Gerry Adams and Martin McGuinness. Many republicans who served long sentences are more than aware that McGuinness, Adams and others served only short periods in jail. Dixie is not alone in believing that those who hold the reins in Sinn Féin have benefited from the struggle while other ex-prisoners like himself are abandoned, having given the best years of their lives to imprisonment and unemployment. They are alone, not recognised in the peace process and ignored by the present leadership. He sees himself and other ex-prisoners as victims. In an interview with Kitty Holland of *The Irish Times* he memorably said that 'Sinn Féin have no more in common with the ideals of Bobby Sands than the modern Labour Party has with the ideals of James Connolly.' Dixie's observations on conventions were borne out. The result was rigidly controlled, this time by Mary Lou.

Derry had been a test of her mettle. The paranoid secrecy of internal manoeuvres within Sinn Féin makes it impossible to reveal the full detail of all the exchanges, calls and caucuses that took place to draw a close to this bitter episode. It was a triumph for Mary Lou. She had faced down a significant internal challenge, with the help of Gerry Kelly and other members of the old guard. Not a single prominent member of Sinn Féin, not a single member of the late Martin McGuinness's family, put their head above the parapet to defend Martina Anderson, previously a goddess in the republican pantheon. It is, however, inconceivable that Mary Lou would have acted without the guidance of her mentor, Gerry Adams. She had admitted in her 2020 interview with Hugh O'Connell in the *Sunday Independent* that she spoke to Adams weekly because she valued his wisdom. This battle for Derry had been waged for many months. At no point in her three years of leadership did she need Adams more. She emerged from the challenge as a ruthless giant-killer. Sinn Féin Derry was tamed. The elections due in May 2022 would tell if her hard-heartedness had secured the seats occupied by the two dispossessed MLAs.

If anything, Mary Lou's victory over Martina Anderson had lifted the party higher in the Southern polls. Sinn Féin rarely dipped below 30 per cent between June and September 2021. The party still consistently led Fine Gael and Fianna Fáil. On 8 July, the party's candidate in the Dublin Bay South by-election, a traditional Fine Gael stronghold, former MEP senator Lynn Boylan, had finished a respectable third.

It was business as usual in the Dáil. On the first day after the summer recess, Sinn Féin exploited Simon Coveney's bungled attempts to appoint his former cabinet colleague and friend

Katherine Zappone to a tailor-made special envoy's post at the United Nations by putting down yet another vote of no confidence. Mary Lou made her single transferable speech on cronyism, once again attacking Micheál Martin for propping up Fine Gael. Micheál Martin responded in kind, accusing her of hypocrisy: 'Some of the statements made by Deputy Mary Lou McDonald in the past few days are genuinely breathtaking in their cynicism and the double standards involved. She even went so far as to say yesterday that Sinn Féin were forced into putting down the motion, because they were not prepared to look the other way. Not prepared to look the other way? Sinn Féin?' Coveney won by ninety-two votes to fifty-nine. It was an ugly debate.

Mary Lou looked forward to her autumn party conference with the wind at her back. Rarely can any Irish political leader have approached an ard fheis with greater confidence. As Saturday 30 October approached, I decided to don my journalist's cap and head out to the Helix Theatre in Dublin City University, the place where Mary Lou had abandoned her PhD. I wished to witness her in action among the faithful. I was particularly interested in whether or not the shadowy figures, the ageing former military men from the North, the six guys who carried Bobby Storey's coffin, would be there. Or did they simply come out for showpiece occasions? The word on the street was that Adams was staying away so as not to steal Mary Lou's thunder and that Martin Ferris was in hospital with a back injury. But what about the other four? Would Gerry Kelly show his face? Was Seán 'Spike' Murray a scarlet pimpernel? Would Seán 'The Surgeon' Hughes venture from his south Armagh den? And what about Martin 'Duckster' Lynch, the one-time driver for Gerry Adams, sentenced to ten years in jail for possession of a Russian rocket launcher? Would they be there keeping a watching eye on Mary Lou, the woman who never joined their army? And, even more intriguing, would Martina Anderson turn up to salute her newly despised leader as she was soaking up the admiration of so many republicans? Surely they would all be told to stay away? They were not part of the programme. Nor were they intended to be caught by the cameras. That was not their role.

I didn't have long to wait. I was in the premises at 9.30 a.m., before the proceedings started, watching the delegates arriving and passing through security. The occasion was almost festive. Suddenly I spotted a man little known to the public, inconspicuous and almost shabby, small in stature. I recognised him instantly. This anonymous delegate was Spike Murray. Murray had been sentenced to twelve years in jail in 1982 for explosive offences. In 2005 *The Sunday Times* named him as a member of the Army Council.

I went into the main annex, the large DCU foyer where the delegates socialised and drank coffee. After a brief visit to the adjoining Helix Theatre itself, I settled in the crowded café. It was not long before I spotted two other familiar faces. Sitting right in the centre of the same area was another of Storey's coffin-carriers, Duckster Lynch, in deep conversation with a third, Seán 'The Surgeon' Hughes. Three out of the four available pall-bearers, all former IRA Army Council chiefs, were in attendance. It didn't take long for the fourth to appear. Gerry Kelly, the man who delivered the bad news to Anderson and Mullan, floated between the stage and the café. Kelly, an active MLA with an Army Council and prison record, was busy preparing for another volte-face, a speech in favour of dropping the party's long-standing policy of outright opposition to the Special Criminal Court, the non-jury court previously so hated by Sinn Féin. The other three ex-IRA chiefs appeared uninterested in the action inside on the stage. They were holding a watching brief from the sidelines, in the shadows.

I didn't see Mary Lou or Pearse Doherty all day, except on the stage. They were presumably in another room being 'handled' for the media. Michelle O'Neill appeared frequently to mix with the troops sitting in the foyer area. She socialised most comfortably with Duckster Lynch, The Surgeon Hughes and other Northerners such as former IRA prisoner and current MLA Carál Ní Chuilín. O'Neill spent a lot of time talking to Martina Anderson's successor in Foyle, Ciara Ferguson. In turn, Ní Chuilín spent most of the lunch break with Spike Murray, who was hosting a table for much of the day where Northern Ireland members of Sinn Féin, including Niall Ó Donnghaile, the senator from Belfast's Short Strand, joined them.

I briefly spoke to Martina Anderson, all alone, early in the morning, when she assured me that she was not avoiding me but I should contact the press office if I wanted to speak to her. She cut a sorry figure. I didn't see her or her niece Elisha on the platform at any time during the day. Nor did she speak. Hers looked like a token appearance, followed by a rapid disappearance.

I asked Duckster Lynch and Spike Murray to talk to me about Mary Lou. Lynch was affable, protesting with a smile that he was 'a very quiet person', but he referred me to Sinn Féin's bottomless black hole, the press office. Murray told me he 'didn't really know Mary Lou'. I changed the subject, telling him that I had recently enjoyed lunch in An Cultúrlann, the cultural centre on the Falls Road, with former Sinn Féin finance minister Máirtín Ó Muilleoir. 'Who paid?' he asked. 'Máirtín,' I replied. 'That's a first,' he responded.

When I cornered Gerry Kelly with a request to chat about Mary Lou, he told me that he would have to talk to her first. 'She's grown in stature,' he volunteered. 'I've watched her over the years. I've heard nothing negative. She's very popular North and South.' He was rapidly 'rescued' by Duckster Lynch, who politely pleaded that Gerry was urgently needed elsewhere. A few seconds later Kelly was in a huddle with The Surgeon Hughes. South Armagh's Conor Murphy, another ex-army MLA, joined Michelle and Duckster for lunch.

My biggest surprise of the informal part of the day was that the Northern and Southern members of Sinn Féin hardly mixed at all. One exception was Donegal's Pádraig Mac Lochlainn, albeit a border-county TD, talking to south Armagh's Seán Hughes. Sinn Féin North and South looked like two separate parties with a titular head.

The Southern TDs were there in the same room. At tables well distanced in a different part of the foyer from their Northern comrades sat Eoin Ó Broin, Aengus Ó Snodaigh and Seán Crowe together, Rose Conway-Walsh, Louise O'Reilly, Lynn Boylan, David Cullinane, Donnchadh Ó Laoghaire, Denise Mitchell and others. The army made little effort to bond with the non-combatants.

Inside the main hall, the formal proceedings were stage-managed to the last second. The platform party was meticulously picked for every minute of the day, always certain to include the right balance of North and South, male and female, and as few reminders of the IRA as possible. The speakers were specially chosen for each debate. Stormont ministers queued up to speak along with ordinary delegates. The motion on the Special Criminal Court was the most keenly anticipated. A few dissenting speakers were chosen, giving the appearance of a debate, but Gerry Kelly made a fine speech, designed to comfort the hardliners.

After the Special Criminal Court debate ended, I was sitting high up in the gallery out of sight. The lights were turned out when all the delegates had gone for lunch. I sat in the dark and watched the stage. The entire audience had left the theatre. On the stage only Mary Lou and Michelle O'Neill remained, chatting. Suddenly, from the back of the theatre, Duckster Lynch joined the leader and her deputy on the stage. He entered into a robust discussion with Mary Lou, as Michelle very attentively brushed some dandruff off his jacket. Duckster, reputedly the last chief of staff of the IRA, still retained instant access to the top of the party. It was the only spontaneous event on the stage all day. Unfortunately, the microphones were off and their voices didn't carry to the back of the theatre.

The rest of the proceedings went like clockwork. It was interesting that more speakers queued for the housing debate than for the item on a united Ireland. As would be expected, Mary Lou's speech was impeccably crafted and superbly delivered. The podium party for her performance was fascinating. There was no longer any Martina Anderson, cast into outer darkness, no longer any Elisha McCallion, still in disgrace, no room for ex-prisoner Carál Ní Chuilín, not even a place for Gerry Kelly, the man who had delivered Martina Anderson's head on a plate. Sinn Féin didn't want to see Gerry's face on the RTÉ *Six One* news that evening.

John Finucane, whose father Pat had been murdered by loyalist paramilitaries, did the warm-up for Mary Lou. There was only one face from the old IRA days, a minimal gesture in their direction: the ex-IRA prisoner from south Armagh Conor Murphy, minister for finance in the Stormont executive, whose history was unfamiliar to the average RTÉ viewer. He would hardly spook them the way a Gerry Adams or even a Martin McGuinness did. He was no Martina Anderson, nor even a Gerry Kelly, who didn't make the cut, despite his help in dragging the Special Criminal Court motion over the line earlier in the day. There were six women, four from Northern Ireland. Ciara Ferguson, the replacement for Martina Anderson in Derry, was placed prominently on the stage, not just for the leader's speech, but at other points in the day. She badly needed exposure for the forthcoming contest in Foyle. It was a masterpiece in choreography.

The Sinn Féin shop window, the platform party, were presented as a government-in-waiting in the South, alongside a few younger female Northern activists, far too young to have been involved in the Troubles. On the platform, they looked like an undivided family. Outside in the foyer, they hardly broke bread together.

It was Mary Lou's finest hour. She was unassailable, regularly showing up in opinion polls as the most popular political leader in the South. She had successfully mobilised an entire party – North and South – behind her united Ireland mission and message. She was making all the running on the unity train, leaving Simon Coveney, Micheál Martin and other Southern leaders trotting behind her. Sinn Féin's shadowy figures still existed, but would obviously accept her as their vehicle to power and influence, as long as she was surfing the current wave of popularity.

The obstacle to unity lay elsewhere. In the North. It was time to interview the forgotten people of Northern Ireland about the Sinn Féin leader. I resolved to talk about Mary Lou McDonald to a few non-Sinn Féin political influencers in Northern Ireland. I started with Dame Arlene Foster, the former first minister, who was forced to resign as leader of the Democratic Unionist Party in April 2021. She told me over coffee and scones in Belfast's Europa Hotel that she gets on 'OK with Mary Lou on a personal level. She's easy to talk to, but she's a very focused, very determined person. And she can be quite – well, I don't think I'm easily bullied . . . but if you were weak, she would walk all over you. You have to be quite strong with her. She would always persistently push it.'

As an example of Mary Lou 'pushing it', Arlene Foster cites an occasion when she was at a meeting with Mary Lou, Michelle O'Neill, Secretary of State Brandon Lewis and others. 'There was an occasion when we were engaged with Brandon Lewis, back before the reintroduction of devolution. Mary Lou was up [from Dublin]. She always wanted everyone to understand that she was the leader, not Michelle. We were having a round table. What usually happens is the leader is there and one other. Naomi Long was there, probably with Stephen Farry [deputy leader of the Alliance Party]. Steve Aiken [UUP] was there. Mary Lou was there with Michelle, and the Secretary of State came to me first, as first minister. And then he went to Michelle as deputy first minister. And Mary Lou said: "I'm the leader. Michelle will speak later." She always asserts her authority over Michelle when she's there. All the rest of us were sitting back going: "Well, we know who's the boss . . ."'

There seems to be a pattern of self-importance about Mary Lou when it comes to negotiations. Foster recalls that 'She left most of the negotiations to Michelle and Conor [Murphy] and then she would fly in, like Adams, at the end with "I'm blessing this agreement" . . . in a sort of grandiose way. I mean she does have that "I'm actually a step above all this" aura. She would come up here at key points and you would always know she was here because they would announce it as though it was the arrival of the Queen of Sheba!'

Foster doesn't recall much about Mary Lou until 2009 when she became deputy leader: 'I think that's when she came to prominence more. But we didn't really have any interaction until she was made leader.' She recalled: 'You remember back in the eighties there was always a lady behind Gerry Adams and Martin McGuinness in any press conference. And the lady never spoke. She was always just there to show that there were females involved in the movement. Mary Lou wasn't that sort of person. She was obviously capable and could speak very well.'

The former first minister says that unionists are wary of Mary Lou: 'From a unionist point of view, they get very irritated when they see her at Stormont, because they will say to us: "What's she doing up here? She's not from here. She doesn't represent anybody here, standing here in Stormont, speaking." So it really irritates unionism here when they see somebody from Dublin coming up and standing in Stormont and, you know, it's emphasising "I'm the leader".'

However, Mary Lou is not as irritating as Foreign Affairs Minister Simon Coveney. 'Mary Lou,' says Foster, 'is leader of the party that wants a united Ireland. We understand that, but it's more offensive when Simon Coveney interferes in Northern Ireland because he's an actual government minister. Simon doesn't respect the protocols. He doesn't even tell people when he's coming. He just appears. It's as if it's part of the wider green field. He is hated in unionist and loyalist areas, make no mistake about it. On a personal basis, I get on with Simon. If you go up the Shankill, you will see pictures of Simon Coveney about how much he is hated. I've told him on occasions, "A little less from you, Simon, would be very helpful!"'

Foster and her unionist flock are unimpressed by Mary Lou's constant appearances at commemorations. Foster explained: 'She doesn't have that sort of Sinn Féin background. I think sometimes Mary Lou works quite hard at proving that she is one of them. The military section probably think she isn't one of them but recognise that she does have the ability to progress in today's society. So every time there's an anniversary of a hunger striker's dying, Mary Lou's tweeting about it, Michelle's tweeting about it. No recognition that these guys were involved in some heinous crimes and they were in jail for a reason. When I challenge about glorifying terrorists, they say they "have to remember our dead". And that's why victims get so angry. You can be an activist; you can support terrorism without actually being involved in it yourself. Everybody in Sinn Féin passively or otherwise supports what they did here in Northern Ireland for forty years.'

Foster believes that, despite Mary Lou's assumption of the leadership, 'Adams still has power within Sinn Féin. He would claim otherwise, of course. He tries to present himself now as a poet, philosopher!' Foster also believes that there is still an Army Council, 'but it's not performing the functions it did before.' On 'shadowy figures', she comments that 'it's all about definition. There are people behind Mary Lou who aren't in the public eye, so they are shadowy figures. I mean, Bobby Storey was a shadowy figure. I always understood that he was on the Army Council.'

Finally, Foster is sceptical about Mary Lou's attitude to gay rights and abortion. 'Sinn Féin,' she says, 'under two females has moved policy away from some of the traditional policy areas, including abortion and gay rights. They have done it quite seamlessly, because they say, "Right, this is the direction of travel of society, so we need to be ahead of that, we need to be the ones leading it." Abortion and gay rights are issues they moved position on very quickly.'

There seems to be very little meeting of minds.

Sir Jeffrey Donaldson, Foster's successor in the DUP, was not optimistic that Mary Lou will initiate a new era of republican–unionist understanding. He was typically direct in our interview. He first remembered her from 'a couple of programmes, in particular RTÉ's *Questions & Answers* with John Bowman. At the time she didn't seem used to the rough and tumble associated with Sinn Féin. She didn't, on the surface, fit the Sinn Féin bill. I recognised that she was articulate, although she initially seemed more focused on the social than the constitutional issues. She clearly felt that the constitutional issues were important too.'

Donaldson emphasises that 'she was not involved in the conflict, but she has never accepted that terrorism was wrong. There is only a small degree of difference between someone who was involved in violence and those who seek to defend or excuse it.'

Donaldson sees her at the Northern Ireland Executive's party leaders' forum meetings. 'As leader of Sinn Féin, she will sometimes turn up. That can make for difficult conversation in discussions targeted at Northern Ireland-specific topics. She talks about Southern issues. I don't see how she can sit on the Northern Ireland leaders' forum if she is Taoiseach. If she does get the job, unionists are clear. We will not accept interference in our affairs. Will Mary Lou then blur the lines between Strands One and Two?' (Strand One in the Good Friday Agreement refers to the internal affairs of Northern Ireland while Strand Two is the relationship between North and South.)

Donaldson goes further than Arlene Foster in describing Mary Lou's relationship with Michelle O'Neill. Not only does 'Michelle defer to Mary Lou, but all Northern Ireland Sinn Féin ministers are clearly subservient to her'. He insists that 'Gerry Adams had much more influence than she has within the Republican movement, especially the volunteers. She does not have that credibility, gained from being in the IRA.'

'As a bystander', Donaldson believes that 'tension between Sinn Féin North and South remains. The Northern division tends to defer to the needs of the Southern leadership. They look over their shoulder at Southern Sinn Féin and undoubtedly the growth of Sinn Féin in the South has become the overriding priority of the republican movement.'

Finally, I asked Donaldson if Mary Lou and he had any informal contact – often the oil that greases the wheels of political stalemate. Does she ever pick up the phone to him for a chat?

He shook his head. 'She kindly sent condolences on the death of my father. That was it.'

Social Democratic and Labour Party leader Colum Eastwood agreed to be interviewed just before the May 2022 Assembly election. He says he first remembers Mary Lou 'at a meeting of our parties' youth wings in Liberty Hall in Dublin. She was a member of the European Parliament at the time. I have met her a number of times over the years. She is always impressive, more impressive than others in Sinn Féin. I have obviously dealt more with Michelle O'Neill.'

Like Arlene Foster, Colum Eastwood says that 'I get on fine with Mary Lou on a personal basis. She's a tough opponent and very capable.' His knowledge of her at close quarters is mostly confined to party leaders' meetings: 'She often attends party leaders' meetings here. Sinn Féin asked that they have two representatives at these meetings, meaning Mary Lou and Michelle. So, they both attend.' Eastwood, like both Foster and Donaldson, says that 'Michelle definitely defers to Mary Lou who is always across her brief.' He confirms what others say about her arrival at party leaders' meetings: 'Sometimes when we feel we are moving towards a solution at leaders' meetings, progress can disappear when Mary Lou arrives. At a couple of them, when she appeared, the talks paused.'

Eastwood, who represents Derry, says that 'there was anger in the Sinn Féin ranks against Martina [Anderson]. Lots of community jobs went to Sinn Féin members.' And then, acknowledging the dark secrets that surround the episode: 'We will never know what really happened to Martina and Karen.'

Eastwood is dismissive of the shallow politics of Sinn Féin. 'They are not radical. They are populist, whatever they need to be. Populism is easy. I don't think the Provisional movement ever had politics. They spend their whole time in the Dáil trashing their opponents. They are more interested in power than in a united Ireland.'

On the issue of whether there is still an Army Council, Eastwood is damning. Stating that 'I'd be astonished if she thinks of herself as Adams's boss', he believes that there is still 'a structure which is divided into political and financial entities. They have mountains of money. It's unreal. Enormous. It's not just money from America. They have money,' he adds mysteriously, 'from elsewhere. It is still true that the army gets protected.'

Perhaps Eastwood's most perceptive comment was on the commemorations issue, a point where he departs from his nationalist rival. 'She can't,' he asserts, 'say she is reaching out to unionism and commemorate at the same time. It goes back to – the Army comes first. There are lines that cannot be crossed. She's proved time and time again that Sinn Féin is an outfit where organisation comes first.'

Former Ulster Unionist Party leader Lord Empey says he does not know Mary Lou personally, except for a few 'hellos' in TV studios. 'She seems plausible to a point,' he allows. 'There is a fundamental clash between the appearance of a new chapter for republicanism and her being forced back to justify and eulogise those involved in terror in the past. As far as I am concerned, there is no escape for her from that past. It will take at least another generation to achieve.'

Mary Lou has a lot of convincing to do with those individuals whom she wants to unite into one nation. Perhaps she will soon try a less confrontational approach to them. She is politically secure south of the border, where Sinn Féin has continued to dwarf all three government coalition parties individually. In the eight months following the October 2021 ard fheis, Sinn Féin had exceeded 30 per cent in every Red C poll, leading the other parties by a comfortable margin. It had begun to score higher figures than Fianna Fáil and Fine Gael combined. In June 2022 Sinn Féin squatted on an all-time high of 36 per cent.

The political narrative south of the border remained similar for many months. The cost of living replaced housing and health as the burning issue. Inflation, particularly in fuel, energy and food prices, rose to thirty-eight-year highs in response to the war in Ukraine. Mary Lou and Pearse Doherty exploited the resulting fall in living standards with the same populist rhetoric that has worked wonders for Sinn Féin in the housing space.

In the post-election period there were fewer hiccups on the Northern front. However, in December 2021 a revealing event reminded us of where power still resided in Sinn Féin. The party's boy wonder, housing expert Eoin Ó Broin, who has played a significant role in giving Sinn Féin serious credibility, lost the run of himself.

Gerry Adams, an aspiring poet in retirement, had made a controversial 2021 Christmas video sketch in which he sang the words 'Tiocfaidh ár lá' and wished people 'a Gerry Christmas'. There were protests from IRA victims, deeply upset at the republican slogan being used. The company behind the video withdrew it. Eoin Ó Broin went on the radio and suggested that Adams should apologise. He prefaced his suggestion with a patronising piece of advice that 'people should be careful with their language with reconciliation in mind'.

Patronising Adams, retired or not, is hardly a recommended career move within Sinn Féin. The following day, heavyweight TDs David Cullinane and Matt Carthy rallied to their former leader's side, insisting that Adams had nothing for which to apologise. They knew which way the wind blows in Sinn Féin.

They were followed by Mary Lou. She answered a media question very decisively. It was a put-down for the boy wonder. 'As far as I am concerned, I wouldn't be asking somebody, anybody, Gerry Adams or anyone else, to apologise for doing something for a good cause and with a good heart.'

Nothing had yet changed. Eoin Ó Broin, the quintessential new face of Sinn Féin from the South, had foolishly chosen to lock horns publicly with the old guard from the North. Adams and Mary Lou McDonald swatted him away. Ó Broin was put back into his housing box. The new dawn would have to wait.

Ó Broin's spat with Adams did little to reduce public support for Sinn Féin, as measured by the polls. Nor did other setbacks that dominated Sinn Féin's coverage by the media in the early weeks of 2022. Russia's invasion of Ukraine might have embarrassed the leader of any other party with Sinn Féin's history of such close relations with Putin's regime. Not Mary Lou. She reacted with typical devil-may-care populism. She happily called for the expulsion of Russia's ambassador to Ireland. Sinn Féin even removed much of the archive from its website, effectively shredding easy access to information about its pro-Putin past.

A far more awkward problem in the long term could be the loss of one of Mary Lou's 'accidental TDs', Violet-Anne Wynne. A new Clare deputy, she resigned from the party in February 2022, alleging 'psychological warfare' from local Sinn Féin members. The background was not ideal for either Sinn Féin or herself. Violet-Anne, a poll-topper in the 2020 general election, had incurred a debt of €12,126 for unpaid rent. The story of her difficulty broke in the local media two days before the general election. A judgement had been issued against her. She had failed to repay the debt.

Ever since her election, there had been serious tensions between Violet-Anne and the party, centred not just on her housing problem, but on other familiar complaints, including the party's insistence on choosing its TDs' staff and maintaining a rigid control over its neutered deputies.

Violet-Anne told me: 'Mary Lou had phoned me three months after the election and said Sinn Féin would lend me the €12,126 debt which I owed elsewhere. We reached an agreement, but the other problems persisted.' Seven months after her election in December 2020, Violet-Anne had secured a meeting with Mary Lou to sort out a host of difficulties. It went badly.

She outlined the situation to me: 'I had a pre-Christmas 2020 meeting with Mary Lou. I explained all the difficulties which I faced. Mary Lou heard everything,' she said, 'including my personal circumstances.' Violet-Anne had outlined her insecure housing situation, a sick partner and five children. The debt was still hanging over her head, but because she now had a TD's salary, she had agreed repayments of €1000 a month to Sinn Féin.

Violet-Anne continued: 'She didn't take my problems seriously. She took notes and promised to look at what could be done. I was watching her facial expressions. I felt I didn't get enough over to her. I feel, as a woman, that she let me down. I feel her feminism is a façade.'

Violet-Anne's revelation that she had been lent €12,126 by Sinn Féin raises many questions for Mary Lou. Is the party in the habit of arranging loans to TDs? How many other Sinn Féin deputies or their family members are in debt to the party for housing or rent or for any other purposes? Has Mary Lou herself or any member of her family ever received a loan from the party for housing or improvements or any other purpose?

Loans from political parties to their TDs are not illegal. Nor, according to the Standards in Public Office, are they unknown, albeit rare; but the implications of the hold a party could have over its indebted deputies or senators should be seriously considered. Would an unscrupulous centralised party be able to exert improper, compromising pressure on an indebted TD?

In July 2022, Violet-Anne Wynne had not yet discharged her obligations to Sinn Féin. Strangely, the party had not contacted her about the overdue payments since her resignation.

Such regular outbreaks of internal difficulties never deflected Mary Lou from the big picture; the Assembly elections were fast approaching in May. Eoin Ó Broin's faux pas had enabled her, yet again, to very publicly keep Adams onside for the big test.

Offending the godfather of the party would hardly make sense ahead of a key battle in his home territory. Adams was still her 'wise' confidant, her mentor and the key to her acceptability in the North. The bar for the Assembly elections was high because commentators had fuelled expectations that Sinn Féin would win the most seats and capture the first minister's job. After the humiliation of Martina Anderson, Mary Lou could not afford to cause further offence to any powerful hard-line republicans lurking in the long grass. It was essential for her that the replacement candidates in Derry held the seats of the discarded duo. It was even more important that she, not Michelle O'Neill or Gerry Adams or indeed Gerry Kelly, was the first person identified with the Sinn Féin success that she anticipated in the May polls. She wanted Northern nationalists to see her, a Dubliner, as their leader.

Sinn Féin triumphed in the 2022 Assembly elections. They won more seats than any other party. Crucially, they held both seats in Foyle. Mary Lou spent several days in Northern Ireland celebrating the result. She seized the moment, chaired every available press conference, grabbed every microphone and plunged into a spate of media interviews in Northern Ireland, in Britain with Beth Rigby on

Sky News, with ITV's *Good Morning Britain*, with Sky's *Sophy Ridge on Sunday* and with many others. She invited Tory MPs to listen to her plans for a united Ireland in the Houses of Parliament where Sinn Féin, ironically, refuses to take its seats. At Westminster, as she strode out of the meeting, she was flanked by two MLAs and two MPs, John Finucane and Michelle O'Neill on one side, Conor Murphy and Chris Hazzard on the other, all four from Northern Ireland. In the photographs, the four elected representatives walked a step behind Mary Lou, their leader from the South, striding purposefully ahead of them. She may not have had a personal mandate from Northern Ireland, but there was no disguising the message. She was living the dream.

Next, Mary Lou jetted into Brussels to deliver a shared anti-British message to willing listeners on the EU Commission, tired of fighting the protocol battle. In her interview with Joe Duffy in May 2021, she had concluded with an answer about a question on her 'legacy'. The mask slipped for a moment. She wanted her legacy to be that 'I did my part, I contributed to a united Ireland. That is the reason I get up and go to work every morning.'

It was pretty early to be talking about her legacy. She was not even yet a minister, but she was emerging as the leader of the biggest party in the island of Ireland. She wanted everyone to recognise it. Her egoism and her republicanism were blossoming in parallel. They were comfortable bedfellows.

Perhaps that is a clue to the riddle of Mary Lou. Few people believe that her lip service to feminism, to socialism or any other ideology is more than threadbare. Her critics dismiss her purely as an opportunist. They are convinced that she never believed in anything bar her own promotion, that her decision to join Sinn Féin was no more complicated than a good career move from a restless, but ambitious, young woman who had been unable to settle in any job for long. Yet there is a consistency about her desire for a united Ireland. It is in keeping with her family background and her decision to join Fianna Fáil, even if the hunger-strike story is a stretch.

Eamonn McCann, the veteran Derry journalist, former MLA, Marxist and impeccably non-sectarian campaigner, defends Mary Lou McDonald on the opportunism charge. He says she is 'no more opportunistic than Micheál Martin or Leo Varadkar. A bit of opportunism comes with the party. She is more sure-footed than other political leaders.'

McCann recalls Bernadette McAliskey denouncing Mary Lou by name for Sinn Féin's failure to have a policy on the thorny subject of abortion before the 2018 referendum. 'Within weeks,' he remarks approvingly, 'Sinn Féin had done a giddy U-turn. For many years Sinn Féin was not a populist party.' He elaborates: 'It is impossible to tell what she believes in. I'm not saying she's a bad person. I'm sure she's a lovely person.' McCann predicts that 'by the time of the next election there will be a strong appetite for putting a woman into power'.

Mary Lou's Dublin Central constituency colleague and Fine Gael minister for finance, Paschal Donohoe, thinks that she 'believes in a united Ireland, but not in the Sinn Féin mantra that Ireland is a failed state'.

Few people doubt that she entered the party as a creature of Gerry Adams, some suggesting that she was a participator in a cult of the leader's personality. Many are certain that he and his coterie are still a big influence. Others will never forgive her for supporting Adams's stances on crucial issues, including those of his paedophile brother Liam, the rape of Máiría Cahill and the murder of Jean McConville.

One member of her family told me that she has the pugilist instincts of her father, but is sadly distanced from him nowadays. It is likely that her difficult home life and parents' separation have left their mark and may explain aspects of her behaviour.

Deep suspicion surrounds her inexplicably late republican vocation, reawakened only when she was close to the age of thirty.

A question mark still hangs over the source of the funds that paid for the conversion of the family home in Cabra from a humble bungalow into a modern gaff fit for a millionaire.

She is talented, well educated, middle class and nakedly ambitious. Not a single person, of the hundreds interviewed for this book, dismisses Mary Lou McDonald as evil in the way that many speak of Gerry Adams. On the contrary, they are almost unanimous that she is likeable and charming. Some, like Killian Forde, who have worked at close quarters with her say that she is not 'knowable'. Sceptics suggest that her core battle cry of a united Ireland is one we can all share, until we are confronted by the cost.

When I started writing this book, I wrote to Mary Lou's mother, Joan, seeking an interview. I asked her to tell me about Mary Lou's childhood. Joan politely replied, in handwriting on a pleasant card, that she felt a biography was 'premature'.

I suspect now that I understand what she meant. Mary Lou's ambitions reach skywards. First, she wished to lead Sinn Féin into being the largest party in the state. Second, she wanted to be the first woman Taoiseach. Finally, she wished to unite Ireland. Perhaps there are at least two volumes left in this remarkable woman.

ACKNOWLEDGEMENTS

FAREWELL FROM THE FALLS ROAD

It was 12 July 2022. Orange parades and marches were being held all over Ulster. I was having lunch in the Felons' Club on the Falls Road, Belfast, writing these words of thanks to those who have made a biography of Mary Lou McDonald a live project.

Mary Lou, the leader of Irish republicanism, North and South, still does not qualify for membership of the Felons'. She was never a republican prisoner nor interned for her beliefs.

I am grateful to the management and the customers in the Felons' for indulging me during two visits to the premises, the heart of republican Belfast. I thank Gerry Scullion, currently treasurer of the club and former republican prisoner, for shepherding me around this monument to republicanism, a hostelry steeped in the history of the Provisional movement.

It is far from the Felons' Club that Mary Lou McDonald was reared. There are 1916 proclamations on the walls, murals commemorating the hunger strikers and a stained-glass window depicting a local armed IRA unit. A book about the life of the late IRA commander Bobby Storey is sold over the counter for £7. Damien, one of the customers in the bar, was wearing an Aidan

McAnespie T-shirt. McAnespie was killed by the British Army at a border post in 1988 when passing through the checkpoint on his way to a GAA match.

Another customer, perhaps surprisingly, was sporting an Irish Rugby Football Union T-shirt. Earlier on the same day – 12 July – he had cheered on the All-Ireland rugby team as they beat the All Blacks in New Zealand.

I asked several of the customers about Mary Lou McDonald. Damien, a member of Sinn Féin, was adamant: 'Mary Lou is a smart girl', he volunteered admiringly. His companions muttered in agreement.

His words were echoed by virtually all the other customers. 'She is very popular' insisted another. A middle-aged 'regular' watching the horse-racing on TV was a big fan. He had met her when she visited the Felons'. In this shrine habituated by Northern republicans, there was no resistance to the woman from Dublin taking over the mantle from their local Belfast hero, Gerry Adams.

'Ah,' I said, offering an opening for dissent, 'but would you vote for her if she stood as a candidate in West Belfast?' The answer was a unanimous 'Yes'. Not a hint of hesitation.

I am equally grateful to the Andersonstown Social Club PD (Prisoners' Dependants), half a mile up the road – even deeper in West Belfast – who kindly allowed me to take similar sample soundings for my research on the same day. The bar was occupied by members from the Andersonstown district relaxing on the 12 July bank holiday afternoon, a celebration that republicans do not share. The walls are decorated with republican images, most prominently a picture of former chairman the late Bobby Storey. The members of that club, with a republican history to match the Felons', spoke of Mary Lou with respect. One member told me that his entire family 'of forty-two' people loved her. Another voiced the opinion of his companions and himself that 'Mary Lou had not forgotten the north of Ireland while others have.' It was a dig at Micheál Martin and Leo Varadkar. They were all cheering for Mary Lou to win a victory in a 'vote of no confidence' in the southern government in the Dáil later that same evening. As it happened, Sinn Féin lost the vote.

Mary Lou's methodical cultivation of Northern republicans has worked. A few months earlier when former Sinn Féin finance minister and Belfast Media Group publisher, Máirtín Ó Muilleoir, invited me to conduct an *Andersonstown News* 'vox pop' – seeking a verdict on Mary Lou from customers in West Belfast's Kennedy Centre – I was surprised at the findings. Most of the shoppers not only knew who Mary Lou was, but positively approved of her. The suggestion that she was somehow an outsider from a well-off Dublin background, making sporadic visits to the less privileged Falls, did not arise. There was one instance of hostility to her, but it was based on Sinn Féin's u-turn on abortion. There was apathy among a few younger voters, but the overall reaction to the Sinn Féin leader was enthusiastic.

I want to thank Máirtín, the Felons', the Andersonstown Social Club PD and the management of the Kennedy Centre for providing me with this opportunity to sample, at first hand, grass roots, West Belfast opinion about Mary Lou McDonald.

Most of the other people to whom I owe thanks would be mortified if they were publicly named as enablers of this biography. Many of the interviews have been undertaken in exchange for solemn pledges of confidentiality. A majority of sources have insisted on anonymity. I have interviewed more than two hundred people on the subject of Mary Lou McDonald over the past year. Whether it is her family, her fellow pupils, her teachers, her contemporaries at Trinity College Dublin, her lecturers, her adult friends or her early employers, many have asked not to be named. Not to forget the clandestine meetings with members of Sinn Féin itself. Mary Lou's private and public life were shrouded in mystery, long before she joined the most secretive of all Irish political parties.

The Mary Lou trail does not go cold when she joined the republican movement. While the initial united wall of silence from nervous party members was impressive, it proved far from impregnable and happily short-lived.

As the months went by, the workings of the republican movement became increasingly apparent. I want to thank those members of Sinn Féin – past and present – who assisted in painting a more accurate account of Mary Lou's life as a republican and about the inner workings of the party she joined.

I can however say – because they spoke in more formal interviews on the record – that I am particularly grateful for the experiences shared by former Democratic Unionist Party First Minister Dame Arlene Foster, and to her successor as party leader, Sir Jeffrey Donaldson, for his update on how he sees a future with Mary Lou. I am similarly appreciative of the time taken by Social, Democratic and Labour Party (SDLP) leader, Colum Eastwood, to give his views on the president of Sinn Féin. I am also in the debt of other former nationalist party leaders for their advice and briefings. Former Ulster Unionist Party leader Lord Reginald Empey gave an illuminating account of the unionist perspective on Mary Lou.

Many Sinn Féin members, TDs, senators and councillors past and present, disillusioned defectors or true believers, spoke to me in depth. It would cause a sensation if I were ever to publish the names of some of those strangers who visited my home in Wicklow over the dark winter evenings of 2021/22. I will not be doing so but suffice it to say that highly unlikely characters came calling. In particular, I must thank one member of the IRA Army Council (whether former or current remains a matter for debate) for meeting me at an unnamed, distant location in rural Ireland. He was helpful on many issues, but significantly for one of the fabled 'hard men', he was full of loyalty to Mary Lou McDonald. When I asked him if the IRA Army Council still existed, he winked at me, looked innocent and asked me how I could possibly think that he would know?

To another old-style republican, Martin McAllister from Crossmaglen, I offer my thanks for making me aware of the Byzantine nuances of south Armagh before I set out on my research in this extraordinary region. To his delightful wife Mary, many thanks for her warm hospitality.

Local knowledge was priceless in deepest Tipperary where Mary Lou spent so many long summer holidays with her mother's family. Independent Tipperary councillor Joe Hannigan gave generously of his time to assist my task and introduced me to Pat Moroney, the former schoolteacher whose knowledge of the history of the Glen of Aherlow is probably unsurpassed. With the help of both men, I was fortunate to meet Mary Lou's mother Joan's relatives, the Hayes family, who are steeped in local history.

To the many brave victims of violence on both sides of the border and of the political divide, it was a sad privilege to hear your stories of suffering; but thank you for sharing them with me.

To the multitude of journalists who have provided information, thank you for sharing your expertise and often your unique local knowledge.

I have interviewed several recent Ministers for Justice about Mary Lou, Sinn Féin and the IRA Army Council's existence or otherwise. None will emphatically state that the old army apparatus is dismantled. Several politicians – North and South – are of the view that Mary Lou is still in thrall to shadowy figures in Northern Ireland. She insists that she is not. While politicians from the South have been invaluable, I could not possibly name them all. One exception is former Taoiseach, Bertie Ahern. His willingness to mark my card, sharing his unparalleled insights into both the intricate nuances of Northern Ireland politics and the Dublin Central constituency which he shared with Mary Lou, has been priceless. Academics too have been helpful. In particular Associate Emeritus Professor in Social Policy at Trinity College Dublin Anthony Coughlan, veteran campaigner against the European Union, offered a refreshing perspective on republican history and on Mary Lou herself.

But the viability of this book is enhanced not so much by the, sometimes predictable, murmurings of politicians who have contributed, but by the people on the ground, who have watched Mary Lou in action from early childhood to the present day. Some members of her family have been helpful in providing information about her early years, education and youth. I am grateful to them. People within Fianna Fáil and the Irish National Congress (INC) have filled many of the obvious gaps in her incomplete narrative about her pre-Sinn Féin life. Her Dublin Central constituency rivals, while mostly reluctant to go on the record, have provided many significant missing details.

A lot of the material in this book is new. For that, credit is due to Seamus Haughey, formerly Research Librarian in the Oireachtas Library. It was a stroke of good luck that Seamus took early retirement just as the biography was beginning. He has been with me on the entire journey. His scholarly approach and ability to source archival material were invaluable.

The amount of work done by Fiona Fitzsimons – director of Heritage Services company, Eneclann – in tracing family histories cannot be overstated. Hers was a thoroughly professional job.

Particular recognition is due to Julien Dorgere of Super8 Productions Limited in Galway. Julien is Ireland's leading 8mm film specialist. Without his skills, several of the most important photographs in the book may have been lost.

Others to whom heartfelt gratitude is appropriate include Aoife Sherwin of My Secretary, Secretarial Agency, who typed the entire work; the Webb team of Tom and Sarah, who researched subjects and questions to be put to interviewees; and consultant Jim

Dorgan, who fact-checked many of the more obscure parts of the transcript.

To the publishers Atlantic Books, led by Clare Drysdale, Will Atkinson and Simon Hess, thank you for having the faith to promote a second book about Irish politics within two years. Their commitment to the project from day one has been a constant tonic in the face of obstacles. To Deirdre Roberts for her assistance in publicizing the book, a word of thanks.

Finally, the most important person of all, literary agent Jonathan Williams has been available, wise and unbelievably helpful at every stage. Owing to the limitless extent of his exertions, I am still unsure of the exact boundaries of a literary agent's duties, but the amount of work Jonathan has undertaken so willingly has been utterly selfless. A perfectionist, he is not afraid to correct my flawed grammar, punctuation, spelling and syntax, a challenge that would drive a less tolerant mortal up the wall. His support was particularly appreciated when he was recovering from sickness in the later weeks while the book was being completed; but he managed to summon up enough energy to school an uncertain author through the hardest of hurdles. Thank you.

INDEX

abortion, 71, 97, 103, 117, 250, 289, 322–9, 345, 386–7, 399
  referendum (2018), 322, 324–6, 333, 338, 340, 395
Adams, Áine, 211–15, 221, 249, 254, 263, 266, 269
Adams, Gerard, 2, 7, 9–10, 12, 15, 88–91, 99, 107, 111–12, 115, 118, 173, 198, 254, 362–3
  abortion, views on, 323, 324
  Ansbacher affair (2014), 243, 249
  Ardboyne meeting (2009), 205–8
  assembly elections (2004), 134
  assembly elections (2007), 161–2
  brother's sexual abuse scandal (2009), 211–15, 221, 249, 254, 263, 266, 269
  bullying scandals (2015–17), 304–5
  Cahill rape allegations, 262, 266–70
  Cahill's funeral (2004), 258, 259, 260, 286
  Christmas video sketch (2021), 390–91
  Derry review (2021), 378
  economics, knowledge of, 251
  European elections (2004), 129, 139, 142
  general election (2007), 152–3, 165, 173
  general election (2011), 217–22, 230
  general election (2016), 291–6
  Gregory's funeral (2009), 169, 170
  IMC report (2004), 139
  Joxer Daly's party (1994), 189
  longevity, 115
  McConville murder interview (2014), 273–4, 286
  McDonald's transition, 113, 121–2, 124, 127–30, 134
  McElduff incident (2018), 284, 286
  McGuinness's funeral (2017), 308
  Murphy conviction (2015), 282
  presidential election (2011), 287–8
  Quinn murder (2007), 279–80
  resignation (2017–18), 315
  Share the Wealth in Budget (2001), 122, 124, 129–30
  succession (2016–18), 296–8, 304–5, 311, 315
  Westminster election (2010), 196
  Working Together conference (2002), 127
Adams, Liam, 211–15, 221, 249, 254, 263, 266, 269
Aer Lingus, 37, 75
Ahern, Bartholomew 'Bertie', 97, 110, 128, 137–8, 154–5, 165–6, 183, 362
  general election (2007), 156, 158, 161, 162, 164–6
  McGuinness's funeral (2017), 307
  retirement (2008), 165, 220
Ahern, Maurice, 170
Aiken, Steve, 384
Alderdice, John, 139
Alliance Party of Northern Ireland, 341, 384
Amsby, Alan, 34–5
An Cultúrlann, Belfast, 381
Anderson, Martina, 10, 11, 306, 309–10, 343, 346, 358–9, 371–8, 380, 383, 389
Andrews, Barry, 342
Anglo-Irish Bank, 57
Ansbacher Cayman Limited, 183, 242, 244–9
Anti-Austerity Alliance, 252, 291
Aontú, 328, 344, 354
ard fheis, 113, 115, 161, 297, 329, 358
  2004 137
  2007 161
  2009 173
  2010 214
  2011 231
  2014 325
  2015 323–4
  2017 315
  2018 315–18, 328
  2021 345–6, 379–84
Ard na Gréine, Rathgar, 49–50, 61, 67
Ardboyne meeting (2009), 205–6
Ardlinn, 54
Arms Trial (1970), 89

Army Council, 9, 11, 113, 118, 225, 360, 372, 386, 389, 400–401
  Adams and, 89
  Ard Chomhairle members, 114–15
  Cahill and, 257
  Derry review (2021), 372
  disbandment, 6, 7, 113
  Ferris and, 337
  Hughes and, 310
  Kelly and, 340, 380
  Murray and, 380
Ashe, Thomas, 187
Ashington Heath, Dublin, 182

Bacik, Ivana, 71, 142, 170, 172
Bagnall, Patrick, 45
Baker, Sam, 337–8
Balcombe Street gang, 310
Ballagh, Robert, 90, 100
Bank of Ireland, 116, 180, 182, 193
Banotti, Mary, 36, 70–71, 95–6
Barrett, Seán, 243–6, 248, 252–4
Barrett, Sylvester, 246
Barron Inquiry (2004), 134
Barry, Kevin, 93, 96, 108
Basque Country, 60, 74, 233
Behan, Thomas, 43
Belfast An Cultúrlann, 381
Belfast Féile an Phobail, 313
Belfast Project, 272–3
Bell, Ivor, 273–4
Bhreatnach, Lucilita, 262
Bielenberg, Kim, 203
Bird, Charlie, 139
Black, Alan, 285
Black, Frances, 259, 260
Black, William, 42
Black and Tans, 41, 42, 339, 349
Blair, Anthony 'Tony', 128, 134, 198
Blaney, Neil, 89
Bloody Sunday (1972), 2
Bodenstown, Co. Kildare, 311
Boland, Kevin, 89, 90
Bonar Law, Andrew, 34
Bord Gáis Éireann, 81, 191
Boston College Belfast Project, 272–3
Bowman, John, 387
Boylan, Lynn, 290, 333, 342, 378, 382
Brady, Cyprian, 156–7, 162, 163, 164
Brady, Philip, 23–4
Brady, Royston, 136, 139, 140–41
Bréadún, Deaglán de, 36, 52, 73, 74, 107, 219
Breen, Daniel, 37, 40
Brexit, 349, 373
Briscoe, Ben, 23–4
Britain's European Question, 78
British–Irish Parliamentary Body, 225
Broadcasting Authority Act (1960), 111
Brolly, Áine, 54, 324, 328
Brolly, Francie, 324, 328
Brosnan, Joe, 139
Browne, John, 189–90
Brún, Bairbre de, 58, 135, 142, 146–8, 174, 175–6, 196, 206, 259, 260
Buchanan, Gerard, 23–4
Buckley, Margaret, 319
bullying scandals, 299–305
Burke, Christopher, 152–3, 160, 161, 171–3, 186–7, 200, 221, 258–9
Burke, Sharon, 374–5
Burton, Joan, 85, 125, 252–5, 264, 267–70, 290, 294, 327, 337
Bush, George Walker, 198
Butler, Joan, 20, 61–3
Butler, Ray, 243

Byrne, David, 187
Byrne, Michael, 82

Cabra, Dublin, 179–85, 191–4, 201–2
Cahill, Annie, 260
Cahill, Joe, 88–9, 91, 144, 256–61, 286, 309
Cahill, Máiría, 5, 133–4, 255, 256, 259, 261–72, 282, 395
Calleary, Dara, 356, 368
Callinan, Martin, 234–9
Cardiff, Kevin, 231
Carey, Sarah, 71–2
Carmody, Ross, 202
Carpenterstown, Castleknock, 84
Carron, Tom, 89
Carson, Sile, 104
Carthy, Matt, 7, 56, 290, 342, 351, 391
Casey, Peter, 334, 335
'Cash for Ash' project, 307
Cass, Gary, 313
Castleknock, Dublin, 81, 84, 93, 96, 108, 123, 151, 166, 182, 192
Catholicism, 36, 53, 323, 366
Cayman Islands, 183, 242, 244–9
Central Remedial Clinic controversy (2013), 65, 234, 239–40
cervical cancer, 329, 334
Charleton Tribunal report (2018), 330–31
Cherish All the Children Equally, 324
Christian Democrats, 146
Citizens' Assembly, 325
Clancy, Áine, 221
Clarke, Frank, 3, 241
Clarke, Paul, 189
climate change, 149, 345
Clinton, William 'Bill', 307, 308
Cohen, Michael, 55
Colleary, Padraig, 244
Colley, George, 155
Collins, Áine, 269
Collins, Gerard, 245, 248
Collins, Liam, 64
Colombia, 99, 312
'Come Out, Ye Black and Tans', 360
Comhairle Dáil Ceantair, 91, 96
Comhdháil Náisiúnta na hÉireann, 89–90, 94, 96, 100–109, 234
Comiskey, Joe, 87
Comiskey, Nora, 87–94, 99, 100, 105, 107, 320
Committee on Procedure and Privileges, 240, 248, 249
communism, 147, 148
confidence and supply agreement (2016–20), 298, 338
confidence votes, 329–30, 339, 347–8, 369–70
Conlan, Brian, 234, 239
Connolly, James, 105, 339, 378
Connolly, Niall, 99
Conroy, Greg, 190
Conservative Party (UK), 328
Conway, Ciara, 269
Conway-Walsh, Rose, 7, 11, 351, 382
Coonan, Noel, 243
Cooper, Matt, 209
Coppinger, Ruth, 269
Corrib gas field, 57–60
Corrigan, John, 231
Corrigan, Peter, 311
cost of living crisis (2022), 390
Costello, Joe, 155, 158, 163, 170, 221, 247
Coveney, Simon, 349, 378–9, 384, 385–6
Covid-19 pandemic, 358, 363, 367–70
Cowen, Barry, 368
Cowen, Brian, 169, 208, 216
Cox, Brian, 68–9
Cox, Patrick, 209
Coyle, Margaret, 180
CPL Resources, 54
Cranny, Máire, 68
Criminal Law Jurisdiction Act (1975), 93
Cronin, Réada, 11
Crossmaglen Rangers, 311
Crowe, Seán, 11, 118, 130, 137, 164, 195, 351, 382
Cuffe, Ciarán, 342

Culhane, Michael, 235
Cullinane, David, 11, 12, 137, 142–3, 216, 295, 332–3, 336, 360, 362–3, 382, 391
Cumann na mBan, 41, 311
Cunningham, Ted, 196–7
Curragh Camp, Co. Kildare, 43–5
Currie, Austin, 85

Dáil centenary (2019), 338
Dáil elections, see under elections
Dáil McDonald's suspension (2014), 24, 252–4
Dáil, 150–66, 249–55
Daly, Clare, 147, 323, 327
Daly, Frank, 231
D'Arcy, Mary, 93
Davis, Mary, 289
Davison, Gerard 'Jock', 198
de Valera, Eamon, 252
Deasy, John, 228, 247
Delargy, Pádraig, 376
Democratic Socialist Party, 147
Democratic Unionist Party (DUP), 149, 196, 288, 307–8, 328, 341, 365, 376, 384, 387
Derry Sinn Féin, 358, 359, 370–78
Derry, Ulster Easter commemoration, 311, 313
Derry Volunteers dinner, 305–6, 313
Devereux, Eoin, 75
Digney, Monica, 328
divorce referendum (2019), 342
Dobson, Bryan, 278
Doherty, Patrick, 114, 123, 173
Doherty, Pearse, 7, 11, 12, 137, 199–200, 362
    ard fheis (2010), 214
    ard fheis (2021), 380
    Cahill rape allegations, 268
    cost of living crisis (2022), 390
    Derry convention (2021), 376
    Donegal South-West by-election (2010), 215
    European elections (2004), 142–3
    general election (2011), 216, 217–19, 220, 224, 230
    general election (2016), 295, 296
    general election (2020), 351
    IRA, views on, 367
    leadership transition (2016–18), 297, 304, 315, 317, 320
    Lisbon referendum (2009), 210
    Seanad Éireann seat 203, 206, 207
Doherty, Regina, 265–7, 269
Doherty Ryan, Deirdre, 91–2, 125–6
Donaldson, Jeffrey, Sir, 376, 387–8
Donaldson, Kenny, 314
Donegal South-West by-election (2010), 215
Donohoe, Paschal, 155–6, 158, 162–4, 170, 172, 221, 349, 395
Doris, Brendan, 309
Doris, Tony, 309
Dowdall, Jonathan, 186–7
Dowds, Robert, 247
Doyle, Pascal Vincent, 50
drink-driving laws, 3
Drumm, Máire, 319
Dublin Bay South by-election (2021), 4, 378
Dublin Central constituency, 3, 39, 151–66, 168–73
Dublin City Council, 102–3, 152, 154, 156, 179–80
Dublin City University (DCU), 53, 79, 80, 85–6, 105, 127, 366, 379–84
Dublin Mid-West by-election (2019), 347, 351
Dublin West constituency, 85, 108–9, 118, 119, 122, 123, 252, 290–91, 294
Duffy, Gavin, 335
Duffy, Joe, 367, 394
Dugdale, Bridget Rose, 312
Durkan, Mark, 358
Dwyer, John, 137, 142

East Germany, 147
Easter Rising (1916), 93, 188, 297, 305, 311, 313, 364
Eastwood, Colum, 341, 358, 371, 388–9
Edwards, Rodney, 74, 86, 365
Egan, Barry, 61

Eighth Amendment, 322, 324–6, 333, 338, 340, 395
Éirígí, 56–60, 199, 200, 209
elections
  1973 general election, 23
  1983 Dublin Central by-election, 155
  1997 general election, 110, 111, 120; Westminster
    elections, 116
  2002 general election, 105, 118, 120, 123–6, 151, 152,
    156, 158, 171, 182, 195
  2003 Northern Ireland assembly election, 134
  2004 European elections, 129, 131, 133, 134–42, 154,
    157, 195, 201, 225, 260; local elections, 140, 143,
    195
  2007 Northern Ireland assembly election, 161–2, 196;
    general election, 120, 151–66, 171, 187, 195, 199,
    205, 230
  2009 Dublin Central by-election, 168–73; European
    elections, 167, 168, 171, 173–7, 186, 196, 201, 205
  2010 Westminster elections, 196; Donegal South-West
    by-election, 215
  2011 general election, 181, 182, 201, 216–23, 293;
    presidential election, 287–9, 293, 294, 332, 334, 335
  2014 European elections, 290, 293, 334, 336; local
    elections, 290, 293, 343; Dublin West by-election,
    252, 290–91, 294
  2016 general election, 249, 291–6, 312; Northern
    Ireland assembly election, 312
  2018 presidential election, 331–8
  2019 European elections, 320, 338, 342, 344, 347, 354;
    local elections, 320, 338, 342–4, 354; Dublin
    Mid-West by-election, 347, 351
  2020 general election, 319, 320–21, 338, 348–54
  2021 Dublin Bay South by-election, 4, 378
  2022 Northern Ireland assembly election, 371, 373,
    393–4
Electoral Reform Society, 222
Electricity Supply Board, 251
Elizabeth II, Queen, 162, 334
Elliott, Thomas 'Dixie', 376
Ellis, Desmond, 93, 124, 151, 351, 356, 360
Empey, Reginald, Baron, 389–90
Enniskillen bombing (1987), 112, 133
Erasmus Programme, 76
Ericsson, 59
Europe for a Union of the Nations, 146
European Central Bank, 290
European Commission, 290
European Council, 154
European Court of Human Rights, 90
European Free Alliance/Green Group, 146
European integration, 75–7
European Parliament, 57, 58, 76, 77, 130, 144–50, 159,
  173–7, 185, 373
  2004 elections, 129, 131, 133, 134–42, 154, 157, 195,
    201, 225, 260
  2009 elections, 167, 168, 171, 173–7, 186, 195, 201, 205
  2014 elections, 290, 293, 334, 336
  2019 elections, 320, 338, 342, 344, 347, 354
Evening Herald, 63, 93, 148
Ewart, Sarah, 323
extradition, 88, 89, 93, 189

Fanning, Ronan, 78
Farage, Nigel, 209
Farrell, Mairéad, 303
Farry, Stephen, 384
Feehily, Josephine, 231, 243
Féile an Phobail, 313
Felons Club, 1–2, 10, 212, 358
feminism, 170, 253, 270, 300, 324, 327
Ferguson, Ciara, 376, 381, 383
Ferris, Martin, 7, 114, 115, 118, 128, 153, 164, 225, 337,
  351, 356
Ferris, Toiréasa, 199
Fianna Fáil, 13–15, 23, 37, 47, 49, 87–109, 110, 115–16,
  119–20, 123, 289
  confidence and supply agreement (2016–20), 298, 338
  Covid-19 pandemic, 368–70
  Dublin Central by-election (1983), 155
  Europe for a Union of the Nations, 146

Fitzgerald confidence motion (2018), 330, 331
  general election (2007), 156–7, 158, 160, 162–6
  general election (2011), 219, 220, 221, 222–3
  general election (2016), 292, 293, 294, 298
  general election (2020), 349, 350, 352–3, 354, 355–7,
    365
  Harris confidence vote (2019), 339–40
  Lisbon Treaty referendum (2009), 210
  Murphy confidence votes, 329–30, 347–8
  polling, 370, 390
  presidential election (2018), 331
  republican wing, 87–95, 110, 115
  rezoning rows (1990s), 184
Fine Gael, 3, 49, 88
  confidence and supply agreement (2016–20), 298, 338
  Covid-19 pandemic, 367–70
  European elections (2019), 342
  general election (2007), 155–6, 158, 162–3
  general election (2011), 219, 220, 222
  general election (2016), 292, 293, 294, 298
  general election (2020), 349–50, 352–3, 354, 355–7,
    365
  Murphy confidence votes, 329–30, 347–8
  polling, 367–8, 370, 390
  presidential election (2018), 331, 332
  rezoning rows (1990s), 184
  Varadkar confidence vote (2020), 369–70
  Zappone affair (2021), 379
Finucane, John, 332–3, 383, 394
Finucane, Patrick, 149
Finucane, Seamus, 263
Fitzgerald, Frances, 253, 269, 327, 330, 331, 342
FitzGerald, Garret, 78
Fitzgerald, Martina, 335
Fitzgibbon McGinley 180
Fitzpatrick, Dermot, 156
Fitzpatrick, John, 140
Fitzpatrick, Kevin, 20
Fitzpatrick, Mary, 156–7, 162, 163, 164, 221
Flanagan, Brendan, 179, 182, 193
Flanagan, Charles, 349
Flanagan, Luke, 147, 288
Flannery, Frank, 241
Fleming, Tom, 288
Flynn, Padraig, 83
Forde, Killian, 145, 200–205, 396
Foster, Arlene, Dame, 307–8, 365, 384, 385, 386
Foyle, Derry, 312, 346, 358, 371
Freeman, Joan, 335

al-Gaddafi, Muammar, 258
Gallagher, Seán, 289, 335
Galligan, Yvonne, 222
Garda Síochána, 234–9
gas, 57–60
Gas Networks Ireland (GNI), 191–2
Geoghegan-Quinn, Máire, 245, 248
Gernika Group, 60
Gildernew, Michelle, 346
Gillespie, Patsy, 306
Gillespie, Paul, 78
Gilmore, Eamon, 169, 290
Glen of Aherlow, Co. Tipperary, 38–47
Golfgate (2020), 369
Good Friday Agreement (1998), 56, 105, 110, 137, 195,
  209, 258, 275, 374, 387
Gorman, Tommie, 279
Gormley, John, 169
Green Book, 204
Green Left Group, 147
Green Party of Ireland, 59, 90, 136, 157, 222–3, 293, 342,
  344, 349, 354, 356
Gregory, Tony, 155, 158, 161, 163, 167, 168–70
Grieve, John, 139

Halliday Square, Dublin, 80, 84, 192
Halligan, Brendan, 77
Halligan, John, 299–300
Hamilton, George, 271, 340
Hanafin, Mary, 337

Hannigan, Joseph, 41, 45
Harney, Mary, 176, 242, 244, 248
Harrington, Maura, 60
Harris, Simon, 339–40, 348, 368
Haughey, Charles, 89, 90, 155, 160, 183, 244
Hayes, Breda, 42, 43, 46
Hayes, Brian, 291
Hayes, James 'Jimmy', 42, 46
Hayes, John, 42
Hayes, Liam, 42, 46–7
Hayes, Marian, 46–7
Hayes, Molly, 38–41, 42, 45, 47, 86–7, 118, 365
Hazzard, Chris, 394
healthcare, 160, 344
Healy-Rae, Michael, 288
Hennessy, Mark, 125, 161
Higgins, Joe, 85, 125, 136, 142, 167, 173
Higgins, Michael D., 111, 219, 289, 307, 331–6
Holland, Kitty, 377
homelessness, 349–50
homosexuality, 386–7
housing crisis, 131, 344, 350
Howell, Ted, 362
Howlin, Brendan, 250, 252
HPV vaccine, 334, 335
Hughes, Brendan, 187, 273
Hughes, Seán, 7, 310, 372, 379, 380, 381, 382
Hume, John, 189, 196, 319, 371
Hutch, Gerry, 187

Independent Alliance, 299–300
Independent Monitoring Commission (IMC), 138–9
inflation, 390
Institute for British–Irish Studies, 56
Institute of European Affairs, 106, 135
Institute of International and European Affairs (IIEA), 77–9
International Monetary Fund (IMF), 215, 220, 290
Irish Business and Employers Confederation (IBEC), 106, 210
Irish Civil War (1922–3), 37, 40, 41, 42–7
Irish Congress of Trade Unions (ICTU), 106, 120, 126, 210
Irish Film Board, 51
Irish Free State (1922–1937), 40, 41, 42–7
Irish language, 4, 10, 70
Irish Language Act (proposed), 4
Irish National Congress (INC), 89–90, 94, 96, 100–109, 234, 320
Irish Productivity Centre (IPC), 106, 120
Irish Republican Army (IRA), 1, 6, 73, 111–15, 360–63
    arms smuggling, 257–8, 281
    Army Council, see Army Council
    Balcombe Street gang, 310
    Cahill rape allegations, 5, 255, 259, 261–72
    Cahill's funeral (2004), 256–61
    ceasefire (1994), 366
    Civil War (1922–3), 37, 40, 41, 42–7
    Colombia Three, 99, 312
    Enniskillen bombing (1987), 112, 133
    extraditions, 88, 89, 93, 189
    Green Book, 204
    hunger strikes (1981), 13, 47, 65, 70, 72, 203, 256
    Kingsmill massacre (1975), 56, 112, 284
    McCartney murder (2005), 197–8, 219
    McConville murder (1972), 249, 272–5, 286, 294, 395
    Mountbatten assassination (1979), 112, 281, 361
    Mountjoy Prison escape (1973), 187
    Northern Bank heist (2004), 6, 184–5, 196–7, 219
    pensions, 197
    proxy bombing, 306
    Quinn murder (2007), 275–80, 353
    Rathbride column, 43
    Russell commemoration, 97, 131–2, 141, 309–10
    Sinn Féin, relationship with, 111–15, 117, 118, 123, 137–8, 204
    Smith commemoration, 123, 130
    Storey's funeral (2020), 6, 360, 363, 379
    Tohill kidnapping (2004), 137
    Troubles (1966–98), 13, 56, 111, 123, 132, 256–8, 306, 313, 314

War of Independence (1919–21), 37, 41, 42, 360
Warrenpoint ambush (1979), 281, 361
Warrington bombings (1993), 112
Weston kidnapping attempt (1983), 152
Irish Republican Socialist Party, 89
Irish Times, The, 134, 139
Irish War of Independence (1919–21), 37, 41, 42, 360
Irish Women Workers' Union, 89
Israel, 205, 328, 373

John Paul II, Pope, 36
Johns Hopkins University, 51
Johnston, Jackie, 45
Joxer Daly's pub, Dublin, 189

Keane, Eamon, 218
Kearney, Declan, 373
Kearns, Nicholas, 215
Keatinge, Patrick, 77
Keena, Colm, 117
Keenan, Brian, 131–3, 141, 258, 309–10
Kehoe, Nicky, 123, 130, 151–4, 156, 158, 161, 163–5, 171, 189, 200
Kehoe, Paul, 243, 248–9
Kelleher, Billy, 342
Kelly, David, 289, 354
Kelly, Fiach, 238, 239
Kelly, Gerry, 7, 8, 12, 114, 115, 340, 372, 373, 377–83
Kelly, Peter, 241
Kelly, Seán, 258
Kemp, Richard, 282
Kenny, Enda, 169, 243, 244, 264, 294, 307, 308, 335
Kerins, Angela, 3, 234, 240
Kerr, Dick, 139
Kilmichael ambush (1920), 360–61
Kinahan gang, 187
King, Cathal, 290–91
Kingsmill massacre (1975), 56, 112, 284

Labour Party, 60, 71, 77, 105, 128, 146, 155, 203, 205
    Dublin Central by-election (2009), 169, 170
    European elections (2004), 136, 138, 139, 142
    European elections (2009), 173
    general election (2007), 163
    general election (2011), 219, 220, 221, 222–3
    general election (2016), 292, 293, 294
    general election (2020), 356
    Lisbon Treaty referendum (2009), 209
    local elections (2014), 290
    presidential election (2018), 331
Lacey, Dinny, 40, 46
Laguiller, Arlette, 147
Lanigan, Ann, 81
Lanigan, Bernadette, 81
Lanigan, Carmel, 82
Lanigan, Geraldine, 81, 82
Lanigan, Gerard, 160, 192, 194
Lanigan, Martin, 4, 5, 13, 14, 16, 63, 74, 80–85, 120, 146, 166, 318, 364–5
    Bodenstown commemoration (2013), 311
    Cabra mansion, 179–85, 191–4, 201–2
    childcare, 133
    marriage, 76–7, 79
    politics, interest in, 123
Lanigan-McDonald, Gerard, 16, 160, 166, 311, 318
Lanigan-McDonald, Iseult, 16, 130–31, 133–4, 146, 166, 311, 318
Lawlor, Liam, 85
Leeson, Brian, 57
Legion of Mary, 61
Lenihan, Brian Jr., 15, 85, 88, 93–4, 119, 120, 125
Lenihan, Conor, 81
Lennon, John, 69
Leonard, Tommy, 155
Lewis, Brandon, 384
Libya, 257–8, 281
Liffey Valley, Dublin, 83
Lifford, Co. Donegal, 314
Lisbon Treaty referendums (2008–9), 167–8, 173, 175, 177, 206–11

Lisnagaul ambush (1920), 41, 42, 46
Lisvernane, Co. Tipperary, 38–41
Little Sisters of the Poor, 68
Long, Naomi, 341, 384
Looby, Carmel, 67
Loughlin, Elaine, 343
Love Both, 325
Lowry, Michael, 183
Lynch, Andrew, 208
Lynch, Martin, 7, 372, 377, 379, 380–81, 382

Mac Lochlainn, Pádraig, 382
Mackin, Desmond, 114, 117
MacManus, Chris, 147
MacSharry, Ray, 245, 248
MacThomais, Shane, 204
Magee, Patrick, 258
Magill, 21, 57, 229
Maguire, Michael, 270
Mahon Tribunal (1997–2012), 165
Maillot, Agnès, 352
Mallon, Kevin, 187
Mandela, Nelson, 69, 89–90, 328
Mangan, Patrick, 45
Mansion House, Dublin, 101, 118
Marathon, 58, 59
Markievicz, Constance, 319, 339
Martin, Eamon, 323
Martin, Micheál, 169, 210, 226, 232, 249, 264, 294, 384
    confidence and supply agreement (2016–20), 298, 338
    Covid-19 pandemic, 368, 369, 370
    Fitzgerald confidence motion (2018), 330, 331
    general election (2020), 348, 352, 354, 355–7
    presidential election (2018), 335
    Zappone affair (2021), 379
Maskey, Alex, 114
Massereene Barracks shooting (2009), 57
May, Theresa, 373
McAliskey, Bernadette, 89, 90, 395
McAuliffe, Paul, 350
McCabe, Jerry, 294
McCabe, Lorraine, 331
McCabe, Maurice, 234, 238, 242, 330–31
McCallion, Declan, 359
McCallion, Elisha, 11, 183, 184, 339, 346, 358–9, 361, 363, 371, 383
McCann, Eamonn, 395
McCann, Jennifer, 264
McCann, John, 124
McCarthy, Cathal, 100–106
McCartney, Andrew, 307
McCartney, Raymond, 376–7
McCartney, Robert, 197–8, 219
McCauley, Martin, 99
McCionnath, Brendan, 98
McClements, Freya, 13
McConville, Jean, 112, 133, 249, 272–5, 286, 294, 395
McCrory, Agnes, 263
McDonagh, Brendan, 231
McDonald, Beatrice, 19, 21, 24, 29, 32, 51, 66–7, 68
McDonald, Joan, 4–5, 14–16, 19, 20, 29, 36, 37, 42, 50, 61, 66, 69, 133, 318
McDonald, Joanne, 4, 14, 22, 29, 51, 52–60
McDonald, Maeve, 20, 63–6
McDonald, Mary Lou
    abortion, views on, 323–9
    Catholicism, 53, 366
    childhood, 35–47, 48, 60–66
    Dáil suspension (2014), 24
    'Damascus moment' 13, 14, 38, 70, 72
    debating skills, 67–9, 70, 72
    education, 13, 14, 24, 32, 48, 49, 50–51, 67–77, 79, 85–6, 95, 366
    feminism, 170, 270, 300, 327
    finances, 185–91
    grandmother, relationship with, 38, 47, 86–7, 118, 365
    leadership transition (2016–18), 297, 304–5, 311, 315–21
    parents' separation (1979), 4–5, 36, 61, 66, 69
    racism, views on, 204–5
    republicanism, 38–47, 67, 70
    sexism, views on, 204–5
    Sinn Féin transition, 94–109, 110, 118–19
    socialism, views on, 148, 339
McDonald, Nora, 20, 66
McDonald, Patrick (brother), 4, 22, 29, 51–2
McDonald, Patrick (father), 4–5, 14, 15, 19–36, 37, 49, 50, 61, 66, 69, 318
McDonald, Phyllis, 20, 66
McDowell, Michael, 139
McElduff, Barry, 56, 284–6
McElvanna, Peadar, 313
McEnery, Ted, 227–8
McGee, Harry, 196, 198
McGeough, Gerry, 97, 328
McGinley, Denis 'Dinny', 243
McGrath, Finian, 105–6, 127, 172, 216, 234, 307
McGrath, Michael, 227, 355
McGreehan, Erin, 207
McGrory, Barra, 270
McGuinness, Declan, 328
McGuinness, Dodie, 134
McGuinness, John, 3, 226–9, 231–3, 238, 247, 249
McGuinness, Martin, 2, 15, 88, 91, 99, 111–15, 118, 121, 124, 134, 173, 198, 328
    abortion, views on, 323, 324
    Ardboyne meeting (2009), 205–6
    assembly elections (2007), 162
    Cahill's funeral (2004), 258, 259
    death (2017), 307–9, 313, 315, 365
    Derry and, 306, 371, 374
    leadership ambitions, 305
    presidential election (2011), 288–9, 293, 294, 305, 332, 334, 335, 354
    resignation (2017), 307
    Westminster election (2010), 196
McIntyre, Anthony, 101, 272–3
McKenna, Patricia, 59, 90, 129, 136, 139–40, 141–2
McLaughlin, Mitchel, 114, 115, 149
McLellan, Sandra, 243, 268, 299–301, 302, 323
McManus, Edward, 108
McManus, Frank, 89
McManus, Liz, 265, 276–7
McVerry, Michael, 313
McVerry, Peter, 169
Meaning of Life, The, 366
Merrigan, Matt, 90
Mhic Mhathúna, Emma, 329
Minihan, Louise, 200
Mitchell, Denise, 337, 382
Mitchell, Gay, 129, 136, 139, 142, 143, 173, 177, 289
Moloney, Ed, 272–3
Molony, Senan, 265, 336
Monaghan, Jim, 99, 312
Montessori school, 24
Mooney, Mary, 82
Moore, Aoife, 364
Moore, Brian, 45
Moran, Brian, 261
Moran, Mary, 265
Morgan, Arthur, 10, 118, 153, 164, 216–17, 224, 225, 356
Moroney, Pat, 46
Morris, Martin, 263–4, 271
Morris, Séamie, 302–3, 343
Morrison, Daniel, 10
Morrissey, Tom, 125, 126
Mountbatten, Louis, 1st Earl, 112, 281, 361
Mountjoy Prison escape (1973), 187
Mr Pussy (Alan Amsby), 34–5
Mullan, Karen, 372–6, 380, 389
Murphy, Conor, 10, 12, 128, 275–80, 286, 297, 305, 309, 316, 353, 381, 383, 385, 394
Murphy, Eoghan, 329–30, 347, 350
Murphy, June, 300, 301
Murphy, Patrick, 256
Murphy, Paul, 138, 252, 291, 294
Murphy, Thomas 'Slab', 281–3, 286
Murray, Seán, 7, 9, 379, 380, 381

Narrow Water ambush (1979), 281, 361
Nash, Gerald, 268
National Treasury Management Agency, 231
natural gas, 57–60
Nazi Germany (1933–45), 131–2, 141
Neville, Dan, 243
New Cabra Road, Dublin, 179–85, 191–4, 201–2
New Hollande Band, 82
New York, United States, 340–41
Ní Chuilín, Carál, 346, 381, 383
Ní Ghadhra, Máirín, 76
Ní Riada, Liadh, 290, 333, 334–6, 342
Nolan, Carol, 117, 319, 325–6
Nolan, Patrick, 45
Nordic Green Left, 147–8, 176
Norris, David, 73, 289
Northern Bank heist (2004), 6, 184–5, 196–7, 219
Northern Ireland, 121, 384–8
    elections, *see under* elections
    Executive collapse (2017–20), 307, 349
    extraditions, 88, 89, 93, 189
    Good Friday Agreement (1998), 56, 105, 110, 137, 195, 209, 258, 275, 374, 387
    IMC report (2004), 138–9
    Irish Language Act (proposed), 4
    McConville murder (1972), 249, 272–5, 286, 294, 395
    Quinn murder (2007), 275–80, 353
    Renewable Heating Incentive scandal (2017), 307
    Troubles (1966–98), 13, 56, 111, 123, 132, 256–8, 281, 306, 313, 314
Notre Dame des Missions, Dublin, 13, 14, 48, 49, 50, 67, 69–70, 72, 95
Novartis, 54–5

Ó Broin, Eoin, 12, 205, 295, 320, 347, 350, 351, 362, 382, 390–91, 393
Ó Caoláin, Caoimhghín, 97, 116, 118, 122, 128, 134, 164, 206, 220, 225, 229–30, 243, 287
Ó Clochartaigh, Trevor, 303–4
Ó Donnghaile, Niall, 357–8, 381
Ó Laoghaire, Donnchadh, 11, 295, 351, 358, 382
Ó Muilleoir, Máirtín, 381
Ó Riada, Seán, 334, 335
Ó Snodaigh, Aengus, 11, 118, 122, 131, 151, 164, 196, 225–6, 243, 297, 351, 382
O'Brien, Denis, 307
O'Brien, Jonathan, 243, 300
O'Callaghan, Jim, 355–6
O'Callaghan, Miriam, 353
O'Connell, Hugh, 300, 361–2, 365, 378
O'Connor, James, 41, 42–7
O'Dea, Willie, 160
O'Doherty, Shane Paul, 73–4
O'Donnell, Marie-Louise, 68
O'Dowd, John, 345–7
O'Dwyer brothers, 40, 46
O'Hagan, Joe, 187
O'Hanlon, Éilis, 265
O'Hanlon, Siobhán, 263
O'Hare, Dessie, 313
O'Hare, Rita, 90, 101, 114, 309
O'Loan, Nuala, 272
O'Mahony, John, 235
O'Malley, Desmond, 242, 244, 245, 248
O'Malley, Donogh, 67
O'Maoileoin, Brendan, 21–2, 24–5, 28, 32–3
O'Neill, Gerry, 343
O'Neill, Melissa, 301
O'Neill, Michelle, 7, 284, 308–9, 316, 318, 345–6, 374, 380–82, 384, 387–8, 394
O'Neill, Sorcha, 301
O'Reilly, Louise, 188, 295, 340, 351, 382
O'Reilly, Ray, 153
O'Rourke, Seán, 294–5
O'Rourke, Stella and Una, 83
O'Sullivan, Grace, 342
O'Sullivan, Maureen, 161, 169–72, 221, 269
O'Sullivan, Nóirín, 235
Obama, Michelle, 337
Oireachtas Health Committee, 324

Oklahoma, 68
On the Banks of the Dodder (Walsh), 49
Orange Order, 102, 105, 110
Orde, Hugh, 197

Paisley, Ian, 288
Palestine, 205, 328
Party of European Socialists, 146
Patten Commission (1999), 101
Pearse, Patrick, 133, 339
People's Democracy, 90
Perry, Cieran, 221
Phelan, Vicky, 328–9
Pius XII, Pope, 249
Plaid Cymru, 146
Police Service of Northern Ireland (PSNI), 197–8, 211, 263–4, 270, 273–4, 340
polling, 367–8, 370, 378, 383, 390, 391
Poppy Day, 112, 334, 335
Portadown, Co. Armagh, 97
Porterstown, Castleknock, 93, 96, 108
Portlaoise prison, County Laois, 123, 152, 171
Power Play (Bréadún), 36
Price, Dolours, 273
Progressive Unionist Party, 138
proxy bombing, 306
Public Accounts Committee (PAC), 3, 226–55, 329, 361
Putin, Vladimir, 391

Quayle, James Danforth 'Dan', 115
Quinn, Frank, 191
Quinn, Martin, 38–41
Quinn, Paul, 275–80, 353
Quirke, Esther, 41, 43, 44

Rabbitte, Pat, 60, 128, 251–2
rape, 5, 254–5, 259, 261–73
Rathgar, Dublin, 48
Rathmines Senior College, 70, 74
Reade, Michael, 317
Redmond, Brendan, 162
Regan, Mary, 175
Registration of Lobbying Bill (2014), 250
Rehab Group, 3, 66, 232, 234, 240–41
Reid, Odran, 78
Reilly, Kathryn, 268
Reilly, Noeleen, 301–2, 343
Renewable Heating Incentive Scheme, 307
Revenue Commissioners, 231, 242, 243
Reynolds, Albert, 189, 258
Ridge, Sophy, 394
Rigby, Beth, 394
Riverwood, Castleknock, 123, 126, 182, 192
Robinson, Peter, 264
Ronaghan, Gary, 54, 59
Rossa, Proinsias de, 129, 136, 139, 142, 173, 177
Rossnowlagh, County Donegal, 62
Rossport Five, 58
Rowley, Angela, 100
Royal Dutch Shell, 57–60
Royal Irish Constabulary (RIC), 319, 348–9, 360–61
Royal Ulster Constabulary (RUC), 88, 97, 101, 110, 257, 262, 269, 271, 311
Ruane, Caitríona, 90
Ruane, Kenneth, 235
Rubicon Films, 52
Russell, Seán, 97, 131–3, 141, 309–10
Russian Embassy, Dublin, 25–7, 34, 49
Rutledge, Una, 68
Ryan, Eoin, 129, 136, 139, 140, 141, 173
Ryan, Gerard, 242–3, 247
Ryan, Patricia, 357
Ryan, Patrick, 89
Ryan, Philip, 343
Ryan, Richie, 245

Sands, Robert 'Bobby', 70, 89, 149, 203, 249, 328, 339, 377–8
Sarkozy, Nicolas, 168
Scallon, 'Dana' Rosemary, 289

Scottish Nationalist Party, 146
Seanad Éireann, 21, 99, 119, 203, 224, 238, 288, 295, 303, 357–9
Share the Wealth in Budget (2001), 122
Sheehan, Maeve, 187
Sheehy, Lisa Marie, 302–3
Shell to Sea campaign, 57–60
Sheridan, Kathy, 220
Sinn Féin, 1, 4, 5, 49, 94–109, 110–14
    Ard Chomhairle, 103, 104, 113–14, 115, 117, 124, 151, 317, 359
    ard fheis, see ard fheis
    Ardboyne Hotel conference (2009), 205
    Basque Country, relations with, 60
    Broadcasting Authority Act (1960), 111
    bullying scandals, 299–305
    Éirígí split (2006), 58–9, 199
    Irish National Congress conference (1990), 90
    Irish Republican Army, relationship with, 111–15, 117, 118, 123, 137–8, 204
    leadership transition (2016–18), 297, 304–5, 311, 315–21
    National Officer Board, 113–14, 117
    O'Dowd's challenge (2019), 345–7
    partitionist strategy, 121, 195, 198–9
    polling, 367–8, 370, 378, 383, 390, 391
    rape allegations, 254–5
    Share the Wealth in Budget (2001), 122
    socialist wing, 58–9, 199, 200
    United Left membership, 147–9
    votes of no confidence, 329–30, 339–40, 347–8, 379
    Wynne resignation (2022), 391–3
Small Grant Scheme, 359
Smith, Brendan, 116
Smith, Tom, 123, 130
Smithers, Tony, 200
Smyth, Robbie, 139, 140
Smyth, Sam, 180, 183
Social Democratic Labour Party (SDLP), 121, 134, 196, 271, 319, 341, 358, 388
Social Democrats (Ireland), 293, 356
socialism, 16, 48, 57, 105, 146–9, 199, 204, 339
South Africa, 69, 89–90, 168, 328
South-East Fermanagh Foundation, 314
Spain, 73, 74
Special Criminal Court, 282–3, 294, 367, 380, 382, 383
St Bridget's National School, Castleknock, 81
St Louis school, Rathmines, 52
St Mary's College, Rathmines, 51, 67, 68
St Patrick's Day, 340–41
Stafford, John, 155
Stafford, Mary, 179
Stanley, Brian, 56, 360–61, 363
Starmer, Keir, Sir, 264, 270
Statoil, 58, 59
Stoneybatter, Dublin, 80, 84, 153, 192
Storey, Robert 'Bobby', 6, 197, 258, 261, 360, 363, 386
Strabane, Co. Tyrone, 314
Strawberry Beds, Dublin, 80–81, 82, 84, 87, 192, 194
Strawberry Hall pub, Dublin, 81, 87
Strictly Come Dancing, 46

Taaffe, Anne, 191
Teeling, Dermot, 187–8
Teeling, Vera, 187, 188
Templeogue College, Dublin, 51
Terry, Sheila, 125
There's Something about Mary (Banotti), 36, 70–71, 95–6
Thompson, William, 97
Tipperary, Ireland, 38–47, 61, 66, 95
Tohill, Bobby, 137
Tóibín, Peadar, 117, 319, 325–8, 338, 354
Tone, Theobald Wolfe, 94
trade unions, 75

Travellers, 334
Traynor, Des, 244
Treacy, Seán, 41
Treaty of Nice (2001), 123
Trinity College Dublin, 14, 16, 49, 50–51, 53, 70–74, 79, 320, 366
Troubles (1966–98), 13, 56, 111, 123, 132, 256–8, 281, 306, 313, 314
Troubles in the Glen, The, 41, 46
Troy, Maurice, 82
Troy, Patrick, 81, 83, 84
Trump, Donald, 55
Tubridy, Ryan, 364
Tuffy, Joanna, 269
Twomey, John, 235
Twomey, Seamus, 187
Tyaransen, Olaf, 71, 107
Tynan, Noel, 191
Tyrell, Áine, 211–15, 221, 249, 254, 263, 266, 269
Tyrone Volunteers, 314

Uí Mhurchadha, Pádraigín, 89
Ukraine, 390, 391
Ulster Unionist Party (UUP), 341, 384, 389
Ulster Volunteer Force, 311
united Ireland, 2, 6, 12, 14, 47, 78, 100, 111, 118, 214, 233, 311, 328–9, 371, 384, 395
    Fianna Fáil and, 90, 94, 105, 107, 110
    general election (2020), 356
    presidential election (2018), 334, 335
United Kingdom Independence Party (UKIP), 209
United Left, 147–8, 176
United Nations, 379
Unity, 89
University College London, 51
University of Limerick, 74–7, 79, 135, 366
University of Liverpool, 53
Upper Bann Association, 359

Varadkar, Leo, 336
    confidence and supply agreement (2018), 338
    confidence vote (2020), 369–70
    Covid-19 pandemic, 368, 370
    general election (2020), 348, 350, 354, 355, 356, 357
    local elections (2019), 342
Villa Park Road, Dublin, 166, 182, 193
votes of no confidence, 329–30, 339, 347–8, 369–70

Wall, Chris and Myra, 166
Wallace, Mick, 147
Walsh, Ged, 49
Ward, Mark, 347, 351
Warrenpoint ambush (1979), 281, 361
Warrington bombings (1993), 112
water charges controversy (2014), 252, 290–91
Waterways Ireland, 349–50
Weslin Construction, 180, 193
Weston, Galen, 152
Whelan, Noel, 337
White, James, 87–8
White, Mary, 98–9, 105
White, Stephen, 45
Wilson, Desmond, 89
Wilson, John, 238
Wilson, Padraic, 258, 263
Wolfe Tones, The, 360
Wolfhound Pictures, 52
women's suffrage anniversary (2018), 336–7
Working Together for a New Ireland conference (2002), 127
Wren's Nest pub, Dublin, 81, 82–3, 93, 120, 123
Wright, Briege, 263
Wynne, Violet-Anne, 391–3

Zappone, Katherine, 379